A Christian Samurai

Sketch of the Shimabara banner by Robert J. Schroder. Reprinted by permission of the artist.

A Christian Samurai

THE TRIALS OF BABA BUNKŌ

William J. Farge, SJ

Foreword by Kevin M. Doak

The Catholic University of America Press

Washington, D.C.

The paper used in this publication meets the minimum requirements of American National Standards for Information Science–Permanence of Paper for Printed Library Materials, ANSI Z39.48-1984.
∞

Library of Congress Cataloging-in-Publication Data
Names: Farge, William J., author. | Doak, Kevin Michael, writer of foreword.
Title: A Christian samurai : the trials of Baba Bunkō / William J. Farge, SJ; Foreword by Kevin M. Doak.
Description: Washington, D.C. : The Catholic University of America Press, 2016. | Includes bibliographical references and index.
Identifiers: LCCN 2015048886 | ISBN 9780813228518 (pbk. : alk. paper)
Subjects: LCSH: Baba, Bunkō, 1718–1759. | Baba, Bunkō, 1718–1759. Tōdai Edo hyaku bakemono. | Christianity—Japan—History. | Catholic church—Japan—History. | Japan—Church history—To 1868. | Japan—Social conditions—1600–1868.
Classification: LCC BR1306 .F37 2016 | DDC 275.2/07092—dc23
LC record available at http://lccn.loc.gov/2015048886

Ad Majorem Dei Gloriam et Beatae Virginis Mariae
Honorem et Martyrum Iaponicorum Venerationem

Contents

Foreword

Rarely do historians actually make original discoveries, and even more unusual is it for a Western historian of Japan to uncover something new and important in Japanese history. The closest example I can think of is Ronald Toby's discovery in *State and Diplomacy in Early Modern Japan* (Princeton University Press, 1984) that Tokugawa Japan (1603–1867) was not a closed country, as historians had believed. Toby's revision pointed out that the term "closed country" (*sakoku*) was not in use in Japan when the event allegedly happened, but was in fact a retranslation by a nineteenth-century Japanese scholar working from Engelbert Kaempfer's 1729 *History of Japan* to describe what supposedly happened in 1639. This was a seismic shift for Western historians of modern Japan. But Japanese historian Tashiro Kazui had already noted the anachronism of sakoku in 1982, two years prior to Toby's book (to be fair, Toby's contribution was not limited to this conceptual point but built on it to illustrate Japan's openness to East Asian, especially Korean, cultural influences through diplomatic relations). What Farge has accomplished here is more original, more important, and more startling in its implications than even Toby's work. And in fact, it substantially undermines the revisionist anti-sakoku argument. At the same time, Farge also completely undermines the basis for the original "closed country" position, most notably made in George Elison's *Deus Destroyed: The Image of Christianity in Early Modern Japan* (Harvard University Press, 1973). Elison argued that Tokugawa Japan was "closed" because it had eradicated Christianity from Japan. What Farge has done through careful research into primary sources is to demonstrate both that Japan had not eradicated all traces of Catholicism during the Edo period and yet that its continuing brutal suppression of Japanese Catholics justifies the earlier characterization of Tokugawa Japan as a "closed country." To appreciate the significance of Tokugawa Japan as a closed country, we need only consider the fate of the thirty thousand Catholics who emerged from this brutal persecution in 1865 and finally found freedom in the "open country" of Meiji Japan in 1873. Tokugawa Japan was not a "closed country" because there were no Catholics in Japan but precisely because there were. Here, in Farge's subtle hands, we begin to see that "closed" was more an ethical failure than a cultural or political issue.

But let us not overlook what Farge has discovered: proof of the existence of a Japanese Catholic in eighteenth-century Japan. This is an extraordinarily important find in and of itself. Historians of both the Elison stance and the Toby revision have largely accepted the underlying premise of Japan during its "early modern" period as free from Christianity. Both the term and the concept of early modern Japan as a "sakoku" was directed at the fact of Japan's government closing the country to Christianity in the early sixteenth century. Not even the revisionist "sakoku deniers" took issue with that historical fact. But Farge's careful historical and textual analysis has uncovered strong evidence that Baba Bunkō (1718–59) was not only in all probability a believing Catholic, but that his Catholic values were expressed publically and were even incorporated into early modern Japanese literary and cultural history. I'm completely persuaded by the case Farge makes for Baba's Catholicism: direct evidence like his reference to the Eucharist as a person, and a range of circumstantial evidence, including his arrest and execution (when the only crime that fit this punishment was being Catholic), and the substantive nature of his views that can only be explained with reference to Catholic values. While there may still be holdouts who will simply refuse to accept Farge's argument (mainly due to anti-Christian bias in the field of Japanese studies that Farge notes below), open-minded scholars of Japanese history and of Christian history will be very impressed by Farge's original work and his discovery of Baba Bunkō, the eighteenth-century Hidden Catholic.

I hope that Farge's study will restore Baba Bunkō to his rightful place in Japanese history, even while forcing historians to reconsider the "closed country" debate and to recognize the viability of Christianity in Japan under some of the harshest persecutions the world has ever seen. But we should not overlook how Farge's work brings back to the forefront the universality of the Catholic faith in surprising ways. His book will not only be an essential text for historians and literary scholars of early modern Japan, but for scholars of modern and early modern East Asia, historians of Christianity in East Asia, comparativists working on early modern Christianity, and anyone interested in the history of Christianity, particularly Catholicism. Whether scholars of Christianity outside East Asia will take notice will tell us much about how open-minded the field of Christian studies in general is toward the historical realities of East Asia.

Kevin M. Doak
Georgetown University

Preface

Baba Bunkō (1718–59), a samurai from Iyo domain in Shikoku, set out in 1751 to begin a new life in the capital of Edo (now Tokyo) as a bureaucrat in the government of Tokugawa Ieshige (1711–61), the Japanese shogun.[1] Bunko's career as a government functionary did not last long before he abruptly left his post, renounced his samurai status, and began writing and lecturing on the hypocrisy and corruption in the most important offices of the Tokugawa *bakufu* (government).

Bunkō is an unknown figure among most Western historians of the Tokugawa (or Edo) period (1603–1868). In Japan, however, he has been acclaimed as the most outstanding storyteller and lecturer (*kōdanshi*) in early modern Japan and has been praised as "the great man of Edo satirical style."[2] As an Edo resident, Bunkō's proximity to the seat of power and his daily exposure to the presence of *daimyō* (territorial lords), scholars, and artists, as well as peasants and commoners from around the country, solidified his defiant outlook toward those who controlled politics and culture in the capital.

A number of mysteries surround the circumstances of his life. The reasons behind his arrest, trial, and execution have never been examined in

1. Personal names in Japanese begin with the family name followed by the given name. Thus, "Baba" is the family or last name; Bunkō is the given name. Likewise, "Tokugawa" is the family name; "Ieshige" the given name. Because the family name Baba, like many family names in Japan, is shared by a large number of people who are not necessarily related, historical personages are often referred to by their "first" or given name.

The date of Bunkō's death is usually given as 1758 since he died in Hōreki 8. However, because the day of death was the twenty-ninth day of the twelfth month in the lunar calendar, the actual date of his death would have been January 27, 1759, in the western Gregorian calendar.

2. Sekine Mokuan, *Kōdan rakugo konseki dan* (Tokyo: Yūsanbō, 1923), 7. Mitamura Engyo, *Mitamura Engyo zenshū* (Tokyo: Chūō kōronsha, 1975), 10: 45.

any English-language scholarship. Not least among the unsolved mysteries of Baba Bunkō's life is the suspicion that he may have been a hidden Christian. Close analysis of the writings of his later life yields considerable evidence that Bunkō was certainly knowledgeable about the most important doctrines of Christianity and sympathetic to its moral teachings.

For the first time, important writings of Baba Bunkō are presented in English translation. Among the literary works examined is his collection of satirical anecdotes, *Contemporary Edo: An Album of One Hundred Monsters* (*Tōdai Edo hyaku bakemono*, 1758), in which he pursues his struggle with "monsters," exposing the hypocrisy of well-known and lesser-known officials of the government, Confucian teachers, and Buddhist and Shintō religious leaders.[3] In the preface to *Contemporary Edo: An Album of One Hundred Monsters*, Bunkō describes these "monsters" as individuals who grotesquely transform their appearance in order to manipulate society and other people. The monster is someone, he says, who is always changing his position, both physically and intellectually, because he never holds to any conviction. "Under the guise of being human, he ensnares people in his deceptions."[4] The complete translation of *Contemporary Edo: An Album of One Hundred Monsters* is included as an appendix at the end of the book.

Baba Bunkō became a focal point of dissent in Japan in the 1750s and "the first person to pierce the iron curtain of Tokugawa secrecy."[5] He presents a revolutionary view of the history of the Tokugawa period, a view that is so different from the conventional one offered by Western historians that he and his writings will certainly be the subject of research, discussion, and debate in the future.

3. There are some published translations of short selections from Baba Bunkō's works. "One Hundred Monsters in Edo of Our Time," appeared in Sumie Jones and Watanabe Kenji, *An Edo Anthology: Literature from Japan's Mega City, 1750–1850*, 103–13, and "Aged Geisha and 'Young' Kabuki Actors" appeared in *Two Lines: A Journal of Translation*, June 2006.

4. Baba Bunkō, *Tōdai Edo hyaku bakemono*, in *Shin Nihon koten bungaku taikei*, vol. 97, *Tōdai Edo hyaku bakemono, Zaishin kiji, Kana sesetsu*, ed. Tajihi Ikuo and Nakano Mitsutoshi (Tokyo: Iwanami shoten, 2000), 3.

5. Yamada Tadao, "Seiji to Minshūbunka," *Rekishi hyōron* no. 465 (1989): 26–27.

Acknowledgments

My attempt to take a fresh look at the history of Christianity in early modern Japan and to reevaluate the long-term impact of Catholic missionary activity in the late sixteenth and early seventeenth centuries led me in unexpected directions. I did some exploration beyond the so-called "Christian century" and tried to find what, if anything, might have remained of Christianity and Christian influence in the eighteenth century after the missionaries had been expelled and Christians had gone underground. As a result of my research, I have taken a stand against some of the assumptions that have long been held by the most eminent scholars and historians in the field of Japanese history. I offer my findings here with some trepidation but also with excitement and with gratitude to all of those people—scholars and the academic professionals as well as friends—who have given me much support and encouragement to pursue this study.

I would like to thank especially Prof. Kevin Doak and Fr. Stephen Fields, SJ, of Georgetown University, who were the first to encourage me to continue down an unchartered path of discovery that led to the writing of this book. They kept me going when I had doubts and spurred me on to bring this project to its conclusion. Mr. Thomas Aylward II and his family offered me accommodations during the summer and fall of 2013 and gave me the space and time to work. Prof. Yamaguchi Michihiko of Nihon University encouraged me not to be afraid of opposition to my thesis but to state my own findings clearly and forcefully. He gave me insights into the Japanese texts that helped me to do this.

There are many other people I would like to thank. Dr. Jennifer O'Sullivan spent hours reading various drafts of the manuscript and offered suggestions that helped me to clarify my arguments. Mr. Rene Miller and his wife, Michele, offered me technical assistance. Dr. Donald Boomgaarden, Mr. Julio Minsal-Ruiz, SJ, and Fr. Aaron Pidel, SJ, offered helpful suggestions and advice. Mr. Robert Schroder kindly did the illustration of the Shimabara banner. The book cover design is the work of Mr. Daniel Mitsui. Mr. Otis Burkell and his wife, Kirsten, offered inspiration and support. I am also grateful to Mr. Bruce Hoefer, who gave me opportunities to articulate my thoughts and opinions on many different topics.

Finally, I would like to express my thanks to Loyola University New Orleans for offering me the time to write, free from teaching and the other responsibilities normally involved in university work. Loyola also provided me the necessary funding to complete this project. I am grateful for the support of the Jesuit community at Jesuit High School, as well as to the pastor of St. Patrick's Church in New Orleans, Fr. Stanley Klores, and to the parishioners of the church for their continued support and encouragement.

Summary of Chapters

Chapter 1: Deus Restored

A general introduction of the Tokugawa period (1603–1868) is presented for readers who may be unfamiliar with three major characteristics of Japanese society during this time: a strict hierarchical social order, a national policy of isolationism (*sakoku*), and the persecution and suppression of Christianity.

As the title of the chapter indicates, "Deus Restored" is a rebuttal of the common understanding of the place of Christianity during this period that was put forward by George Elison in his 1973 book *Deus Destroyed: The Image of Christianity in Early Modern Japan* and which has persisted in the historical scholarship of the Tokugawa period until today. According to this understanding, the fact that almost all Christians were killed, exiled, or had apostatized by the 1640s proves that the Christian mission in Japan was a failure, and that even though there was a tiny group of "hidden Christians," they were of little importance. By the 1660s, according to this view, Christianity was virtually eradicated, and its influence on Japan was never of any real significance.

One reason why this has been the standard view of the history of Japanese Christianity is because historians, by the very nature of their scholarship, choose certain "facts" that they consider relevant and ignore other "facts" that they determine are irrelevant to the history they wish to write. Historians will leave out some historical data and personages that do not seem to fit into the story they are creating.

Baba Bunkō is one of those historical personages who does not fit with the history of the Tokugawa period as it has been conceived up to this time. Nor do his writings fit in with the existing corpus of Tokugawa popular literature. The writings of Baba Bunkō provide data that have been overlooked by historians, resulting in their failure to see the place of Christianity in the mid-eighteenth century. His references to central Christian beliefs, such as the doctrine of the Eucharist and the sacrament of confession, invite a serious literary analysis of his writings and a reexamination of the Tokugawa period as a whole. This book will challenge the historian and the literary critic to take a second look at Tokugawa culture and to reevaluate the influence of Christianity and the Christian mission in Japan.

The reasons why the strategy the shogunate used in the first decades of the Tokugawa period to arrest, torture, and execute Christians and suspected Christians was partially abandoned in the latter half of the eighteenth century and why the existence of Christians was even ignored by local officials in some areas are explained.

Chapter 2: Tokugawa Christianity

The policy of the bakufu to extinguish Christianity was a failure. Christians continued to be found throughout Japan, and the fear of Christianity persisted. Local officials were sometimes shocked that Christians were still being found throughout the Tokugawa period, not only in areas that were known to have been Christian before the persecution began, but in many other areas of Japan as well.

Baba Bunkō's last work, an essay titled "A Collection of Useless Grumblings," was a direct affront to both the shogunate and the imperial institution. His criticism of the Shinto and Buddhist religions and his praise for the symbols of Christianity and Christian prayer are surprising to the modern historian, who might have thought that no Christian literature had been composed in eighteenth-century Japan. Bunkō's understanding of Christian doctrine provides a challenging new perspective through which to consider the history of Christianity in early modern Japan.

Chapter 3: Popular Games and Monster Stories

Bunkō did not only write explicit Christian literature. In fact, most of his writings are satirical tracts that condemn or humorously belittle specific government officials, Confucian scholars, Buddhist monks, and even the shogun himself, many of whom he calls "monsters." Bunkō's collection of anecdotes, *Contemporary Edo: An Album of One Hundred Monsters*, is based on a popular game called "One Hundred Monsters." He uses the framework of the monster tales and ghost stories from this game to write much of his social and political satire.

Bunkō's designation of contemporary daimyō, samurai, and members of the elite classes as "monsters" and "demons" who have the power to bewitch people into thinking that they are wise teachers and just rulers reveals his own understanding of morality. His perception of moral and immoral conduct runs contrary to the contemporary values that historians usually associate with the Tokugawa era and with the popular literature of the period.

Chapter 4: Raindrops Falling in the Forest

When arresting and charging Christians, Tokugawa authorities in the latter half of the eighteenth century often did not make a direct accusation that a person was a Christian. Rather, it was common to accuse suspected Christians of other crimes. By not specifically mentioning the crime of being a Christian, officials did not have to acknowledge the presence of Christians in their jurisdictions or be concerned about reporting them to the bakufu authorities in Edo. Officials in Edo by all means wanted to avoid public acknowledgement of the existence of Christian influence and consequently did all they could to avoid using the term "Christian" in any legal proceedings.

Baba Bunkō was arrested after having given a series of lectures, titled "Raindrops Falling in the Forest," about a peasant uprising in Gujō (in present-day Gifu prefecture), which had begun as a tax dispute between peasants and the daimyō, Kanamori Yorikane (1713–63) of Mino-Hachiman.[1]

The judgment handed down against Bunkō by the bakufu high court (*hyōjōsho*) explicitly declared that he had committed no crime deserving of death, and yet he was condemned to be beheaded. If Bunkō had actually been put to death simply for his criticism of officials, or for the man-

1. Kanamori Yorikane was daimyō from 1736 to 1759 (Hōreki 8. 12. 25). Dates will be designated by year, month, and day; thus, Hōreki 8. 12. 25 is the eighth year of the Hōreki period, twelfth month, twenty-fifth day.

ner in which he had criticized Kanamori Yorikane for his cruel treatment of the peasants in his domain, or for other writings judged to be subversive of the regime, he would have been the only person in the Edo period to suffer death for such a reason. It therefore seems likely that the crimes mentioned in the high court's declaration sentencing him to death were not the crimes for which he was condemned. There was another unstated reason for his condemnation.

Chapter 5: Baba Bunkō's Political and Social Dissent

Why did Bunkō think that he would be able to get away with criticizing by name specific government officials, not to mention the shogun himself? Perhaps it was because he correctly saw that the enforcement of government censorship was sporadic and not very effective during the 1750s. Perhaps Bunkō spoke openly and wrote directly about forbidden topics because he saw no one else being prosecuted for doing the same.

There was definitely a growing atmosphere of dissent in Edo. Graffiti and popular satirical verses (*senryū*), which were commonly distributed, made fun of samurai. It was this environment that opened the way for Bunkō's satirical writings. His attacks on officials, including shogun Tokugawa Ieshige, his senior counselors (*rōjū*), and Confucian teachers, such as Miwa Shissai (1669–1774), are unique in the literature of the period and provide a rare glimpse into the nature of political opposition in the Tokugawa period.

Chapter 6: The Decline of Tokugawa Neo-Confucianism

The Neo-Confucian social ethos that had provided the foundation for the strict hierarchy of classes in Tokugawa society was disintegrating. Samurai were becoming less credible as rulers, and commoners were less willing to remain passive and submissive to their authority. The perceived lack of genuine virtue among the samurai class was becoming increasingly evident to the urban commoners of Edo in the 1700s, deepening their cynicism and distrust.

The traditional Neo-Confucian philosophy no longer gave the samurai the rationale or the support they needed to rule in an increasingly commercialized society beset by growing discontent and doubt. The absence of any system of ethics to replace Confucianism and the relativism of the period opened a window of opportunity for Baba Bunkō to criticize the political, religious, educational, and cultural institutions of his day. Examples from Bunkō's writings illustrate his perception that Neo-Confucian orthodoxy was collapsing.

Chapter 7: Baba Bunkō's Literary Heritage

The distinction made in Western literature between fiction, which is supposedly imaginative, and nonfiction, which is presumed to be historical or factual, does not apply to the literature of the Edo period. Early modern popular literature in Japan, known as *gesaku*, is actually a variety of different kinds of writings, which includes essays and anecdotes that have both fictional and historical elements.

While Bunkō's writings can be compared to gesaku, and the influence of the contemporary popular literature on his literary style is apparent, the content of his works is quite different from gesaku. In fact, he did not see himself as a gesaku writer at all but as a writer focusing on current events and popular history. He did use some of the literary conventions of gesaku, however, such as *mitate* (incongruous associations), to show that there are "monsters" among us in high positions of political, religious, or academic authority.

Chapter 8: Kabuki Actors, Monks, and Courtesans

Samurai, Buddhist monks, Confucian scholars, and even daimyō were involved in secret liaisons with male actors of the kabuki theater, particularly the *onnagata* (female impersonators), and with the courtesans and prostitutes of the Edo "pleasure" district known as Yoshiwara. Even though the Tokugawa authorities and the Confucian elite condemned Yoshiwara as a place of immorality, they perpetuated the system that kept women enslaved by their patronage of the various establishments. Though Yoshiwara may have been unsavory, in Bunkō's opinion, the immorality was not primarily the business in which the courtesans were engaged. It was rather the practices of the elite that made Yoshiwara a place of immorality. Indeed, Bunkō praises some of the courtesans for their virtue and engages the reader's sympathy in their plight.

Bunkō takes some well-known Buddhist monks to task for condemning the women of Yoshiwara for their lack of virtue while at the same time taking advantage of the diversions they offered. He presents his critical views of the Buddhist establishment as a whole, pointing out the monks' character weaknesses and moral flaws, and satirizing the contrasts between "the sacred" and "the profane" aspects of their lives.

Chapter 9: The Breakdown of Social Order

The shogunate took measures to safeguard and preserve the traditional status relationships and class distinctions in Japanese society, but the moral decline of the samurai class continued through the eighteenth century, even accelerating during the shogunate of Tokugawa Ieshige.

Since the Confucian social order, by which commoners and peasants also lived, had its foundation in the interdependent relationships between a daimyō and his samurai, the morals at every level of society were only as strong as the lord-retainer relationship. Bunkō perceived that there were fundamental and obvious flaws in the human relationships at this upper stratum of society. Since the lord-retainer relationship was clearly on the point of breaking down in the 1750s, the collapse of the other Confucian relationships, Bunkō predicted, would follow.

Chapter 10: The Christian Question

Can the satirical anecdotes and essays that Baba Bunkō composed be classified as Christian literature? Scholars in the West have restricted the genre of Japanese Christian literature to the so-called "Christian century" of the late 1500s and early 1600s. The general consensus among historians and literary critics today is that an eighteenth-century Christian literature would not have been produced. Any thesis affirming the existence of Christian literature at that time would not be compatible with the history of Christianity in Japan that historians have constructed. However, Christian proclamations of faith in the latter half of the Tokugawa period challenge historians to reexamine the question of whether or not there are, in fact, texts that can be called "Christian" during that period.

Most of the works of Baba Bunkō conceal any specific Christian belief and avoid using any vocabulary that would be construed as Christian. However, the definition of "Christian literature" must change depending on the social and political conditions at different times in history. During a time of persecution Christian literature would be very different from texts written during a time of religious freedom. The historian today is challenged to take a second look at the preconceptions and assumptions that he or she has projected onto the literature of the Tokugawa period. Some works have long been assumed to be Christian. Others, such as the essays and anecdotes of Baba Bunkō, have been presumed to be non-Christian. However, if Bunkō's works are based on absolute moral principles that are Christian, rather than Confucian or Buddhist, his writings must be classified as Christian literature of eighteenth-century Japan.

A Christian Samurai

1 | DEUS RESTORED

Christianity has exerted an influence on Japanese society and culture far greater than one might expect from a religion of its paltry size.

A.H. ION

The Christian Century in Japan

Tokugawa Ieyasu (1542–1616) officially established the Tokugawa shogunate with its capital in the city of Edo (present-day Tokyo) on March 24, 1603 (Keichō 8. 2. 12). Ieyasu was the first of fifteen Tokugawa shoguns who ruled Japan, along with the country's approximately three hundred daimyō, for over 250 years. The shogunate ended, and a new government took shape on January 3, 1868, when the emperor was restored to partial political power in what has been called the Meiji Restoration.

The Tokugawa, or Edo, period was characterized by a strict hierarchical social order in which the samurai class ruled over the peasant, artisan, and merchant classes. Outside of these four classes were the so-called *eta* (filthy persons), whose professions as butchers, tanners, or undertakers violated the precepts of Buddhism and relegated them and their descendants to an outcast class. There were also *hinin* (non-persons), who served in the capacity of guards, street cleaners, and executioners. Others outside the four-class structure included beggars, entertainers, and prostitutes.

Epigraph is from A. H. Ion, "Japan and Christianity: Impacts and Responses by John Breen, Mark Williams," book review, *International History Review* 20, no. 1 (1998): 160.

In addition to, theoretically at least, a strict class separation, the Tokugawa period was distinguished by its policy of isolationism (*sakoku*). The shogunate under Tokugawa Iemitsu (1604–51), the third shogun and grandson of Ieyasu, promulgated a number of laws between 1633 and 1639 that prohibited, under pain of death, any Japanese from traveling outside of Japan and anyone who was already abroad from ever returning home. Japan was not totally isolated during this time, however. Limited trade did continue with the Dutch factory on the tiny artificial island of Dejima in Nagasaki. China was given trade privileges at the Nagasaki port, and there were commercial exchanges with Korea on the island of Tsushima, and between Satsuma domain and the Ryūkyū Islands.[1] The policy of sakoku remained in effect until 1853, when Commodore Matthew Perry arrived from the United States and forced Japan to open to Western commerce.

A third characteristic of the period, which was a result of Japan's isolationist policy, was an intense persecution of Catholicism. Catholicism had been brought to Japan by the Jesuit missionary Francis Xavier (1506–52) in 1549 and flourished for about a century. Nagasaki, on the island of Kyushu, and nearby Kagoshima, where Xavier landed, along with other areas of Kyushu and Shikoku, became centers of Japanese Catholicism. The Christian daimyō maintained strong cultural and religious ties to Portugal and Spain. Charles Boxer (1904–2000), distinguished historian of Japanese history, designated this period between 1549 and 1650 the "Christian century."

The policy of sakoku not only severed trade relations with the West, it also marked the beginning of the end of the free practice of Catholicism. The expectation that a Christian daimyō would be loyal to the shogunate or that samurai and commoners would be subservient to the local lord precluded the possibility that anyone could also be loyal to the Western religion. Catholicism came to be perceived as an attack on the samurai's allegiance to his lord and a threat to the strict social order. By 1612 the shogun had ordered his samurai retainers and all commoners to renounce Catholicism. Those who remained faithful were hunted down,

1. Satsuma is in modern-day Kagoshima and Miyazaki prefectures. Ryūkyū Islands are present-day Okinawa.

arrested, and executed. Finally, the Closed Country Edict of 1635 (*sakoku rei*) forbade any missionaries from entering the country.[2] Many Japanese converts to Catholicism were brutally tortured and killed for their faith. In 1622, 120 missionaries and Christian converts were executed in Nagasaki in what is known as "the great martyrdom."[3]

In 1637 Catholic peasants and samurai rose up in rebellion against the shogunate at Shimabara in Kyushu. It has been argued that the causes of that rebellion were primarily political and economic in nature rather than explicitly religious.[4] However, the rebel banner, a representation of the chalice and host of the Eucharist, shows that the loyalty of many, if not most, of the insurgents was to their religious faith. (See an illustration of the banner in the front of this book.) The rebellion was crushed after a year-long siege of Hara Castle in 1638, and from that time on Christians were able to survive only by going underground, keeping their faith hidden. Rewards were given to those who were willing to report or turn in Christians. Those suspected of practicing the Christian faith were subject to investigation by being forced to tread on a sacred icon (*fumie*) of Jesus or Mary, in an act that was meant to show they were not Christians. Anyone who refused to step on the fumie—thus associating himself or herself with Christianity—was severely punished, whether by being boiled alive in the hot springs of Unzen, by being hung upside down for days in a hole filled with excrement (*ana-tsurushi*), or by being crucified. When Christianity was officially banned in 1638, there were more than two hundred thousand Christians in Japan. The persecution continued until Christianity was again legalized in 1873, five years after the end of the Tokugawa shogunate.

The generally accepted interpretation that is presented in most modern histories of the "Christian century" is that while missionary activity flourished in Japan for a time, after 1650 virtually all the Japanese Christians had been tortured and executed, had apostatized and reverted to

2. The edict was not called "Closed Country Edict" (*sakoku rei*) at this time. It is a term that came into use at a later date.

3. Hubert Cieslik, "The Great Martyrdom in Edo, 1623: Its Causes, Course, Consequences," *Monumenta Nipponica* 10, no. 1/2 (1954): 1–44.

4. Michael S. Laver, *The Sakoku Edicts and the Politics of Tokugawa Hegemony* (London: Cambria Press, 2011), 132.

their former Buddhist practices, or had gone into seclusion, and the missionaries' efforts to convert the Japanese eventually ended in a complete failure.

This interpretation of the "Christian century" is put forward by George Elison in his book *Deus Destroyed* and is typical of the story that most Western historians have presented: "In short, the missionaries left no lasting influence.... [T]he Christians [were] exterminated by the despotic Tokugawa regime.... The Christians' heroism could not avert this fate: they could do nothing to arrest this force, and were ground up before it."[5]

This view was again put forward in 1991 by Elison in *The Cambridge History of Japan*, in which he stated that by 1644, after the last Jesuit missionaries had been killed or had apostatized, Christianity was eradicated and was no longer of any importance in Japan.[6] More recently, Constantine Nomikos Vaporis in his 2014 book *Voices of Early Modern Japan* has presented the same argument, asserting that Christianity was eradicated in Japan.[7] This view, however, has been countered by other historians, such as Haruko Nawata Ward, who focuses on alternative historical personages and events in her book *Women Religious Leaders in Japan's Christian Century, 1549–1650*. She shows that the Christian mission had a significant cultural and social impact on Japan and convincingly argues that the Jesuit mission was in fact successful in ways that have been overlooked by historians. Christianity, she asserts, was instrumental in empowering women to make their own decisions about their lives and provided them with opportunities to exercise leadership in ministries of Christian teaching, apologetics, preaching, and works of mercy, all of which were perceived as a threat and a challenge to a strongly Neo-Confucian society.[8]

The historians who hold the conventional, majority view that the Christian mission was a failure prefer not to look at history beyond the

5. George Elison, *Deus Destroyed: The Image of Christianity in Early Modern Japan, rev. ed.* (1973; repr., Cambridge, Mass: Harvard University Press, 1988), 248, 249, 253.

6. J. W. Hall and J. L. McClain, *Early Modern Japan*, vol. 4 of *The Cambridge History of Japan* (Cambridge: Cambridge University Press, 1991), 370.

7. Constantine Nomikos Vaporis, *Voices of Early Modern Japan: Contemporary Accounts of Daily Life during the Age of the Shoguns* (Boulder, Colo.: Westview Press, 2014), 211.

8. Haruko Nawata Ward, *Women Religious Leaders in Japan's Christian Century, 1549–1650* (Surrey, UK: Ashgate Publishing Company, 2009), 15.

"Christian century" as it has been traditionally understood, because there is a scarcity of historical materials from the later seventeenth and eighteenth centuries. However, it is the later period that provides the evidence that Christianity did not simply fade away but continued to have an impact on politics and an influence in society. Evidence of Christian activity in the 1700s would not be consistent with the thesis of missionary failure and the subsequent demise of Christianity in Japan that has been constructed. Thus, there is a wide, unexplored historical gap between the end of the Christian mission in Japan in the 1640s and the surprising reappearance of a small group of Christians who emerged from seclusion in March 1865 when the French missionary Fr. Bernard Petitjean encountered them at Oura Church in Nagasaki. (Japan had again opened to foreign contacts in 1853, though complete freedom of religion would not be introduced until 1873.)

The story of the generations of Japanese Christians who survived during this "gap" after the persecutions of the early 1600s and remained in hiding, all the while passing on their faith to succeeding generations, has not been closely studied. It should not be assumed that Christian history in the Tokugawa period ended at the close of the "Christian century" and then suddenly started up again in 1865. Admittedly, there are few historical records that tell the story of Japanese Christianity in the intervening decades, but this lack does not justify ignoring important historical artifacts that do exist only because they would introduce an inconsistency in the long-held story of Christian missionary failure. What Fr. Petitjean did not realize when he met the small group of Christians on the steps of Oura Church was that there were approximately fifty thousand other Christians whose descendants had been in hiding for over two hundred years. Western historians of the "Christian century" and of the Tokugawa period cannot justifiably ignore the 1700s and 1800s when there were generations of Japanese Christians who lived ostensibly normal lives and successfully practiced their religion in secret, undetected by the authorities.

What Is History?

Why have historians ignored this middle period of Japanese Christian history? It goes without saying that all historians construct a history, which is perhaps a respectable way of saying they fabricate a story. How a historian arranges the elements that he or she believes to accurately describe the past and puts them in a logical sequence depends on a number of factors, including the point of view or particular emphasis on which the historian wishes to focus, as well as the values and assumptions of the readership for which the historian is writing. The writer of history has an intention to present a particular historical slant, and a slant or bias cannot be avoided. No written history is completely objective or totally without bias. It all depends on the message the historian wishes to communicate. Thus, Ralph Waldo Emerson can say, "There is properly no history, only biography."[9] The biography he is speaking of is, of course, the biography of the historian who is writing.

This may be obvious to the intelligent reader of history; but a historian who is taken up with writing a literarily polished historical narrative wants to make sense of his or her data and, as a consequence, is not always attentive to the inevitable connection between the selection or exclusion of data and the resulting interpretation. The historian obviously cannot present a particular view of history, call it objective reality, and then consider it closed to questioning or to further study. The actual past, independent of the historian's interpretation, involves the actions of human beings and consequently does not always follow a rational or orderly sequence of events. In other words, it may not always make logical sense. In fact, the closer a historical narrative is to what some might call objectively factual events that correspond to reality, the less perfectly the narrative will be characterized by order and precision.

Understandably, historians put credence in their own interpretation of events of the past and trust their own ability to choose and select which facts are significant and which are irrelevant to the history they are writing. Hayden White made us all aware that the effort to represent "reality" through historical narrative "arises out of a desire to have real events display the coherence, integrity, fullness, and closure of an image of life that is and can only be imaginary."[10] The causes and the results

9. Ralph Waldo Emerson, *Essays: First Series* (Boston: Houghton, Mifflin Co., 1841), 15.

10. Hayden White, *The Content of the Form: Narrative Discourse and Historical Representation* (Baltimore: Johns Hopkins University Press, 1987), 24.

of historical events in the past, as well as the events themselves and the personalities that shape those events, are all filtered through the preferences and personal values, whether conscious or unconscious, of the writer of history. The historian necessarily must choose to focus on a particular individual or group of individuals out of the vast pool of historical personages and to highlight some of their deeds and actions while leaving others out. The writer of history makes choices about whom he or she will include and who will be excluded based on which individuals are assumed to have more significantly influenced the course of history as the historian sees it. In addition to the events and people that are chosen, there are many more that are disregarded, forgotten, or purposely ignored, because their inclusion would disrupt the logical sequence of occurrences that come together to form the historical narrative. This way of proceeding, however, should not necessarily be faulted. After all, who would read a history book that lacked coherence or made no logical sense? The historian must be faithful to the goal of recording a comprehensible and rational history to achieve coherence and consistency in his or her written text. Nonetheless, it is important for the reader to be aware that the stories historians write never give a complete picture of the past.

This book will examine the Christian history in early modern Japan, when Christianity was not only persecuted but almost totally hidden and practiced only in secrecy. Not surprisingly, this was a period about which little historical research has been attempted because of the scarcity of primary written resources. It is a period of history that has long been practically invisible to modern historians, not to mention almost completely concealed even from the Japanese who lived at that time. A study of this period certainly would seem to be a nearly impossible task. However, a close analysis of the only writer who was executed by the bakufu during the Tokugawa period specifically for his writings provides a window on the situation of Christianity during this dark period. The case will be made that Baba Bunkō was in accord with at least some of the more important doctrines of Christianity, and his works give evidence of values and perspectives on government, culture, and society that stood out in sharp contrast to the conventional views of other contemporary writers and thinkers.

First, however, a few pieces of the puzzle of this obscure period of particularly enigmatic and mystifying Christian history will be laid out so that a fuller picture can gradually take shape.

Evidence of the Failure of the Shogunate's Anti-Christian Policies

In 1790 a certain village headman in the Nagasaki area by the name of Sakujirō brought accusations against nineteen villagers suspected of being Christians. The accused defended themselves before the Nagasaki city magistrate, Mizuno Tadamichi (1747–1823), by insisting that every year, in accordance with the law, they had submitted to the routine religious inquisition and trampled on the Christian religious image (*fumie*) that was put before them in the presence of the intendant (*daikan*).[11] They had thus proven to the satisfaction of the magistrate that they were not Christians. Their names had been written in the Buddhist temple register, and they had made regular offerings to the Buddha as required by law, giving additional evidence of their Buddhist affiliation.[12]

Sakujirō presented as evidence for his case against the suspected Christians statues of "Santa Maruya" (Holy Mary) and "a crucified Buddha" that he claimed had been in the possession of the accused. An innkeeper by the name of Yasuzaemon, speaking on behalf of the Christian defendants, told the magistrate that the statues had been planted in their homes by an unknown party and did not actually belong to them. As implausible as this excuse was, the magistrate judged that Sakujirō had, for whatever reason, fabricated the evidence in an attempt to prove that the suspects were Christians. The judgment passed down by the magistrate declared the nineteen innocent, and they returned to their homes. As for Sakujirō, he was convicted for bringing false accusations against his neighbors, was tattooed, given a hundred lashes, and expelled from Nagasaki. Incredibly, the Nagasaki city magistrate never investigated or

11. The intendants were senior Tokugawa officials who supervised police and judicial matters, gave moral guidance to people, and most importantly, collected taxes.

12. Urakawa Wasaburō, *Urakami Kirishitanshi* (Zenkoku shobō, 1943), 22. Also cited in J. L. Breen, "Heretics in Nagasaki, 1790–1796," in *Contemporary European Writings on Japan: Scholarly Views from Eastern and Western Europe*, ed. Ian Nish (Woodchurch, UK: Paul Norbury Publications, 1988), 10.

even asked from where the religious statue of Mary or the crucified Buddha had come. He was anxious both to bury the incident and even to discourage further informants from coming forth with reports of suspected Christian activities.[13] This outcome is quite surprising since the bakufu had for some time posted public notices (*kōsatsu*) of monetary rewards for anyone who reported the presence of Christians.

The strategy of the shogunate in the first decades of the Tokugawa period to arrest, torture, and execute Christians and suspected Christians was often ignored in the latter half of the eighteenth century. The policy towards Christians had unofficially changed, and officials turned a blind eye to the existence of Christians in their jurisdictions. Like the Nagasaki city magistrate in 1790, other provincial officials were known to have sometimes looked the other way when faced with the prospect of having to enforce the anti-Christian edicts and arrest a Christian.[14] The territorial lords were lax in this matter not because they had become sympathetic to the forbidden religion or because they had come to see Christians as members of a harmless religious sect. Quite the contrary. Daimyō simply feared the consequences of having to report to the shogunate the presence of Christians in their jurisdictions because they were concerned that the Edo government might censure, punish, or possibly even remove them from their positions.

In 1792 Yasuzaemon, the innkeeper mentioned above who testified in support of the accused Christians, was himself reported for trying to convince guests at his inn to join his "sect."[15] At times, he reportedly would have a friend, Heisuke by name, bring him water in a bowl over which he would make a sign of the cross. Yasuzaemon would then pour the water over a person's head. This is a clear reference to Christian initiation and baptism. The authorities suspected that Yasuzaemon's inn was a front for a Christian organization, but nothing was done to deter Yasuzaemon from what was obviously proselytizing.[16]

One of Yasuzaemon's followers, a certain Risuke, confessed to a repre-

13. J. L. Breen, "Heretics in Nagasaki, 1790–1796," 10.

14. Miyamoto Tsuneichii et al., eds., *Minkan hūkyō*, vol. 18 of *Nihon seikatsu shomin shiryō shūsei* (Tokyo: San'ichishobō, 1972), 771.

15. Ibid., 795.

16. Ibid., 95.

sentative of the Nagasaki city magistrate that he worshipped a "crucified Buddha" while chanting the words "Amen Iezusu" (Amen, Jesus). The magistrate, Mizuno Tadamichi, reported this suspicious activity in his 1796 report to the bakufu but surprisingly declared Risuke's "Buddha" on a cross to be insufficient proof of actual heretical or subversive activities.[17] This was certainly a radical departure from the policy of brutal persecution that had been carried out in the early 1600s. This had been the second incident in which the judgment of the Nagasaki city magistrate showed a shift from brutality to apparent embarrassment that there were still Christians in his jurisdiction. Modern historians of this period of Japanese history have overlooked such incidents because they do not fit in with the general interpretation and understanding of the later Tokugawa period as a time practically devoid of Christianity as a result of systematic persecution.

Seventy years after the nineteen Christians were found innocent of any crime, Fr. Bernard Petitjean encountered the hidden Christians at Oura Church in Nagasaki in 1865. He and the European priests with him, assuming that Christianity had completely died out two hundred years earlier, were astonished to find that there were still Japanese who were faithful to their Christian beliefs. The presence of Christians was no surprise to the Tokugawa shogunate, however. The Japanese government had long known of the existence of communities of Christians because they had emerged from time to time throughout the Tokugawa period, just as they had in 1790 when Sakujirō discovered them in his village. After a century of laws proscribing Christianity, it was evident to the shogunate that their effort to wipe out the forbidden religion had not been a success. The Nagasaki city magistrate had seen the wisdom of not giving the shogunate information that there were still Christians in his jurisdiction. It had been politically expedient for him to bury the Sakujirō case.

Since Christianity had not been wiped out, the question arises whether or not certain historical personages, who are well known to historians of the period, could have been influenced to some degree by the Western religion. This question has rarely been asked and has never been thor-

17. Ibid., 832. Also cited in Breen, 13.

oughly investigated. Conrad Totman, one scholar who has raised this question, has pointed out that the philosopher Nakae Tōju (1608–48) confessed that he worshiped T'ai-i shen, the great original god who created all things. Totman has suggested that a suspicious critic could reasonably associate Nakae's religious view with the proscribed Christian teaching about a transcendent creator God to whom one must pray and owe allegiance.[18] Totman's suggestion does not fit the mold of the conventional conceptions of the political or popular culture of Tokugawa Japan. Consequently, the idea that Nakae Tōju might have been influenced by Christian teachings would not be consistent with the story the majority of historians have traditionally recognized as the conventional history of the Tokugawa period. No historian would suggest that Nakae Tōju, even if he had been influenced by Christianity, was in fact a Christian. Such an assertion could never be proven. All Japanese Christians at the time kept their faith secret. The study of Christianity, suspected Christians, and their writings in the later Tokugawa period is a new area of exploration and a highly controversial one, even if there are some extant texts that reveal Christian convictions or sympathies veiled behind highly nuanced language.

Baba Bunkō lived during this period when Christianity is thought to have been nonexistent in Japan, and his writings are the principal focus of this book. He hailed from Iyo domain in what is today Ehime prefecture on the island of Shikoku. Bunkō is known as a political satirist, and most of his writings make no mention of Christianity. However, his references to a few central Christian beliefs, including the doctrine of the Eucharist, suggest a persistent influence of Christianity in the eighteenth century and invite a reexamination of his writings and of the period as a whole. A study of his works challenges the historian to take a second look at Tokugawa policies vis-à-vis political dissidents and also to reevaluate the influence of Christianity and the Christian mission in Japan. In addition to being a literary study, this book will attempt to go beyond the conventional assumptions with which historians have long understood Tokugawa history and propose a new interpretation of both the Christian

18. Conrad Totman, *Early Modern Japan* (Berkeley: University of California Press, 1993), 178.

and secular history of Japan in the early modern period. Baba Bunkō has rarely been mentioned in modern Western histories simply because there has never been a logical place for him in the historical narrative that has been constructed up to this time. The goal of this book is to construct a different history of the period by presenting historical evidence that has usually been left out of the narrative. Placing Baba Bunkō and his critique of the Tokugawa government and of the popular culture of the day into a new context will hopefully contribute something important to the more conventional histories of early modern Japan.

Baba Bunkō is not a familiar name even to Western scholars and historians of the Tokugawa period. The oversight is perplexing since Bunkō was the only person in the Tokugawa period to have been executed specifically for his writings. He was not executed explicitly for being a Christian or for any Christian sympathies. He was, however, the only person in the middle of the eighteenth century to give written evidence of having understood certain elements of Christianity, such as the Eucharist, that would have been unfamiliar to anyone who was not a Christian.

A Biography of Baba Bunkō

Bunkō was born Nakai Bun'emon in 1718. At an early age he became interested in the art of storytelling (*kōdan*). His father was proficient in the craft, and the young man grew up listening to the tales his father would tell. By the time he was six or seven years of age, he had heard much from his parents about the famous raconteur (*kōdanshi*) Fukai Shidōken (1680–1765), a feisty satirist whose bawdy renditions of exploits in the "pleasure" quarters attracted large audiences. He provocatively waved a wooden baton that resembled a phallus to attract passersby.[19] Shidōken's antics and his abrasive personality aroused both indignation and amusement. The young Bun'emon was fascinated by Shidōken and begged his father to tell him as much as he knew about this famous storyteller.[20]

Bun'emon's father was something of a family historian, as well as being a storyteller. What he recounted to the young boy about the ad-

19. Iida Takesato et al., eds., *Hōsei ronsan* (Tokyo: Dai Nippon tosho, 1903–4), 1422.

20. Many Japanese writers of the Tokugawa period are referred to by their given name–for example, "Saikaku" for Ihara Saikaku. I have adopted the same custom to refer to Fukai, and others in the book, by their given names (*gagō*).

ventures of his samurai forebears is not known; but Iyo, the area where his ancestors had served as domainal retainers, had been the center of Christian activity in Shikoku. The first Christian missionaries, among them the Jesuit Gaspar Vilela (1525–72) landed at Horie Beach, about six miles west of the town of Iyo in 1559. The Jesuit historian Luis Frois (1532–97) baptized the first six Christians of Iyo in 1564. Kobayakawa Takakage (1533–97), a samurai retainer of Toyotomi Hideyoshi (1536–98), built the first Christian church there; and a priests' residence was constructed at Dōgo (in present-day Matsuyama) about the same time. Kobayakawa took his half-brother, Hidekane (1566–1601), as his adopted son and had him baptized in 1587 and given the Christian name Simeão.[21]

The hidden Christians (*kakure kirishitan*) of Iyo retained their Christian identity throughout the Tokugawa period not so much by learning the prayers that were passed down to them, as did the Nagasaki Christians, but by keeping Buddhist statues marked with disguised or hidden crosses and by venerating the graves of their Christian ancestors. In 1975 some graves of underground Christians were discovered in Iyo by children who reported seeing "strange rocks" in the underbrush. The children reported their find to a local Christian, Norimatsu Masanori, who investigated and identified the gravestones as those of Christian samurai from Iyo.[22]

It would be surprising if the samurai forebears of Baba Bunkō, who had served a Christian lord, had not themselves become Christian and passed on their faith to their descendants. It had been customary that if the lord were Christian, peasants and retainers would become Christian as well. A historical researcher today, however, would certainly be hard-pressed to prove conclusively that the Nakai family, of which Bunkō was a descendant, was or was not Christian. This is because if the family had been Christian, they would have concealed their religious beliefs precisely so that their faith would never be known.

The sociologist Georg Simmel has explained the dynamics of both individual secrecy and group secrecy that were integral to Japanese

21. Hidekane was the ninth son of Mori Motonari (1497–1571). The daimyo's wife was a daughter of the Christian samurai Otomo Sōrin (1530–87).

22. See the website of Matsuyama Board of Education, http://www.matsuyama-edu.ed.jp/~s.horie/rekisi/kirisitan.htm

Christian religious praxis. The secret—that is, one's Christian faith—determined the relationships between the ones who preserved the secret and those who did not.[23] Secrecy became part of the fabric of life in the "deep cover" (*fukaku kakure*) of the underground Christian communities.[24] There could never be conclusive evidence that Nakai Bun'emon was a Christian, but a study of his writings after he changed his name to Baba Bunkō will point to suggestions of his hidden beliefs. Unlike the Christian peasants of the Nagasaki area in the early seventeenth century, hidden Christian samurai, such as the Nakai family, would have had recourse to an option other than the choice of either apostasy or martyrdom. Higashibaba Ikuo, scholar of religious culture in early modern Japan, has shown that there was a third alternative, the result of a bit of casuistry known as "faith by external apostasy," which allowed a samurai to hold his faith in good conscience without practicing it in any external way. Although this option would have gone against the instructions of the Church, it was the most reasonable and practical solution if one wanted to continue to believe and practice the faith secretly without being detected.[25]

In 1751 Iyo domain was still reeling from a series of economic disasters that had begun twenty years earlier during the Kyōhō famine (1732). Iyo, along with forty-six southwestern domains, had lost nearly 75 percent of its crops. Twelve thousand people had starved to death, and over 2,600,000 had reportedly suffered from hunger due to the effects of the famine. Iyo was one of the worst hit areas.[26] It was in this year that Nakai Bun'emon left his home in this traditionally Christian area and journeyed to Edo, the shogunal capital.

Just before his departure for Edo, Nakai changed his given name from Bun'emon to Samaji. Later, he took on an entirely new name, Ba Bunkō, which he changed again, not long after, to Baba Bunkō, the name by which he would become known to the audiences who heard his lectures and read his essays and anecdotes. It was also the name by which

23. Kurt H. Wolff, *The Sociology of Georg Simmel* (Glencoe, Ill.: The Free Press, 1950), 345.

24. Murai Saiai, *Bakuhansei seiritsu to kirishitan kinsei* (Tokyo: Bunken shuppan, 1987), 73.

25. Ikuo Higashibaba, *Christianity in Early Modern Japan: Kirishitan Belief and Practice* (Leiden: Brill Academic Publishers, 2002), 155.

26. Totman, *Early Modern Japan*, 237.

he would become known to the Tokugawa authorities. The practice of changing one's name was not uncommon at the time (or even now). It was meant to signify a change of direction of one's life or of one's status. After arriving in the capital, Bunkō found a position working as a low-ranking bureaucrat in the service of the government. However, what might have become a promising career in Edo took an unexpected turn. For unknown reasons, he ended up leaving his position after only a few months. Unemployed, he began to make regular visits to Gojiin Temple (in present-day Kanda-bashi, Tokyo) to observe the street vendors and listen to the entertainers telling their tales. It was not a long time before Bunkō himself, on the grounds of the large Asakusa Temple (Sensōji in present-day Taito-ku, Tokyo), sitting behind a small raised platform in the manner typical of the many storytellers in Edo at the time, began recounting his own tales, telling war stories, and reciting selections from the Japanese classics. These included the two famous tales of rivalry between powerful families, *The Tale of the Taira* (*Heike monogatari*, thirteenth century) and *The Tale of the Soga Brothers* (*Soga monogatari*, fourteenth century). Bunkō also used material from the well-known collection of Buddhist essays and anecdotes titled *Essays in Idleness* (*Tsurezuregusa*, fifteenth century) to spice up and give depth to his lectures and stories.

All of these classic works had long been part of the typical repertoire of the kōdanshi, but Bunkō took this form of entertainment to another level by interspersing his recitations of the tales with anecdotes about the vices prevalent in contemporary society and the hypocrisy of named public officials. He castigated in particular the immorality of the samurai and members of the elite governing class of the Tokugawa bakufu, with whom he had worked for a short time, and called them "monsters." The Catholic novelist and critic Inoue Hisashi (1934–2011) composed a hypothetical lecture in the style of the oral performances that Bunkō delivered at Asakusa Temple. Inoue's fictional re-creation, which clearly presents the attitude of confrontation with which Bunkō spoke and wrote, captures the essence of Bunkō's presentations.

> My good people, who have come here tonight to Asakusa Temple: I tell you there are many monsters roaming about. Beware, all of you. When I say

"monsters," you may think of enchanted foxes, demon serpents, or giant rats. But these are not the monsters to be feared. More frightening and much worse than these are people! Human beings, I tell you! They are what you should be afraid of![27]

The combination of criticism of the privileged on the one hand and support of the victimized poor and weak on the other became an important characteristic of his style. His satirical exposés directed against dishonest public officials revealed a familiarity with government bureaucrats and the political situation in Edo that offers important insights into the history of the Tokugawa period. Blatant corruption in the government, which Bunkō strongly denounced, may have been one of the reasons he not only resigned his government post after only a few months. He also renounced his samurai status, turning his back on a social position with which he could no longer in good conscience associate himself.

A contemporary account by a person who witnessed Bunkō lecturing in the Kanda district of Edo would indicate the little importance he placed on his former samurai status:

In Kanda there lives a raconteur of old war tales by the name of Ba Bunkō. Until recently he was a samurai in the service of the government. Now he goes about unkempt, with disheveled hair. What could have happened? Though a *rōnin* [masterless samurai], he does not seem to be very educated and has no visible means of support. And yet he has the leisure to give lectures and tell old war tales. Recently, he has begun to devote himself to the writing of *kanazōshi* [small pamphlets sold by peddlers].[28] His last recorded place of residence was in Matsushima-chō [present-day Tokyo, Chūō-ku, Nihonbashi, Ningyō-chō 1-chōme].[29]

Though this early account of Bunkō's activity reports that he appeared uneducated, this was clearly a false impression. Bunkō had studied *haikai* (popular linked verse) under the prominent Edo poet Nakagawa Sozui (1684–1744), which allowed him to hone his skills at oral performance.

27. Inoue Hisashi, *Gesakusha meimeiden* (Tokyo: Chūō kōronsha, 1979), 192.

28. *Kanazōshi* were short stories or tales written in the indigenous Japanese kana script rather than in Chinese characters and hence could be easily read by the less educated commoner. This genre of literature was produced in Kyoto from approximately 1600 to 1680.

29. Hōreikan, *Bokuteki ruisō*, manuscript in National Diet Library, Tokyo, folio 30 front.

Though lecturing and storytelling was the safer medium and less subject to government censorship than the written word, he branched out to become a writer of political satire. The style and content of his political writings bear the marks of a well-informed, educated writer who was openly critical of the government and its officials. There were many itinerant lecturers and storytellers who tried to scrape out a living on the grounds of the Asakusa Temple and at other temples, as well as in the neighborhoods of Edo. Bunkō's style, however, gradually became noticeably different from that of the other kōdanshi who entertained the crowds because he departed from fiction and became more of a social critic.

About this time, Bunkō was fortunate enough to make the acquaintance of a wealthy rice broker, Iseya Sōshirō, who offered the fledgling kōdanshi his support. Bunkō was soon earning his own living by lecturing and preaching in the didactic style typical of other kōdanshi. He continued to develop a talent for delivering dramatic recitations, telling anecdotes, reporting the latest spicy rumors, and lecturing on current topics. His entertaining monologues became more and more popular, but it was especially for his oral presentations given under the title "An Account of the Disorder in Japan" (*Dai Nippon chiranki*), which he delivered at Unemegahara in what is today the Ginza area of Tokyo, that he drew the largest crowd.[30]

Bunkō's essays reveal a knowledge of politics and ethics, and also a familiarity with the modus operandi of Edo officials that would have been beyond the knowledge of the typical kōdanshi. In spite of having been a provincial samurai and now a newcomer to Edo, he was obviously familiar with the inside workings of the political establishment and at the same time was well-versed in Edo popular culture. Consequently, the content of his kanazōshi essays was quite different from other works in that genre. Rather than the typical stories about the past or contemporary accounts that were presented as fiction, Bunkō's stories were about real people, most of whom would have been known to his readers.

30. This is the area of Ginza 5-chōme, to the south of Sūkiyabashi Gate and east of Kobikichō 4-chōme. Few daimyō had their residences in this area, which was mainly made up of places of entertainment for the commoners: show tents, street entertainers, and places for eating and drinking.

A significant event for Bunkō took place on the grounds of the Asakusa Temple. It was there that he first met his childhood hero and the most famous kōdanshi of the time, Fukai Shidōken. This was the legendary storyteller about whom his father had spoken to him when he was a boy, and he was excited now to finally meet the star of oral storytelling who had fascinated him so much. After a time, however, Bunkō became disenchanted with Shidōken and even quite critical. It became clear to him that though Shidōken was educated and talented, he seemed to have no practical sense of morality, of right or wrong. Bunkō calls Shidōken a "pseudo-monk" who deceives people because he is ignorant of good and evil. "Everything he says is a repudiation of the sound sense of Heaven.... What makes this so terrible is that he is leading the world astray, destroying the love between fathers and sons and between older and younger brothers. He is a criminal, no different from the most heinous of villains."[31]

Bunkō came to the conclusion that Shidōken was a fraud who repeated the same tales again and again but had not learned any lesson from them that could be applied to correcting one's moral behavior or improving one's way of life. Shidōken, for his part, would taunt Bunkō, criticizing him for being cowardly, fickle, and afraid to tell the truth. The jeers and gibes that came from his mouth did much to embolden Bunkō to become more fearless in his own lectures, and it was probably due, at least in part, to Shidōken's negative evaluation of him that Bunkō resolved to be afraid of no one. Shidōken turned out to have been an important figure in Bunkō's life even though the two never got along.

Baba Bunkō was not the only samurai to leave his home province and travel to Edo, nor was he unique in abandoning "the way of the warrior" to become a teacher and public speaker. In fact, three or four out of every ten rōnin who went to Edo from the provinces no longer lived as samurai but adopted the lifestyle of the commoner.[32] Most of these immigrants to Edo were proud of their samurai heritage but found themselves attracted to the diversions and entertainments of commoner culture. Bunkō also

31. Baba, *Tōdai Edo hyaku bakemono*, 39.

32. Najita Tetsuo, "History and Nature in Eighteenth-Century Tokugawa Thought," in *Early Modern Japan* , vol. 4 of *The Cambridge History of Japan*, ed. John Whitney Hall et al. (Cambridge: Cambridge University Press, 1991), 646.

became familiar with the popular culture but did not allow himself to become immersed in it. Not only did he not flaunt his former samurai background, but he distanced himself as much as he could from it. While other samurai were jealous of the growing wealth of the merchant class and indignant at the lack of respect they were shown by commoners, Bunkō did not identify with their complaints or insist on commoners' respect. Most samurai in the 1750s might have been envious of the popular pastimes of the kabuki theater and the Yoshiwara "pleasure" quarters that wealthy commoners could afford, but though Bunkō was very familiar with both of these entertainment centers and wrote about them extensively, he did not begrudge the wealth of the merchants or the opportunities for the diversions in which they indulged. Rather he was quite critical of the values and the influence that these institutions had on society. Quite unlike other former samurai, he had a clear vision, purpose, and direction for his life. Bunkō gradually saw that it was his calling to knock the bottom out of the traditional belief in the moral superiority of the samurai—a crucial assumption that the Tokugawa bakufu propagated in order to uphold its legitimacy and keep political control in the hands of the samurai class.[33]

Baba Bunkō was influenced by the philosophy of Arai Hakuseki (1657–1725), who argued that the shogun must be the sole, ultimate source of authority,[34] but if the shogun were powerless, his government would not be legitimate.[35] This was the reason that, in Bunkō's view, the government of the contemporary shogun, Tokugawa Ieshige (ruled 1745–1760), was illegitimate. Ieshige was indeed the perfect example of "a powerless ruler" and consequently, as Bunkō saw it, his government was unlawful and corrupt. In *A Confidential Record of Current Little-Known Facts* (*Tōji chinsetsu yōhiroku*, 1756), Bunkō gives a scathing account of the shogun's "immoral" lifestyle:

> Tokugawa Ieshige, the ninth shogun from Ieyasu, eldest son of the previous shogun, Yoshimume, born in Kii, has been a punishment inflicted on the en-

33. Ibid.

34. Kate Wildman Nakai, *Shogunal Politics: Arai Hakuseki and the Premises of Tokugawa Rule* (Cambridge, Mass: Council on East Asian Studies, Harvard University, 1988), 183.

35. Matsumura Akira et al., eds., *Arai Hakuseki, Nihon shisō taikei*, vol. 35, *Arai Hakuseki, Toshi yoron* (Tokyo: Iwanami shoten, 1975), 428.

> tire realm. He became ill in the prime of his life, no doubt due to his excesses in sex and alcohol. He has sexual relations with the maids of his court. He gives extravagantly sumptuous banquets. All of this is a contributing factor to his poor health. He has led an utterly dissolute life, and his propensity for sex and alcohol has only increased as he has gotten more and more ill. He wakes up very late in the morning but is always tired. He is inarticulate [because of a speech defect], and so he never gives any commands unless [his spokesman] Ōoka Tadamitsu [1709–60] speaks for him.[36]

Ieshige's lifestyle would not necessarily have been judged immoral by the standards of the time. Bunkō's description of the shogun's "utterly dissolute life," even though perhaps extreme in Ieshige's case, was easily overlooked and considered typical of the conduct of officials in the shogunal court at the time.

Bunkō, judging from a completely different moral standard, maintained that the weak, and thus illicit, government of Ieshige rendered the entire system of samurai dominance illegitimate, and the illegality was further proven by the open corruption of samurai officials. Bunkō would not have dreamed of a complete overthrow of the Tokugawa shogunate, but he strongly advocated changes within the bakufu structure that would allow only moral officials and a virtuous shogun to rule. Bunkō considered the previous shogun, Tokugawa Yoshimune (r. 1716–45), such a virtuous ruler.

Though Bunkō was familiar with Hakuseki's works, his criticisms of society and government were not based primarily on philosophical grounds but more on his own personal observations. The causes of the failure of officials to govern in a just manner were their hypocrisy, their lack of ethical and moral understanding, and their immoral behavior. In *Contemporary Edo: An Album of One Hundred Monsters* (*Tōdai Edo hyaku bakemono*, 1758), Bunkō critiques the lifestyle of a number of these officials, one of whom is Mizoguchi Naoatsu (1714–80), also known as Shibata Baikō, the seventh daimyō of Shibata, Echigo domain (in present-day Niigata prefecture) between 1732 and 1761.

"Among all the fools in Edo," Bunkō writes, "there is the one called

36. *Tōji chinsetsu yōhiroku*, in Kokusho kankōkai, eds., *Sōshō Edo bunko*, vol. 12, *Baba Bunkō shū*, ed. Okada Satoshi (Tokyo: Kokusho kankōkai, 1987), 177–80.

Shibata Baikō." This was a daimyō who was in the habit of going out in search of erotic exploits in total disregard of his highly respected position.[37] Because of such open condemnation of important officials, Bunkō would eventually become an embarrassment to the shogunate and a threat to the image of social stability that it wished to project.

Fortunately, the proprietor of an Edo lending library, one Eizō by name, recorded Bunkō's lectures and circulated the manuscripts widely. Though Bunkō's writings were never published in his lifetime, they did circulate in the form of handwritten manuscripts, and many remained in circulation even after his death.[38] A copy of "The Tale of a Tribute from Morioka" (*Mitsugi Morioka monogatari*, 1757), for example, a tract which deals with a dispute in the Tokugawa shogunal castle between the senior counselors and officials of Nanbu domain, contains a label indicating that it was circulated by a commercial lending library as far away as Kanazawa, about two hundred miles from the capital. This is evidence that Bunkō's works traveled well beyond the boundaries of Edo.[39] The Tokugawa government destroyed or confiscated many of Bunkō's written works after his death, but not all. Isaac Titsingh, the head of the Dutch factory of the Dutch East India Company from 1779 to 1784, knew of Bunkō's writings long after the satirist's death.[40]

As the reader will see, Bunkō's satirical attacks on corruption in the government, the nature of his denunciation of the immorality in contemporary popular culture, and the reasons for his repudiation of the hypocrisy in the religious establishments of Buddhism and Confucianism all point to the moral principles on which he based his writings. His essays would be impossible to fully comprehend without reference to these moral principles and an understanding of their source in the Japanese Christianity that persisted in secrecy throughout the Tokugawa period.

37. Baba, *Tōdai Edo hyaku bakemono*, 7–8.

38. Timon Screech, ed., *Secret Memoirs of the Shoguns: Isaac Titsingh and Japan, 1779–1822* (New York: Routledge, 2006), 67.

39. Peter F. Kornicki, *The Book in Japan: A Cultural History from the Beginnings to the Nineteenth Century* (Honolulu: University of Hawaii Press, 2000), 108–9.

40. Screech, *Secret Memoirs of the Shoguns*, 67.

2 | TOKUGAWA CHRISTIANITY

> *. . . the Bakuhan state may have taken a relaxed approach to the enforcement of the anti-Christian policies. . . . Their existence would have been de facto evidence that either the official or his predecessor had been derelict in the exercise of their responsibilities.*
>
> PETER NOSCO

Enforcing the Anti-Christian Edict

With his military victory at the battle of Sekigahara (present-day Gifu prefecture) in 1600, Tokugawa Ieyasu consolidated his power over the Western territorial lords, brought an end to the conflicts of the Sengoku (warring states) period (1467–1573), and became the de facto ruler of Japan. Among Ieyasu's vanquished foes was Konishi Yukinaga (1555–1600), the territorial lord of Higo domain (present-day Kumamoto prefecture) in Kyushu, which was a major center of Christianity. Yukinaga had sided against Ieyasu with a coalition of daimyō from western Japan under the command of Ishida Mitsunari (1559–1600), the lord of Sawayama (now a part of Hikone). After the defeat of the western forces at Sekigahara, Yukinaga fled into the mountains in the vicinity of Mount Ibuki (in

Epigraph is from Peter Nosco, "Secrecy and the Transmission of Tradition: Issues in the Study of the 'Underground' Christians," *Japanese Journal of Religious Studies* 120, no. 1 (1993): 23.

present-day Gifu prefecture). It was there that he was captured and ordered to commit suicide. However, because of his Christian faith, Yukinaga refused to obey the order and was executed.

Other Christian daimyō managed to escape Yukinaga's fate after their defeat at Sekigahara and fled Japan. It is estimated that between three and four hundred samurai, most of whom had become Christians on their own or at the behest of their lords, made their way across the seas to safety in the Philippines, Macao, Siam, Burma, and other areas of Southeast Asia. In 1640 the Jesuit Antonio Farinha, on arrival in Arakan in Burma, reported that well over one hundred Japanese immigrants had been living there for thirty years, and almost all were Catholics.[1] It was known to the shogunate that many Japanese Catholics had fled and were living abroad, and that there was a high probability that any returning Japanese would likely be Christian. The presence of Japanese Christians living abroad remained a concern for the shogunate throughout the Tokugawa period.

In 1611 Yamada Nagamasa (1590–1630), a palanquin bearer to the lord of Numazu (in present-day Shizuoka prefecture), had sailed to Siam on a ship that was licensed by the shogunate to establish trade relations, but he was prevented from returning to Japan because of Ieyasu's 1613 edict forbidding the repatriation of Japanese who were living abroad. Nagamasa eventually became the chief of the royal bodyguards for the king of Ayutthaya, Somdet Phra Songtham (r. 1611–28). In that capacity, he commanded eight hundred Japanese and twenty thousand Siamese troops in a series of battles to secure the throne for the king's son, Somdet Phra Chetthathirat II (r. 1628–29). Of the eight hundred Japanese serving under Nagamasa's command, as many as half were Catholics. They made their living as merchants in peacetime and soldiers when needed.[2] Nagamasa and over fifteen hundred Japanese inhabitants resided in the settlement known as "Ban Yipun" (the Japanese quarters) in Ayutthaya. The Christian community of Ban Yipun numbered about four hundred samurai in addition to Christian commoners.[3] A Jesuit priest, Antonio Francisco Cardim (1596–1659), administered sacraments and celebrat-

1. Iwao Seiichi, *Nanyō Nihon machi no kenkyū* (Tokyo: Iwanami shoten, 1966), 139–43.

2. Ibid., 143.

3. Madalena Ribeiro, "The Japanese Diaspora in the Seventeenth Century according to Jesuit Sources," *Bulletin of Portuguese/Japanese Studies* 3 (2001): 53–83, 75.

ed Mass for the Christian community in the 1620s and 1630s. Japanese Christians remained in Ban Yipun well into the later Tokugawa period.

Not all of the Christians in Japan at the time of the 1613 edict left the country. Even after Christianity was officially proscribed, samurai who had accepted the faith took up posts in the bakufu and carried out their assigned bureaucratic tasks without giving any indication they were Christian. This is proven by the fact that, even after Tokugawa Ieyasu's anti-Christian edict of 1613, Christianity continued to infiltrate many of the domains in southwestern Japan and even into a circle of Ieyasu's own guards in his castle at Sumpu (in present-day Shizuoka prefecture).[4] When their presence became known, Ieyasu, recognizing the threat to shogunal authority, strengthened security within his ranks. Increased surveillance led to the discovery of tens of Christian *hatamoto* (bannermen) who were in service to the shogun.[5] These ostensibly loyal samurai had been engaged in a profoundly subversive activity.

What continued to alarm the government was that in spite of the close vigilance, pockets of Christians continued to be discovered many decades after the expulsion edict. More than five hundred Christians were arrested in Bungo province in southern Japan between 1660 and 1670. Christians were found in all but eight of the sixty-six major provinces of Japan, and a large number of arrests were made in districts in central and northern Japan in the late 1600s where no flourishing Christian communities had ever been thought to have existed.[6] In 1667 more than two thousand Christians were arrested in Mino and Owari in central and northern Japan. In 1697 another group of thirty-five Christians were arrested and put to death in Mino (in present-day Gifu province), where the official position of the domain was that Christians had been completely wiped out thirty years earlier.

The number of hidden Christians living in Japan in the 1700s is not known for certain, but Peter Nosco has estimated that "tens (if not hundreds) of thousands of Christians continued to defy the state by sustaining

4. Nam-lin Hur, *Death and Social Order in Tokugawa Japan: Buddhism, Anti-Christianity, and the Danka System* (Cambridge, Mass.: Harvard University Asia Center, Harvard East Asian Monographs, 2007), 40.

5. Ibid.

6. Joseph Jennes, *A History of the Catholic Church in Japan: From Its Beginnings to the Early Meiji Era* (Tokyo: Oriens Institute for Religious Research, 1973), 162.

the traditions, practices, and creed of their forebears, veiling it in Buddhist folk religion and for the most part outwardly living the lives of near-model citizens."[7] As shown above, their existence has been confirmed by discoveries throughout the Tokugawa period. Christians were in Nagasaki and its environs, of course, but also in Settsu (now part of Hyogo prefecture and Osaka), Nanbu, and Sendai domains, and in other areas of Japan.

Contemporary political theorist and critic of Christianity Miura Baien (1723–89) articulated the fear of a spread of Christianity even as late as 1784. "In the third year of Genki [1572]," he wrote, "devotees of this [Christian] sect entered our country from the lands of the southern barbarians and gave the people gold and silver. They displayed magical arts to them and deceived them. Within eleven years this doctrine had gradually spread, and everyone was a Christian."[8] Toward the end of his life Miura again expressed a popular view of Christianity that had prevailed for over a century, since the first decades of the Tokugawa period: "In planning to conquer a country Christians first help the weak and restore the poor to prosperity with gifts of gold, silver, grain, and cloth; then heal the sick with various incantations and beguile men's eyes and ears with their wiles and finally bedevil their hearts with the doctrine of the Lord of Heaven."[9]

Baien reported that he had heard of "five or six Japanese boys studying for the priesthood in Luzon, Philippines, and twelve studying in Macao, all of whom were planning to be sent back to Japan."[10] Such reports confirmed the shogunate in the wisdom of its policy that no Japanese should return to Japan from abroad. Baien expressed surprise that not only were there Japanese Christians living abroad, but there were also Christians who had somehow managed to remain in Japan even long after the proscription of the religion. He wrote: "How is it that even now in 1784, we occasionally hear of cases where the followers of the evil sect rouse the spirits of the deceased at night in abandoned places?"[11]

The fear of Christianity persisted throughout the Tokugawa period. A

7. Nosco, "Secrecy and the Transmission of Tradition," 25.
8. Miura Baien, *Samidare-sho*, trans. Leon Hurvitz, *Monumenta Nipponica* 8, no. 1 (1952): 289–326, 292, 314.
9. Ibid., 292.
10. Miura Baien, *Samidare-sho II*, *Monumenta Nipponica* 9, no. 2 (1952): 330–56, 337.
11. Ibid., 347.

pamphlet written in 1757 titled *Real Record of the Arrival of the Christian Sect in Japan* (*Kirishitan shumon raichō jikki*) asserts that "the term *bateren* [padre] is derived from the missionaries' ability to perform magic and miracles through demonic power over Heaven.... By means of this foreign religion and miraculous powers the bateren are able to bring the people of Japan into total submission." The work accuses the missionaries of having brought a "demonic religion" from the land of the barbarians and of using powers they acquired from evil gods and demons to subvert the minds of the Japanese.[12]

The Real Record of the Arrival of the Christian Sect in Japan blames Oda Nobunaga (1534–82) for allowing Christianity to spread in the first place:[13]

> Nobunaga was an unprincipled and perverse man. He tore down the Shinto and Buddhist temples and seized their possessions. His obstinate and unrestrained conduct was so great that the good gods turned their eyes away, and the evil gods and demons, taking advantage of their opportunity, introduced false doctrines and wicked rites by bringing over the *Kirishitan*, the demonic religion from Nanban [the land of the southern barbarians], whereby an untold number of people were destroyed.[14]

The fear of the evils brought by Christianity intensified in the 1750s—rather than diminishing, as one might expect—since the religion had supposedly been eradicated a century before. In the eighteenth century Christianity was still perceived as a political threat to the social order.[15] *The Real Record* perpetuated frightening myths about the bateren in particular, long after they had been expelled from the country. "They [the bateren] taught the Christians to perform various miracles, such as how to change a handkerchief into a horse, to make a bird out of dust, to make a withered tree blossom, to turn clods of earth into pearls, to sit upon the air, to descend into the earth, or to cause clouds to rise and make it rain or snow."[16] The author explains that by analyzing the three Chinese characters that

12. M. Paske-Smith, *Japanese Traditions of Christianity: Being Some Old Translations from the Japanese, with British Consular Reports of the Persecutions of 1868–1872* (Kobe: J. L. Thompson, 1929), 6.

13. Oda Nobunaga initiated the unification of Japan in the late sixteenth century.

14. *The Real Record of the Arrival of the Christian Sect in Japan*, Waseda University manuscript, 1755, 1. Also in M. Paske-Smith, *Japanese Traditions of Christianity*, 6.

15. Kiri Paramore, *Ideology and Christianity in Japan* (Abingdon, UK: Routledge, 2009), 109.

16. Paske-Smith, *Japanese Traditions of Christianity*, 27–28.

are used to make up the word "bateren," one can easily prove that the missionaries were engaged in evil magic. "The character *BA* means to destroy; *TE* is a contraction of *Ten* meaning the heavens; and *REN* means to pass through the clouds.... By means of their foreign religion and miraculous powers, the bateren destroy heaven and are able to pass through the clouds and bring the people of Japan into submission."[17]

However, in fact, these were not the three characters that were used in the sixteenth century for the term "bateren." The actual Sino-Japanese characters that were used were the characters for "companion," "heaven," and "group," designating "the group of companions that live according to heaven." The above text reflected the commonly held belief that the bateren were unworldly creatures who had come to destroy traditional Japanese beliefs.

One of the best known and most widely read of the anti-Christian works of the period was *Tales of the Christians* (*Kirishitan monogatari*, 1639). Written by an anonymous author, this book was the first in a genre of anti-Christian literature and was read throughout the Tokugawa period. *Tales of the Christians* begins with a grotesque portrayal of the first missionaries to arrive in Japan: "In the reign of ... the 108th emperor, a Southern Barbarian ... trading vessel came to our shores. From this ship for the first time emerged an unnamable creature, somewhat similar in shape to a human being, but looking rather more like a long-nosed goblin or the giant demon Mikoshi Nyūdō [a genie]. Upon close interrogation it was discovered that this was a being called *bateren*."[18]

The Confucian scholar Aizawa Seishisai (1782–1863), in a work on national policy titled "New Thesis" (*Shinron*), argued in 1825 that Christianity was still a threat after so many years, even though it had been long forbidden:

> The immunity of superior men to Christianity does not permit complacence. Again the dimwits argue, "Stupid commoners cannot be deceived and converted today because Christianity is strictly prohibited. Though the barbarians may display trifling shrewdness, there is no cause for alarm." The barbarians have been unable to work their wiles on us up to now only because

17. Ibid., 9–10.
18. *Kirishitan monogatari: Anonymous Chapbook*, in Elison, *Deus Destroyed*, 321.

> the bakufu has strictly outlawed Christianity. And I might add, the people of the realm are very fortunate that it has. Nevertheless, the fact remains that the mysterious evils are spreading throughout the land today.[19]

Japan never completely rid itself of the fear of Christianity during the Tokugawa period. The reality behind this fear was, as Aizawa wrote, the spread of Christianity "throughout the land." Rumors about Christians continued to persist for more than three hundred years, long after Christianity was purportedly eradicated. The continuing propagation of Christianity was still occurring late in the Tokugawa period during a time that historians today have discounted as having any importance in the history of Christianity in Japan.

Hidden Christians

Not all Japanese Christians were poor, oppressed peasants cowering in their huts on isolated islands off the coast of Kyushu, waiting in fear for the authorities to discover them. The descendants of samurai who had converted to Christianity, either out of their own conviction or because the daimyō under whom they served was a Christian, also kept their faith after Christianity was proscribed. Though the evidence of persecution directed against peasant Christians is much more available than direct evidence for the persecution of Christian samurai, it cannot be assumed that all of the Christian members of the samurai class were exiled, fled Japan, or immediately gave up their faith. In fact, the samurai who were "hidden Christians" would have been quite capable of keeping their faith secret, if only because by the late 1700s even the domainal authorities wanted to keep the fact of the existence of Christians hidden from the shogunate.

It is understandable that many historians of early modern Japan have come to the conclusion that Christianity was virtually wiped out. This was the propaganda disseminated by the Tokugawa shogunate. However, the conclusion that the bakufu no longer considered Christianity a threat in the eighteenth century is false. The shogunate continued its

19. Bob Tadashi Wakabayashi, *Anti-Foreignism and Western Learning in Early Modern Japan: The New Theses of 1825* (Cambridge, Mass.: Council on East Asian Studies, Harvard University, 1991), 211–12.

efforts to enforce its anti-Christian statutes and to make sure domainal administrators enforced them as well, since the existence of the Christian religion was still perceived as a menace. As late as 1688 the bakufu required all daimyō to submit two registers of suspected Christians: one listing the names of those who had died and another enumerating the descendants of Christians who were still living. Of course, those still living, even if their ancestors had been Christian, may not necessarily have been Christian themselves, but the government insisted that they be scrutinized simply because the blood of the *Kirishitan* flowed in their veins. The bakufu reintroduced particularly stringent regulations pertaining to Christians as late as 1695. Twice a year local officials were required to report to the bakufu any changes in the status of the descendants of Christians, such as the birth of children, marriages, adoptions, and deaths.[20] As late as 1776, Senior Counselor Matsudaira Yasuyoshi (1719–89) was concerned that some local officials were being negligent with regard to scrutinizing descendants of Christians and ordered reports to be made twice a year.[21] This is clear evidence that the government was still perplexed about Christian influence remaining in Japan and that neither the Christian creed itself nor those who professed it were successfully eradicated, despite one-and-a-half centuries of systematic persecution.[22]

In 1827 a woman in Kyoto by the name of Toyota Mitsugi was found to be in possession of Christian books that had been published by missionaries in China and then smuggled into Japan. The government was shocked at the revelation that she had secretly taken over the organization of a Christian group that had been in existence since the 1780s. The government tried to conceal the fact that she was somehow connected with the forbidden religion. Tokugawa law stipulated that Christians, if discovered, were to be condemned to death. There were, of course, other crimes for which criminals were executed during the Tokugawa period. The crime of arson, for example, or the theft of a large sum of money, or

20. Nam-lin Hur, *Death and Social Order in Tokugawa Japan*, 101–2. While I am grateful to the author for the information supplied here, I come to a very different conclusion. Nam-lin Hur asserts that since Christianity was virtually extinct, the shogunate was not worried about its influence. I find that the shogunate was very much worried and fearful of Christianity throughout the Tokugawa period and into the Meiji period. This was the reason for its continued surveillance.

21. Nam-lin Hur, *Death and Social Order in Tokugawa Japan*, 400.

22. Peter Nosco, "Secrecy and the Transmission of Tradition," 25.

actually plotting the overthrow of the government incurred an automatic death sentence. Local authorities could use any one of these crimes as a pretext to execute a Christian without having to report to the bakufu that a Christian had been discovered. To let the truth be known that Toyota Mitsugi was a Christian would have been tantamount to an admission that two hundred years of attempts to exterminate Christianity had been a failure and put the local officials, including the Shogunal Deputy in Kyoto (*Kyōto shoshidai*), at risk of being reprimanded or removed from office. This is why the local government never publicly or explicitly accused Toyota of being a Christian, but people living in the Osaka and Kyoto area where Toyota was known spoke of the incident as "the Christian affair."[23]

Baba Bunkō's Christian Literature

Baba Bunkō's last collection of essays, written only one month before his arrest on the sixteenth day of the ninth month of 1758, summarizes opinions and convictions that he had expressed in much more subtle ways in prior writings. In 1758 Bunkō no longer took the precautions he had taken earlier to avoid arrest, and consequently his essays in this last collection give evidence of Christian sympathies in a clearer and more direct manner.

The work in question, titled "A Collection of Useless Grumblings" (*Guchishūi monogatari*, 1758. 8), is a synopsis of his views of contemporary Japanese society, the imperial establishment, the shogunate, and Christianity. The purpose of the rather undignified title of the work may have been to deter the attention of the authorities. However, it may also be a reference to Bunkō's statement that "people were told Christianity was completely useless." The title could also refer to the futility of praying to the Shinto deities and Buddhas, since Bunkō calls this type of prayer "vain and useless."

The work begins with an introduction that gives various reasons for the moral decay in the contemporary society:

> Looking at the world [i.e., Japan] today, people are drawn to a myriad of excesses and extravagances.... People have lost a sense of right and wrong.

23. Joseph Jennes, *A History of the Catholic Church in Japan*, 189.

> They are so immersed in the pursuit of their own pleasure that they can hardly bear even to catch a cold.... Even though the laws of Confucius strongly forbid wearing indecent dress and using foul language, such habits are seen everywhere nowadays. There have been publications that call for a restoration of obedience to the traditions of the ancient [Chinese sage] kings, but these are ignored.[24]

Bunkō is referring here to the decline in samurai morality and respectability and to the deterioration of Neo-Confucian orthodoxy that had long been the moral underpinning of society and government. This moral decline in Tokugawa society, which Bunkō laments in much of his writings, will be explored in greater detail in the following chapters. After the introduction to "A Collection of Useless Grumblings," Bunkō explores the specific, concrete causes for the decline in morality, suggesting that the coat-of-arms of the emperor (the imperial chrysanthemum) and the coat-of-arms of the shogun (the paulownia) may in some way be responsible for this moral decline:

> From ancient times, the emperor's crest was a design based on the sun or the moon.... Then later the chrysanthemum, which is a pattern that resembles the sun, came into use. The paulownia is the crest of the shogunate. It has been said that the paulownia has the power to counteract various vices, such as the three poisons of covetousness, anger, and foolishness. The ancient sage kings (*seiō*) believed that it protected against the ten evils and bestowed the ten goods.[25] These crests of our country, the chrysanthemum with sixteen pedals, also known as "the hermit's flower" (*in'itsuka*), and the paulownia are believed to have some hidden meaning, but they actually make little sense and are really inferior (*soryaku*) things.[26] Even so, people today are very submissive to the shogunate (*marunouchi*).... Such crests are pointless, and they look foolish. Both crests should be abolished and the designs for them redone. They have brought unexpected misfortune rather than protection.[27]

24. Baba Bunkō, *Guchishūi monogatari*, National Diet Library MS; also in Mitamura Engyo, ed., *Mikan zuihitsu hyakushu* (Tokyo: Chūō kōronsha, 1977), 9: 12.

25. The ten evils are killing, stealing, adultery, lying, clever talk, duplicity, slander, ill-will, covetousness, perverted views. The ten goods are their opposites: not killing, not stealing, nonlicense, not telling a lie, not breaking faith, not backbiting, not using lascivious language, not being greedy, not being angry, not holding wrong ideas.

26. In the Jin Dynasty (266–420), the poet Tao Yuan-ming (365–427) used the chrysanthemum to symbolize hermits who upheld integrity and honor.

27. Baba, *Guchishūi monogatari*, 19–20.

Bunkō's disdain for the symbols of the imperial house and the shogunate is apparent, but more importantly he proceeds to introduce another crest which, in his opinion, is more worthy of respect than either the imperial chrysanthemum or the Tokugawa paulownia. This section of his work contains a number of references to Christianity:

> Now, let me ask: Is it proper to have destroyed what was for all human beings the most important symbol of all? That crest was one that was simple and proper. It showed the body of a person (*hito no karada o arawasu*). Chikamatsu [Monzaemon], who is held in high regard in our country, wrote about a certain uprising, which was a tragic disaster, in one of his plays. This play was the beginning of his bad luck. Everyone knows the *haikai* "The crest was the beginning of the end of his good fortune" (*shindai no kuzushi-hajime wa mondokoro*).[28]

"A certain uprising" to which Bunkō alludes is found in Chikamatsu Monzaemon's puppet play, "A Battle of Frogs in Shimabara" (*Keisei Shimabara kairu* [i.e., *kaeru*] *gassen*, 1719). In the play, a son of Fujiwara no Hidehira (1122–87) is said to use a form of Christian magic to conjure up a plague of frogs. He eventually takes the name of Nanakusa Shirō, an obvious reference to Amakusa Shirō, the young leader of the Christian uprising in Shimabara (1637–38).[29] The uprising to which Bunkō refers above is obviously the Shimabara rebellion.

What Bunkō calls "the most important symbol of all," the one that should take precedence over the imperial chrysanthemum and the shogunal paulownia, is the symbol that "shows the body of a person." Continuing his discourse, Bunkō clarifies the meaning of this symbol, which he also calls the crest of the "Christian champion" (that is, Amakusa Shirō):

> In Kanei 14 [1637] in Amakusa in Hizen province, the crest of the Christian champion (*taishō*) Watanabe Shirō Tokisada, in accordance with ancient belief, was the principal image of the Christian Lord of Heaven (*Kirishitan tentei no honson*). This image was made the crest of his movement. After Christianity was forbidden, no one used this crest. If anyone did use it, it was assumed he was a Christian. People were told Christianity was completely useless and

28. Ibid., 12.

29. Keiko Suzuki, "The Making of Tōjin: The Construction of the Other in Early Modern Japan," *Asian Folklore Studies* 66 (2007): 83–105, 98.

> that if they had the crest in their possession, they would be burned. This so frightened people that they would publicly declare that Christianity was certainly an erroneous religion.[30]

This crest to which Bunkō is referring is the battle flag of the Shimabara rebellion. This battle flag does not literally show the figure of the body of a person, as Bunkō indicated. It is rather the representation of a chalice and a round "host," or wafer of bread—the objects of the sacrament of the Eucharist used in the Catholic Mass that are believed by the faithful to be the body and blood of Christ. To the eyes of a non-Catholic the chalice and bread on the banner would not have actually been "the body of a person." For Bunkō, however, the crest of the Shimabara rebellion depicted "the body of a person" who was the "Christian Lord of Heaven." He obviously has a Catholic understanding of the meaning of the chalice and the host on the Shimabara banner because he refers to the wafer of bread as "the body of a person."

At the top of the banner is the inscription in Portuguese, "Praised be the most holy sacrament," in capital letters (LOUVAD[O] SEJA O SANTISSIM[O] SACRAMENTO). This is the crest that Bunkō describes as the "most important of all," the banner that should replace the imperial and shogunal crests that are "pointless," "look foolish," and "should be abolished."

In addition to his assessment of the Shimabara banner, Bunkō makes explicit mention of Christianity in a reference to the Catholic practice of confession. Calling attention to this practice was an important element in Bunkō's writing because it served to counter the common anti-Christian view of confession as one example of the many harmful practices in Christianity. The author of the anti-Christian diatribe *Tales of Christians* (cited above), for example, condemns confession as a cruel practice, the purpose of which is to severely punish wrongdoing:

> There is *confissan* [confession]: In the "Room of Repentance" the bateren and an *iruman* [catechist] and other adherents all sit in a circle while the penitent standing in the center publicly proclaims contrition for his sins and misdeeds. He begs forgiveness, subjecting himself to severe humiliation. Thereupon the bateren, taking into his hands the *penitencia* [whip], flogs the

30. Baba, *Guchishūi monogatari*, 13.

> sinner, causing the blood to flow. Then he wipes the blood off with a piece of cloth and, without washing his hands, offers up prayers. And they call this a great deed! But this is what the *Kirishitan* sect actually believes.[31]

In *Deus Destroyed* Fabian Fucan, a lapsed Catholic who is more familiar with the practice of confession, also condemns it, calling it the work of the devil:

> At the time of *confissan* the individual and the bateren meet privately. It is just the two of them, and no one else is allowed to draw near. The individual penitent declares his offences, leaving nothing out. Even if a man has perpetrated banditry or piracy; even if he has killed his father and his mother and has committed the Five Unpardonable Sins; even if he has been guilty of treason and rebellion in plotting to subvert the state, or has committed other capital crimes—if the bateren upon hearing him forgives his offences, his sins are nullified. So they claim. A devilish doctrine, indeed![32]

Bunkō's essay *A Confidential Record of Current Little-Known Facts* contains a rebuttal to these familiar condemnations of Catholic confession. While the author of *Tales of Christians* presents confession as having originated in Buddhism and then being corrupted in its Christian form, Bunkō sees confession as having originated in Christianity and subsequently being taken over by Pure Land Buddhism (*Jōdō shū*) and corrupted. He writes:

> In the summer of Hōreki 5 [1756] the Pure Land Buddhist sect perpetrated a devilish fraud—the practice of confession (*dozō sōden)* [literally, transmission of secrets in the storehouse]. This practice, which they were recommending, was in every way in imitation of the Christian practice. It is like this: One is led into a small room and made to confess the evils he has done during his whole life. He is then made to stand before a large bronze mirror and when his face is reflected in it he appears to be a dog, a horse, a beast, or bird.... The foolish are tricked, their money is taken, and they are taught to be grateful for this. This is another way the Pure Land sect makes money—by bestowing forgiveness for sins (*tsumi shōmetsu*). They call the practice "transmission of secrets in the storehouse."[33]

31. *Tales of Christians*, in Elison, *Deus Destroyed*, 331.
32. Ibid., 288.
33. Baba, *Tōji chinsetsu yōhiroku*, 227–30.

Bunkō's description of the penitent's face being reflected in a mirror as some kind of animal pokes fun at the description of Catholic confession as it is described in *Tales of Christians*. The belief that a monstrous image of the penitent is reflected in a mirror persisted as a common Japanese superstition well into the late 1700s. Miura Baien mentioning the phenomenon in *Musings During the Early Summer Rain* (*Samidare-sho*, 1784) wrote, "We occasionally hear of cases where the followers of 'the evil sect' ... show people monstrous images in magic mirrors, and delude them into evil."[34] Bunkō takes the superstition that Christians use a mirror to show "monstrous images," which was current at the time, and turns it against the Buddhists, claiming that in their practice of confession the face of the penitent is reflected as a dog, horse, beast, or bird.

This essay has the rather cumbersome title "The Transmission of Secrets in the Storehouse according to the Pure Land Sect and the Examination of Conscience of Nakayama Eichika and Matsushita Useki (*Ikkō shū dōzō sōden Nakayama Dainagon dono sasen, nōhitsu Useki go-kyūmei no koto*, 1756).[35] In his counterattack on Buddhism, Bunkō discusses first the "corrupt" practice of Buddhist confession and then proceeds to condemn the efforts of the Buddhists to have Shinran (1174–1268), the founder of the Pure Land Buddhist sect, posthumously bestowed with the title of "*Kenshin daishi*" (Great Master who reveals the truth). Bunkō attacks the corruption involved in the fundraising campaign to honor Shinran that was organized by Matsushita Useki (1700–1779) and Nakayama Eichika (1708–62), both contemporaries of Bunkō:

> Useki was engaged in a plot to make money by graft and corruption. One day the two of them went to see the wealthy Kyoto merchant Kuwana Saburōemon, an active follower of the Pure Land Buddhist sect. Useki said to Kuwana, "I am a follower of the Pure Land sect, the same as you, and for many years I have thought it a shame that Master Shinran has never been proclaimed 'Great Master.' I have come to Kyoto for the purpose of promoting his cause. What do you think?"
>
> Now Kuwana was one of those foolish Buddhist followers. He listened to Useki's plan and replied, "There is no greater happiness than to be devoted to the Buddhist law. Let's do that."

34. Miura Baien, *Samidare-sho* II, 347.
35. Baba, *Tōji chinsetsu yōhiroku*, 227–30.

Useki went on to explain the details of his plan to Kuwana: "I hope to raise money for the project, and I would like you to help me. After all, it is useless to pray and to ask for favors if you do not make offerings of money, right? And if we do not get suitable bribes from court nobles and Edo officials, our noble plan to get the title of 'Great Master' bestowed on Shinran will not be successful. Money is necessary for the progress of the Buddhist law, is it not?"

Kuwana replied, "I will be happy to do all I can to help, and so I will donate money for that purpose." Kuwana gave three hundred *ryō* of his own money and raised five hundred ryō from acquaintances.[36] Useki took the money but used all of the eight hundred ryō for his own obscene pastimes. He even went to the brothels at Shimabara in Kyoto and Maruyama in Nagasaki and lived a life of luxury off the donated money. He had his own dream of glory with the unlicensed prostitutes as well.

All the while, he was preaching his plan to other wealthy men of Kyoto and taking their money. He had the court nobles completely fooled as well. His scheme was never investigated because he bribed officials and acted like he was their friend, so they didn't do anything. He had even deceived the nobleman Nakayama Eichika, a counselor of the first rank in the imperial court (*dainagon*), convincing him that there was nothing wrong with carousing with prostitutes as long as one could pay for it. Lord Nakayama spent extravagantly at the most famous brothels. He built a new room onto his mansion, which he converted into a shrine and installed a Buddhist altar where he placed a newly carved statue of Shinran on a beautiful stand in the middle of the shrine. He placed an offering box in front of the image of Shinran to collect funds for the cause.

People came from all over, from the environs of Kyoto, from Osaka, Sakai, Fushimi, and the Gokinai region to give money to Useki and to worship at Lord Nakayama's little shrine and put money in the offering box.

Meanwhile, for about the next six months Useki and Nakayama were spending all the money they had collected at the brothels. Everything was going well for them until some merchants in Edo who had given money to Useki began to complain that there was too much delay in the declaration of the honorary title for Shinran. The merchants went to the Honganji Temple [Buddhist headquarters] in Kyoto to ask whether Shinran had yet been named "Great Master," and they were told, "There has certainly been nothing like that done here at Honganji Temple. You are without doubt the victims of

36. Though the value of the ryō fluctuated considerably throughout the Edo period, one ryō was generally considered to be the equivalent of one koku, the amount of rice that could feed a person for one year.

> a fraud." The merchants informed the Shogunal Deputy in Kyoto, Sakai [Tadamochi, 1722–75], and requested that Useki and Nakayama be investigated.
>
> Their plot was finally exposed, and their evil plan came to light. Nakayama was exiled to Iyo and demoted in court rank. Useki was executed. Kuwana gave back all the money he had collected and was banished. What they did was the worst kind of evil.[37]

Bunkō is drawing a parallel here between two examples of "Buddhist fraud." The practice of the Pure Land Buddhist confession and Matsushita Useki's blatant dishonesty in the fundraising campaign, both of which were done out of greed for money, exposed the hypocrisy of Buddhism.

This essay was duplicated eighty years after Bunkō's death by Sawa Chikane (1788–1838) in a collection of writings titled *Dreams on a Spring Night: Informal Talks* (*Shunmu dokudan*, 1837).[38] Sawa's essay is a word-for-word reproduction of Bunkō's text above, but in addition to Bunkō's criticism of the practice of confession in the Pure Land Sect and of the fundraising campaign, Sawa also includes a condemnation of confession in the Nichiren Buddhist sect, which allegedly used the practice to extort money in return for a promise that sins would be forgiven. Sawa reports that his father had expressed the opinion that the Nichiren monks who perpetrated this fraud were evil and deserved the death penalty. "Both Shinran and Nichiren," Sawa writes, "will end up at the end of the world numbered among the accursed."[39] Christian confession was a common target of anti-Christian tracts from shortly after the edicts of expulsion until the end of the Tokugawa period. Bunkō and Sawa turned this common anti-Christian attack around and made it into a criticism and denunciation of corruption in Pure Land and Nichiren Buddhism. This later collection of essays by Sawa Chikane is evidence that Bunkō's writings were still in circulation and consulted even as late as 1837.

"A Collection of Useless Grumblings" includes a lengthy treatise on prayer. Bunkō first advances the opinion that Buddhist and Shinto prayer are "exceedingly pointless," but Christian prayer, on the other hand, has the characteristics of "good prayer." He writes:

37. Baba, *Tōji chinsetsu yōhiroku*, 227–30. Emperor Meiji honored Shinran with the title of "*Kenshin Daishi*" in 1877, 615 years after Shinran's death.

38. Sawa Chikane was a disciple of *kokugaku* scholar Murata Harumi (1746–1811).

39. Sawa Chikane, *Shunmu dokudan*, 256–58.

> People ought to reconsider praying to various [Shinto] gods and buddhas. If a person tries not to purposely say embarrassing things to others, why would he open his heart to gods and buddhas?... Samurai pray to the gods and buddhas to get ahead in life, to receive an increase in their stipend or to be promoted, to be able to put themselves before everyone else, or to be able to force a rival into early retirement and acquire his position. Samurai pray so that they will be able to crush everyone else for their own purposes. A person with such a heart will say spiteful things about others without remorse. That's the type of person who will pray to [Shinto] gods and buddhas. How much more would such men want to make the one pure God (*yuitsu seijō no mi-kami*) conform to their own evil will...?
>
> Officials today and well-placed persons delight in receiving bribes from the lowly, just like the gods and buddhas are inclined toward receiving offerings of money. Not only samurai, even farmers, artisans, and merchants raise up their own selfish prayers to gods and buddhas. All of this is exceedingly pointless.
>
> There is nothing stranger than the prayers of some women who, for their entire lives, think only of their appearance. They cover their faces with make-up even in the presence of close relatives. They use hateful language and all the while are making pilgrimages to the temples in Asakusa and Zōshigaya. They pray and pray. How surprising it would be if their prayers actually reached the ears of any gods or buddhas at all. It is all vain and useless. They are simply multiplying their selfish deeds....
>
> Adulterers want to meet other people and think about how they can cheat on their spouses without being discovered. They want to go to the [kabuki] theater. They follow any possible chance for romance at the drop of a hat. And all the while, all they really want is money. How shocking! What a foolish life they lead!
>
> Such people offer prayer tablets to the gods and buddhas to try to get what they want, just as the daimyō offer a sacred horse plaque (*shinme*) at the temples and shrines. This has been a custom in Japan from olden times. Because it's difficult for a commoner to purchase a real horse to offer at a shrine or temple, they will buy a picture of a white horse and offer that. That's the origin of those votive wooden tablets with the white horses painted on them (*ema*).[40]

Bunkō's disdain for Buddhism is again apparent from the following anecdote in "A Collection of Useless Grumblings":

40. Baba, *Guchishūi monogatari*, 19–20.

> There is a retainer, Nagai Fujizaemon, who lives in the Honjō area. His only son was very ill with smallpox. He asked a monk from Hiraitomyōji Temple to bathe him in oil and pray that he have a long life. No matter how much the monk prayed, it didn't do any good. Eventually the monk said, "You have to trade someone else's life for the life of your son." Fujizaemon agreed and left.
>
> Now this samurai had long been an unfilial and unjust person. This is why he agreed with the monk to take someone else's life to save the life of his son. But since there was no one whose life he could take, he whispered in secret to the monk, "I'll take the life of my aged mother in order to save my son."
>
> What an unfilial heart he has! There is no one who has ever been worse in either China or Japan. How could the monk agree to such a plan unless he was consorting with the devil (*maō*)? In the end, his son died anyway.

Bunkō then contrasts such prayer to the gods and Buddhas with Christian prayer:

> As everyone knows, the Christian sect (*kirishitan-shū*) has been prohibited, so there was a plan to change the sect's name and, under the guise of being followers of the Nichiren [Buddhist] sect and have the [Catholic] padres (bateren) dress like Nichiren monks to offer their prayers....
>
> The prayer of the padres is good because it has the three characteristics of real prayer. Real prayer is like building a fire: first, one needs good, dry tinder; secondly, a good flint; and thirdly, a successful strike with the flint. Even the short prayers that have these three elements are good prayers. If one of the three characteristics is a bit weak, the other two might sometimes make up for it. In prayer, the dry tinder corresponds to the faith of the petitioner; the flint is his prayerful devotion; and the strike is the text that he prays. All three must be joined together—faith, devotion, and a well-composed prayer. It is said that if any of the three elements is lacking, the prayer will not be answered.
>
> If the tinder [i.e., faith] in prayer is damp, how could the person praying make a fire? He must first examine the tinder to see that it is dry, that is, unadulterated and pure, and then he can light the fire and set out the lamp.[41]

The importance Bunkō places on prayer, faith, and devotion in this text is a kind of last testimony in which he explains why, as a public speaker and writer, he has been so devoted to a firm belief that ethics

41. Ibid., 21–22.

and morality are not only important to society and in government but of ultimate value. Bunkō's criticism of Shinto and Buddhist prayer, his praise for the symbols of Christianity and Christian prayer, and his understanding of Christian doctrine provide a challenging new perspective with which to study the history of early modern Japan. Like Toyota Mitsugi and others who were known to be Christians but were never charged as such, Baba Bunkō was never accused of being a Christian or Christian sympathizer or charged with any other capital offense. The magistrate who tried him insisted that he had done nothing deserving death, but as will be seen, Bunkō was arrested and executed in Edo in January 1759. Before examining more closely the reasons for his execution, it will be necessary to study more of his writings in depth.

3 | POPULAR GAMES AND MONSTER STORIES

Don't believe there is no such thing as a monster in this world. Human beings are monsters that really do exist.

IHARA SAIKAKU, 1685

Let's Play "One Hundred Monsters"

Gossip about the samurai class and rumors of scandal in the private lives of public officials were constantly circulating in the capital. Baba Bunkō took advantage of his listeners' interest in the comings and goings of the ruling elite, giving lectures and distributing manuscripts that provided his commoner audience not only with humorous and entertaining stories, but also with the latest shocking information about the improprieties, misconduct, and outrageous behavior of bureaucrats and Buddhist monks, teachers, and scholars. The capital was the perfect location for him to do this since there was a much larger percentage of samurai in the population of Edo than in any other city in Japan. No more than 7 to 10 percent of the general population was of the samurai class, but in Edo in the 1700s the samurai comprised well over half of the population, and their estates occupied about 65 percent of the land area.[1]

Epigraph is from Ihara Sakaku, *Son of an Amorous Man, Saikaku's Accounts of Various Places, Twenty Cases of Unfilial Children* (*Kōshoku nidai otoko, Saikaku shokoku hanashi, Honchō nijū fukō*, 1685), ed. Fuji Akio, Inoue Toshiyuki et al. (Tokyo: Iwanami shoten, 1991), 264.

1. Vaporis, *Voices of Early Modern Japan: Contemporary Accounts of Daily Life during the Age of the Shoguns*, xxvi.

In his collection of anecdotes about incompetent bakufu officials, lazy Confucian scholars, and indigent Buddhist monks titled *Contemporary Edo: An Album of One Hundred Monsters*, Bunkō explains to his reader that even though the number of "monsters" he writes about is fewer than one hundred, he uses this number in the title of his book anyway.[2] The modern reader will immediately notice that there are nowhere near a hundred monsters in the work (there are actually twenty-six), but Bunkō's contemporary reader would have immediately associated the number "one hundred" with the well-known party game, "one hundred monster stories" (*hyaku monogatari*), a popular amusement that was all the rage during the Kyōhō period (1716–36).

This game can be played by any number of people and always follows the same general pattern. The participants, each carrying a lighted lantern, gather together in a circle outside at night or in a dark room. One person begins to tell a ghost story or a tale about monsters or demons. When the tale is finished, the storyteller extinguishes his or her lantern. One after another each person takes a turn relating a frightening tale. Gradually, as each ghost story is finished, the area becomes darker and darker as lanterns are extinguished one by one until finally all the lanterns have been put out, and there is complete darkness. At this point the tension has reached its peak, and everyone waits in silence to see if a real ghost or demon might appear. The players become more and more anxious, anticipating the arrival of some kind of terrifying phantom or apparition until someone shrieks, "The ghost! The ghost!" and everyone screams out in genuine (or feigned) terror. This experience might then become the subject of a new ghost story to be related at the beginning of the game the next time it is played. Some Edo-period *ukiyoe* (woodblock print) artists have portrayed this climactic moment at the end of the game when a monster supposedly appears.[3]

There are a number of literary works that copy the structure of this game. *One Hundred Tales of the Great Peace* (*Taihei hyaku monogatari*, 1732), for example, is a collection of twenty-nine ghost stories, most of

2. Baba, *Tōdai Edo hyaku bakemono*, 3.

3. Katsushika Hokusai [1760–1849], *Newly Published Perspective Picture: One Hundred Ghost Stories in a Haunted House (Shinpan uki-e bakemono yashiki hyaku monogatari no zu)* (Eijudō, Edo: Nishimuraya Yohachi, 1790); http://www.mfa.org/collections/search_art.asp?recview=true&id

them about enchanted animals. *One Hundred Eternal Tales* (*Bansei hyaku monogatari*, 1751) and *One Hundred Tales Ancient and Modern* (*Kokon hyaku monogatari*, 1751) were similar collections of stories of the supernatural that were originally in oral form but later came to be written down. Players of the game often took stories from these collections.

Bunkō uses this framework of monster tales told in the game to write much of his social and political satire. The contemporary reader certainly found amusement in his essays, stories, and anecdotes, but Bunkō not only wanted to entertain, he wanted to instruct his reader as well. Any of his anecdotes could stand alone, but taken together they open the reader's eyes to systemic corruption and injustice in society in a way that is meant, like a ghost story, to be shocking and frightening. In order to play Bunkō's "game," the reader must follow the "rules," that is, have some familiarity with the background of the real historical personages who are the objects of his satire and also be familiar with political and social events and trends of the time. The "rules" also include applying an interpretive strategy with full knowledge of the literary conventions and techniques of early modern Japanese literature: comparison and contrast, metaphor, allegory, literary reversals, and incongruous associations (*mitate*), as well as understatement and exaggeration, all of which go into the formation of a successful early modern tale of horror, whether it be completely fictional or shockingly true.

In *Contemporary Edo: An Album of One Hundred Monsters*, Bunkō describes the type of "monster" he will be dealing with: "a monster is someone who grotesquely transforms his appearance in order to manipulate society and other people.... Under the guise of being human, he ensnares people in his deceptions."[4] Bunkō's "monsters" are invisible to the eyes of human beings because they appear in the likeness of holy Buddhist monks, wise Confucian scholars, wealthy merchants, saintly women, and noble officials. They are exposed as frauds and hypocritical "monsters" when Bunkō strips away their sanctimonious deceptions and exposes their true identities.

This collection of anecdotes is very much in the literary style of the

4. Baba, *Tōdai Edo hyaku bakemono*, 3.

contemporary genre of monster stories known as *kaikidanmono*. This genre was strongly influenced by ghost tales from China and was popular in Japan in the 1750s. The tales are entertaining but are often quite graphic and have the gruesomeness of horror stories. The kaikidanmono had evolved into its written form from the oral hyaku monogatari stories that came out of the game described above. Bunkō took verbatim or with minor changes some of the lines from a number of the kaikidanmono. *Hyaku monogatari* (One hundred stories, 1658–61), for example, was a series of monster stories, each of which ended with a frightening warning: "There are more of these monsters now than in the past" or "Such horrible events are on the rise."[5] Bunkō ends a number of his anecdotes about notable people in *Contemporary Edo: An Album of One Hundred Monsters* in the same way: "He is indeed a strange monster," or "The world is becoming even more filled with these great deceivers." Bunkō reports that the fiends and "demons" in Edo are similar to the strange and terrible creatures in the kaikidanmono. "Although it acts human, this is a monster that will deceive humans" (*hito ni shite, hito o bakasu mono*) is a line which recurs in a number of the Edo ghost stories that Bunkō uses in his satirical exposés about real people.

Bunkō greatly expanded the scope of the kaikidanmono genre, giving it a greater significance than that of a simple horror story. His tales are not meant just to scare or entertain but also to make people aware that they are being taken in by real monsters, not just pretend ones in games or in fictional ghost stories but by living, breathing monsters that exist in society and particularly in the renowned institutions of the Tokugawa government. His monsters are real human beings who have the ability to transform themselves into creatures that are repulsive and frightening not because of their physical appearance, but because of their moral hypocrisy and spiritual degradation. Bunkō makes City Magistrate Tsuchiya Masasuke (r. 1754–67), for example, one of his prime examples of such a monster.

5. Takada Mamoru, ed., *Edo kaidanshū zen san satsu* (Tokyo: Iwanami shoten, 1989), 2: 20, 45.

Two City Magistrates

As an example of how Bunkō's literary "game" is played, let us consider "The Case of the Monster Magistrate," an anecdote that openly maligns the south Edo city magistrate, Tsuchiya Masasuke. This is the official who would eventually be responsible for Bunkō's conviction and execution. Bunkō opens his piece with a quote from an early writer of satirical sermons (*dangibon*), Masaho Nokoguchi (1655–1742), in which Buddha, along with the Chinese sages Yao and Shun, is portrayed as a fraud who was able to convince people that he was virtuous, but actually was nothing of the kind. The Buddha spent his entire life, Nokoguchi writes, simply imitating virtuous people, and so was perpetuating a deception.[6]

Bunkō agrees with Nokoguchi's assessment of Yao, Shun, and the Buddha, but goes further. He gives Nokoguchi's argument a political twist and puts it in a new context. He uses Nokoguchi's criteria to evaluate City Magistrate Tsuchiya Masasuke's performance in office and then concludes that Tsuchiya is no different from the sage kings or Buddha. They all give the impression of being virtuous, but actually they do not practice any virtue at all. Bunkō accuses Tsuchiya of imitating a truly virtuous man, former City Magistrate Ōoka Tadasuke (1677–1751), in order to give the impression that he is also virtuous.

Ōoka Tadasuke had been known for his just and wise decisions. His appointment to the office of Edo city magistrate in 1717 had been part of Shogun Tokugawa Yoshimune's plan to reorganize the government. As the shogun's chief legal adviser, Ōoka had been instrumental in a number of reforms, such as the promulgation of a statute of limitations on criminal offenses and improvements in prison conditions. His role in carrying out these reforms was well known to the common people, among whom favorable stories about Ōoka were still circulating long after he had left office.[7]

Like most people at the time, Bunkō was also enamored with Ōoka Tadasuke. The reputation of Ōoka that has come down to us from history is that of a magistrate who was untainted by any suspicion of impropri-

6. Baba, *Tōdai Edo hyaku bakemono*, 9.
7. Hall, *The Cambridge History of Japan*, 4: 446, 448.

ety or misconduct. Having risen to political power from humble origins, Ōoka was loved and respected by the people of Edo. In 1712 he had been the magistrate of Yamada, a small but politically significant village owing to its proximity to the Grand Ise Shrine, the most important Shinto shrine in Japan. The office of Yamada magistrate, however, was an ill-paid post and did not offer many possibilities for advancement, so his appointment to the position of Edo city magistrate in 1717 caused much surprise in Tokugawa officialdom, since such a promotion was entirely unprecedented.[8]

It had been Ōoka's courageous judgment in a boundary dispute between some farmers of Kishū domain (in present-day Mie and Wakayama prefectures) and peasants in Yamada domain that had drawn the attention of shogun Tokugawa Yoshimune and won for Ōoka the coveted position of Edo city magistrate. The boundary dispute had been going on for some time prior to Ōoka's appointment as Yamada magistrate, but all previous magistrates avoided making a judgment as to where precisely the border between Yamada and Kishū should lie for fear of antagonizing shogun Yoshimune, who himself was from Kishū.[9]

On being appointed to the Yamada post, Ōoka promptly rendered a verdict in the dispute that favored Yamada against Kishū. Far from being offended or feeling that his home province had been slighted, Shogun Yoshimune praised Ōoka's sense of impartial justice and rewarded him with the appointment as south Edo city magistrate, one of the most important positions in the bakufu civil service. After he was transferred to Edo, Ōoka continued to render just and wise decisions, and his reputation as a courageous and impartial judge spread quickly. It was his judgment in the boundary dispute that drew Bunkō's attention and convinced him that this magistrate was a man of superior moral character. Many officials who appear in Bunkō's writings are evaluated by the standard of impartial justice that Ōoka Tadasuke set. Unfortunately, many people in Edo were deceived by Tsuchiya Masasuke and were of the opin-

8. James Murdoch, *A History of Japan* (London: Routledge and Kegan Paul, 1949), 3: part 1, 333.

9. Kii domain was assigned as a fief to Tokugawa Yorinobu (1602–71), the eighth son of Ieyasu, in 1619. Yorinobu founded one of the three houses from which future shoguns would come. Yoshimune was from this branch (Kii) of the Tokugawa family.

ion that he was like Ōoka, unaware that he was not only incompetent but the epitome of the corrupt bureaucrat. Tsuchiya's imitation of Ōoka was nothing more than an attempt to disguise his own incompetence in office and perpetuate the lie that he was capable and virtuous.

Bunkō gives a number of examples to show how Tsuchiya attempted to show that he was as upright as Ōoka Tadasuke. Tsuchiya issued proclamations and decrees on the same type of paper (Nasu paper) that Ōoka used.[10] He tried to appear just as relaxed and in control of himself when dealing with litigation and finance issues as had Ōoka. At trials he judged with leniency, handing down merciful punishment even to the guilty, just as Magistrate Ōoka was reputed to have done. Bunkō goes on to apply Nokoguchi's condemnation of the sage kings and Buddha to the city magistrate and shows that the magistrate, who is held in high esteem by people, just as Buddha and the sage kings were, is merely giving a false impression of being honest and irreproachable. Bunkō is unrelenting in his satirical attack on Tsuchiya. He calls him "Tsuchi" and asks the reader, "Doesn't that name sound like 'dirt'?" (Tsuchi means earth, ground, or dirt in Japanese.) "He is as different from Magistrate Ōoka as heaven is different from earth (*tsuchi*)." Bunkō goes on to point out that Tsuchiya has "no principles at all," so when a person who had actually known Magistrate Ōoka sees Tsuchiya, "Tsuchi's facade evaporates, and the monster is unmasked."

Bunkō asks, "So how did Tsuchiya manage to become Edo city magistrate in the first place?" He answers that it was because he was constantly focused on seeking attention and giving a good impression. He is highly respected, just as Buddha is, but he has completely fooled the people of Edo![11] The satirical jibes thrown at Tsuchiya are also directed against Buddha, showing how utterly despicable both are in comparison with someone who is genuinely virtuous, such as Magistrate Ōoka Tadasuke.

In the context of Nokoguchi's condemnation of the Chinese sage kings,

10. Nasu paper is made in Echizen. Tsuchiya used it in imitation of Ōoka Tadasuke, whose official title was "lord of Echizen."

11. Sakai Tadamochi, the thirteenth lord of Wakasa, was daimyō between 1740 and 1757 and Commissioner of Temples and Shrines from 1747. 3 to 1747. 12. He was the bakufu representative in Kyoto (*Kyōtō shoshidai*) from 1752. 4. 7 to 1756. 4. 7.

Yao and Shun, and Buddha, Bunkō makes it clear that just as Confucianism and Buddhism were foreign philosophies based on the ideas of men who only imitated the virtues of others but did not actually practice virtue themselves, so too the Office of the City Magistrate is held by a man who can do no more than attempt to imitate the greatness of the virtuous former city magistrate. Confucianism and Buddhism are both condemned as teachings that can do no more than offer a kind of pseudo-wisdom and "perpetuate a deception," as Nokoguchi expresses it, because they were founded on the teachings of imposters. Bunkō had witnessed himself the wisdom and the just judgments of Ōoka Tadasuke and was of the opinion that the former city magistrate's sense of moral justice far surpassed that of the ancient Chinese sages Yao and Shun, and his righteousness went beyond that of Confucius and Buddha. Bunkō presents his startling condemnation of Confucianism and Buddhism as the opinion of Nokoguchi, but it is clear that it was Bunkō's opinion as well.

Bunkō claimed that even the disreputable Sakai Tadamochi (1722–75), who served as the shogunal deputy (*shoshidai*) in Kyoto from 1752 to 1756, thought Tsuchiya was totally debased.[12] Sakai despised Tsuchiya, even though he himself was a corrupt official. When Tsuchiya was city magistrate of Kyoto, before he was transferred to Edo, his tenure in office was marked by dishonesty and double-dealing that went beyond anything Sakai had done. Though Tsuchiya was ill-qualified for his post even in Kyoto, he managed to hold on to power only because of his finesse at taking and giving bribes. Sakai, as shogunal deputy, was Tsuchiya's superior and was charged with evaluating Tsuchiya's performance in office. Though his evaluations were quite negative, for some reason unknown to both officials, Tsuchiya was promoted ahead of Sakai to the position of Edo city magistrate. According to Bunkō, Tsuchiya's sudden promotion was due to his ability to transform himself in the blink of an eye, just like a monster in a ghost story, and appear to be wise and virtuous.

A "monster" such as Tsuchiya Masasuke, Bunkō writes, must continually be on the move in order to hide his crimes and avoid being seen

12. The post of Kyoto deputy, usually given to a middle rank *fudai daimyō*, a rank which Sakai held, involved overseeing the affairs of the imperial court and of the many temples in the city. The *shoshidai* was also responsible for the administration of justice in the adjacent provinces by supervising the city magistrates of Kyoto, Fushimi, and Nara.

for what he really is. When Bunkō describes Tsuchiya as a person who "moves from place to place," he is not speaking of a change of geographical location. He is referring more particularly to an axiological movement, a constant change of moral criteria and value judgments that reduce sound morality to relativism, deceit, and a hypocritical show of virtue.

This city magistrate, Bunkō writes, was able to "transform his outward appearance" (*onore ga sugata o ikei ni shite*) by disguising himself, not with costumes or make-up, but rather by imitation of the external habits and manners of people who were morally superior to him. He carries out his impersonations hoping that people, not seeing his faults and weaknesses, will come to respect and admire him. Throughout his professional life, this strategy allowed Tsuchiya to advance to high positions and maintain the deception that he was a man worthy of his status. Tsuchiya, the "monster-official," Bunkō declared, and others who possess a mere facade of virtue, lead people into moral decay and corruption. Bunkō was not writing a typical ghost or monster story, though the form of his writing resembled that genre. He was obviously writing a "monster" story based in reality. As the reader will see, "The Case of the Monster Magistrate" deeply insulted and angered Tsuchiya, and he did not let Bunkō get away with this affront to his pride.

Bunkō's writings did not always mirror the opinions of commoners, as is illustrated in this essay about the two magistrates, but he did give voice to the popular attitudes toward the bakufu that the people of Edo could not articulate, either because of the fear of punishment or because they did not have a moral foundation on which to base their criticisms. Bunkō put many of the townspeople's voiced and unvoiced complaints against officialdom into a moral framework that offered an alternative to samurai, Confucian, and Buddhist theories of ethics and morality. The nature of right and wrong, moral and immoral are the themes that run through much of his writing and are central to his discussion of the two magistrates. He exposes the contradictions between the regime's claim to virtue on the one hand and its crude actions, arrogance, and dishonesty on the other. He opens to view what people might have suspected but could not always see clearly: the flaws and foibles, deceit and corruption in the private lives of public persons. As Bunkō directed his keen vision toward specific individuals, he exposed contradictions and incongruities between what the members of the ruling class professed to be and what they actually were.

Obviously, Bunkō is not interested in literature solely as an amusing game or fictional monster story. His purpose is to elicit a deeper awareness of the realities behind the external appearances of officialdom and to expose the criminality behind the façade of decorum and virtue perpetrated by members of the samurai class. The satirical contrast that Bunkō constructs between the "monster" Tsuchiya Masasuke and the "virtuous official" Ōoka Tadasuke, for example, is one of the most interesting and historically significant of his political satires. Both Tsuchiya and Ōoka held the same office, of course, but the manner in which each man conducted himself in office could not have been more different. The contrast between them provided Bunkō with provocative material with which he would go on to display with penetrating insight the character and conduct of other elite members of society. Bunkō had excellent powers of observation and an ability to ferret out information—skills that he had acquired and developed by telling fortunes of passersby on the grounds of Asakusa Temple after he had first arrived in Edo from his home in Iyo. His encounters with many different kinds and classes of people encouraged him to write powerful satire about the hidden, dark underside of the lives of the members of the ruling class.

By satirizing contemporary political officials and making them characters in the popular game of ghost stories, Bunkō not only exposed corruption, he also showed Edo politics to be like a game, an ugly game that involves real monsters. He communicated his conviction that high public officials are human only in appearance and are in reality deceivers and tricksters. Readers of Bunkō's satire saw that public officials were not unlike the mysterious and frightening creatures of ghost tales and very different from real human beings like themselves.

Officials of the government, like Tsuchiya, held the general opinion that the townspeople were less than human, incapable of virtue; but Bunkō has turned the tables on the officials, showing that actually it is the elite who are less than human. This reversal of what might be called conventional wisdom among the elite adds an element of bitter irony to his anecdotes. What would otherwise simply be an entertaining monster tale becomes subversive social critique and a threat to traditional views of the social hierarchy. His hypothesis that the "monster" is a creature who exists only in "the guise of a human being" but who is able to "grotesquely change his appearance" conveys a deep skepticism, if not fear, of the authorities and a warning that extreme caution is warranted when dealing with them. It must have been quite shocking to suggest that Edo, the city of samurai where people lived out their everyday lives, was actually a demonic realm that was reminiscent of horror tales and ghost stories. Bunkō's presentation of a world in which "monsters live among us" demonstrated that Tokugawa officials, such as Tsuchiya, who could not be considered a true human being, represented a serious threat to the safety and well-being of the populace.

Lost in the Land of Demons

Another popular ghost story and well-known play, *The Legend of the Haunted Mansion* (*Banshū Sarayashiki*, 1741), is the source for Bunkō's satire directed against Aoyama Tessan, an official who had held the office of fire and theft investigator (*hitsuke tōzoku aratame*) from 1623 to 1651, during the shogunate of Tokugawa Iemitsu.[13] Bunkō's version of the story is titled *A Record of Doubts and Questions about the Legend of the Haunted Mansion* (*Sarayashiki bengiroku*, 1758).[14] Bunkō had heard the original version of the story from his father when he was eight or nine years old.[15] It is the story of a servant girl, Okiku, who is continually being tormented by her samurai master, Aoyama Tessan. Aoyama had been an official long before Bunkō came to Edo, but he uses this former fire and theft investigator as a character in his story to represent the man who holds the same office in his own day, Yamada Asaemon Yoshitsugu (1705–70).

The first part of Bunkō's story is identical to the plot in the original, in which Aoyama's wife has become so terribly jealous of her servant

13. Tessan was the chief retainer of Hosokawa Katsumoto, the lord of Himeji Castle in Banshū (Harima domain, in present day Hyōgo prefecture).

14. Baba, *Sarayashiki bengiroku*, in *Kinsei jitsuroku zensho, ed. Waseda daigaku shuppanbu* (Tokyo: Waseda daigaku, 1917), 1–22.

15. Ibid., 1.

Okiku's beauty and innocence that she torments her by tying her up with ropes and poking her with a short sword. Like her husband, she is a heavy a drinker and "did not have the gentleness of a woman," a detail that Bunkō adds to the story. She treats all the servants cruelly, but it is especially poor Okiku who suffers the brunt of her brutality. The other servants are shocked at their mistress' inhumanity. Many of them flee, but Okiku, who had been given to the Aoyama family as a servant for life as punishment for an unmentioned crime committed by her father, is forced to remain in the Aoyama household. Bunkō describes what it was like for Okiku to live in the Aoyama residence: "The poor girl felt like she was lost in the land of demons (*Kikaigashima*)."[16]

One day Okiku accidently drops an heirloom dish, which is one of the prize possessions of Aoyama's wife. She expects a terrible punishment for her mistake. Aoyama's wife immediately chops off the middle finger of Okiku's right hand. Bunkō comments that such treatment is contrary to Confucian ethics, which Aoyama supposedly professes. Confucianism, as Bunkō reminds his reader, teaches that "one's body is received from one's parents, and it is a crime against the virtue of filial devotion to harm even a single hair of one's head."[17] If this is true for one hair, Bunkō reasons, is it not even more true for a finger? He poses the moral question: How could Aoyama and his wife perpetrate such a cruel deed if they are people of high status? "They are the masters; Okiku is the servant. According to the Confucians, Aoyama, as master, takes the place of Heaven and Earth for his servants. He should be their guardian and protector. But he is a master who looks upon his servants as filth. It would be understandable if Okiku looked on her master as an enemy."[18] Bunkō explains that since Okiku's treatment is a clear violation of the Confucian morality that Aoyama publically professes, he is a hypocrite and a "monster."

Bunkō emphasizes his own belief that those who have been relegated to inferior positions in society, such as housemaids and menservants, should always be treated justly; but Aoyama Tessan, as an official of the Tokugawa government, represents the bakufu, and his violation of Con-

16. Baba, *Sarayashiki bengiroku*, 13.
17. Ibid., 16.
18. Ibid.

fucian norms in dealing with a commoner is a crime of the Tokugawa bakufu. The government was known to cover up crimes of its officials by appealing to the rights of samurai. This is exactly what Aoyama does. He cites the heroism of Musashibō Benkei (1155–89), a Japanese warrior monk of great physical and moral strength, to justify his own cruelty.[19] Benkei, Aoyama declares, loved nature so much he gave notice that if anyone broke off a single flower from a tree, he would deserve to have his finger cut off. Aoyama insists that his wife's heirloom dish was worth much more than any flower, and so the punishment for such a crime should be at least as severe. After her finger was severed, Okiku ran out of the house in pain and humiliation. All the years of abuse had finally caught up with her. She gathered up some heavy rocks, put them in her sleeves to weigh her down, jumped into a well, and drowned.

Later that month, as the story goes, Aoyama's wife gives birth to a baby boy. Strange things begin to happen from the moment of his birth. Otherwise healthy, the child is born without a middle finger on his right hand. Every night from dusk to dawn, a light comes from the well where Okiku drowned, and a sad voice is heard counting from one to nine and then wailing loudly, "The tenth is missing! The tenth is missing!"[20] The incessant counting continues all night long, night after night. Terrified at the sound of the ghostly cries, the retainers, the servants, and all the members of the Aoyama household can do nothing but put their hands over their ears in a desperate attempt to block out the awful weeping and howling, but the persistent voice resounds inside of their heads even during the day.

The shogunal authorities come to investigate the situation, but they hear no sounds. They judge that Aoyama and his wife, along with all the servants, have gone mad. They conclude that Aoyama can no longer be of any service to the government. He is charged with incompetence, and all his possessions are confiscated.[21]

A Record of Doubts and Questions about the Legend of the Haunted Mansion follows this same sequence of events as the original story, but

19. Benkei was the principal retainer of the Minamoto no Yoshitsune (1159–89).
20. Baba, *Sarayashiki bengiroku*, 18.
21. Ibid., 19.

the reader's attention is focused not so much on the dramatic developments of the action as on the injustices that are perpetrated by Aoyama and his wife and the consequences of their cruelty. Bunkō's version is not just a ghost story, as is the original. What is even more frightening than the wailing of the ghost of poor Okiku or the cruelty of Aoyama and his wife is the brutality of Yamada Yoshitsugu, the fire and theft investigator of Bunkō's own time, whom Aoyama represents. According to Bunkō, Yamada, like Aoyama, also had a reputation for cruelty. Nicknamed "the wolf who takes children" (*kozure-ookami*), Yamada imprisoned in a dungeon in his own residence people accused of having committed a crime. The dungeon was even equipped with its own torture chamber. The bakufu had no hesitation in making use of Yamada's brutality and gave him the responsibility for carrying out the punishments and death sentences of convicted criminals. Yamada reveled in his assignment, even volunteering to take on the most irksome task that could be delegated to an executioner—apprehending criminals of the eta (outcast) class. Yamada relished taunting and tormenting the outcasts before beheading them.

Bunkō draws other comparisons between Aoyama Tessan and Yamada Yoshitsugu. Like Aoyama, Yamada was a heavy drinker. Both men were known to frequent the various establishments of the Yoshiwara bordello district. Both gave saké to their subordinates, the policemen (*yoriki*) and the constables (*dōshin*) while they were on duty. Bunkō reports that it was not uncommon to see them intoxicated as they made their inspection rounds. The law enforcement officers who worked under Yamada were afraid that they themselves might become victims of his cruelty, so they would arrest innocent people and accuse them of arson or theft just to please their chief, who was thirsty for the blood of victims on whom he could inflict the greatest torments in his torture chamber. Bunkō writes that while police and constables went around harassing and abusing innocent people, real criminals remained at large; and thievery and arson were out of control.[22]

Another official who appears in Bunkō's version of *Legend of the Haunted Mansion* is Kumeno Heinaibyōe (d. 1683), a well-known martial

22. Baba Bunkō, *Tōsei Buya zokudan*, vol. 86 of *Mado no susami zen*, *Buya zokudan zen*, *Edo chomonshū zen*, ed. Tsukamoto Tetsuzō (Tokyo: Yūhōdō shoten, 1932), 7–8.

arts instructor, who had been one of Yamada's subordinates.[23] Kumeno had impressed the Tokugawa authorities with his skill in martial arts, particularly with his swordsmanship. Bunkō explains, "Kumeno wanted nothing more than to use his martial abilities to chop the heads off criminals."[24] Bunkō's disdain for Yamada and Kumeno is unmistakable, but it was because of the immoral misuse of authority that Bunkō's fear of such men, whom he calls "monsters," was greater than his disdain. Though both law enforcement officials were of samurai status, Bunkō considered them to be no different from the outcasts who customarily carried out the death sentences and buried the bodies of condemned criminals. Yamada and his underlings did the same work as those who had been classified as pariahs, but since they were samurai, they turned law enforcement itself into a despised, rather than a respected, function of government.

Bunkō writes of the eventual death of Kumeno and his alleged resolve to make amends for his cruelty in the afterlife: "At last, after a life of many evil deeds, Kumeno Heinaibyōe died of an illness. His only surviving son said that he had seen his father in a dream, and his father asked him to have a [Buddhist] *kannon* statue carved to make up for the evil deeds he had done when he was alive.[25] His son complied and put the statue in Asakusa Temple. How foolish the boy was to listen to a dream!"[26] Bunkō implies that Kumeno's son was foolish not only to have listened to a dream but also to have believed that a Buddhist statue placed in a temple would have any power at all to absolve Kumeno from a life of terrible cruelty. The short anecdote about Kumeno Heinaibyōe which concludes this section of *The Legend of the Haunted Mansion* is an indictment not just of the cruelty of Aoyama Tessan, Yamada Yoshitsugu, or Kumeno Heinaibyōe. It is rather a condemnation of the Tokugawa government that they served and was the source and promoter of their cruelty.

23. Baba, *Sarayashiki bengiroku*, 7.

24. Ibid., 8.

25. Kannon is a Buddhist bodhisattva associated with compassion and usually depicted in Japan as a female.

26. Baba, *Sarayashiki bengiroku*, 9.

Mukōsaki Jinnai, a Healer of Many People

In the mid-Edo period Tokugawa punishments had lost their power to strike fear in the hearts of the common people, and crime was rampant. One reason for this was the proliferation of pardons, so criminals were no longer afraid of punishment.[27] In the 1750s a notorious samurai went on a killing rampage, terrorizing areas of Edo. His name was Mukōsaki Jinnai, and he is the subject of a satirical essay in which the police and local constables are accused of doing nothing to try to stop him. Bunkō reports:

> Mukōsaki Jinnai came here from Tsukuba [in present-day Ibaraki prefecture] and settled in the Aoyama district of Edo [a samurai residential district]. He was a very powerful man, skilled in swordsmanship and jujitsu and had many disciples to whom he taught his arts. This samurai was in the habit of testing his sword on passersby, stalking them for sport, and cutting them down in cold blood. Such crimes have been forbidden since [Tokugawa] Ieyasu's time. The city magistrate investigated, but no action was taken, and the police and constables were unable to detain Jinnai simply because they were no match for his strength. It appeared as though the authorities were unable to control this rogue samurai.[28]

Bunkō claims that it had long been illegal for a samurai to cut down a commoner, but actually the Tokugawa code that was enforced in the 1700s did allow samurai to take the life of a commoner if the samurai felt he had been insulted. This custom, known as *burei-uchi*, allowed the killing of a commoner who did no more than use abusive language or act in an insulting way toward a samurai. As Eiko Ikegami notes in *The Taming of the Samurai: Honorific Individualism and the Making of Modern Japan*, burei-uchi exempted the samurai from any official accusation, but as peace continued in the Tokugawa period, the samurai who took recourse to burei-uchi were often regarded as cruel and ill-bred, and limits were put on the use of this privilege.[29] This may have been the reason

27. Daniel Botsman, *Punishment and Power in the Making of Modern Japan* (Princeton: Princeton University Press, 2005), 89.

28. Ibid., 10.

29. Eiko Ikegami, *The Taming of the Samurai: Honorific Individualism and the Making of Modern Japan* (Cambridge, Mass.: Harvard University Press, 1995), 245.

why Bunkō thought that the custom was illegal and that Mukōsaki Jinnai's indiscriminate killing of commoners should have been a reason to apprehend him.

Bunkō acknowledges that Jinnai was a criminal, but what he sees as worse than this samurai's murdering rampage were the incompetence and cowardice of the law enforcement officials, particularly of Yamada Yoshitsugu, at apprehending Jinnai and putting an end to his random killings. This case was clear evidence for Bunkō that officials would not or could not enforce peace and security in the city. "There was a turn of events that finally caught up with Jinnai and ended his killing spree. One day Jinnai was ill and quite weak due to a high fever. Investigator Yamada saw his chance, ordered him arrested, and had him put into prison. His illness was treated, and after he recovered, Jinnai vehemently protested, 'I resent being arrested when I am sick.'"[30] He was eventually sentenced and condemned to be crucified at the execution grounds at Senju-Kozukappara (present-day Minami-senju, Arakawa-ku, Tokyo). As he was dying, Jinnai screamed out from his cross: "I was captured without any warning when I was ill with a fever. It's unfair. I hereby swear that I will be the god of this place, and if any sick person prays to me, he will recover." Bunkō concludes, "Compared to the officials who arrested and condemned him, Jinnai was 'a holy sage' because before he died, he had sworn that he would aid the ill and the weak who prayed to him." Thus, Bunkō writes, "The criminal Jinnai became a healer of many people."[31] By calling Jennai "a holy sage," Bunkō is declaring him forgiven and redeemed; and even though he had been a criminal, he is now morally superior to the Tokugawa officials who arrested and executed him.

This assertion, of course, is completely inconsistent with the contemporary Japanese sense of morality and justice. Bunkō's point that compared to the Tokugawa officials even a horrendous villain like Jinnai can be looked upon as "a holy sage" flies directly in the face of the Japanese understanding that criminals could never be forgiven and were forever a source of spiritual pollution (*kegare*).[32] This is why criminals were driven

30. Baba, *Sarayashiki bengiroku*, 11.
31. Ibid., 11, 12.
32. Botsman, *Punishment and Power in the Making of Modern Japan*, 23.

out of their communities and their houses were burned to the ground. It was not just to punish them but, more importantly, to purify and cleanse the area that the criminal had "desecrated" by his presence.[33] Jinnai, however, became "a healer of many people." This attitude toward Jinnai strikingly aligns with the Christian belief in the intercessory power of the dead, particularly that of saints. Their death is reverenced, and prayers of petition are addressed to them. In Japan in the seventeenth and eighteenth centuries, honoring the gravesites of the Christian martyrs was actually more important than the *orationes* (the prayers that were passed down from generation to generation). As Konuma Daihachi notes in his book *Hidden Christians of Iyo*, this was particularly true in Iyo domain, the area from which Bunkō came, that the graves of Christians were the preferred sites for prayers.[34]

Japanese Buddhists saw the death of their own faithful in a completely different light. They regarded honoring even their own martyrs as the worship of devils.[35] Such an idea that saints could be implored for aid or healing was incomprehensible to Japanese at this time. The branch of the Hokke Buddhist sect referred to as *fuju-fuse ha*, for example, never attributed any religious significance to the suffering or even the martyrdom of its followers, even though it was persecuted and many of its monks and followers were killed by the bakufu.[36] In *Death and the Afterlife in Japanese Buddhism*, Mark L. Blum states that the Christian practice of revering its saints has no parallels in Buddhism. It is true, he says, that the notions of *junshi* (following one's lord in suicide) and *junkyō* (giving one's life for one's faith) are Confucian beliefs, but these terms refer not specifically to the actions of saints but to forms of ritual suicide.[37] The term *junkyō* has taken on the Christian meaning of martyrdom in recent times, but as a Buddhist term it refers more to the "extinguishing of evil

33. Ibid., 23

34. Konuma Daihachi, *Iyo no kakure kirishitan* (Ehime: Ehime ken bunka shinkō zaidan, 1998), 166.

35. Neil S. Fujita, *Japan's Christian Encounter with Christianity* (New York: Paulist Press, 1991), 189.

36. Ibid.

37. Mark L. Blum, "Collective Suicide at the Funeral of Jitsunyo: Mimesis or Solidarity?" in *Death and the Afterlife in Japanese Buddhism*, ed. Jacqueline Ilyse Stone et al., 137–74 (Honolulu: University of Hawaii Press, 2008), 141.

passions" (*bonnō*) or to the ending of the cycle of birth and rebirth rather than being killed for one's faith. Bunkō's description of an executed criminal as a person to whom one could pray for healing reflects an attitude that runs counter to Japanese cultural beliefs and religious traditions of the time.

The conclusion that can be drawn from the story is that Bunkō saw two sides to Mukōsaki Jinnai. One the one hand, he had been a notorious criminal because of his killing of innocent people. One the other hand, he became a holy sage at his death because he had promised to aid the sick and also because he was killed by the bakufu. His execution somehow exonerated and absolved him of his crimes so that after death he could be a healer for those who appealed to him. He was in a sense a martyr, because those who put him to death were, as Bunkō claims, worse than he. This anecdote was obviously insulting to the civil authorities, but it would also have been offensive to the Buddhist establishment.

The Law of Karma

A sad and frightening tale of adultery, murder, and abortion titled "The Case of the Old Woman at the Storehouse" (*Okura mae obaa ga den, 1756*) offers another example of Bunkō's unconventional and critical assessment of Buddhism in Tokugawa society in the eighteenth century.[38] Bunkō begins with a tongue-in-cheek jab at the Buddhist doctrine of karma (the belief that deeds done in the past or in past lives determine present and future experiences):

> If you don't pray to Heaven, you will spend your whole life as a fool, probably surpassing the foolishness of most other people. Isn't that the meaning of the Buddhist law of *karma*—to be more foolish than other people?
>
> Speaking of foolishness, everyone knows the old lady who hangs around the Asakusa rice storehouse nowadays and is seen sometimes in the vicinity the shogun's palace, acting rather strange and foolish. She has been wandering around Ryōgoku Bridge and the Asakusa area since sometime in the Kyōhō period [1716–36]. She is very ugly, always covered with dirt. She climbs down into ditches and gets completely covered with mud. She sticks her face right up to the rear end of horses. When she saw a mother with a little boy,

38. Baba, *Tōsei Buya zokudan*, 358–60.

> she went up to the boy, pulled at his penis and started laughing like a crazy woman. . . . Unfortunately, she did have a child of her own once.[39]

Bunkō proceeds to tell the story of this woman and her child. Many years previously the woman's husband, a man by the name of Izumiya Yohei who was deceased by the time Bunkō is writing, had been a well-to-do merchant in the Asakusa district of Edo. For a long time the couple had been unable to bear children. Yohei often blamed his wife for her infertility as the cause of their childlessness, and she would express her consternation and sadness to her younger sister. As the years passed, Yohei and his wife remained childless. Out of frustration with his wife's barrenness, Yohei allowed himself to become romantically involved with his wife's younger sister, and it was not long before she became pregnant. Yohei's wife, now burning with jealousy, blamed her disgrace on her sister and beat the poor girl repeatedly.

By the seventh month of her little sister's pregnancy, Yohei's wife was so desperate for revenge that she resolved to use any means possible to end her shame. Hoping to kill the child before it was born, she administered an abortion-inducing potion to her sister. Instead of killing just the baby, however, the concoction also killed the young mother-to-be. Yohei's wife had not intended this result, but she had no strong regrets and thought that it was karma, and it was meant to be. At least the cause of her shame was gone.

Exactly one year later, in the very same month that she had killed her pregnant younger sister and the baby with the abortifacient, Yohei's wife finally became pregnant herself. She was overjoyed that after so many years she was finally going to bear a child. Later that year she gave birth to an apparently healthy baby boy. She rejoiced that the horrors of her shame were now all in the past. She and her husband were happy beyond belief, and they loved their young son very much. Not all was right, however. By the time the boy had turned two years old he was still unable to speak.

Yohei and his wife had always been devout Buddhists and prayed faithfully to Buddha and to the Shinto gods. They burned incense before the Buddhist altar and frequently visited the Shinto shrine to pray for their son,

39. Ibid., 358.

but even by the time the child was four years old he was still not speaking a word. Finally, in the spring of his fifth year, the boy said his first word. Looking at his mother, he cried out, "Auntie." From that time on, he always called her "Auntie," and as he grew older he would never acknowledge her as his own mother. The boy never called his parents "mommy" or "daddy."

All of this seemed very mysterious to Yohei and his wife, until one day it suddenly occurred to her that the child must not be her own. The little boy she had borne was actually the child with whom her younger sister had been pregnant at the time of her death, the child whom she had killed. She concluded that the spirit of the fetus had somehow entered her own womb at the very moment she had murdered her younger sister, and the child was conceived a second time. The refusal of the boy to call her "mother" was the retribution that she would have to suffer for her entire life for her remorseless killing of the unborn child of her younger sister. Bunkō writes that her "son's" cold attitude toward her was her punishment not only for the abortion of the child and the murder of her sister but also for her husband's adultery. The joy of having a son was no more, and Yohei and his wife realized thereafter that they were raising the child of another person. They grieved for the rest of their lives over their fate of never being able to have their own child. They would never be real parents.

In his commentary on the tale, Bunkō makes sure his readers understand that even the households of the elite cannot escape punishment for their crimes. Though the wealthy and powerful seem to have everything they want, their happiness is only temporary. Their lives, hidden from the view of commoners, are filled with evil, shame, regret, and sorrow. Bunkō concludes his tale with the following observation: "The prayers of Yohei and his wife at the temples and shrines did them no good. The gods and buddhas could not save them from their own cruelty or from the consequences of adultery and murder. From then on Yohei and his wife, following the Buddhist custom, wore black in mourning.... Few people know the background of the crazy woman whom they see every day wandering around the Asakusa storehouse. So I have recorded the story of Yohei's wife here."[40]

40. Ibid., 359–60.

The "one hundred monsters" are respected members of the privileged classes of society, but at the same time are perpetrators of deceit, fraud, corruption, adultery, abortion, and cruelty of all kinds. Samurai, such as City Magistrate Tsuchiya Masasuke, the law enforcement officials Aoyama Tessan and Yamada Yoshitsugu, and wealthy merchants, like Yohei and his wife, are immoral "monsters" who have no sense of true virtue or honor, even though they believe themselves to be morally superior. Bunkō's satire points out the moral deficiencies of the highborn but praises the qualities and virtues of those who are generally despised and thought to be low-class, such as the servant Okiku, and even criminals, such as Mukōsaki Jinnai.

4 | RAINDROPS FALLING IN THE FOREST

Crimes of the pen were met with punishments ranging from home confinement in manacles and confiscation of personal assets to imprisonment and exile, the most egregious example being the execution in 1758 of Baba Bunkō.

NORIKO MIZUTA LIPPIT, 1993

The Fall of Kanamori Yorikane

The "monster" that attracted Baba Bunkō's attention as no other was the daimyō Kanamori Yorikane. Between October and November of 1755, Kanamori had arrested more than five hundred peasants from ninety-five families because of their vocal opposition to his oppressive taxes. He banished them into the mountains, sending them toward Shirakawa village in Hida domain, about fifty miles from their village. Unable to support themselves along the journey, most of the exiled villagers starved to death in the mountains during the particularly severe winter of 1755.

Even the early autumn in eastern and northern Honshū was particularly cold in 1755. Zhang De-Er of the National Climatic Center in Beijing suggests that the anomalous weather conditions and the severe cold

Epigraph is from Noriko Mizuta Lippit, Sekine Eiji, Japan-United States Friendship Commission, et al., *Monogatari no Yokubō,* Proceedings of the Second Midwest Research Pedagogy Seminar on Japanese Literature, November 13–14, 1993, Purdue University, 55.

and famine in both China and Japan that year may have been the result of a number of volcanic eruptions around the world.[1] The eruption of Mount Etna in Italy on March 9 the same year continued for six days. The eruption of the Mount Katla in Iceland on October 17, 1755, lasted 119 days. The Asama volcano, on the border between Nagano and Gunma prefectures in Japan, erupted in August the year before and again in 1755. L. M. Cullen blames a "premature climatic cooling" for the bitterly harsh winter.[2]

Baba Bunkō had long been highly critical of the government's role in the worsening economic conditions in the rural farming areas. He became a spokesperson in Edo for the peasant population and instrumental in bringing the bakufu's oppression of the peasants in Kanamori's domain to the attention of commoners in the capital. Bunkō had learned the details of the plight of the exiled peasants of Gujō through contacts he had made with peasants who were coming to Edo—whether to bring their goods to market or to lodge appeals and complaints with the government at the "complaint box" in front of the bakufu high court (*hyōjōsho*). (The system of direct appeal had been instituted under the shogunate of Tokugawa Yoshimune in 1721.) The creation of chartered trade associations (*kabu nakama*) had made travel to the capital from the rural areas more common. Before then travel had primarily been the privilege of the provincial daimyō and their entourages, but as a result of the establishment of the trade associations, merchants and artisans began traveling to and from the provinces to trade their wares. Conrad Totman points out that, through this trade, some of the wealthier merchants became almost like minor daimyō, possessing specific commercial "fiefdoms" not unlike domains.[3]

Peasants who came to Edo would often gather in Unemegahara (present-day Ginza 5-chōme, Chūō-ku). It was there that Bunkō had opportunities to meet and speak with travelers from the provincial areas, including from Gujō, and hear what they were saying about the growing

1. Zhang De-Er, "A Study of the Large Scale Flooding over Eastern China in 1755," *Advances in Climate Change Research* 3 (March 2012): 128–37.

2. L. M. Cullen, *A History of Japan, 1582–1941: Internal and External Worlds* (Cambridge: Cambridge University Press, 2003), 91.

3. Totman, *Early Modern Japan*, 301.

discontent in their home domains. City dwellers who attended Bunkō's lectures heard his reports and the latest news about tough economic conditions in the countryside and the resulting peasant uprisings, which were becoming more and more frequent.

"Raindrops Falling in the Forest"

In his work "Raindrops Falling in the Forest: A Hiragana Record" (*Hiragana Mori no shizuku*, 1758), Bunkō gives an account of the beginning of the peasant uprising in Gujō domain in 1754 and concludes with the final resolution of the problems at the end of the uprising in 1758.[4] The Japanese title of his work (*mori no shizuku*) is taken from "A Collection of Poetry for Her Former Majesty" (*Chōshū eisō*), written by Fujiwara Shunzei (1114–1204) in 1178.[5] The specific poem in question, titled "First Love," describes the heartfelt pain and humiliation of unrequited love:

Tears of shame	*Morashite mo*
fall like raindrops	*sode ya shioremu*
in the forest,	*kazu naranu*
fading the sleeves	*mi o hazukashi no*
of a foolish person	*mori no shizuku wa*

"Tears falling on one's sleeves," a common image in classical Japanese poetry, expressed a woman's shame and sadness at being neglected or abandoned by her husband or lover and her subsequent loneliness. The shame of rejection, the loss of one's status and security, and the destruction of one's household is implied by the term "*mori no shizuku*" (falling raindrops). Bunkō uses the same expression to describe the shame and the fall from grace of the daimyō of Gujō, Kanamori Yorikane.

The complete title, "Hiragana mori no shizuku," is an obvious pun on the name Kanamori: since there are no spaces between the words in the Japanese title, it could be read as "Hira Kanamori no shizuku." The character "*hira*" was used to refer to a samurai as one who was "low," "common," or "average." Thus, the title could be translated as "The fall of the

4. The introductory word "*hiragana*," which is one of the two Japanese syllabaries, indicates that the work is meant to be an easy-to-follow text for a popular audience.

5. "*Chōshū*" was an appellation for the wife of the former sovereign, Emperor Horikawa (r. 1086–1107), whom Shunzei, at least nominally, served.

low-class Kanamori," which would sum up the content of this six-page document.

In the ninth month of 1758 Bunkō began a series of lectures in Kuremasa-chō (present-day Chūō-ku, Nihonbashi, 3-chōme) in Edo that was based on this written text about the Gujō uprising. The manuscript itself is no longer extant, but the content of the introduction and other details are known from a number of sources. A section of *Records of the Tokugawa* (*Tokugawa jikki*), the official history of the Tokugawa shogunate, titled "Mori no shizuku," contains material that was taken from Bunkō's notes and used at his trial as evidence against him.[6] The notes are written in a style similar to Bunkō's own writing in other works that deal with disturbances in daimyō houses (*sōdō*), such as "The Tribute from Morioka" (*Morioka mitsugi monogatari*, 1757) about the conflict between the *bakufu* and Nanbu Toshikatsu (1725–79), which will be discussed in chapter 9.[7]

The lecture series itself was titled "A Martial Arts *Taiheiki*: Little-known Facts of Raindrops Falling in the Forest" (*Butoku Taiheiki Chinsetsu mori no shizuku*) and described the unjust treatment and horrific suffering that the peasants of Gujō had endured for the previous four years at the hands of Kanamori. Bunkō points out that the uprising was one of the largest since the beginning of the Tokugawa shogunate. More than three thousand peasants from over one hundred and twenty villages marched on Hachiman castle, the stronghold of Kanamori, demanding a reduction in the oppressive taxes. Every evening from the hour of the rooster (5:00–7:00 p.m.), on seven consecutive days from the tenth to the sixteenth, Bunkō spoke to local townspeople who gathered at the dry goods store, which was owned by a certain Yasuemon, about the current situation in Gujō. The number of people attending his presentation increased every evening until, on the seventh and final day, a crowd of about two hundred people had gathered.[8]

The final lecture moved from an account of the family lineage of

6. Yamada Tadao, "'Hiragana mori no shizuku' no yukue," *Nihon no rekishi geppō* 20 (September 1975): 13.

7. Other works in the same vein include *Akita Suginao monogatari* and *Akita chiranki*, both of which record the humiliations suffered by Satake Yoshimine (1690–1749), lord of Akita, at the hands of fellow daimyō.

8. Sekine Toshio, ed., *Sekine bunko shinshū, dai ikki*. This work, in manuscript form, was edited by the author's eldest son, Masanao, and published upon his father's death in 1893. In vol.

Kanamori to condescending praise, followed by an outline of the serious crimes he had committed and then ending with a strong indictment of his misuse of authority. Kanamori's claims of noble ancestry and cultural refinement were contrasted with his administrative incompetence, arrogance, and cruelty. Bunkō concludes that his indulgent and irresponsible behavior as daimyō, in spite of his distinguished lineage, eventually brought about his personal downfall and his family's fall into oblivion:

> The lord of Gujō castle in Mino, Kanamori Yorikane, a daimyō of a 38,000-koku domain and Junior Assistant Minister of War (*hyōbushōyū*) of the Minamoto clan, was descended from the illustrious house of the Toki family and ruled over the Hida domain [present-day Takayama City, Gifu prefecture] which had been inherited in the time of Oda Nobunaga. After many generations, the glory of the domainal house has turned to ashes, as has the fame and honor of Yorikane himself. He had become obsessed with unbridled greed. He indulged his own pleasures unceasingly, and he inflicted great suffering on the people.[9]

Ōta Nanpo (1749–1823), an Edo-period fiction writer, mentions "Hiragana Mori no Shizuku," the pamphlet from which the above paragraph is taken, in his essay "At Kanasogi" (*Kanasogi*, 1809). Ōta describes his search for a copy of Bunkō's original lecture notes and concludes that the document, written before the Ieshige government confiscated the Kanamori domain in January of 1759 (Hōreki 8.12), had probably been seized by the government and destroyed. In 1980 Takada Eitarō, a scholar of Japanese history, also made an extensive search for "Hiragana mori no shizuku," but like Ōta Nanpo before him, could not find a single copy. He came to the conclusion that there was no original copy of the document to be found.[10] The Imperial National Archives in Tokyo possess an 1827 document titled "Mori no shizuku" which in part duplicates the content of the official Tokugawa record of Bunkō's denunciation of Kanamori and may or may not be identical to Bunkō's original document.

206, "*Gunsho kōdan jireki*" (An oral history of war stories), can be found the information included here about Baba Bunkō's last days before his arrest.

9. *Mori no shizuku*, folio 1 front and reverse, 1827, in manuscript in the Imperial Archives (*Kunaicho shoryōbu*), Tokyo, and in a copy of the same manuscript in Gifu Prefectural Library.

10. Takada Eitarō, "Baba Bunkō o ou: 'Hiragana mori no shizuku' no koto," *Gujō shidanshi* 38 (April 1980): 3.

Peasant Uprising in Gujō

The peasant disturbances in Gujō began as a tax dispute between agitated impoverished peasants and Kanamori. The daimyō was a cultured man who loved poetry and painting but was a failure as an administrator. His grandfather, Kanamori Yoritoki (1669–1736), had been lord of the castle at Hida and a personal attendant of the shogun, Tokugawa Tsunayoshi. Yoritoki fell out of favor in 1698, was removed from his post, and sent north to Kaminoyama city (in the southeast part of present-day Yamagata prefecture) in Dewa domain. He was transferred again by order of the shogun to Gujō. On the death of his grandfather in 1736, Yorikane succeeded to the headship of the family and acquired Gujō, then a domain of twenty-four thousand koku and Echizen, Ono-gun, a domain of fifteen thousand koku. The Kanamori clan was rehabilitated by the bakufu, and Yorikane was given the honorary title of grand chamberlain (*sōjaban*) in 1747.[11] His political career undoubtedly would have advanced further had it not been for the poor financial condition of his family. Their fiscal problems were due in large measure to his grandfather Yoritoki having been forced to change fiefs twice. However, the prolonged depressed state of the family finances, which affected the entire domain's financial situation, was not completely the doing of the bakufu. Yorikane's lifestyle was nothing short of luxurious. The debts he incurred because of his excessive personal expenses accumulated beyond his means to repay them.[12] He attempted to resolve the crises in both his personal accounts and the domain's treasury by a reform of the taxation system.

In his lecture series Bunkō did not concern himself with the intricate financial details of the taxation system in Kanamori's domain or with the question of how it should or should not be reformed. He was concerned with directing his audience's attention to the inept machinations of domainal officials and their failure to relieve the financial disorder they themselves had created through bureaucratic mismanagement, which

11. *Kaneshi kaseiroku*, folio 31, in *Kyōto daigaku zō: Taisohon kisho shūsei*, vol. 6, ed. *Kyoto daigaku bungakubu kokubungaku kenkyūshitsu* (Kyoto: Rinsen shoten, 1994). The *sōjaban* announced the names of daimyō, bannermen, etc., who came for an audience with the shogun.

12. *Kaneshi kaseiroku*, folio 32.

was a direct result of the immoral lifestyle of the daimyō of Gujō. Bunkō tried to elicit the audience's sympathy for the suffering of the peasants and their indignation at the bungling of the tax reform program.

The attempted reform was to be financed by placing a new and oppressively heavy tax burden on the peasants. Not surprisingly, this provoked the violent reaction against Kanamori's rule. In 1754, just prior to the first uprising, officials of Gujō domain announced that the fixed rate (*jōmen*) system of taxation, which had been used up to that time, would be abolished.[13] This tax system had been introduced in 1724 and had allowed a peasant's tax rate to remain the same for a fixed period of usually three, five, or even ten years without an increase. Under this system peasants were able to cultivate new land without being taxed for it, thereby increasing their production and allowing them to pay lower taxes in real terms over the fixed period. Kanamori's new proposal was to replace this arrangement with the *arige kenmi* system, a progressive tax by which the amount to be paid would be determined by an inspection of the year's crop and based on the yield from one *tsubo* (approximately 3 ft. by 6 ft.) of land. Under this progressive tax system any increased production or cultivation of new areas would be taxed. Thus, property that had not been assessed under the old system would become taxable under the proposed reform. The bakufu had already enforced this new system over all Tokugawa-owned lands by 1749, arousing strong resistance among the peasants in those areas, but the opposition had been contained. With the bakufu as a model and under his advisers' recommendations, Kanamori attempted to proceed with similar reforms.

To implement the changes in the taxation procedures, senior officials of Gujō first consulted with the magistrate of finance (*kanjō bugyō*), Ōhashi Chikayoshi (r. 1754–58), in order to get his advice on the best way to implement the progressive tax. Ōhashi recommended Kurosaki Saichiemon, a tax consultant for a number of other domains that had implemented the same system. Yorikane hired him and paid him two hundred koku to begin work on the reform of the tax system. Ōhashi kept in close touch with the shogunal representative in Mino (*Mino gundai*), Aoki

13. Hall, *Cambridge History of Japan*, vol. 4, *Early Modern Japan*, 495.

Jirōkurō (dates unknown), and followed his recommendations. In the following year, 1755, the peasants, disturbed over their domain's persistent determination to adopt the progressive taxation system, sent representatives to Edo where they made an appeal to the senior counselor, Sakai Tadayori (1705–66).[14]

Sakai passed the appeal on to the north Edo city magistrate, Yoda Masatsugu (r. 1753–68) for examination.[15] Yoda investigated the peasants' appeal and concluded that there were indeed some grounds for a complaint against Kanamori; however, no concrete response to the appeal was forthcoming. The standoff between the peasants and Kanamori did succeed in obstructing the progress of the tax reform, and the problem was still not resolved three years later at the beginning of 1758.

In the fourth month of 1758, fifty Gujō peasants representing twenty-eight villages secretly entered Edo. Six of them had been appointed to bring another appeal, this time claiming injustice on the part of the government of Kanamori. They dropped the petition into the "complaint box." Three months later Senior Counselor Sakai finally ordered the case to be heard. The first decision Sakai made was to order two of the peasants who had placed the appeal in the complaint box to be jailed. Though he had acknowledged earlier that the peasants' appeal was justified, a complaint directed against the regime often meant that a prison term or other punishment was unavoidable, even if the appeal proved to have merit. The dispute over the tax reform was still not resolved.

The Itoshiro Disturbance

The serious situation in Gujō was further complicated by another crisis that had started much earlier than the peasant unrest over the proposed tax reform. In 1746 Uemura Buzen (d. 1758) attempted to solidify his control as village headman over Itoshiro and its main Shinto shrine Hakusan Chūkyo, both of which were in Kanamori's jurisdiction.[16] The shrine had been important since the Nara period (710–94), but it was

14. Sakai was senior counselor from 1749 (*Kan'en* 2) 9.28 to 1764 (*Meiwa* 1) 5.16.

15. Hayakawa Kōichirō, *Uzu no hirogari: Hōreki sōdō to Kanamori Yorikane o chūshin ni* (Gifu: privately printed by the author, 1974), 101.

16. Itoshiro was located on the border between Echizen and Mino on the Nagara River in what is today Gifu prefecture.

only in the Edo period that the bakufu recognized the headship of the shrine as a hereditary position under the Uemura family. The village of Itoshiro was being administered by twelve families of the *otona* (head farmer) class and supported by about one hundred fifty other families. Since Hakusan Chūkyo Shrine was entrusted to the Kanamori house, the bakufu did not levy any land taxes on it. In 1746 Uemura Buzen was headman of the village, but the hereditary custodian (*kōtō*) of the shrine was a member of the Sugimoto family. Both of these families, the Uemura and the Sugimoto, were jointly authorized by the bakufu to administer the shrine, while not ignoring the wishes of twelve other families who were charged with its day-to-day operation.

Uemura Buzen's complaints about this collective rule and his desire to consolidate control over both Hakusan Chūkyo Shrine and Itoshiro village under his authority alone had been threatening the stability of Kanamori's domain for the previous twelve years.[17] Uemura's scheming toward the goal of having both civil and religious authority in his own hands finally came to a head and caused a break in the long-established alliance between the leading Kyoto Shinto families, the Shirakawa and the Yoshida. The Tokugawa government had given jurisdiction over all Shintō shrines in the country to these two families and recognized them as the authorities over all Shintō ritual. Uemura formed an alliance with the Yoshida family against the Shirakawa in order to solidify his own control of both the village and the shrine.

The custodian of Hakusan Chūkyo Shrine, Sugimoto Sakon, and the villagers of Itoshiro opposed Uemura's attempt to seize complete control, insisting that from ancient times the shrine had belonged to the Shirakawa Shrine Bureau (*Shirakawa shingihaku no mon*). Uemura, they felt, was overreaching his authority. Uemura decided to bribe Kanamori's official in charge of shrines and temples, Neo Jinzaemon, in order to strengthen his position and the power of his ally, the Yoshida house, so that he could neutralize the Sugimoto faction. Sugimoto Sakon complained to Kanamori's domainal government about the illegal activities of Uemura but found his appeals ignored by Kanamori's officials. In the eighth

17. *Mori no shizuku*, folio 10–13.

month of 1754, representatives of the Sugimoto faction had no other recourse but to make a secret trip to Edo and appeal to the commissioner of shrines and temples (*jisha bugyō*), Honda Tadateru (r. 1749–58). Honda was a close friend of Kanamori and a supporter of his tax reform and had no reason to support the appeal from the Sugimoto faction. Honda reported the Sugimoto "agitators" to Kanamori.

Three years later supporters of the Sugimoto made a second appeal, this time to Senior Counselor Matsudaira Takechika (1716–79), as well as a second entreaty to Honda Tadateru.[18] Early the following year, 1758, another appeal was made to Matsudaira.[19] More written pleas were again placed in the complaint box in the sixth month of 1758, beseeching the bakufu's aid and denouncing Kanamori's acceptance of bribes and the illegal scheming of Uemura Buzen. These continual direct appeals over a period of several years finally resulted in an inquiry before the bakufu high court in the eighth month of 1758. The timing could not have been worse for Kanamori, as this was only one month after the investigation into the peasant complaints over his proposed tax reform. The bakufu was growing impatient with Kanamori's inability to preserve peace and tranquility in his domain.

The shogunal government in Edo was now investigating two cases: the peasant dispute over the proposed tax reform and the controversy over the administration of Itoshiro village and the domainal shrine. The Gujō peasants and the villagers had drawn the attention of the bakufu to Kanamori Yorikane's apparent incompetence, to the unreasonable and excessive force that he had used to drive the peasants from their land in 1755, and to his unsuccessful attempts to put down the uprising and resolve any of the disputes. Bunkō reported the details of these disturbances in his lectures to his Edo audience.

There were approximately 3,300 incidents of peasant uprisings in the Edo period. The Gujō disturbance was the only one brought before the bakufu high court and the only one that ended in the dismissal of a domainal lord and the replacement of a senior counselor and other high officials in the government.[20] The bakufu confiscated Kanamori's terri-

18. Ibid., folio 13–17.

19. Ibid., folio 28–39.

20. http://www.rd.mmtr.or.jp/~asashi/newpage636.htm

tories and moved him to Morioka domain in the far north. Three months later and two days after Bunkō's execution, the government declared that Kanamori and his descendants would suffer the loss of samurai status in perpetuity. Gujō domain passed into the hands of Aoyama Yoshimichi (1725–79) on the same day in early 1759 (Hōreki 8. 12. 27).

Other high shogunal officials were also punished for complicity in Kanamori's failed reform measures, for corruption, and for failure to keep order. Senior Counselor Honda Masayoshi was dismissed (1758. 9. 2) and confined to house arrest.[21] Kurosaki Saichiemon, the consultant who had participated in planning the tax reform, underwent severe questioning and torture and eventually died in prison.[22] Honda Tadateru, the commissioner of shrines and temples, was forced to resign from office and lost his samurai status, as did the magistrate of finance, Ōhashi Chikayoshi. Two shrine officials who were colleagues of Uemura Buzen were executed, as was Uemura himself, who was found guilty of the crime of instigating the Itoshiro Disturbance. The supporters of Sugimoto Sakon and others who had opposed Uemura were given light sentences for creating disorder, and the control of Hakusan Chūkyo Shrine was given over to the Yoshida family.

The punishment handed down against the Gujō peasant leaders for their responsibility in instigating an uprising was severe. Ten were executed, four imprisoned, and thirty-nine sent into exile.[23] The penalties meted out to both officials and peasants were the unfortunate result of Kanamori's ineffectiveness in dealing with the tax reform dispute and his failure to settle the shrine issue in an expeditious manner. According to Bunkō, however, "This daimyō's propensity to being a womanizer and a drunk was the primary cause of his political ineffectiveness."[24] The bakufu, of course, never raised morality issues of this kind during its investigation of Kanamori's personal life.

Soon after the Kanamori Affair, popular lampoons appeared in Edo directed against the daimyō of Gujō, Ōhashi Chikayoshi, and Aoki Jirōkurō, the shogunal representative in Gujō. One lampoon went as follows: "Led astray by Kanamori, that flunky of the fallen Ōhashi, Aoki Jirōkurō has

21. *Mori no shizuku* (1827), folio 57.
22. Ibid., folio 60–68.
23. Ibid., folio 87–92.
24. Ibid., folio 31.

ended up in prison suffering."[25] Contrary to the literal sense of the lampoon, Aoki was actually never imprisoned, nor did he end up suffering. The lampoon uses a pun that plays on Aoki's first name, Jirōkurō, as a combination of two homonyms: prison (*jirō*) and suffering (*kurō*). The anonymous writer is expressing his belief or hope that Aoki would eventually be punished, suffer, and end up in disgrace.

The year following Kanamori Yorikane's loss of samurai status, bakufu officials held a meeting at which an extraordinary confession was made.[26] Among those assembled were the new Senior Counselor Akimoto Suketomo (r. 1760–64) and Ōoka Tadamitsu, who was Shogun Tokugawa Ieshige's grand chamberlain. Ōoka realized that once Ieshige was gone (the shogun was less than a year away from death), his own political power would be severely limited, and his authority as the grand chamberlain would soon pass from his hands to another. Ōoka also feared that the discovery of corruption in the bakufu, which had been tolerated by high officials for so long under Ieshige, would be brought to light and would adversely affect Tokugawa predominance over the domainal lords. The participants at the meeting issued a declaration acknowledging corruption in the administration in which they conceded that officials had been receiving bribes.

The declaration was presented to Shogun Ieshige. Included also was the promise that from that time forward reception of political favors and gifts would no longer be tolerated. Akimoto, Ōoka, and the other officials were well aware that because of Kanamori's incompetence, not only was his lineage ended, but many of the prominent figures of his domainal government and numerous officials in the shogunal government who had been implicated in his incompetent handling of affairs were brought to ruin. The Itoshiro Disturbance and the resulting verdicts against the officials involved in that debacle had been the reason for this declaration against bribery and confession of corruption. It was just as Bunkō had said: "This ruler [Kanamori] who at one time had been respected became an object of indignation and fear." It was not fear of Kanamori, however, but fear for the survival of Tokugawa power.[27]

25. Hayakawa, *Uzu no hirogari*, 63.
26. *Mori no shizuku* (1827), folio 1 front and reverse.
27. Ibid., folio 1 front and reverse.

The Arrest

As Bunkō was coming to the end of his final lecture on these events, on the last night of the series, a constable making his usual rounds patrolling the neighborhood entered Yasuemon's dry goods store. While Bunkō was speaking, Yasuemon called over to Takeuchi Genkichi, one of Bunkō's companions, whom everyone called Bunchō, and signaled that a constable was in the room.[28] As the audience of about two hundred people was being worked up into a state of indignation at Bunkō's description of the plight of the starving peasants in Gujō, Bunchō became fearful for his own safety as well as for that of Bunkō. He continued to use gestures to try to direct Bunkō's attention to the presence of the constable in the room. Bunkō either did not see the signals or, because he was coming to the end of his lecture, did not want to stop speaking. He had never been worried about the government taking notice of his writings or the content of his talks before and was not concerned that a passing constable would pay any attention to what he was saying. His only audience on the previous six evenings, as far as he had been aware, was made up of townspeople, peasants, and rōnin. The constable on duty had not come in at any time on the previous six evenings.[29]

Bunkō finally finished his talk around 10:00 p.m., having spoken for about four hours. He then gave out free copies of his notes, "Hiragana mori no shizuku," to about ten people who had been chosen by lot. Other copies were sold for three hundred mon, approximately the amount that would buy rice for one person for twenty-five days.[30] The high price for such a short, six-page, unpublished pamphlet is an indication that it was in great demand. Its unusual subject matter, one of the largest peasant uprisings in Tokugawa history and Bunkō's call for a daimyō to relinquish power, made it worth the price for anyone who could afford it. It is understandable that the bakufu would have wanted to seize every

28. Okada, *Baba Bunkō shū*, 310.

29. Sekine Shisei, *Shisei airoku*, describes in vivid detail the events leading up to Bunkō's arrest.

30. It is difficult to give an exact equivalent to the value of three hundred mon. In the Hōreki period one ryō fluctuated between fifty and eighty mon, though sometimes the words "mon" and "ryō" were used interchangeably. In Saikaku's day, an eggplant could be bought for two mon. See Ihara Saikaku, *Nippon eitaigura* (1688), ed. Higashi Akimasa, 44.

last copy of such an inflammatory manifesto and use it later as evidence against him, which in fact was done.

When the lecture ended and most people had left the store, Bunkō was beginning to relax with a cup of tea. It was at that time that the constable approached and informed him that he was under arrest. Bunkō protested in his characteristic loud voice, "What do you think you're doing? Can't you see I'm about to have a cup of tea!"[31] The constable quickly restrained him by tying his hands and admonishing him not to get violent. Well aware that it was illegal to speak about official policy or about peasant uprisings, the constable warned him, "You must be crazy to give a lecture like that." Though forcibly subdued, Bunkō smiled at the constable. "I'm not the one who's crazy," he said. "We are all sane here, it's you people who are the crazy ones."[32]

The Law and Legal Precedents

In the 1750s the two Edo city magistrates had only about 120 policemen and constables at their disposal to keep watch over a population of almost one-and-a-half million commoners. These law enforcement officers were not an intimidating presence in Edo, and it was not uncommon for townspeople to be disrespectful toward them. The constable who arrested Bunkō was a dōshin, a samurai officer of lower hereditary rank with a smaller stipend than a yoriki (policeman). He was from the office of the north city magistrate, Yoda Masatsugu, who was on duty at the time. Bunkō did not seem to feel threatened by the constable who arrested him, possibly because Magistrate Yoda was known to be lenient and had the reputation for passing judgment with a degree of compassion.[33]

Though rude to the arresting officer, there is no evidence that Bunkō purposely exposed himself to actually being charged with a crime. He had been able to get away with criticizing public officials for years and had spoken about the Gujō uprising often. Bunkō's lecture notes had been privately circulated without incident because the laws governing publication were not very effective in enforcing censorship and were

31. Okada, *Baba Bunkō shū*, 306–7.
32. Ibid.
33. Baba, *Tōji chinsetsu yōhiroku*, 243–44.

even less effective when it came to controlling the distribution of unpublished manuscripts. The government had not seemed particularly interested in Bunkō or his writings up to the time he was apprehended.

Bunkō, like the general population in Japan in the eighteenth century, was not well informed about the specifics of the criminal code. Only the punishments that would be inflicted on those guilty of the most serious offenses were commonly known. It was understood, for example, that the death penalty was reserved for those who had committed murder, engaged in fraudulent business practices, such as counterfeiting money, sold poisons as medicines, had sexual relations with the wife of a man of a higher class, committed arson, or stole an amount of money greater than ten ryō.[34] Of course, being a Christian meant automatic execution as well. People only knew that if someone committed one of the major crimes or was found to be a Christian, that person would receive a death sentence. They did not know with certainty what punishment would be meted out for lesser crimes. Even the constables who were charged with the enforcement of the law often did not have a detailed knowledge of the specifics of the criminal statutes.[35]

The criminal code issued by Senior Counselor Matsudaira Norimura in 1742, titled "The Edict in 100 Sections" (*Osadamegaki hyakkajō*), was "not allowed to be seen by anyone but the magistrates."[36] It was not addressed to the people subject to its provisions and, in fact, was deliberately kept from them. Only the court nobility at Kyoto, the daimyō, and high-ranking samurai had access to texts of the shogunate's officially promulgated criminal laws, and even that access was partial and restricted. The bakufu saw no necessity to communicate any more than the barest outlines of the criminal code to the common people. Since Bunkō was doubtless unaware of the specifics of the law, he wrote and spoke without too much fear of reprisal. He had never heard of anyone being executed for something that he had written. He probably knew of the possibility that he could be manacled for a few days or even sent into

34. Ishii Ryōsuke, *Edo no keibatsu* (Tokyo: Chūō kōronsha, 1964), 202.

35. Totman, *Early Modern Japan*, 335.

36. John Carey Hall, trans., "The Edict in 100 Sections," part 4 of "Japanese Feudal Laws III: The Tokugawa Legislation," 683-804, in *Transactions of the Asiatic Society of Japan* 41, part 5 (1913): 804. This code was revised by Matsudaira Takechika in 1767 and issued as *Kajō ruiten*.

temporary exile, a common punishment for violating censorship laws, but he was willing to accept that risk.

Two verdicts typical of the rulings that Magistrate Yoda passed down will illustrate the leniency with which he dealt with crimes involving both samurai and commoners and explain why Bunkō was not worried about the constable from Yoda's office.[37] In one case a commoner by the name of Rokusuke, who had come from Shinshū (in present-day Nagano prefecture) and was employed as a servant at the residence of a constable in Hatchōbori (in present-day Chūō-ku, Tokyo), threatened his employer with a knife and attempted to take money and other valuables. In an effort to defend himself and his home, the constable struggled with Rokusuke but was unable to take the knife away from him. Rokusuke stabbed the constable and then assaulted his wife and ran away, leaving them both for dead. The constable died from his wounds, but his wife survived the attack and reported the break-in and assault to authorities.

Rokusuke was apprehended. City Magistrate Yoda summoned the relatives and co-workers of the murdered constable and promised that Rokusuke's crime would be thoroughly investigated, and if found guilty, the criminal would be executed. In his final verdict, however, Yoda declared that Rokusuke could not be judged according to the same standards by which samurai were judged because he had the status of a servant; and such being the case, he could not be expected to have any sense of discipline or loyalty. Since he could not have actually owed allegiance to the constable whom he had killed in the same way that a samurai would owe allegiance to his lord, the guilt of his crime was mitigated to a certain extent. Yoda judged that his punishment would be a fine and confiscation of his property.[38] Understandably, the family of the murdered constable was outraged. They had demanded that Rokusuke be paraded through the city, exposed for three days, and then crucified. Murder was one of the crimes that was automatically punished by death, but Magistrate Yoda still insisted that Rokusuke was only a servant and could not legally be executed. Under continued pressure, however, the magistrate eventually did give in to the family's demands.

37. Baba, *Tōji chinsetsu yōhiroku*, 243–44.
38. Ibid., 242–43.

Another incident involving City Magistrate Yoda would also have led Bunkō to conclude at the time of his arrest that he could escape severe punishment. The wife of Uesugi Shigesada (1720–98), lord of Bishū and head of the Bureau of the Shogunal Kitchen (*ōi no kami*), was standing one day on the bank of the Meguro River (present-day Setagaya-ku, Tokyo) in front of her mansion watching the boats go by. On the opposite bank four or five townsmen from Asakusa, who were on their way to Meguro Shrine, were getting into a boat to cross to the opposite bank where Lady Uesugi was standing. As they were approaching, the townsmen stood up on the bow of the boat and proceeded to urinate in her direction, laughing at her derisively. Lady Uesugi immediately left and reported the incident to her husband's retainers. She expected that they would immediately put the insolent townsmen to the sword, but since the retainers could not agree on what to do, she demanded that Magistrate Yoda arrest the townsmen and have them executed. Yoda heard her complaint and judged in her favor. They were to be put in jail for fifty days and then executed.

It seemed that Lady Uesugi would see justice served. However, the jailed hooligans called on a prostitute who was known to be a favored companion of Lord Uesugi to help them, begging her to intercede on their behalf and plead their case before him. Uesugi listened to her plea and brought a petition to Yoda to spare the lives of the men who had insulted his wife. Yoda released the prisoners even before they had served their fifty-day sentence.[39] The magistrate's judgment, not to mention Lord Uesugi's relationship with the prostitute, caused a rift between him and his wife as well as a split between Uesugi and his retainers. As a result of such cases, Yoda was perceived to be an official who could be persuaded to forgo strict enforcement of the law. Bunkō reasonably concluded that he had nothing to fear from such a judge.

Bunkō had not committed a crime as serious as murder, nor had he been as criminally offensive as the five townsmen who had insulted the wife of a prominent bakufu official. Unfortunately, instead of being tried while Magistrate Yoda was still on duty, Bunko was tried three months

39. Ibid., 243–44.

later, and Magistrate Yoda was no longer engaged with the business of the Office of the City Magistrate. Bunkō had been in detention during Yoda's term, but by the end of the year when Bunkō faced judgment and sentencing, it was the south city magistrate, Tsuchiya Masasuke, who was on duty and who would act as judge in Bunkō's case.

The respective jurisdiction of the north city magistrate and the south city magistrate was not a function of geography but of temporal terms of office. Both officials alternated in having responsibility for administering and policing the affairs of the commoners on a monthly basis. Since it was a constable from the office of the north city magistrate who apprehended Bunkō, Yoda Masatsugu began the proceedings against him. A senryū (satirical poem) current at the time condemned the north city magistrate because it was one of his constables who had arrested Bunkō for speaking publically about Kanamori Yorikane: "Preoccupied by the Kanamori affair, the city magistrate [Yoda Masatsugu] has made a mess of everything and heaped shame upon himself."[40]

As a rule, the magistrate worked on a case only during his month on duty. It was customary that the legal proceedings and any other business he was working on would be suspended until he resumed his office the following month.[41] The proceedings against Bunkō should have been put on hold and reopened when Magistrate Yoda was again on duty, but in an unusual move Magistrate Tsuchiya took over Bunkō's case and brought it to a conclusion himself. Tsuchiya wanted his revenge and decided to handle the case because Bunkō had maligned and discredited him in "The Case of the Monster Magistrate."

After his arrest on the day of his last lecture (1758. 9. 16), Bunkō was kept in detention and interrogated for three months. This in itself was also highly unusual, as punishments in Edo were usually administered quickly. The purpose of the long period of detention could only have been to give the government the time to force Bunkō to recant statements he had made. There is unfortunately no public record of precisely what the government's questions or his answers were during this time of detention. All that can be surmised with relative certainty is that the question-

40. Hayakawa, *Uzu no hirogari*, 63.
41. Hanasaki Kazuo, *Ōedo monoshiri zukan* (Tokyo: Shufu to seikatsusha, 1994), 96.

ing went on for an unusually long time, indicating that Bunkō refused to recant or submit to the demands of the government, whatever they were. The bakufu's investigation into the peasant uprisings in Gujō was continuing during the entire time Bunkō was being held in detention, but the government was not interested in defending or protecting Kanamori.

The Judgment against Baba Bunkō

After Bunkō's case was transferred from the jurisdiction of Yoda Masatsugu to that of Tsuchiya Masasuke, it was then brought before the bakufu high court. The decision in the case was passed down in early 1759 pronouncing Bunkō guilty of crimes punishable by exile. In its official judgment (*mōshiwatashisho*), which was signed by Tsuchiya Masasuke, the high court declared:

> Baba Bunkō (age 41), raconteur of old war stories, who lectured in Matsushima-chō, is very poor and does not make enough money to even buy clothes. He begged from those who gathered at his lectures about current government investigations and other serious topics. He put out a placard and passed out written materials, selling them by lot, and distributing them to book dealers.
>
> A number of people who attended his evening lectures wrote down every word he said and carried these notes outside of Edo, spreading views that are strange and unconventional [*isetsu nado* 異説など]. This was a dishonorable act. Although he was ordered to stop and desist from spreading rumors about current problems, he continued his lecturing, thus holding the shogunate in contempt. The penalty prescribed for these crimes is exile.
>
> However, since he has long been critical of the shogunate and has no respect for officials, he is to be imprisoned and executed. He will be beheaded at Asakusa and his corpse will be paraded around town.
>
> —Given by order of: [south city magistrate] Tsuchiya Echizen [Masasuke] and Matsudaira Ukon no Shōgen [Takechika, senior counselor and lieutenant of the inner palace guards] on this day of Hōreki 8.12.25 [January 23, 1759].[42]

42. *Bakufu jidai mōshiwatashi shōroku* (Collection of notices and announcements from the bakufu period), in *Hyakuman tō*, ed. Nakane Shuku (Tokyo: Kinkōdō, 1892), National Diet Library MS, vol. 9, 30–31. Also cited in various modern editions: *Edo Bungaku Kenkyūkai*, eds., *Edo monogatari* (Tokyo: Sanseisha, 1927), 2–3; Okada Satoshi, ed., *Baba Bunkō shū*, 309; and *Hikkashi*, in *Miyatake Gaikotsu chōsaku shu*, ed. Tanizawa Eiichi et al., 4: 59–60.

Bunkō's death sentence was carried out at Kozukappara execution grounds in what is now Minami-senju, Arakawa-ku, Tokyo.[43]

The first issue the high court raised in its condemnation of Bunkō was his poverty. This, of course, was not a crime in itself, but the bakufu in the 1750s did see the poor as a threat to order in the capital. In 1742 when city officials were concerned that vagrants were responsible for setting a number of fires, all the "wild beggars" (*nobinin*, that is, beggars outside of the supervision of a *hinin* boss) were ordered to be rounded up.[44] Anxiety that the poor were a possible public menace would come to a head in 1790 when Senior Counselor Matsudaira Sadanobu (1759–1829) began to make plans for the Stockade for Laborers out of concern for maintaining order among the "lowly people."[45] Bunkō, however, was not considered to be nobinin, nor was he considered to be one of the "lowly people." Thus his poverty, never considered to be a problem and never raised as an issue until he was condemned to death, was obviously an excuse to hide a more serious reason for his execution. There was also no evidence for the court's assertion that he "was ordered to stop and desist from spreading rumors." As already mentioned, Bunkō was taken by surprise at the time of his arrest because he had never been approached by a constable or policeman before.

There were many itinerant lecturers in Edo who put out placards and sold their materials just as Bunkō had done without being arrested, so this would not have been the real reason for his sentence of capital punishment either. His real crimes were the content of his lectures on the ongoing government investigations and the ridiculing of officials, but those had not officially been capital offenses. The "dishonorable act" of spreading "views that are strange and unconventional" (isetsu nado), however, was another matter entirely. What exactly those "views" were was not specified in the official judgment of the high court, but Ohashi Yukihiro of Waseda University has pointed out that the term "isetsu nado" was sometimes applied to the crime of being Christian.[46] In order to avoid a

43. In present-day Arakawa-ku, Kozukappara is commonly referred to as "Asakusa" since the execution grounds actually were in Asakusa until 1667.

44. Botsman, *Punishment and Power in the Making of Modern Japan*, 98.

45. Ibid., 107.

46. Ohashi Yukihiro, "Kinseijin to kirishitan [4] kakushi nembutsu to Kyōzaka kirishitan ikken," June 18, 2013, 1–2.

public execution for practicing Christianity, a vague charge of holding "strange and unconventional views" was issued instead.

Bunkō maligned, discredited, and ridiculed officials as high as the shogun himself, but those offenses were cited only in general terms. More significantly, they were not considered to be deserving of the death penalty. As the high court declared: "The penalty prescribed for these crimes is exile." The crime for which he was condemned is not specified in explicit terms. Knowing that he was probably not committing a capital crime, Bunkō continued writing and lecturing for almost five years. The government did not act against him. His writings were widely dispersed, as the high court admitted, and he attracted large crowds, particularly to his last lectures on the peasant uprising in Gujō. These lectures were delivered without incident for six continuous days. It was only by an unfortunate circumstance that the constable happened to walk into the dry goods store and arrest him on the seventh day of the lecture series.

If his comments to the constable at the time of his arrest are any indication, Bunkō did not show in any way that he might have had regrets or second thoughts about his criticisms of the shogunate or the personal attacks he had made against officials, nor did he have any fear of serious reprisals. His open disrespect of Tokugawa Ieshige and his bold defamation of City Magistrate Tsuchiya Masasuke, into whose hands he eventually fell, would certainly have incurred the anger of the magistrate, but Bunkō was obviously not afraid of that.

Bunkō may or may not have known that City Magistrate Tsuchiya, in fact, was not authorized to impose a penalty more severe than exile.[47] Senior Counselor Matsudaira, who also signed the judgment passed down by the high court, would have had no personal reason to have Bunkō executed. Bunkō had actually praised Matsudaira for "carrying out his duties faithfully and wisely."[48] He probably would not have agreed to Bunkō's death for any of the stated reasons. Bunkō, noting particularly the compassion that Matsudaira had for those below him, refers to him as a gentleman (*kunshi*).[49] There was no reason for the senior counselor

47. Hanasaki, *Ōedo monoshiri zukan*, 102.
48. Baba, *Tōji chinsetsu yōhiroku*, 191.
49. Ibid., 192.

to condemn Bunkō to death, since he was convicted of crimes that by law only warranted exile.

The wording of the document shows that Bunkō's sentence was a matter of controversy among the officials involved in the case. It was not necessary for the court to say that "the penalty prescribed for these crimes is exile" if there was a consensus to put him to death. The document could have simply decreed the death penalty without the irrelevant excuse of his poverty, putting out a placard, lecturing, and distributing materials. The only justification for the death sentence was "isetsu nado"—that is, his "strange and unconventional views." This was the crime not explained in the condemnation. There were no details offered to explain it, no list of offenses that might shed light on the reasons for capital punishment. If he had been put to death simply for his lectures and writings critical of the regime, he would have been the only person in the Edo period to suffer death for such a reason, which makes it even more unlikely that the crimes mentioned in the declaration were the crimes for which he was condemned.

As the reader has already seen, officials had long used the same tactic when arresting and charging Christians. Instead of making a direct accusation of being a Christian, it was common to accuse suspected Christians of other crimes. The bakufu's dealings with Christians were usually not made public, and the accusations made against those suspected of being involved with the "forbidden sect" were not made explicit.[50] As noted above, by not mentioning Christianity directly, officials did not have to acknowledge the presence of Christians or report them to the bakufu authorities. Officials in Edo by all means wanted to avoid public acknowledgement of the existence of Christian influence and consequently did all they could to avoid using the term "Christian."[51]

An interesting example of this is an incident that occurred in 1792. One Kumejirō traveled to Edo where he submitted an appeal (*kakikomi-uttae*) to the bakufu to have villagers who had been accused of "strange views" released from prison.[52] Presenting a kakekomi-uttae was only al-

50. Joseph Mitsuo Kitagawa, *Religion in Japanese History* (New York: Columbia University Press, 1966), 164.

51. Ohashi, "Kinseijin to kirishitan," 1.

52. Toya Toshiyuki, *Kirishitan nōmin no keizai seikatsu: Hizen no Kuni Sonogi-gun Urakami-mura yamazato no kenkyū* (Tokyo: Itō shotenkan, 1943), 12.

lowed in the most serious cases when it was absolutely necessary to circumvent regular court procedures. The bakufu was well aware that there had been irrefutable evidence of Christian practices among the villagers on whose behalf Kumejirō was appealing, but neither Kumejirō nor the bakufu made any reference at all to the Christian practices or to their "strange views" in the proceedings to accept or reject the appeal.[53]

In the case of Bunkō, the bakufu made no attempt to justify the radical punishment handed down by the high court. The reader has seen Bunkō's verbal attack on the city magistrate, his condemnation of senior counselors for bribery and immorality, and his mocking of shogun Tokugawa Ieshige, but these "offenses" are not mentioned in the judgment handed down, making it appear that these insults against bakufu officials were not the primary cause of the death sentence. All of Bunkō's crimes seem to be covered under the generalization of "holding the shogunate in contempt," but that crime was not judged to be deserving of the death penalty.

Other writers had committed offenses as serious as Bunkō but had not been punished with death. The Shintō scholar Takenouchi Shikibu (1712–67), for example, was detained for questioning under the suspicion that he had disparaged the shogunate, charges similar to those raised against Bunkō. When interrogated by the bakufu's shogunal deputy in Kyoto on whether or not he had said that the bakufu showed signs of corruption and was in danger of collapse, Takenouchi coyly replied, "Indeed, I believe that these are precarious times."[54] Taking Takenouchi's reply as an affirmative answer to their question, the city magistrate and the public officials present at his hearing became quite upset.[55] For his "crime" of publicly expressing his conviction that the bakufu was corrupt and beginning to show evidence of political and moral decay, Takenouchi was given only a "minimal sentence."[56] He was banished from Kyoto, where he had been lecturing to young court officials, and was sent into exile in Hachijōjima. He died before he reached his destination, however. Several court nobles who were under suspicion of supporting Takenouchi were

53. Ibid.
54. Maruyama Masao, *Studies in the Intellectual History of Tokugawa Japan*, 276.
55. Ibid., 277.
56. Totman, *Early Modern Japan*, 337.

dismissed from their positions and put under house arrest. This would have been the punishment for Bunkō's "crimes" as well, but there were other offenses not mentioned in the high court's decision for which he had been found guilty.

The same year that Bunkō was executed, Yamagata Daini (1725–67) denounced the inefficiencies of Tokugawa rule in his *New Thesis of Ryūshi* (*Ryūshi shinron*, 1759), a highly critical work that had revolutionary implications.[57] He even went so far as to write that the assassination of a "prince" could at times be best for the country. Yamagata continued to teach his ideas but was never arrested or reprimanded, again leading one to question whether Bunkō's "defamation of public officials" and his "contempt of the bakufu" were the real reasons for his execution.

New Thesis of Ryūshi remained in manuscript form and was not published until 1763, so one might argue that the government did not know of it or simply saw fit to ignore it. However, the work did become public in 1763, and still nothing was done to Yamagata until 1767 when he was executed, but not for his writings; it was for proposing that a popular army be raised in the countryside, that it capture a regional domain, and from there implement a rebellion against the bakufu center.[58] If Bunkō had advocated such a treasonous uprising, the reasons for his execution would have been apparent, but he had done no such thing. The high court did not convict him of any capital crime. It simply condemned him to death.

The Disciples of Baba Bunkō

After his execution, some of Bunkō's followers distanced themselves from their former mentor. Morikawa Bakoku (1714–91), for example, expressed opinions on the art of public speaking that seemed to be a reprimand of his former teacher and friend and a repudiation of his past association with Bunkō. Morikawa wrote about Bunkō: "To go so far as to put lies into your speech or to ramble on about this and that, even if it is true; or harping on every little point about this person or that is not acceptable any longer. Such a speaker may be intelligent, but he is not wise or care-

57. Naramoto Tatsuya, ed., *Kinsei seidōron*, vol. 3 of *Nihon shisō taikei* (Tokyo: Iwanami shoten, 1976), 392–419.

58. Najita, "History and Nature in Eighteenth-Century Tokugawa Thought," 645.

ful. As the senryū goes, 'There was never a liar like a professional lecturer.'"[59] Bakoku's rejection of Bunkō did not only bring him official approval. Bakoku was also given a government stipend that provided him with the financial means to take care of himself and eight other people in his house in Bakuro-chō, the same neighborhood where Bunkō had lived.

Bakoku had become a successful lecturer in his own right, even while Bunkō was still alive. He told war stories in the traditional style, but after being exposed to Bunkō's manner of lecturing, he started to report on various disturbances and confrontations between lords and retainers in daimyō households in Edo and gave his own frank opinions on the pretense and arrogance of some officials. Not long after Bunkō's execution, however, the content of Bakoku's lectures changed and contained less direct political commentary and social satire and increasingly took on the characteristics of innocuous entertainment.[60] His newfound prudence brought him some success and made him popular with bakufu officials, and he credited his success to the new, less confrontational approach that he adopted. Bakoku was even invited on a number of occasions to speak before Senior Counselor Matsudaira Sadanobu. Sadanobu, who was responsible for censorship of publications, came to admire Bakoku. The fact that Bakoku was one of the senior counselor's favored speakers is evidence that this former disciple of Bunkō had abandoned the principles he had learned from his mentor. Bakoku had achieved financial security and had built a favorable reputation for himself. However, he never seemed quite as content as he had been before Bunkō's execution. He increasingly sought consolation in alcohol, and by the end of his life had lost much of the respectability that he had previously won among both the officials and the Edo townspeople.[61]

After Bunkō's death there were other kōdanshi who chose to direct their rhetorical and literary talents toward simple amusement, avoiding direct criticism of the government. Yoshida Ippō (d. 1779), for example, had been a close acquaintance of both Bunkō and Bakoku and had learned much

59. Sekine Mokuan, *Kōdan rakugo konseki dan*, 44.
60. Nomura, *Honchō wajin den* (Tokyo: Kyōei shuppan kai, 1944), 29.
61. Sekine Mokuan, *Kōdan rakugo konseki dan*, 44.

from them about satirical techniques in speaking and writing. He decided, however, to change his style of public lecturing from teaching and giving commentaries on contemporary events to speaking solely for the sake of entertaining his patrons. Adults gradually stopped attending his lectures, and his audience increasingly became young children, whose mothers brought them to hear his amusing, easy-to-understand fairy tales and anecdotes.[62]

A much more talented kōdanshi than Ippō was Yoshida Tenzan (dates unknown), who was active in Osaka during the Meiwa-An'ei period (1764–81). He too made a decision after Bunkō's execution to restrict his public performances to recitation of the traditional war stories and commentaries on famous people of the past.[63] His kōdan entitled "Tenshinki" (A record of the heavenly gods, 1779), for example, was a Muromachi-era rehash of a Shintoist apology that included anecdotes from the life of Sugawara no Michizane (845–903), a scholar and poet of the Heian period (794–1186), and his son Koreyoshi (812–80). Characteristic of a number of the kōdanshi who had once followed Bunkō, Tenzan no longer had anything to say about contemporary politicians. These former disciples of Bunkō, who had modeled their kōdan performances on those of the master, gradually lost the critical spirit and courage that had been characteristic of their mentor.

Censorship

Censorship of literature became more systematized with the publication of *The Index of Forbidden Books* (*Kinsho mokuroku*) in 1772. The bakufu banned "Chinese books" (a code word for publications pertaining to Christianity) and the buying or selling of 122 titles that "contained confidential information, unfounded rumor, and erotic content."[64] Three works by Baba Bunkō were included in this list: "A Record of Contemporary Public Secrets" (*Kindai kōjitsu genpiroku*, 1754), "The Tale of Akita Suginao" (*Akita Suginao monogatari*, 1758), and "An Investigation of Re-

62. Iguchi Hiroshi, "Yoshida Ippō," in vol. 6 of *Nihon koten bungaku daijiten*, ed. Ichiko Teiji et al. (Tokyo: Iwanami shoten, 1984), 153.

63. Ueda Kazutoshi, *Shinkō Gunsho ruiju*, *Shinkō Gunsho ruiju* (Tokyo: Naigai shoseki 1938), 1: 475–89.

64. Nagasawa Kikuya, *Nihon shomoku taisei*, vol. 4 (Tokyo: Kyūko shoin, 1975), 209–17.

cent Rumors" (*Genmitsu keijitsu uwasa*, 1758). Many works, in spite of the fact that they were on *The Index of Forbidden Books*, circulated widely, and a number of copies have survived.[65] Some twenty manuscript copies of Bunkō's *A Record of Contemporary Public Secrets*, for example, are still extant, suggesting it was widely distributed even after it was banned. One copy found its way into the hands of Isaac Titsingh (1745–1812), the intermittent head of the Japan factory of the Dutch East India Company from 1779 to 1784, who told colleagues that he had read a work of one "Bababun Kō [sic]."[66]

Hayashi Shihei (1738–93), a student of Western military science, and Santō Kyōden (1761–1816), gesaku author and artist, were among a number of writers who were censured by the government in the eighteenth century. Shihei was arrested after his publication of *Military Talks for a Maritime Nation* (*Kaikoku heidan*, 1791). This work proposed a radical departure from the traditional education of the samurai that would introduce military strategy rather than martial arts. The bakufu considered Hayashi's work unacceptably critical of government policy, and since it was published without the permission of the bakufu, the woodblocks were confiscated and destroyed. In 1792 Matsudaira Sadanobu ordered Shihei to be put under house arrest, and he died the following year.

Santō Kyōden incurred the anger of the shogunate for his illustrations in Ishibe Kinkō's satire *Reflections of Right and Wrong* (*Kokubyaku mizukagami*, 1789), but he was simply fined one ryō, five mon. Kyōden was ordered by the bakufu to be manacled for fifty days, the maximum sentence under the law, after publishing "erotic" books about the Yoshiwara "pleasure" district. The following year the bakufu issued edicts further restricting the publication of gesaku fiction in order to curb the dissemination of what it judged to be unedifying materials.

Neither Hayashi nor Santō Kyōden received the death penalty. Bunkō might have escaped the ultimate punishment as well, except for the unmentioned crime, which the government was afraid to bring out into the open. Bunkō may have been simply reprimanded in the same way as others, but he threatened the security of the bakufu in some unstated way

65. Kornicki, *The Book in Japan*, 110.
66. Screech, ed., *Secret Memoirs of the Shoguns*, 66–67.

that could not be tolerated. Only the crime of being a Christian or Christian sympathizer can adequately explain the rationale for his execution. A "hidden Christian," however, cannot be proven to be a Christian, and the shogunate in the eighteenth century wanted to keep it that way.

The next chapter will begin a detailed analysis of Baba Bunkō's social and political satire, the details of his denunciations of the bakufu and its officials, and his critical evaluation of the culture, customs, mores, and values of Tokugawa society in the eighteenth century.

5 | BABA BUNKŌ'S POLITICAL AND SOCIAL DISSENT

Participants in few epochs in history have shown more consistency and resourcefulness in seeking to conceal conflict and the inevitable clash of claims to power than Japanese of the Tokugawa era.

HARRY HAROOTUNIAN

The Atmosphere of Dissent in the Eighteenth Century

Although censorship was enforced sporadically and was never very effective during the Tokugawa period, the bakufu did take measures to ensure that security would not be threatened. Officials kept a close eye on a number of writers, such as Itō Jinsai (1627–1705). At the insistence of the government, Jinsai submitted written materials for inspection in 1683 because he was suspected of violating the proscription against writing about government affairs and policy. Kumazawa Banzan (1619–91) was ordered to be put under house arrest for commenting on public affairs in 1687.[1] A new office assigned to examine imported Chinese books for any references to Christianity was created in 1685 at Nagasaki. These government actions were meant to control the spread of ideas that would in any

Epigraph is from Harry Harootunian, "Ideology as Conflict," in *Conflict in Modern Japanese History: The Neglected Tradition,* ed. Najita (Princeton: Princeton University Press, 1982), 25.

1. Totman, *Early Modern Japan*, 221.

way shed an unfavorable light on the official functions of government and question or raise doubts about the legitimacy of the regime. The shogunate tried to be vigilant in ferreting out and destroying any writings that criticized the bakufu, interfered in policy, or spread heterodox ideas, particularly Christianity.

Provisions Governing Publishing (*shuppan jōkō*), promulgated in 1722, stipulated that the name "Tokugawa Ieyasu" or the name of any other shogun or bakufu official be strictly forbidden to appear in print.[2] In addition, the law forbade the writing and publication of either historical accounts or fictional stories that depicted in any recognizable fashion samurai, their families, or their ancestral lineages. Moreover, writers were not permitted to comment on any recent historical events that might disturb the political, economic, or social status quo. Authors would have to disguise their reports of current events by either setting them in the distant past or changing the names of the principal protagonists, or both. Essayists, playwrights, historians, and biographers were free to make up imaginary tales about samurai, their exploits, their vendettas, or succession quarrels in fictional daimyō households, but stories and reports could not exhibit any recognizable parallels to actual events or persons. It was also illegal for an author to protect his anonymity by using an alias or by leaving his name off of the colophon of the manuscript.

In spite of such meticulously composed censorship laws, or perhaps because of them, a popular literature of dissent arose in Edo. The expression of highly contentious views directed against the government in a satirical manner does not generally occur in a society in which there is political and social freedom, but rather where there is a degree of repression. It is often economic adversity and political intimidation that drive some writers and artists to make their dissenting views known through satire. At times when there are conflicting social interests and changes in traditional intellectual attitudes and conventions, satire arises as an expression of dissatisfaction. Though there may be opposing political opinions expressed during a time of social tranquility and general satisfaction, these opinions and positions are not usually articulated through

2. Tsuji Tatsuya, *Kyōhō tsugan*, 9: 166. Also cited in Nishiyama Matsunosuke, Gunji Masakatsu et al., eds., *Edogaku jiten* (Tokyo: Kōbundō, 1994), 428.

satire. Baba Bunkō wrote satirical essays and anecdotes about incidents in the lives of contemporary samurai and government officials that were historically accurate without changing names or dates to hide any of the identities of his characters. He wrote even about matters related to the personal habits and way of life of a number of officials, including the shogun, Tokugawa Ieshige.

The middle decades of the eighteenth century were socially and politically unsettled years in Japan. It was a time that was ripe for satire and dissent. During the Hōreki period (1751–64) both the economy and social morality were in a perilously unstable state. The bakufu's determination to restore moral order to society and to initiate various economic reforms succeeded only in raising the level of cynicism and sarcasm directed against it. The ultimate failure of the reforms to produce any long-lasting economic recovery or social improvement increased people's skepticism even more, and commoners became more assertive in articulating their discontent.

The denunciations against the government were expressed in graffiti (*rakushu*) and one- or two-line lampoons (*senryū*) that made fun of the ruling elite and of the samurai class. One distinguishing characteristic of the satirical poems, in contrast to the traditional language of classical *waka* poetry, was the absence of romantic metaphors, any depictions of the beauty of nature, or nostalgic references to the different seasons. Rather, these poems depicted the foibles of the elite, specifically of samurai officials, with piercing wit and sarcasm.

Graffiti and senryū were also directed against political corruption.[3] One type of senryū followed the pattern: "If he is a samurai, why does he . . . ?" For example, "If he is a samurai, why has he become a townsman?"[4] This was a reference to the popularity of the prostitute quarters among both low- and high-ranking samurai, even though officially they were discouraged from entering the quarters. The samurai's increasingly poor financial situation and his need to trade rice for cash was satirized in the senryū: "If he is a samurai, why does he go to the storage house to get rice?"[5] The samurai, proud of his birthright and his stipend from the

3. Nishiyama Matsunosuke, *Edogaku jiten*, 47.
4. Goryōken Arubeshi et al., eds., *Haifūyanagidaru*, 57: 118.
5. Ibid., 182.

bakufu, would never admit that he was hungry or needed anything from a commoner. However, more and more often in the 1750s samurai found themselves strapped for cash, often through their own fault or their inability to comprehend the intricacies of finance. They would sometimes have to go to the rice storage facility at Asakusa to exchange their rice stipend for coins so that they could purchase necessities in the increasingly money-oriented economy of Edo. Some of the lampoons could encapsulate the economic situation of the samurai in just a few words, such as: "The officials are starting to sell their offices."[6] The Japanese word for "offices" (*degawari*) in this lampoon is the same expression that was used to designate the role of a kabuki actor. Just as an actor would from time to time change his role in a play, so too the samurai was willing to change or even abandon his official status if he could find a buyer to whom he could sell his office or title.

Scholars, teachers, physicians, and other professionals who received stipends from the shogunate were also made the butt of jokes: "Doctors are supposed to be doctors, but they don't have any medicines."[7] This senryū was composed after its author observed that many samurai physicians were more interested in trying to make a profit by behaving like merchants rather than serving people as healers. Buddhist monks were also made the objects of scorn, as is evident in this verse: "Monks who sell Buddhist images make enough money for even Kōbō Daishi (774–835) to live on."[8] The anonymous author of this senryū observed that there were monks who deceived devout people by claiming that the Buddha statues they were selling were actually made by Kōbō Daishi himself, so that they could charge exorbitant prices for them.

In addition to the lampoons, various rumors spread about the clandestine liaisons that samurai and daimyō were having with Yoshiwara courtesans and kabuki actors. Such gossip nourished a culture of various forms of satirical expression. Of course, people old enough to have lived through the successful administration of Tokugawa Yoshimune (r. 1716–45) and who were still alive when the corrupt Tokugawa Ieshige (r. 1745–60) came to power would have been well disposed to cynicism

6. Ibid., 203.

7. Ibid., 216.

8. Ibid., 203. Kōbō Daishi is another name for Kūkai, founder of Shingon Buddhism.

about the government. The clear-cut differences between these two administrations aroused people's sarcasm concerning the decline in political integrity under Ieshige, after what was perceived to have been a period of virtuous rule under Yoshimune.

When Ieshige came into office in 1745, commoners began to ridicule the samurai more openly and with less caution. Increasingly, samurai were acquiring a reputation for being arrogant in spite of the fact that the majority of them were totally dependent on government rice stipends and ignorant of the intricacies of the money economy that was rapidly developing. Since Edo was populated by a large number of samurai who flaunted their status along with an increasing number of peasants who had come to Edo from rural areas with tales of samurai oppression, commoners in Edo were developing a disgust of samurai pride and an aversion to their offensive manners. As townspeople in the capital were becoming more educated and economically and culturally more sophisticated, cracks were beginning to appear in the strict division of social classes. This meant that commoners were less fearful and more inclined to resist samurai pretensions.[9] This change in attitude and the growing antagonism against samurai officials created an audience for Bunkō's satire. The antipathy that was first expressed in popular lampoons and satirical poems gradually began to be put into a more developed prose form, and Baba Bunkō's political satire grew in popularity.

Bunkō's literary attacks directed against the bakufu and its officials would not have been as popular in a location other than the capital city, where a large number of samurai from the provinces were highly visible to the commoner population. The encounters with members of the elite, such as those described in Bunkō's essays and anecdotes, would not as readily have been part of the daily experience of commoners in a Japanese city other than Edo or in the rural areas where the samurai were more often than not ensconced in their lord's castle and had few encounters with the lower classes. Indeed, the physical location in which satire and dissent can be most effective is the cultural and political capital.[10]

9. Nishiyama Matsunosuke, *Edogaku nyūmon* (Tokyo: Chikuma shobō, 1981), 49.

10. Dustin Griffin, *Satire: A Critical Reintroduction* (Lexington: University Press of Kentucky, 1994), 137.

Bunkō was able to communicate to an audience that understood satire simply because of their experience of living in Edo.

Bunkō's contemporary, Edo humorist Jōkanbō Kōa (flourished 1750s), described the character of the people of Edo at this time in *Didactic Clumsy Sermons Part II* (*Kyōkun zoku heta dangi*, 1753): "The people of Edo act arrogantly, doing exactly what they want to do without fear of any reprisal from those above them.... Merchants act so arrogantly that they appear no different from the great daimyō."[11] Encapsulating in a popular saying the disrespect that many Edoites had for the samurai, Kōa writes: "One need not be afraid of samurai or of lice."[12] Kōa's earlier work, *A Clumsy Sermon on the Present Age* (*Imayō heta dangi*, 1752), had caused quite a stir in Edo and had become popular because of its bold castigation of the elite. "The samurai are a plague on society," Kōa wrote, "and the daimyō have become lazy bookworms."[13] The economic rise of the commoner and the decline of the samurai are evident in Kōa's work. He referred to an advertisement that was seen around Edo for the mortuary services that were provided by a certain Sōshichi, who boasted: "My funerals for commoners nowadays far surpass the ceremonies any samurai can afford."[14] The samurai were even beginning to be perceived as an economic burden on society. More and more the merchants and other townspeople were the ones who were providing the cultural and economic energy that was transforming Tokugawa society, leaving the samurai farther and farther behind.

The official permission to allow the publication of Kōa's *A Clumsy Sermon on the Present Age*, in spite of its criticism of the government, was probably due to the irregular enforcement of censorship or to the inattention of censors. This work included condemnations not only of the samurai, but also of the immorality among actors of the kabuki theater and the corrupt business practices of some wealthy merchants, but its publication was ultimately a testimony to the generally incompetent enforcement of the law under Shogun Tokugawa Ieshige. The publication of the work marked a breakthrough for the Edo publishing world and

11. Noda Hisao, *Kinsei shōsetsu shi ronkō*, 242.
12. Ibid.
13. Nakano Mitsutoshi, ed., *Inaka sōji, Imayo heta dangi*, 127.
14. Ibid., 156.

highlighted the broad popularity of satirical literature. Book sales for the genre grew.[15]

The government tried to fight back and suppress satirical works in order to keep a lid on the growing dissent, which was thought to be undermining society. However, the government's poor attempts to enforce censorship only exposed the weaknesses in the system and the incompetence of prominent officials who could not be consistent in their criteria for censoring the various forms of critical literature that were appearing. The resulting confusion in official circles with regard to dissent only served to enhance the attraction of satire and the popularity of subversive writings. While censorship was ostensibly meant to preserve morality and good order, it was clearly failing to achieve its goals. Actually, the preservation of morality was simply a pretense. The real reason censorship continued to be enforced at all, even if inconsistently, was so that the officials of the government could continue to hold on to some authority over the rising sophistication of the commoner population.

Bunkō, seeing that censorship under Ieshige was inefficient and that Jōkanbō Kōa was not punished for his writings, felt encouraged to write and distribute his own satirical, anti-government essays. There is one important difference between Kōa and Bunkō, however. Kōa kept the targets of his criticism anonymous while Bunkō named names, presented real evidence, drew concrete conclusions, and made direct accusations against very prominent people.

Even though censorship laws that banned heterodox and satirical literature had been in force during the previous administration of Tokugawa Yoshimune, the restrictions on publications had been somewhat relaxed. Yoshimune's desire to even allow some degree of freedom of speech is evident in his reaction to Yamashita Kōnai (dates unknown), a lecturer in military science. Yamashita took advantage of the complaint box, which Yoshimune had instituted in 1721 to allow both commoners and samurai to voice their opinions to the shogun. In his complaint Yamashita criticized inefficiencies in government and in rather blunt terms, attributed the economic failures to Yoshimune's wasting his time pursuing his

15. Ichiko Teiji, *Nihon koten bungaku daijiten*, 3: 205.

hobby of falconry. As the complaint was read out loud the shogun's officials listened in shock and amazement. Remembering that under previous administrations taking such liberty of expression on matters of state would have been dealt with severely, the officials expected Yamashita's immediate chastisement. Yoshimune, however, recognized the courage and the intelligence of Yamashita and ordered that he be rewarded with a gift of three hundred ryō for the advice he had given.[16]

Admonishing the government and its officials was not only permissible under Yoshimune but even encouraged. Tanaka Kyūguemon (1662–1729) also denounced abuses in the bakufu and criticized some of Shogun Yoshimune's economic measures.[17] The shogun recognized the importance of Tanaka's complaints and made him chief of the Kawasaki checkpoint on the Tokaido Road. Later Yoshimune promoted him again to the position of intendant (daikan). Seeing such examples of honest criticism being rewarded by the shogun, Bunkō praised Yoshimune as a shogun who should be respected.

Four years after assuming the duties of shogun, Yoshimune had ordered the first partial lifting of strict censorship. Until that time, censorship had been based on statutes from 1630 when the bakufu had imposed an almost total ban on the importation of Chinese books that dealt with topics in Western religion and thought, particularly Christianity. In the later decades of the 1600s the bakufu had followed a policy of much stricter censorship, imprisoning many writers and imposing a stern ban on foreign publications, including Chinese translations of Western works and even Chinese books that dealt with Western sciences. For almost a century, until 1720, these laws remained in effect. The bakufu continued to put severe restraints on the dissemination of "heretical" ideas that the government feared might circulate among the townspeople in Edo and the peasants in the countryside. The ban against foreign books dealing directly with Christianity remained in force, but Yoshimune was convinced that certain aspects of Western knowledge could be useful in governing.[18] Arai Hakuseki has been given credit for the shogun's change of

16. Totman, *Early Modern Japan*, 330.
17. Ibid., 348.
18. Richard Rubinger, *Private Academies of Tokugawa Japan*, 102.

heart.[19] The relaxation of censorship and the institution of the complaint box were two other reasons that Bunkō held Yoshimune in high regard.

By the 1750s, more than a century before the fall of the Tokugawa bakufu, the verbal attacks on the shogunate were not yet being articulated in terms of loyalist sentiment for the emperor, or in calls for the overthrow of the government, as they would be later in the nineteenth century. Discontent was not yet being expressed in systematic treatises, as it would be later when, for example, Aizawa Seishisai's *New Thesis*, would be interpreted as a call for loyalty to the imperial house.[20] Fujita Tōko (1806–55) would use the terms "*sonnō*" (revere the emperor) and "*jōi*" (expel the barbarian) for the first time in his work *True Record of the Kōdōkan* (*Kōdōkanki jutsugi*) in 1847.[21] Both of these treatises would be seen as a rallying cry for anti-bakufu forces in the waning years of the Tokugawa era, long after Bunkō. However, resentment against those in power can already be seen in the 1750s, several decades before the recognized beginnings of the imperial restoration movement that arose in the 1830s and 1840s. By Bunkō's time there is already a realization that the bakufu is corrupt and ineffectual and resentment against government corruption and injustice is already widespread.

The perception of weaknesses in Tokugawa authority and legitimacy in the 1700s has been difficult for historians to document. This is because the first clear signs that trust in the government was waning cannot be found in the public records or in the writings of the official historians or even in most of the popular fictional literature (gesaku) of the time. The symptoms of the collapse of public confidence in Tokugawa rule appears primarily in the satirical anecdotes and essays in popular literature, but modern historians have for the most part neglected to treat these works as credible historical artifacts. However, it will become clear to the reader that the antagonism and rancor that were ultimately to augur the fall of the bakufu and the restoration of the emperor were expressed as early as the 1750s when Baba Bunkō was writing his satire.

Baba Bunkō's significance lay in his ability not just to promote dis-

19. John W. Hall, *Japan from Pre-History to Modern Times* (New York: Dell, 1970), 223–24.

20. Hashigawa Bunzō, *Nihon no meicho* (Tokyo: Chūō kōronsha, 1974), 29: 293–392.

21. Fujita Tōko, "Kōdōkanki jitsugi," in *Mitogaku*, vol. 53 of *Nihon Shisō taikei*, ed. Imai Usaburō et al. (Tokyo: Iwanami shoten, 1973), 296.

sent but, more importantly, to communicate a moral message through a popular style of Japanese oral performance and written literature for a commoner audience. He attacked directly and with very little restraint those centers of bakufu authority that held the political, intellectual, cultural, and religious power. He was the most outspoken precursor of the sentiments of resistance and the attitudes of defiance that discontented commoners would increasingly exhibit as Japan moved closer to the Meiji Restoration. A close reading of his satire enables one to witness the dishonesty and corruption of individual bureaucrats as early signs of the decline in the Tokugawa system. The official government documents and public records show that his defiance kept officials vigilant during his lifetime and on the lookout, ready to suppress public dissent even after his death and for the next hundred years until the Tokugawa bakufu finally did collapse in 1867.

Tales of Samurai Revenge

Bunkō's written style was influenced by a variety of literary genres that were popular during the Edo period. One of those categories of literature is known as *jitsurokutai shōsetsu* (historical fiction). This popular early modern genre developed directly from oral storytelling (kōdan) and focused on conflicts and disputes among samurai or tales of scandals within samurai households (*goke sōdōmono*). Similar to the modern Western historical novel, the names of real people appeared alongside those of fictional characters; and many of the events, though imaginary, were based on real historical occurrences. The fictional elements of the story should not be dismissed as simply false. Such imaginary components reveal the author's attitude and specific interpretation of the meaning of the actual historical events. Fictional descriptions of characters in the historical novel give the reader a window on the author's understanding of the real personality and temperament, the virtues and foibles of historical personages.

A subgenre of the *jitsurokutai shōsetsu* genre was composed of accounts of samurai vendettas known as *adauchimono*. These stories sometimes included descriptions of the methods samurai used to take revenge on their enemies. In early modern Japan, a vendetta could be officially sanctioned and legally carried out if a samurai kept within specific guidelines. A would-be avenger, for example, had to first secure permission from his own domain's authorities if he wished to take the life of a person who had killed an elder relation or a feudal superior. On the successful completion of the vendetta, the avenger was required to inform the domainal authorities of the outcome or, if the revenge was not successful, to inform the authorities of his failure. If the one being sought fled to another domain, the shogunate would then step in and confirm or rescind the permission originally given for the would-be avenger to carry out his plan in the new territory. By adhering to these restrictions, a samurai who had killed his enemy would not only avoid punishment, he would in fact be celebrated and rewarded by his domain for successfully carrying out the vendetta.[22]

Bunkō bases one of his own anecdotes on an older account of samurai revenge written by an anonymous author and titled *The Vendetta at Takadanobaba* (*Takadanobaba de no kettō*, 1694).[23] This late seventeenth-century *adauchimono* is a partly historical, partly fictional account of a sword fight involving a samurai, Horibe Taketsune (a.k.a. Yasube, 1670–1703), and an unknown commoner.[24] As the story goes, Horibe singlehandedly cuts down sixteen samurai in a revenge killing to uphold the honor of his father-in-law, Sugano Rokuzaemon. The number of men the story reports he killed is probably an embellishment of the historical facts, but the account was meant to illustrate Taketsune's prodigious strength and to honor his heroism. Overstatement and exaggeration to describe samurai courage was typical of early modern vendetta tales.

Bunkō changes the purpose of this classic *adauchimono* in his own retelling of the story, and instead of praising samurai courage and

22. Gen Itasaka et al., eds., *Kodansha Encyclopedia of Japan*, 9 vols. (Tokyo: Kodansha, 1983), 6: 166.

23. In addition to *Takadanobaba kittō*, there are manuscripts of *adauchimono* from the nineteenth century held in the National Diet Library, Tokyo. These include Arakawa Tōbei, *Takadanobaba adauchi* (Tokyo: Kinkōdō, 1887); Tōryūsha Shikō, *Takadanobaba no adauchi* (Tokyo: Kyūkōkaku, 1898); and *Takadanobaba homare no adauchi* (Tokyo: Maruyama Kōjirō, 1885) by an anonymous author.

24. Horibe, the hero of this tale, was one of the samurai who would later be forced to commit *seppuku* (ritual disembowelment) as a result of his participation in the famous vendetta known as the "Forty-Seven Rōnin Incident" in 1703.

strength, he exposes in a humorous fashion a samurai's weakness and cowardice. In Bunkō's adaptation, titled *A Monster in a Duel* (*Adauchi bakemono*), Shimizu Sōjirō, "a handsome boy of sixteen or seventeen" and the son of a wealthy merchant, challenges a seasoned samurai to single combat in order to avenge the death of his father.[25] Ever since he was a small child, Sōjirō had been told that long ago a certain samurai had insulted his father and then cruelly cut him down in the street. As Sōjirō grew older and stronger, he became ever more determined to seek out this cowardly murderer and take his revenge. Eventually, when he found him, he showed great courage in calmly walking up to the samurai and boldly challenging him to a duel.

The scene is set in "the month of the cherry blossoms." The samurai is "a handsome man sporting a braided hat" and "carrying long and short swords that had vermilion-lacquered sheaths decorated with silver"—an indication of his high status. When challenged by the young lad, the samurai arrogantly laughs and ridicules the boy's low-class birth. The reader learns that the boy's murdered father had been a successful merchant who had acquired the family name of Shimizu by purchasing it from an impoverished and desperate samurai who was willing to sell his birthright.

A dialogue ensues between the samurai and young boy in classical warrior-tale fashion, with each identifying himself to his opponent by name. Shinoda, the samurai, accuses the youth of having no manners and violating etiquette by presuming to address him directly. It appears that the hapless young Sōjirō will soon be cut down. The samurai, however, seeing the boy's fierce determination, hesitates and asks that they postpone their duel until the following day. Both agree to meet the next morning at the dueling grounds at Takadanobaba.[26]

Word quickly gets out among the locals that a duel is to take place. Early the next day a crowd of people gathers to witness the battle between the boy, who has no training in the martial arts, and the arrogant samurai. The vividness of the scene and the realism of the dialogue keep

25. Baba, *Tōdai Edo hyaku bakemono*, 13–15.

26. Takadanobaba was a well-known place for dueling, located in present-day Shinjuku-ku, Nishi-Waseda 3 chōme.

the reader in suspense, convinced that the inexperienced young Sōjirō is about to meet a miserable fate. In a surprising departure from the style of the typical vendetta story, however, the samurai fails to show up at Takadanobaba, and the duel never takes place. In the eyes of the townspeople, the samurai has disgraced himself and proven to be a coward.

The literary development of the scene and the detailed description of the characters, which is typical of vendetta tales, lead the reader to assume that an explanation of why the samurai did not appear for the duel would be forthcoming. The reader familiar with the classic plot of the vendetta tales, which inevitably ends with the victory of one mighty samurai over another, might even hope that Bunkō's account would conclude with the victory of the young commoner and the defeat and death of the samurai; but even though no fight takes place, it is obvious that, in the mind of the reader, the boy's valor is victorious over the samurai's cowardliness, and revenge has been won without a killing.

The conclusion of a "revenge tale" without the death of one of the combatants is, of course, atypical of the *jitsurokutai shōsetsu* genre, as is the different social status of the two combatants. The stereotypical tale would begin with one samurai challenging another of equal status and rank. The plot would be similar to the 1740 kodan performance titled *The Revenge of the Thief* (*Tōzokunin no kitō*).[27] In this story there is a duel between two high-ranking samurai, both of whom are equally powerful and have comparable martial skills, and it ends with the death of one. Bunkō's *A Monster in a Duel* does not involve a clash between two equally courageous and skilled samurai but presents a contest between a cowardly samurai and a young commoner who is eager to uphold the honor of his family and exact retribution for his father's murder. Bunkō's point is clear: The reputed courage of the samurai is proven to be a sham in the face of the real courage and determination of a physically weaker opponent. It is the boy's strength of character that defeats the samurai. The samurai, Shinoda Kunizaemon, is humiliated, but his shame is not just his own. In the eyes of the reader his disgrace is the ignominy and loss of dignity that extends to the samurai class as a whole.

27. Mutō, *Rakugo sanbyaku dai jo*, 116.

This tale makes a caricature of the purported honor of *bushidō* (the way of the samurai). Among the bushi class, the vendetta was indeed an honorable pursuit, but Bunkō turns it into a parody. Shinoda Kunizaemon runs away from the fight. He forgoes an opportunity to uphold his reputation and his samurai honor, which was violated when the young Sōjirō rudely accosted him. Bunkō is giving voice to the subversive idea, which was becoming more and more widespread among the commoner class, that samurai are no longer the virtuous, brave, and loyal warriors that they were in the past. Samurai now fail to even show up for a duel to uphold their own honor, proving they are also deceptive and hypocritical. The tale clearly reveals Bunkō's view of the decadence of the Tokugawa-era ruling class.

Bunkō is not only making the samurai an object of ridicule; more importantly he is making light of the noble tradition of legalized vendetta and "just" revenge. He discredits the long-held belief that such a course of action can be honorable. This anecdote is also a parody of the adauchi-mono genre, which typically praised the vendetta, and it shows that the ethics and morality on which the Tokugawa class structure was based is now an object of ridicule.

The custom of the vendetta penetrated deep into Japanese culture at this time and was as much a value respected by the commoner class as it was by the samurai. Some commoners were enthusiastic about the vendetta, and it was often used as a way to uphold their own honor as well. Of the thirty-three acts of blood revenge that were recorded in Edo between the years 1609 to 1703, all but four were carried out by samurai. In the next century, however, from 1703 to 1804, there was a sharp change in this pattern, and a dramatic rise in the number of revenge killings perpetrated by commoners occurred. While nineteen vendettas were carried out by samurai, sixteen were performed by people from the lower classes of society.[28] Admittedly incidents were few, but there was a growing belief in the morality of the vendetta, and its respectability was becoming more and more accepted in popular commoner culture, just as it had long been an important element of the samurai ethical code.

28. Douglas E. Mills, "*Kataki-uchi*: The Practice of Blood-Revenge in Pre-Modern Japan," *Modern Asian Studies* 10, no. 4 (1976): 531.

The contemporary reader of Bunkō's *A Monster in a Duel* would have seen that the townspeople's desire to imitate samurai "morality" by engaging in the vendetta was being mocked. The commoners who heard or read Bunkō's revenge story might have been pleased that the samurai had made a fool of himself, but more importantly Bunkō wants them to understand that it is a mistake to believe that virtue and honor originate with the samurai or that the vendetta is an honorable way to gain victory over one's opponent.

A Tale of Two Shoguns: Tokugawa Yoshimune and Tokugawa Ieshige

Edo experienced a phase of cultural exuberance during the Genroku period (1688–1704). However, the economic prosperity that had characterized the beginning of that period came to an end by the turn of the eighteenth century. In the early 1700s Japan was suffering from hyperinflation, which was the result of wasteful spending under the misguided economic policies of Tokugawa Tsunayoshi (r. 1680–1709). When Tokugawa Yoshimune came to power in 1716 he took various emergency economic measures that were intended to ameliorate the economic decline, but conditions in both the rural and urban areas continued to worsen in spite of his efforts.

Crop failures gave rise to wide fluctuations in the price of rice, and periodic famines caused a dramatic increase in the number of incidents of rioting and social unrest. In the thirty-five year period between 1681 and 1715, there had been 426 outbreaks of peasant revolt. During the following thirty-five year period (1716 to 1750), there were 724 such incidents, an increase of almost 60 percent. What was even more disturbing than the substantial rise in the number of violent incidents was the increase in the scale and scope of the uprisings. A revolt in Iwakitaira (in present-day southwest Fukushima prefecture) in 1738, for example, involved 84,000 farmers.[29] The resulting rise in food prices in Edo strengthened the momentum toward greater opposition to the government, which seemed powerless to curtail the downward economic spiral.

29. Tsuji, *Kyōhō tsugan*, 9: 459.

The financial stability of the bakufu had begun to deteriorate long before Yoshimune became shogun, so the poor economic situation that continued into the 1720s was not completely his fault. In 1721 Yoshimune ordered all government departments to make cuts in expenditures, and he called on the daimyō and upper vassals (*hatamoto*) of the Tokugawa house to lower their own standard of living and cut excessive spending. But all of his attempts to scale down the operations of the bakufu went unheeded. Several years of bad weather resulted in poor harvests in the 1720s and caused a sharp drop in tax revenues. To make matters worse, in the summer of 1732, insects decimated large rice-growing areas, causing over ten thousand people to starve to death.[30] Any government would have been hard-pressed to control the rising price of rice under such circumstances. To his credit, Yoshimune had continually tried to combat graft and corruption in order to relieve the economic hardship, but that policy was not sufficient to stem the tide of continued economic decline. Arguably, Yoshimune's reform efforts in the Kyōhō era (1716–36) may have had some small success in improving, temporarily at least, the financial condition of the bakufu and in stabilizing the income of the samurai, but the reforms irrefutably failed to restore the samurai to the practice of virtue that Yoshimune considered to be of primary importance if there were to be social and economic stability.[31]

Bunkō reports that in 1745 the Wakasa domain (in present-day Fukui prefecture), for example, suffered a revenue shortfall of fifty thousand koku because of the corrupt financial practices of the daimyō Kamio Haruhide (1687–1753). As well as being the domainal lord, Kamio had also been the magistrate of finance for the bakufu since 1737 and would continue in office until 1753. He was responsible for collecting taxes from all the domains and making sure that the revenues were deposited in the coffers of the central government. When Yoshimune was shogun, Kamio was censured in 1745 for "his mismanagement and personal extravagance and told to answer the charges of corruption that were brought against him."[32] Bunkō was not an eyewitness to the legal proceedings

30. Sansom, *A History of Japan*, 164.
31. Totman, *Early Modern Japan*, 305.
32. Baba, *Tōji chinsetsu yōhiroku*, 232.

against Kamio, but in *A Confidential Record of Current Little-Known Facts* he records the beginning of a speech against corruption that he attributes to Shogun Yoshimune: "All the daimyō of this poor country are idle, yet they have been financially blessed. The blessings that we have received are thanks to the hardworking poor who are not themselves blessed."[33] The image of Yoshimune that Bunkō presents is that of a shogun who understands compassion for the poor and laments the moral blindness of the daimyō, who are unable to recognize that their wealth is a blessing and not the product of their own work or virtue. The address of Yoshimune continues: "If we are to make the world [i.e., the realm] peaceful, we [the elite] must humble ourselves."[34] Bunkō, speaking in the persona of Yoshimune, affirms that the way to domestic peace and order is through concern for the poor and through the cultivation of the virtue of humility in the ruler. Bunkō portrays Yoshimune as warning the officials during the corruption trial of Kamio that "they are duty bound to live frugally and humbly, especially now in these difficult times."[35]

Tokugawa Yoshimune left office in 1745 before the deliberations against Kamio could be brought to a conclusion. When Ieshige, Yoshimune's son and successor, took power the same year, the case against Kamio was dropped. Kamio continued as magistrate of finance until 1753 and was never held responsible for the shortfall in Wakasa domain. It was Ōhashi Chikayoshi who succeeded Kamio to the office of magistrate of finance, though as the reader has already seen, Ōhashi was eventually forced out of office due to his responsibility for the failed tax reform in Gujō in 1758. Even though Kamio had been even more incompetent and corrupt than Ōhashi, there were never any charges brought against him during the shogunate of Ieshige.

The picture of Yoshimune that Bunkō presents of a compassionate and humble ruler accords with the historical record. James Murdoch, an early twentieth-century historian, admired Yoshimune for his intimate knowledge of the living conditions of the common people. In fact, Murdoch writes, Yoshimune was known to have been "passionately fond of an active out-of-doors lifestyle and would often meet people of different

33. Ibid.

34. Ibid.

35. Ibid.

classes, including peasants and fishermen."[36] By contrast, Ieshige was a recluse. In poor health throughout his life, he stuttered so badly that his speech was almost incomprehensible, making it nearly impossible to communicate with anyone. Ieshige's every utterance had to be interpreted by Ōoka Tadamitsu (1707–60), the senior counselor and Ieshige's lifelong companion. Ōoka exercised de facto shogunal authority simply by virtue of his ability to understand what the shogun was trying to say. It was due to Ōoka's political skill and in spite of Ieshige's incompetence that the government was able to function at all throughout the 1750s. Under Ieshige, the only way an official would be retained or could advance in the government bureaucracy was to make connections with Ōoka Tadamitsu.[37] Ieshige was totally dependent on his senior counselor, and Tadamitsu had no qualms about flattering the shogun to advance his own career and get what he wanted.

The official explanation for Ieshige's poor health was that he was getting old, even though he was in his mid-forties at the time Bunkō was writing about him. No one other than Bunkō dared to mention that the shogun's physical decline had actually already begun decades earlier when he should have been in the prime of life. Bunkō rejects the notion that old age was at the root of his physical deterioration and emphasizes two other factors responsible for Ieshige's chronic illnesses: "an inordinate amount of drinking and unrestrained sexual practices."[38] These excesses led to various illnesses and disabilities, such as the embarrassing lack of control over his bodily functions. Bunkō writes: "It is not uncommon that the shogun has little accidents in his palanquin, and on one occasion the shogun had to walk out in the middle of a Noh play at New Year's in order to relieve himself. When he returned to his place in the theater, the actors were ordered to start the play over from the very beginning."[39] Bunkō relates the poor state of the shogun's health in highly formal language, using classical grammatical constructions. The contrast between the beautiful language and the base and demeaning content makes the piece quite satirical. In spite of his increasingly poor health,

36. Murdoch, *A History of Japan*, 3: part 1, 316.
37. Baba, *Tōji chinsetsu yōhiroku*, 192.
38. Ibid., 183.
39. Ibid.

Ieshige persisted in his dissolute living and excess. His subordinates, of course, had to defer to him and would never say anything to suggest that the shogun was not living in an honorable fashion. For Bunkō, this was unconscionable, but understandable since many Edo officials lived lives as debauched and immoral as the shogun.

The great shock for Bunkō was to see from his own experience the contrast between Yoshimune's courageous efforts to govern honestly, in spite of economic problems, and Ieshige's complete lack of moral integrity and his apparent unwillingness to even try to govern justly. The disparity between the two shoguns provided Bunkō with a clear, practical understanding of the difference between moral success and moral failure in government. He regarded Yoshimune as having been a legitimate and just ruler and one who was not averse even to humbly accepting criticism from his subjects. He saw Ieshige as a fraud and could not accept the legitimacy of his corrupt government.

Bunkō cited Ieshige's lack of education as an additional reason why he was incapable of being a just ruler. An incident occurred one day in 1755 when Ieshige visited a temple where there were prayers written as *haikai* verses on a pillar. The shogun asked members of his guard about who had written the verses and was told that the poems were those of the well-known *haikai* poets Somaru (?–1795) and Chōsui (1685–1748).[40] The shogun had no knowledge of the two poets and asked a retainer to explain the verses. Somaru and Chōsui were, in fact, the pen names of two of Ieshige's own retainers, Hasegawa Hanzaemon and Sakuma Saburōzaemon. On being told that these two haikai poets were actually his own retainers, Ieshige burst out in a fit of anger. "Why would they use these false names? 'Somaru' and 'Chōsui'—those are such low-class, despicable names," he said. "The gods at this shrine will never answer their prayers if they use such names." Bunkō reports that Ieshige, having no literary appreciation, actually demoted Hasegawa and Sakuma. They "never again advanced and were never successful in the service of the shogun."[41]

40. Somaru and Chōsui were poets whose works are included in the popular *haikai* collection *Goshikizumi* [The five primary colors], which was published in Edo in 1731. This collection of poetry played an important role in the revival of interest in haikai in the period, and it was so popular that a second volume, *Zoku goshikizumi,* appeared in Edo in 1751.

41. Baba, *Tōji chinsetsu yōhiroku*, 250–51.

This anecdote illustrates the arbitrariness with which appointments and promotions were made and the ease with which educated samurai were passed over and prevented from advancement or, as in this case, were even released from service. Bunkō's depiction of Ieshige's lack of literary appreciation is particularly ironic at this time when literacy among commoners was increasing, and the two poets of whom Ieshige said that he had never heard were, in fact, well known among the townspeople of Edo. Bunkō presents Ieshige as more ignorant and boorish than a commoner.

What was worse than poor health or inadequate education was Ieshige's heartlessness. Bunkō's exposé of Ieshige's relationship with his head wife, Oyuki, is a powerful and concrete case in point.

> Oyuki, the mother of prince [Tokugawa] Ieharu [1737–86], is the daughter of the emperor. Ieshige had long been infatuated with her and eventually made her his head wife. She became pregnant and gave birth to Takechiyo [i.e., Ieharu] in Genbun 2 [1737]. She resided in the shogun's palace at Nishinomaru, but Ieshige did not treat her well. He ignored her and exhausted himself in licentious excesses with the maids. This situation was so pitiful for Oyuki. She was so jealous that she became ill.... but Ieshige had no pity on her. In fact, he grew to hate her and finally would never see either her or his son, Ieharu. At present Oyuki shuns the company of others, remains hidden in shame behind her screens, and lives in disgrace, waiting for death.[42]

Bunkō's unconcealed disdain for Ieshige and his obvious compassion for Oyuki reveal the moral standards in which he believes and the determination he has to expose the injustice that has been so blatantly perpetrated by the shogun on his own family.

Yet another indication that Ieshige was ill-suited to govern was his poor treatment of the daimyō. Bunkō notes that Ieshige initiated a succession of territorial and monetary confiscations, beginning with Matsudaira Norimura's loss of ten thousand koku in 1745. The censure of Uemura Tsunetomo of Katsuura (Awa, present-day Tokushima prefecture, Shikoku) and confiscation of his property followed in 1751. Andō Nobutada of Kanō (Mino) was punished with the loss of his domain in 1755, and

42. Ibid., 184–85.

Honda Tadanaka of Sagara (in Kumamoto prefecture) suffered the loss of his territory in 1758.[43] In addition to these, a total of thirty-two financial administrators and local officials were either dismissed or deprived of their stipends between the years 1748 and 1759.[44] In Ieshige's defense, one might argue that for the security of the state the confiscation of the domains was a necessary measure that had to be taken against ineffective domainal lords who were unable to control peasant discord. The removal of Kanamori Yorikane of Gujō also occurred under Ieshige. Incompetence or the failure of local daimyō to successfully control their peasant populations was a problem that had long worried the bakufu.

Whether Ieshige's actions against the daimyō were justified or not, Baba Bunkō focused his readers' attention on the lack of virtue in the shogunate, along with its moral hypocrisy, arrogance, cruelty, incompetence, and general corruption. Bunkō did not, however, limit himself to abstract ethical arguments or to treatises on morality. He presented concrete examples from the lives of contemporary individuals to give evidence of the widespread depravity in society. No one else in Edo at the time dared to make examples of actual people, much less to speak out publically about the shogun. Bunkō was not primarily interested in a political analysis of government policies. He was more focused on the shoguns themselves, Yoshimune and Ieshige, and contrasting their moral behavior and the degree of their faithfulness to moral principle.

A Debate between Two Senior Counselors

Even though Bunkō was highly critical of Tokugawa Ieshige, he did find opportunities to praise some of the functionaries within his administration. Senior Counselor Matsudaira Takechika (1716–79) was one such official whose judgment Bunkō trusted.[45] A conversation between the two senior counselors, Matsudaira and Sakai Tadayori (1705–66), shows that there was a degree of compassion and fairness among some officials who served in Ieshige's government.[46]

43. Tsuji Tatsuya, *Kyōhō tsugan*, 9: 457.

44. Ibid., 458.

45. Takechika was senior counselor from 1747 (Enkyō 4) 9.3 to 1775 (An'ei 8) 7.25.

46. Sakai Tadayori was senior counselor from 1749 (Kan'en 2) 9.28 to 1764 (Meiwa 1) 5.16. The content of the exchange between the two senior counselors is from *Tōji chinsetsu yōhiroku*, 251.

The discussion in question was on the desirability of imposing what was called "correctional fines" (*karyō*) that would allow criminals to avoid an impending prison term or even physical punishment for a crime if they could pay a required fee. According to Bunkō's account, Matsudaira Takechika favored this system, which had been established by Yoshimune in 1718 specifically for commoners who were found guilty of comparatively minor offenses. Sakai Tadayori was opposed to dispensing criminals from physical punishment for any price.

As they were eating and drinking late into the night, discussing the pros and cons of letting criminals off for a fee, Sakai argued that it would be degrading to impose fines on criminals merely in order to raise money for the government coffers. Matsudaira reminded Sakai that fines as a substitute for imprisonment or physical punishment had been normal practice under Shogun Yoshimune and would not be introducing a radically new policy. Matsudaira also pointed out that fines had even been imposed under the Chinese sages as a method of reparation that had greatly benefited society, so there would be no harm in doing the same. In *A Record of Current Little-Known Facts*, Bunkō attributes the following exchange to Matsudaira and Sakai:

> MATSUDAIRA: The money collected from the fines taken from criminals was distributed to the hungry and thirsty who stood begging by the side of the road. The people who were cold were also helped. This is what Yoshimune had in mind when he ordered Ōoka to impose these fines for the first time. How could this be a bad thing?
>
> SAKAI: It may be true that in the age of the sages income from fines was given to the cold and the hungry, but that should not be done at the present time because this is not the age of the sages.
>
> MATSUDAIRA: It is as you say. Instead of clothing the naked and feeding the hungry as in the old days, the government is now more interested in building bridges and roads and using the tax revenues to repair and maintain them.[47]

In Bunkō's account of the exchange between the two senior counselors, Sakai is not convinced that under the present circumstances caring for the poor and hungry is the wisest use of funds. Matsudaira seems to po-

47. Baba, *Tōji chinsetsu yōhiroku*, 251.

litely agree with Sakai that the present is no longer the age of the sages, but he laments that maintenance of bridges and roads for the purpose of making travel to and from Edo easier for the daimyō and their entourages takes precedence over helping the poor.

Though Matsudaira Takechika was a high official in Ieshige's administration, Bunkō presents an image of this senior counselor as one who supports using income from taxes to help the poor and the hungry. This was an issue of concern for Bunkō. Yoshimune had declared that of all his advisers Matsudaira was one of the few he could trust to pinpoint the faults of government and propose solutions. Though the above is an imaginary dialogue, it reflects the values of its author. It is also true that in contrast to many of the advisers with whom Ieshige surrounded himself, Matsudaira did have the reputation of carrying out his duties faithfully and justly. Bunkō praises his compassion for the poor and deplores the fact that Ieshige is shogun rather than Matsudaira Takechika.[48]

The Shogun's Physician, Hattori Kenzui

When the wife of Matsudaira Takechika was in her last month of pregnancy in the tenth month of 1755, there were a number of indications that the birth would be a difficult one. Then, on the day her child was about to be born, she suddenly started choking and gasping for air. Matsudaira ordered the midwife to go out and bring the physician, Hattori Kenzui, to his house immediately. In his essay "Wise Sayings of Lord Matsudaira Takechika" (*Matsudaira Ukon Shogen utagai o omowazaru kakugen no koto*, 1756), Bunkō informs his reader that Hattori was one of the official government physicians appointed by Ieshige himself.[49] Matsudaira had met him before when he would periodically come to the mansion to check on the condition of his wife. On this day, however, Hattori told the midwife that he would be unable to come because he was occupied with "other important matters."

Fortunately, another physician, Takeda Shukuan, not a shogunal physician but only a rōnin who had no government position, happened to be passing in front of the mansion. He was called in and gave Matsudaira's

48. Ibid., 251.
49. Ibid., 221–22.

wife the necessary care and medication that she needed. The treatment relieved her of the asthma-like symptoms from which she had been suffering. Unexpectedly, the delivery of her child was easy, and the senior counselor and his family were grateful for Takeda's assistance.

The next day Hattori Kenzui was out again making his rounds in his usual way and came to the Matsudaira mansion. The senior counselor, understandably still quite angry with him, asked what business was so important that he had refused to come and see his wife the day before, when she needed him. Hattori insisted that the counselor's wife had been in no danger. When told that Takeda Shukuan had seen his wife instead, Hattori belittled the treatment that had been provided by the rōnin, saying that the medicine he dispensed was not needed and probably had no effect at all. The senior counselor angrily replied to Hattori, "If I conducted my official business the way you conduct your medical practice, the government would cease to function."[50]

Bunkō's purpose in relating this incident was to illustrate that the irresponsible conduct of Hattori Kenzui was precisely how officials in Ieshige's government carried on their business; that is, like pitiless malpractitioners who care nothing for those who are suffering and abandon them in their need. Like Hattori, government bureaucrats also make wrong decisions that endanger the lives of others.

The allegorical form in which this anecdote is set draws the reader's attention to the crises in government during Ieshige's rule when uncompassionate shogunal officials were making disastrous economic decisions that affected the lives of many people. Matsudaira Takechika eventually fell into disfavor because of the jealousy of other officials and because of lack of support from Ieshige, but he continued, according to Bunkō, "to carry out his duties with great skill and had compassion for those below him."[51]

Bribery of the Senior Counselor

Senior Counselor Hotta Masasuke (1712–64) was another official whom Bunkō cited for his lack of compassion. Hotta had suggested to Shogun

50. Ibid., 222.
51. Ibid.

Ieshige that the government should release from service ninety samurai, all of whom had been appointed by Shogun Yoshimune in 1745, during the last months of his rule.[52] Hotta argued that taking this action would improve the economic viability of the shogunate and possibly even create a financial surplus. Shogun Ieshige was convinced, and he accepted Hotta's proposal. The ninety samurai were let go, suffered the suspension of their stipends, and were ordered to leave Edo. One of their number was Nakashima Shimbei, a hatamoto who had meritoriously served under Yoshimune.[53] On hearing the news of his dismissal, he went to the shogun's castle and begged Hotta to reinstate him. He was rudely rebuffed.

Nakashima returned to the castle every day for three years, each day appealing to Hotta to allow him to serve Shogun Ieshige. Hotta's disregard for Nakashima and for the other ninety dismissed samurai aroused Bunkō's ire. Although they had been loyal retainers to Ieshige's father and predecessor, Yoshimune, they were now being treated dishonorably. Bunkō writes: "Hotta's action was entirely unjust. He cruelly put these men out on the street without any stipend or any means of survival and left them without the honor due to them."[54] Bunkō made no attempt to conceal his contempt for Senior Counselor Hotta, even though it was a flagrant violation of the law to publicly criticize such a high government official.

It was not only these ninety retainers who were dismissed under Ieshige. All of Yoshimune's advisers, except for Hotta himself, a man reputed to be of "some ability but of inferior moral fiber," were discharged.[55] The other senior counselor in office at the time, Sakai Tadayori, who had argued with Matsudaira Takechika about the imposition of "correctional fines," had attained his position through bribery and flattery, of which Hotta Masasuke had been the beneficiary.[56] Sakai would have his servants prepare extravagant dinners, costing as much as the equivalent of a koku of rice, and bring them to Hotta's residence for him and his guests to enjoy.

One of the corrupt officials who bribed Hotta for an official appoint-

52. Hotta Masasuke was senior counselor from 1745 (Enkyō 2) 11.13 until his death in 1761 (Hōreki 11) 2.8.

53. *Tōji chinsetsu yōhiroku*, 369.

54. Ibid., 194.

55. Murdoch, *A History of Japan*, 3: part 2, 368.

56. Baba, *Tōji chinsetsu yōhiroku*, 235.

ment was Abe Masachika (1716–80). Abe had always wanted to become a high official like his grandfather, Abe Masatake (1649–1704), who had been senior counselor.[57] Bunkō praised the grandfather as "a great intellect of Japan, not at all inferior to [Tokugawa] Mitsukuni (1628–1701), the daimyō of Mito."[58] The younger Abe was, in Bunkō's opinion, typical of the contemporary generation of hypocritical officials:

> Masachika has been appointed shogunal master of ceremonies (*sōjaban*). This is how it happened: One of Masachika's guards advised him, "You should go to see Senior Counselor Hotta Masasuke. Take with you your family's most valuable possession and give it to him. Then Hotta will be well pleased and will promote you to the office of master of ceremonies. Soon after, you will doubtless become senior counselor. You will be like a son to Hotta and have all you want." Masachika then made up his mind to give Hotta a priceless tea canister that had been in his family for generations.[59]

Bribery to attain advancement was, of course, the usual modus operandi in Tokugawa Japan, but Bunkō comments: "This really goes beyond the pale." Bunkō was shocked that the grandson of the great Abe Masatake, whom he so admired, had none of his grandfather's qualities or virtue.

Tokugawa Munekatsu, Daimyō of Owari

For thirty-one years, between 1730 and 1761, Tokugawa Munekatsu (1705–61) was the daimyō of Owari. Located in what is today the western part of Aichi prefecture, including the city of Nagoya, Owari was the largest holding of the Tokugawa family outside of the shogunal properties. As daimyō of Owari, Munekatsu was first in rank among the daimyō of the Three Houses of the Tokugawa branch families (*gosanke*). Bunkō, however, exposes the small-mindedness of this supposedly great daimyō. On one occasion Munekatsu complained to Senior Counselor Hotta Masasuke that the daimyō of the poor domain of Dewa, Uesugi Munefusa (1718–46), had been awarded the primary responsibility for the construction of a new gate, which was to be built at the entrance to

57. Abe Masatake was senior counselor from 1681 to 1704.
58. Baba, *Tōji chinsetsu yōhiroku*, 234.
59. Ibid.

the central hall of Kan'eiji Temple, the burial place for members of the Tokugawa family. Uesugi had generously provided funds out of his own resources to build the gate, which was to be given the name Dewa Gate. This was a great honor for Uesugi, but it was also a sacrifice that, according to Bunkō, caused his family considerable hardship.[60]

Tokugawa Munekatsu thought that he should have been given the honor of building the gate since he was a member of the first of the Tokugawa branch families. Munekatsu asserted that Uesugi "was of low rank, [so] taking charge of the construction of the Dewa Gate was totally beyond his ability."[61] Like most of the elite class at the time, Munekatsu equated low status with a lack of ability. It was Senior Counselor Hotta who had originally assigned Uesugi to the task of building the gate, so when Tokugawa Munekatsu brought forth his complaints and realized that Shogun Ieshige strongly supported him, Hotta was not only embarrassed but afraid that he might be ousted from his position as senior counselor.

Hotta had no choice but to capitulate. He yielded to Munekatsu out of fear of offending the shogun. Bunkō was outraged that Uesugi had been discredited simply because he was "a samurai of low rank" in spite of his self-sacrifice in offering his own resources to build the gate. It was apparent to Bunkō that Senior Counselor Hotta was little more than a sycophant and a corrupt politician who was concerned only about his own status and the favor of Ieshige. This was not, in Bunkō's view, an isolated incident, but a form of corruption that had long been characteristic of the Tokugawa political system. Positions and appointments were given according to birth and rank, not ability, merit, or virtue.

Miwa Shissai, Confucian Scholar

Miwa Shissai (1669–1744), officially appointed as a Confucian scholar and consultant to the bakufu, was naturally a strong proponent of the regime. He worked to uphold the legitimacy of the Tokugawa rank and status system by showing that it was firmly founded on orthodox Neo-Confucian principles. Bunkō asserts that the real reason Miwa Shissai

60. Ibid., 187.
61. Ibid., 187–88.

was such a dedicated promoter of Neo-Confucian doctrine was not because he believed in the teachings, nor because of his loyalty to the bakufu, but because of the status and honor that his position as a Confucian scholar gave him. In fact, it was only by bribing Tokugawa officials that he had been able to acquire his position as a Confucian teacher in the first place. The Tokugawa government provided Miwa with a ready-made career that enhanced his reputation and allowed him to lead a life without financial worry. He had no real qualifications for his position and was a man of little intellectual ability. As Bunkō wrote: "Miwa was a wealthy Confucianist who disseminated erroneous interpretations of Chinese texts that he could not really understand. Even so, he was provided by the bakufu with the service of many pages, personal attendants, and retainers."[62] Bunkō admitted that Miwa was qualified in one sense for the position he held: He was extremely cunning. He managed to have the bakufu support his extravagant lifestyle with generous stipends and with many samurai who would pay well to study under his tutelage. For Bunkō, Miwa was the typical Confucian employed by the government who "not only pursued useless theory but even built a favorable reputation on his erroneous teachings."[63]

Among the samurai who studied under Miwa was Tanaka Heizō. Bunkō reports that Heizō had been summoned to the office of City Magistrate Tsuchiya Masasuke and strongly persuaded to study Neo-Confucianism under Miwa. Tsuchiya reportedly said to Heizō, "All of those who have strong a dedication to Confucian learning are put into powerful positions of authority."[64] Tsuchiya appealed to Heizō's ambition for advancement. In *A Confidential Record of Current, Little-Known Facts*, Bunkō states frankly: "Every fraud in Edo becomes a disciple of Miwa."[65] Miwa hoped that Heizō would be well positioned to help him advance in the bakufu hierarchy. Heizō was after all a descendant of the daimyō of Ōmi, and it was said that his ancestors had received generous stipends and a plethora of aristocratic titles from the government. But Bunkō discloses that this was all little more than unfounded rumor and that, in fact, Tokugawa Iemitsu had demoted Heizō's family, reducing them to hatamoto status in 1623. What was

62. Ibid., 214.
63. Ibid.
64. Ibid.
65. Ibid.

more, even though Heizō was a wealthy man from a formerly noble clan, none of his ancestors had actually possessed any legitimate aristocratic titles for over a hundred years. Bunkō sarcastically refers to Tanaka Heizō as "that aristocratic disciple of Miwa," and by calling attention to the Tanaka family's former glory and exposing his false reputation, Bunkō insults not only Heizō himself but also Miwa, who prided himself on being a teacher of aristocrats.[66]

Tanaka Heizō's summons to the office of City Magistrate Tsuchiya Masasuke was actually a bribe, and Tsuchiya's hypocritical support of Neo-Confucian education was nothing more than a means to gain political capital. By exposing Tanaka as an ambitious fraud, Bunkō was attacking the regime on three fronts: first of all, he called Neo-Confucian orthodoxy "useless theory" and Miwa's interpretation of it "erroneous teaching." Secondly, he mocked the Tokugawa rank and status system by showing that it perpetuated itself through bribery, and lastly, he accused Edo City Magistrate Tsuchiya Masasuke of graft and corruption and declared him to be a "monster."

Hayashi Nobumitsu, Head of the Confucian Academy

Hayashi Nobumitsu (1681–1758), a contemporary of Bunkō, was a descendant of the famous Confucian scholar Hayashi Razan (1583–1657). Nobumitsu held the honorary court title of *chōsan taifu*, an honor of distinction that was not awarded for any meritorious deed or service but was granted solely in order to acknowledge and permanently fix one's rank and status.[67] In his satire titled "The Case of Hayashi, Head of the Confucian Academy" (*Hayashi daigakutō no ben*, 1758), Bunkō cynically contends that even though Nobumitsu was highly esteemed as a great Confucian with this prestigious title, his conduct was totally inconsistent with his position as a supposedly distinguished member of the Hayashi family and as the head of the Confucian Academy, which had been founded by his illustrious ancestor Hayashi Razan.[68] Although Nobumitsu's ancestors had been respected teachers of Neo-Confucian

66. Ibid.

67. Charles O. Hucker, *A Dictionary of Official Titles in Imperial China* (Stanford: Stanford University Press, 1985), 398.

68. Baba, *Tōdai Edo hyaku bakemono*, 20–21.

doctrine for almost two hundred years, Bunkō maintains that Hayashi Nobumitsu was an ideological hypocrite who held no firm convictions in spite of his claim of authority over the shogunate's Neo-Confucian orthodoxy. Bunkō points out the contradiction between his exterior, visible conduct and his hidden, private life, which made a mockery of the humanistic Neo-Confucian ideals of harmonious relationships among individuals and between individuals and the universe. This made him, in Bunkō's view, a fraud and a hypocrite: "Nobumitsu is a member of the Hayashi family, presumed to indeed be upright in his personal conduct, and of course, in the affairs of his office. So no one would suspect that he is a monster."[69] It was Nobumitsu's private diversions and entertainments that were particularly inconsistent with his position and his public persona as a teacher of Confucian morality and decorum: "Nobumitsu is a great monster who prays and reflects only for appearance's sake. He teaches benevolence and righteousness, but this leading Confucian scholar, who is known to the entire country, often brings two or three prostitutes and numerous dancing girls and entertainers up to the front room on the second floor of his residence from where he has a view of the Yayosu riverbank."[70] With this revelation Bunkō did not intend to simply dismantle Hayashi's reputation. More importantly, he wished to expose hypocrisy in the Confucian Academy. Bunkō continues: "On more than one occasion, the raucous laughter of courtesans and the commotion of jōruri singing and samisen playing could be heard coming from Hayashi's quarters."[71] Bunkō does not condemn these pastimes as such. Much worse, in his opinion, was the duplicity of Hayashi, who forbade such diversions to others while at the same time enjoying them himself. Hayashi is duplicitous and hypocritical in other ways as well. At the end of his essay, Bunkō writes, "I guess now real Confucian prayer comes from a Confucian scholar reading Buddhist sutras."[72] This refers to the position Nobumitsu held which claimed that there was no fundamental difference between Confucianism and Buddhism. His lack of real conviction with regard to the doctrinal tenets of Confucianism was further evidence

69. Ibid., 20.
70. This is the east bank of the inner moat going from Hibiya to Wadakura Gate.
71. Baba, *Tōdai Edo hyaku bakemono*, 20.
72. Ibid.

for Bunkō of the hypocrisy of not only the head of the Confucian Academy but of the Tokugawa bakufu itself.

Nobumitsu, as head of the academy, held firmly to this official endorsement of a religious syncretism, but Bunkō was an opponent of this kind of religious eclecticism (*setchūgaku*). He categorized Nobumitsu's custom of carrying a Buddhist rosary and reading Buddhist sutras as "strange and hypocritical." For Bunkō, the contradiction between Nobumitsu's "virtuous and accommodating" public persona on the one hand and his carousing in secret with courtesans and prostitutes on the other was a reflection of the contradictions between his life and the teachings of Neo-Confucianism and Buddhism.

Bunkō's account of Hayashi Nobumitsu contains caustic understatement and a feigned deference to Hayashi's reputation that is more scornful than if he had just condemned him outright. Nobumitsu's tenure in office "has not been edifying," Bunkō sardonically writes, adding sarcastically, "He should be a little more reserved." Actually, Nobumitsu's conduct in office, as Bunkō explains it, was quite scandalous and not merely unedifying. Bunkō called Nobumitsu a "Confucian monster," a fraud who made his living by trying to deceive others. In the end, Hayashi's fraudulent past catches up with him. In 1756 a fire broke out in Hayashi's residence, and his home, along with much of his neighborhood, burned to the ground.[73] Bunkō believed the fire was heavenly retribution for his misdeeds as head of the Confucian Academy.

73. The fire occurred in 1756 (Hōreki 6) 11.25 and burned the Kōjimachi and Yayosugashi areas.

6 | THE DECLINE OF TOKUGAWA NEO-CONFUCIANISM

The sages lived long ago in the past, and their precise teachings have gradually been lost. The scholars of the Han, Tang, Song, and Ming dynasties have misled the world, piling confusion upon confusion. And if this has been true in China, how much the more has it been true in Japan.

YAMAGA SOKŌ (1622–85), *SEIKYŌ YŌROKU*, 1665

Social and Intellectual Trends of the Period

The disintegration of the Confucian social ethos, which had long dictated a strict hierarchy of classes, continued in the eighteenth century. The growth of the commercial economy was accelerating, and the bakufu could not turn back the social changes that were beginning to transform the culture. Samurai were becoming less credible as rulers, and commoners were less willing to remain passive or totally submissive to their authority. The perceived lack of genuine virtue among the samurai class and the failure of many of the provincial daimyō to provide the material necessities for their peasant populations were becoming increasingly evident to the urban commoners of Edo in the 1700s, deepening their cynicism and

Epigraph is from Wm. Theodore de Bary et al., eds., *Sources of Japanese Tradition* (New York: Columbia University Press, 2005), 194.

distrust. Although Neo-Confucianism theoretically obligated samurai to cultivate themselves morally and to "rectify their hearts" through study, as Yamaga Sokō and others advised, the traditional philosophy was too rigid and inflexible to be of practical use in ruling an increasingly literate and commercialized society that was beset by discontent and doubt.[1]

In an attempt to salvage Confucian doctrine and tradition, some samurai scholars rejected the static, lifeless orthodoxy of traditional Tokugawa Neo-Confucianism and advocated a return to what they thought to be the more practical, empirical approach of original Confucianism. Yamaga Sokō was one of the earliest figures in this drive to reform Confucianism by returning to its roots and adapting it to the changing times. Sokō criticized the officially supported school of Neo-Confucianism in his book *Essentials of the Sacred Teachings* (*Seikyō yōroku*, 1665), arguing that the samurai's performance of routine clerical duties, which had formerly never been assigned to members of the elite class, had turned them into passive bureaucrats who had lost pride in their traditions.[2] Peasants, artisans, and merchants had specific tasks to perform that contributed to their own livelihoods; however, it was only the samurai who were no longer obliged or even given the opportunity to carry out the tasks appropriate to their class. They had no actual military duties that involved protecting and fighting for their lord. The virtues of loyalty, courage, and self-sacrifice no longer seemed to have any relevance in their lives.[3] In other words, samurai were no longer samurai.

In order to restore their honor, Sokō proposed that samurai should be obligated to perform some function for the benefit of society as repayment for the stipends that the government was providing for them. He lamented the fact that the samurai, who theoretically were morally superior and singularly qualified to rule, were losing sight of their social obligations and suggested that they serve the nation by again providing a collective example of dedication to duty.

Yamaga Sokō's understanding of the Neo-Confucian ideal of the role of the samurai as loyal defenders of the bakufu contrasted with their of-

1. Yamaga Sokō, *Yamaga Sokō*, vol. 8 of *Sōsho Nihon no shisōka*, ed. Sasaki Moritarō (Tokyo: Meitoku shuppansha, 1978), 82.

2. de Bary, *Sources of Japanese Tradition*, 194–95.

3. Ibid., 192–94.

ten scandalous conduct, which was the primary factor in people's cynicism toward them. The samurai had lost their purpose as defenders of the social order precisely because the official philosophy had remained on the level of theory, moribund and impractical. However, by openly questioning the validity and practicality of Tokugawa Neo-Confucian thought, Sokō was perceived as attacking the ideological foundation of the Tokugawa shogunate itself. Not surprisingly, the authorities banned his book, and Sokō was for a time exiled from Edo. Like Sokō, Bunkō also recognized that Neo-Confucianism was no longer practical, but he strongly disagreed with Sokō that the samurai were in any sense morally superior or singularly qualified to rule. Many of Bunkō's essays and anecdotes come to precisely the opposite conclusion from that of Sokō: the samurai were immoral hypocrites. This is the reason he referred to many of them in his writings as "monsters."

Like Sokō, Kaibara Ekken (1630–1714) was a Confucian scholar who aimed to put some life back into Confucianism. He proposed that the traditional concept of *jin* (compassion, benevolence, humanness) could be reinvigorated as a principle that would restore proper order and stability in society. Though *jin* was a key element in his theory of proper human relationships, Ekken was not successful in applying the principle to the actual living of one's life. In fact, he came to the conclusion that such a principle or any set of principles could not be an ethical guide for one's actions. Bunkō also saw that the Confucian virtue of *jin* remained a theoretical concept that could not be applicable to one's concrete life. He emphasized rather patience, forgiveness, and humility as the virtues that could actually make a practical difference in one's daily life and change society.

Motoori Norinaga (1730–1801), arguably the most influential of the national learning (*kokugaku*) scholars of the time, held the conventional understanding of virtue and morality that was common in the mid-Tokugawa period. Norinaga claimed that Japan had no need of ethical principles at all because in ancient times Japan had been a community in which subjects and rulers naturally lived in perfect harmony with each other and with the deities.[4] It was clear to Norinaga that the ancient national texts that contained the mythological and historical records of the

4. Stanford Encyclopedia of Philosophy; http://plato.stanford.edu/entries/kokugaku-school.

imperial line, that is, the *Kojiki* (*Record of ancient matters*, 712) and the *Nihon Shoki* (*Chronicles of Japan*, 720), as well as the poetic anthology *Man'yōshū* (*The ten thousand leaves*, late eighth century), when rigorously read with a correct understanding of the ancient Japanese language, revealed that ethical principles were actually superfluous to Japan. This was because harmony and peace existed in early society naturally. Holding a position that was totally contrary to this, Bunkō stressed that moral principles were necessary, and that they must be rooted in the inner morality of each person. Harmony and peace do not exist naturally, he insisted. These virtues have to be taught and nourished.

Norinaga was not the only philosopher of the period that held the view that moral principles were superfluous to society. In modern times Maruyama Masao (1914–96) pointed out that Japanese philosophers of the early modern period did not work from fundamental principles at all. Japanese morality during the Tokugawa period was an "empty bag" that no one bothered to fill.[5] Maruyama shows that for Ogyū Sorai (1666–1728), society had no need of ethical norms, because there was, in fact, no so such thing as any absolute principle. There was also no such thing as a moral conscience that one would have from birth.[6] Sorai taught that the norms for political, religious, and civil institutions must be invented anew by the ruler of each new regime, because there are no abstract norms or doctrines that are valid for all times and that would determine the purpose, nature, or conduct of political, educational, and religious institutions in all cases.[7] Following this tradition, no early-modern Japanese philosopher made any attempt to delineate specific and practical absolute moral principles. Baba Bunkō was the only writer to oppose this "conventional wisdom" and insist on the importance of objective morality.

Virtue in Tokugawa Neo-Confucianism could be spoken about only in reference to the samurai class. The merchants and the peasants were not considered capable of practicing virtue, nor of being able to give or receive respect or honor. Consequently, it was believed that they could

5. Kenneth B. Pyle, *Japan Rising: The Resurgence of Japanese Power and Purpose* (New York: Public Affairs, 2007), 58.

6. Maruyama Masao, *Studies in the Intellectual History of Tokugawa Japan* (Princeton: Princeton University Press; Tokyo: University of Tokyo Press, 1975), 212.

7. Ibid., 218.

not be loyal or trustworthy. There were some philosophers who opposed this view. Nishikawa Joken (1648–1724), for example, a scholar of astronomy and Western learning, instructed urban townsmen in his *Merchants' Satchel* (*Chōnin bukuro*, 1719) and rural peasants in *Farmers' Satchel* (*Hakusho bukuro*, 1721) to be more confident of their ability to find their personal value and importance as members of society. He did not, however, offer concrete suggestions about what specific values or principles, if any, they should hold or which virtues they should cultivate.[8]

Like Nishikawa, Bunkō also understood the growing importance of the commoners' place and function in society. However, he also took the radical position not only of affirming that peasants and commoners could be moral and virtuous, he taught which specific virtues should be cultivated: humility, forgiveness, and care for the poor, among others. He filled the content of "the empty bag" with what might be called uniquely Christian virtues.

Yamaga Sokō, Nishikawa Jōken, and Ogyū Sorai all questioned the value of the Neo-Confucian tradition on which the legitimacy of the bakufu system depended. Sorai, in particular, was not concerned about upholding the legitimacy of the shogunate. In fact, he had very little regard for the bakufu ever since his father had incurred the displeasure of Shogun Tokugawa Tsunayoshi and was sent into exile in Kazusa (in present-day Chiba Prefecture). The experience of hardship in exile with his family from 1679 to 1690 had given Sorai some firsthand experience of the blatant injustice in the Tokugawa system.

When Sorai later became an adviser to Shogun Tokugawa Yoshimune (1684–1751), he encouraged practicality and leniency in dealing with the commoner population.[9] He studied the ancient Chinese texts, not as a mere antiquarian scholarly endeavor, as was commonly done, but in an attempt to discover the moral norms that could guide the political order.[10] In the end, however, Sorai concluded that the Neo-Confucianists could not understand or teach the real meaning of virtue because they interpreted the ancient words and expressions using contemporary defi-

8. Najita, "History and Nature in Eighteenth-Century Tokugawa Thought," 622.
9. Totman, *Early Modern Japan*, 364.
10. Najita, "History and Nature in Eighteenth-Century Tokugawa Thought," 602.

nitions rather than trying to discover the original meanings. Their mistaken methods of interpretation led them to misunderstandings in their search for practical rules of proper conduct, and this failure led Sorai to attack the foundations of the government-sponsored philosophy. He was unable to offer any sound alternative, however.

Bunkō saw that Neo-Confucianism was bereft of true moral teachings and that the Confucian institution would never again be able to contribute anything of significance to the benefit of all classes. His empirical analysis of Edo society and government led him to arrive at some of the same conclusions as Nishikawa and Sorai; namely, that merchants and peasants could theoretically possess moral virtue to as great or even greater degree than samurai, that the *bushi* class did not have an inherent right to govern, and that the shogun should not by right have absolute authority. Bunkō, however, also held that morality or immorality should be judged according to specific and unchanging moral standards.

Bunkō agreed with Sorai that one's status by birth did not determine one's sense of morality, but he also taught that political power and the right to determine right and wrong were inappropriately kept in the hands of the samurai class. Sorai articulated his views in the philosophical terms of the educated elite. Bunkō, however, explained his conclusions primarily through concrete examples and by citing his own empirical observations of the daily life of merchants, officials, and the elite in Edo. He judged people, no matter what their class, according to the ethical standards of forgiveness, humility, and justice.

Ishida Baigan (1685–1744) was another philosopher who attempted to adapt Japanese Neo-Confucianism to commoners in order to give them a greater confidence in their own ability to attain virtue. His philosophy was known as *Shingaku* (learning of the mind-heart). When Bunkō was lecturing in Edo in the spring of 1757, he advertised his talks with a placard that read "The interior (*ura*) and the exterior (*omote*) according to Shingaku."[11] Bunkō took advantage of the popularity of Shingaku philosophy and used Baigan's term "*ura-omote*" (the inside and the outside, the hidden and the seen) to contrast the hidden hypocrisy, cruelty, and arrogance of government officials and the good impression they wanted

11. Okada, *Baba Bunkō shū*, 305.

to give the public. Bunkō's lectures exposed the proclivity of the ruling class to speak eloquently about morals and virtue (omote) while at the same time behaving boorishly and immorally, thus revealing the hidden corruption (ura) in their lives. Bunkō's objective, to expose the hidden truth of samurai society, fit in well with Shingaku philosophy and with its emphasis on the importance of establishing a true harmony between one's external actions and one's inner virtue.

Baigan's philosophy presented a theoretical challenge to the Confucian tradition, which was in its death throes. Bunkō, however, took the challenge a step further and applied certain elements of the Shingaku philosophy to actual situations and real bakufu officials. He used the growing confidence of the commoner class as a weapon with which he repeatedly jabbed and poked at the foundations of the Tokugawa establishment. The philosophical, cultural, and literary environment aided Bunkō as well and encouraged him to express his dissent, which went beyond the theoretical philosophies of many of the scholars of the period.

The genre of satire that Bunkō created, rather than philosophical writing, was most effective in bringing the bakufu's hidden corruption to the foreground and in exposing the outward pretense of its Confucian "morality." He concluded that the righteousness or wickedness of actions should not be determined by prestige or social status but by the willingness to acknowledge one's real intentions (ura) without trying to hide them under a cover of pretended motives or false decorum (omote). To Baigan's philosophy, Bunkō added his own observation that if one presents a certain image of himself that contradicts his true persona or identity, he is guilty of a moral failure because he has acted contrary to the virtue of humility. He did acquire important insights from Shingaku, but Bunkō's emphasis on humility was uniquely his own.

Bunkō was exceptional in other ways as well. No other writer raised the issue of just treatment for the eta, the outcast class. He would declare that the government has the responsibility to aid the poor, feed the hungry, and treat the ill. Like the virtue of humility, these are all themes derived from Christianity and are not found in Japanese discourse of the middle eighteenth century or earlier. From where did Bunkō acquire his social consciousness and his sense of morality that was so different from Confucian, Buddhist, or even popular morality of the period, if not from Christian teachings? Though Bunkō was certainly influenced by the thought of many of his contemporaries, such as Ishida Baigan, and was steeped in the culture of his times, he was also convinced that there were absolute moral principles and that had to go beyond the traditional understanding of morality.

Tales of Contemporary Edo 1: Jinzaemon

Bunkō gave voice to his philosophy in stories and anecdotes that illustrated in real life situations the practice of virtue or its opposing vice. In his collection titled *Contemporary Discussions of Worldly Affairs in Musashi* (*Tōsei Buya zokudan*, 1756), Bunkō describes the life of a hatamoto by the name of Jinzaemon who had become quite wealthy. He lived in a splendid mansion in the Edo neighborhood of Honjō, Yoshioka-chō, on what had been the property of a well-known Tokugawa retainer, Kanematsu Matashirō (also known as Matsuyoshi, 1542–1627). In the following excerpt Bunkō presents Jinzaemon as an example of both a victim of injustice and also a teacher of forgiveness and humility:

> One day, Matsudaira Masatada, the magistrate of theft and arson [from 1758 to 1759], who had long coveted Jinzaemon's estate, had him arrested and confined to a small hut behind Ekōin temple [in present-day Ryōgoku, Tokyo]. Matsudaira put Jinzaemon in the custody of a *hinin* [literally, a non-human] by the name of Shohachi.
>
> During his confinement people would bring Jinzaemon food and supplies. Hundreds of people who had served him and had worked for him before his confinement were now unemployed. They went to the magistrate and begged him to release Jinzaemon. Not long after, he was finally pardoned and released.
>
> Before his arrest Jinzaemon had long been respected as a patron of the poor and of prostitutes. He would educate the poor himself, often accompanying them to [Buddhist] sermons and evening lectures. When his employees and servants fought or quarreled among themselves, Jinzaemon said to them: "Even if you are young and strong, fighting is impolite and unbecoming. You should be patient and forgive one another; that is the way of humans. You should also remember that it was because Kenshin [Uesugi, 1530–1578] had great aspirations that he was able to endure great sacrifices."[12]

12. Baba, *Tōsei Buya zokudan*, 376–77. Uesugi Kenshin was a daimyō of Echigo from 1547 to 1578.

Bunkō may have had an idealistic view of Uesugi's character, but he was, in fact, widely known for his honor and virtue. He had been a skilled and compassionate administrator who raised the standard of living among the peasants in his domain of Echigo. The virtues and qualities of this sixteenth-century daimyō, however, are not Bunkō's main point. His comparison of Jinzaemon and Uesugi is meant to highlight specific virtues rather than any individual and to show the importance of compassion, forgiveness, and self-sacrifice, all of which Bunkō held in high regard.

The samurai elite would not have considered Jinzaemon's care for the poor and prostitutes a proper expression of the official Tokugawa Confucian understanding of the virtue of jin. In the Tokugawa period this virtue focused on the cultivation of character through ritual norms, loyalty and fidelity to one's lord, and filial piety within the family. Bunkō emphasizes the importance of humility and forgiveness for all, in contrast to the Tokugawa-period understanding of the Confucian virtue of jin.

Tales of Contemporary Edo 2: Yaoya Oshichi

The tragic love story of the sixteen-year-old daughter of a greengrocer, Yaoya Oshichi (1667–83), became the subject of several kabuki and *bunraku* (puppet) plays. The story begins when a fire breaks out in Edo in the twelfth month of 1682 (Tenna 2). Oshichi, along with neighbors, fled to the open area on the grounds of a nearby temple to escape the conflagration. There she met one of the temple pages, a youth by the name of Ikuta Shōnosuke (a.k.a. Saemon), and fell in love. After the fire, the people of the area returned and rebuilt their homes. For the next year Oshichi could not get Shōnosuke out of her mind. She spent much of her time planning how she could meet her lover again. Her scheme was to start a fire so that she could again "escape" to the temple and meet Shōnosuke. However, before she could start the fire, she was apprehended by the police, tried as an adult, and convicted for the crime of attempted arson. She was condemned to burning at the stake in Suzugamori.

The judge who presided at her case, Doi Toshikatsu (1573–1644), a senior counselor and administrator of shogunal lands (*ōi no kami*) under Tokugawa Iemitsu, knew that if she were one year younger, she would not be tried as an adult, nor would she be condemned to death for her crime. During her trial, Doi had said to her, "You must be only fifteen years old," knowing perfectly well that she was actually sixteen. He tried to be merciful and forgiving, but Oshichi spoke honestly and courageously, confessing that she was indeed sixteen years old and should be punished accordingly.

In his retelling of this familiar story in *A Collection of Tales of Contemporary Edo* (*Kinsei Edo chomonshū*, 1757), Bunkō emphasizes the role of Doi Toshikatsu rather than the crime attempted and focuses on his compassion and desire to show mercy and forgiveness. The general outline of the story would have been quite familiar to the contemporary reader, but Bunkō begins his version by saying, "No one knows the real story of the young girl, Yaoya Oshichi." He changes the name of Oshichi's lover and other details to bring the events into the present.

> She had the nickname "Young Murasaki of Musashi." I went into a library and consulted texts from the Tenna period [1681–84] and the Teikyō period [1684–88] and discovered the truth.... Oshichi was the daughter of a certain Yamase Saburōbei, a retainer of the Maeda house, which controlled Kaga, Nōtō, and Etchū domains. Saburōbei became a rōnin and then renounced his samurai status and became a merchant. He opened a vegetable store (*yaoya*) in Komagome Oiwake Kata-machi [present-day Tokyo, Bunkyō-ku, Mukōgaoka] and took the name Yaoya Tarōbei.
>
> He and his wife had prayed to Hariti, the mother of demon children (*kishimojin*), that they might have a child.[13] When their child was born they named her Oshichi in honor of Hariti's seven demon children.... When Oshichi was fourteen years old in 1681 a fire broke out at Maruyama Honmyōji Temple and everything burnt from Hongo to Komagome. The house of Yaoya Tarōbei also burnt down and the family fled to Enjōji Temple.... There was an attendant at the temple named Yamada Sabei, the second son of Yamada Jūbei, a hatamoto. The boy was confined at the temple as a punishment for having slandered his stepmother.... Yamada fell in love with Oshichi at the temple, and his

13. Hariti is a Buddhist goddess who provides for the protection of children, and also helps with easy delivery and happy child rearing. Originally, Hariti was a cannibalistic demon. She had hundreds of children whom she loved and doted upon, but to feed them, she abducted and killed the children of others. The bereaved mothers of her victims pleaded with the Buddha to save them.

> love became deeper as summer passed into autumn. But they could not stay together. Oshichi left the temple and moved into her reconstructed house.[14]

Bunkō goes on to relate that further results of his research revealed that Oshichi, after she returned home, fell in love with a ne'er-do-well gambler and drunkard by the name of Kichisaburō. He was the one who put it in her mind to set the second fire. "If you really want to meet Sabei again," he said, "burn down your house, and flee to Enjōji Temple again. I will guide you and instruct you on how to set the fire. Only your house will burn down, and then I will extinguish the fire. So there will be no crime. The buddhas forgive evil deeds done for love."

All of this was a deception that Kichisaburō instigated because he was jealous of Sabei and sought to end Oshichi's relationship with him. He tricked Oshichi by having her accused of arson:

> Due to a woman's passion and the demon of love, Kichisaburō was able to trick Oshichi into setting the fire. As she was putting the plan into action, she felt no regret, convincing herself that even if she were to fall into the burning furnaces of Hell, she would still start the fire. As the house began to burn Kichisaburō grabbed her hand and led her out. He also managed to take money and clothes from the cabinets on his way out.[15]

Edo-period playwrights and storytellers made Oshichi a heroine who died for love. Bunkō, however, shows that she was a victim of a demonic temptation and the evil plan of the jealous Kichisaburō.

He then directs the reader's attention to the virtues of the official who judged Oshichi. When faced with the young "criminal" and having to judge her guilty, Judge Doi Toshikatsu is mortified that he has been placed in this position of having to pass judgment in such a case. As he hands down his decision, he expresses his feelings about the case:

> This is a pity. It is so very sad. I am embarrassed that this has occurred during my tenure in office. The people are virtuous. They do not even lock their doors. They yield the right of way to one another on the road. They share their fields. There is never a need to whip them. This is a time when the fire bell should be covered with moss, and the birds should never be frightened

14. Baba, *Kinsei Edo chomonshū*, 431, 432.
15. Ibid., 436.

> by its ringing. But now I must bear my authority as representative of the shogun and rule in the present case.
>
> From ancient times until now it has never been heard that such a young woman would commit as serious a crime as arson. Because she has violated the Great Law, she should be condemned to burning at the stake. But her crime is only because of my own lack of virtue and a lack of virtue in all the rulers. It is an embarrassment for the realm. If she were a minor her crime would be forgiven. Even if her crime had been to set fire to my own house, I would certainly have found her innocent and forgiven her.[16]

Bunkō continues: "Then, the judge released Oshichi and put her in the custody of a certain Nakayama, who cared for her with sympathy and clemency." It was all thanks to "the greatness of spirit" (*kanjin*) of Judge Doi Toshikatsu, who, although aware of the harm a "not guilty" decision would bring to the honor of the bakufu, dealt with the case in a forgiving and merciful manner.

Bunko commends Doi, calling him "a devoted prince" (kunshi) who judged justly. His principle of justice was based on forgiveness more than on a rigid interpretation of the law. As Bunkō presents him, the magistrate was also guided by the virtue of humility. He blamed his own personal deficiencies and lack of virtue for the deficiencies in his people. Forgiveness and humility, the virtues highlighted in Bunkō's version of the Oshichi tale, were not Confucian principles and were not virtues that were esteemed by the samurai class during the Tokugawa period.

As anyone familiar with the actual history of Oshichi knows, she was in fact burned at the stake, having been found guilty of attempted arson. In Bunkō's version Nakayama Kageyu (a.k.a. Naomori, 1633–87), the magistrate of theft and arson, confronted Judge Doi about his lenient application of the law and castigated him: "What kind of ruling is this? Were you taken with Oshichi's beauty and feminine charms? If that is so, you are the criminal."

Bunkō brings his version in line with the historical record by ending his tale with the execution of Oshichi: "There was nothing the judge could do. In light of the evidence, he had no choice. Nakayama reported the Doi to higher authorities, and the decision was made that she had to

16. Ibid., 437.

be executed. Oshichi was burnt at the stake at Suzugamori in the second month of 1682." What actually happened according to the historical account was not as important to Bunkō as the virtues of humility and forgiveness that were exemplified in the conduct of Judge Doi Toshikatsu. Bunkō's purpose was to present him as a model of virtuous behavior that his readers would contrast with the lack of virtue and the hypocrisy of many of the contemporary officials with whom they were familiar.

7 | BABA BUNKŌ'S LITERARY HERITAGE

Twenty-folio volumes will never cause a revolution; it's the little pocket books at thirty sous you have to be wary of.

VOLTAIRE (1694–1778)

Selective History

Modern Western historians have not included Baba Bunkō in their accounts of the Tokugawa period, except occasionally in passing or as a footnote. Perhaps this is because they consider Bunkō's writings to be of little historical importance, anecdotal, idealistic, or purely fictional. His "little pocket books" were after all short manuscripts of only a handful of pages, usually containing four or five anecdotes of a page or two in length. The response that he drew from the bakufu, however, went far beyond what would have been expected. Some of his writings at least were apparently seen as politically subversive.

It is true that Bunkō provides a perspective on the history of the period that is quite different from his contemporaries, particularly in his emphasis on the moral faults and character weaknesses of the leaders in society. Bunkō reported what he observed without embellishment. Other writers of the time presented their observations as fiction or as events that took place in the distant past. His methodology was more like what

Epigraph is from a 1766 letter to Jean le Rond d'Alembert (1717–83); John Fletcher and Nicholas Cronk, eds., *A Pocket Philosophical Dictionary* (Oxford: Oxford University Press, 2011), xvii.

historians do today when they interpret events from a specific perspective.

One of the differences between Bunkō and modern historians may be the degree to which there is an awareness of the moral slant that is being given in the selection of events and people about whom a history is being constructed. Modern historians sometimes write history under the illusion that they are being completely objective, but as explained in the introductory chapter, no historian constructs purely objective history. It is true that many of the details about historical personages and events that Bunkō provides and the moral slant he gives do not appear in the historical writings of his own time, but his accounts are in no way inconsistent with what historians have long known about the history of early modern Japan.

The genre of fiction is often thought to be a representation of the imaginable–that is, of what is entertaining but not true. The genre of history, on the other hand, is considered to be a representation of the actual that corresponds to reality. As Hayden White has pointed out, this is an artificial and misleading distinction and has sometimes been the cause of superficial interpretations of important elements in history.[1] The fiction vs. history distinction definitively crumbles in light of the satirical writings of Baba Bunkō, which contain both the imagined and the actual. What may be embellished anecdotal information or even rumor becomes critical social commentary about historical persons and events and gives a perspective on the period that is much more focused on ethical principles and standards than simply on what happens. Behind Bunkō's satire is a clearly-conceptualized morality and an evaluation of virtue and vice with which he interprets the history of the Tokugawa period. His perspective goes beyond the fiction-history distinction.

The Environment for Satire

The literary critic Dustin Griffin has defined satire as writing that attacks vice and folly by subjecting it to wit and ridicule.[2] Bunkō's ridicule of

1. Hayden White, *Tropics of Discourse: Essays in Cultural Criticism*, (Baltimore: Johns Hopkins University Press, 1978), 98.

2. Griffin, *Satire: A Critical Reintroduction*, 137.

the vice and corruption of his own period certainly marks him as a satirist in this sense. The most important factor that makes any work successful satire, according to Griffin, is a readership that is fairly small and homogeneous. It would be a mistake to judge Bunkō's satirical works as unimportant or insignificant because of the small number of readers he attracted. Because of the repressive environment of Tokugawa Japan, the number of people who heard his lectures or read his manuscripts is impossible to estimate, but his reading audience was probably kept small by the fact that he personally sold his manuscripts only to book dealers and to people who attended his lectures. His small reading audience, however, was a primary factor in his freedom to write at all. Wide publication for a broad audience would actually have had a crippling effect on his writing and on the impact of his satire. If Bunkō had intended for his writings to be published and widely distributed, his work most likely would not have contained the clear and direct attacks on the most well-known figures of the day.

Griffin also states that satiric writing thrives in an atmosphere that is usually more aristocratic than bourgeois. In early modern Japan those distinctions would apply to the samurai (aristocratic) and to the merchant classes (bourgeois). Even though the readers of Bunkō's satire and the audiences who came to listen to his lectures were not primarily of the noble classes, the atmosphere of the city of Edo at the time Bunkō was composing his satire was "aristocratic" or samurai in two respects: culturally and demographically. The "aristocratic" arts, such as the tea ceremony, flower arranging, poetry, and Buddhist meditation that once had signified elite, actual aristocratic status were becoming the common property of a larger number of people in the eighteenth century.[3] Demographically speaking, the population of Edo, which was over half a million in 1657 and which doubled during the next fifty years to well over a million, was roughly half samurai.[4] This demographic made Edo unique among the cities of Japan and was also the characteristic that made it an "aristocratic" capital and, in Griffin's analysis, more open to the production of satire than areas of Japan with a less significant "aristocratic" or samurai presence.

3. Totman, *Early Modern Japan*, 380.
4. Ibid., 153.

Though samurai and commoners did not live in the same neighborhoods of Edo, there was much intermingling of the classes in spite of laws that were meant to keep them apart. Along with increasing numbers of commoners who were becoming interested in Noh drama, which had long been an exclusively elite pastime, there were also samurai who, under disguise, mingled with commoners at the kabuki theater and at the Yoshiwara inns and brothels, where the samurai had ostensibly been forbidden to go. In such an atmosphere, according to Griffin, where the "aristocratic" elements are so pervasive, people who are not of the ruling elite come to appreciate satire that ridicules the social pretense and hypocrisy of "aristocrats" who claim political and social superiority.

Amagasaki Ikko, Samurai-Merchant

Bunkō saw through the pretense of superiority that was apparent among the samurai in Edo. He was also aware that the same attitude of exaggerated self-esteem was filtering down to the wealthy merchants. His story titled "Otsuna at the Tsu no Kuniya Inn" (*Shinagawa Tsunokuniya*, 1758) in *Contemporary Edo: An Album of One Hundred Monsters* is a satirical drama involving a samurai-turned-merchant, his wife, and Otsuna, a Yoshiwara prostitute.[5] Set in the Edo district of Shinagawa at a well-known teahouse, this anecdote introduces Amagasaki Ikkō, a married man of samurai status who has fallen in love with the beautiful courtesan Otsuna. His indiscretion has caused scandal for his family and brings what had been a lucrative business to the point of ruin. Amagasaki's wife, seeing her husband spending much of his resources and most of his time with the prostitute, sends messengers to the inn on a number of occasions in a futile attempt to retrieve her errant spouse. All of her efforts to bring him home, however, end in failure. Finally, having reached the breaking point of frustration and anger, she decides to go herself to the Tsu no Kuniya Inn to demand a face-to-face meeting with her rival, the courtesan Otsuna. Knowing that she would never be allowed to enter the establishment if she appeared to be a customer's wife, she goes to the inn disguised as an old woman and claims that she is Otsuna's aunt. She announces herself at the

5. Baba, *Tōdai Edo hyaku bakemono*, 5–7.

gate and requests to speak with her "niece" immediately: "If you do not mind, I would like to meet the woman who works in this establishment and goes by the name of Tsuna. Actually I am her aunt . . . and since it has been a long time since I have seen Tsuna, I have come to meet her. Would you be so kind as to tell her that I am here?" Amagasaki's wife is allowed to enter, but unfortunately, she lets her pent-up frustrations get the best of her and goes on a violent rampage, breaking everything in sight, making her way to Otsuna's bedroom, and dragging her shocked husband out of the bordello by his collar.

In a short break in the narrative, Bunkō describes the courtesan Otsuna in some detail as a woman who bears a striking resemblance to the well-known kabuki *onnagata* (female impersonator) Nakamura Tomijūrō (1721–86), who was well known for his remarkable feminine-like beauty and who prided himself on his ability to act with more feminine grace than any woman.

As the narrative takes up the action again, the reader realizes that Amagasaki is an obvious reference to an historical person. Though a fictional character in the anecdote, Amagasaki was actually a wealthy merchant of Odawara-chō who was known to have purchased the equivalent of samurai status. He had the reputation of frequenting the inns in Yoshiwara but of never paying his debts.[6] His name differs by only one Chinese character from the fictional Amagasaki. The actual merchant is Amagasaki Ikko (一潮); the fictional character is Amagasaki Ikkō (一候). The fictional Amagasaki Ikkō also hails from Odawara-chō, making it quite obvious that Bunkō is satirizing the actual samurai-merchant Amagasaki Ikko and not simply writing an amusing anecdote about a fictional character.

Bunkō reports that the real Amagasaki Ikko has a long-standing debt that he owes to a certain teahouse proprietor who has come to collect on the invoice. Amagasaki puts him off saying, "Wait a little longer, and I will pay," but the creditor, being particularly impatient, comes back again the same day, this time shouting threats and demanding immediate payment.[7] Amagasaki, appealing to his samurai status, feels insulted

6. Mitamura Engyo, *Mitamura Engyo zenshū*, 13: 368.
7. Ibid.

that the proprietor would dare to come twice in the same day to collect on the debt. He is determined not to forgive the teahouse owner's rude affront to his honor and resolves to make him regret his impertinence.

Amagasaki calls ten of his friends who go with him to the teahouse to teach the proprietor a lesson in "respect." The proprietor, intimidated by this show of force, politely allows the men to come into his establishment, but he asks them to pay in advance for their drinks and entertainment. Amagasaki is insulted by the affront to his honesty. He arrogantly lambasts the owner, screaming how rude he is not to extend credit to a samurai who has long been a regular customer. Amagasaki and his ten ruffians proceed to demonstrate their displeasure by rampaging through the teahouse until everything is in shambles. Bunkō states as a matter of fact, "This was an actual incident." Satirical humor is found in the parallel between the account of Amagasaki's wife ransacking the Tsu no Kuniya Inn and her husband Ikko doing the same at the teahouse. It is a comic but mocking description of what Bunkō would have his reader believe is typical of the members of a samurai or wealthy merchant household.

By relating the humorous, but at the same time outrageous encounter with a prostitute at the inn, Bunkō is claiming that, unbeknownst to all, the real Amagasaki has the moral character of his fictional counterpart. The purpose of the satire is not simply to tell an entertaining story. Bunkō intends to give the reader a behind-the-scenes look at the real Odawara merchant and show he is a morally weak and irresponsible individual, just like the fictional Amagasaki Ikkō. Bunkō has incorporated two themes that were common in gesaku literature: Yoshiwara and the stereotypical figure of the "spoiled son" (*musuko*) who brings the family business to ruin through his extravagance and debauchery in the "pleasure" district.

By alluding to Chinese history and legend in "Otsuna at the Tsu no Kuniya Inn," Bunkō illustrates the difference between gesaku as simply "playful writing" and gesaku as political and social satire. Amagasaki's wife, who had been abandoned by her husband, is compared to Lady Han (Pan Chieh-yū, 48–6 BC), the chief consort of Emperor Ch'eng of Han (51–7 BC). The emperor had long showered his favors upon Lady Han—that is, until he met the beautiful dancer Chao Fei-yen (d. 6 BC). Fei-yen had danced so seductively before the emperor one evening that he fell in love with her and completely forgot about Lady Han.[8] To ensure complete victory over her rival, Chao Fei-yen slandered Lady Han, spreading the rumor that she was a practitioner of witchcraft and then had her expelled from the palace. In spite of her shame and humiliation, Lady Han, though abandoned just like Amagasaki's wife, exhibited a similar strength of character that eventually allowed her to save face in a deadly game of high-stakes palace intrigue. Though Lady Han never again had the love of Emperor Cheng, she did gain an imperial reprieve. The emperor continued to be obsessed with his concubine Chao Fei-yen and, as a result, lost all interest in the affairs of state, just as Amagasaki had lost all interest in the family business. The emperor would do anything Chao Fei-yen asked and even ordered at her behest the executions of some of his senior advisers and high government officials.

Bunkō writes: "[Lady Han,] sleeping alone, wept through the night grieving over the repeated sound of the temple bell."[9] For Bunkō, Lady Han mirrors Amagasaki's wife in the agony of her abandonment: "The jealousy in both of their hearts grew ever more insufferable." Amagasaki Ikko represents Emperor Ch'eng. Both are men who see themselves as powerful but are actually controlled by conniving and jealous women. Otsuna, the prostitute, had power over Amagasaki Ikkō just as Chao Fei-yen was able to manipulate the emperor and make him do exactly what she wanted. The juxtaposed elements among the four characters, the prostitute Otsuna and Chao Fei-yen on the one hand and Amagasaki's wife and Lady Han on the other, as well as the comparison of Amagasaki with Emperor Cheng are typical of Bunkō's satirical style. Bunkō has drawn obvious connections between the corruption and weakness of Emperor Ch'eng and the same defects in the wealthy samurai-merchant Amagasaki. At the conclusion of the story the courtesan Otsuna is given the designation of "monster" because she, like the concubine Chao Fei-yen, stole her rival's husband.

8. Cited in Itō Masayoshi, ed., *Yōkyokushū* (Tokyo: Shinchōsha, 1988), 3: 462. See English translation in Royall Tyler, ed. and trans., *Japanese Nō Dramas* (London: Penguin Books, 1992), 108–9.

9. Baba, *Tōdai Edo hyaku bakemono*, 5. Bunkō's reference to the story of Lady Han (Pan Chieh-yū) is taken from *Wakan rōei shū kenmon* (Observations on *Wakan rōei shū*), a medieval commentary on Fujiwara Kintō's (966–1041) influential collection *Wakan rōei shū* (A collection of Japanese and Chinese poems for chanting aloud, 1013).

Bunkō makes another reference to history and legend in this account of Amagasaki's affair with Otsuna. In the "Swords Chapter" (*Tsurugi no maki*) of the Japanese classic war story *The Tale of the Taira* (*Heike monogatari*, thirteenth century) Watanabe Genshirō no Tsuna (953–1025), a companion-in-arms of Minamoto no Yorimitsu (948–1021), commander in the Imperial Guard and an official in the Ministry of War, is crossing the Midori Bridge at Ichijō Avenue (in Kyoto) when he meets a beautiful woman who wishes to accompany him on his travels. Their passage proceeds without incident until the two reach Gojō Avenue. Without warning the beautiful woman changes into a demon. Watanabe no Tsuna draws his sword, named "Beard Cutter" (*Higekiri*), and manages to cut off one of the arms of the demon just before she flies off to Mt. Atago (Atagosan in northwest Kyoto). Watanabe no Tsuna keeps the severed arm as evidence of his encounter and proof that he had defeated a demon in single combat. Sometime later, after he has returned home, Watanabe no Tsuna's aunt pays him a visit, and he relates to her the story of his encounter with the lovely woman who turned into a demon. Watanabe's aunt asks him to show her the demon's arm that he cut off. On seeing the arm, his aunt reveals herself to be the very monster whose arm had been severed. She stands before Watanabe transformed into a repulsive demon, holding the bloodied stump of her own arm.

The analogy that is drawn between the demon (Watanabe no Tsuna's aunt) and Amagasaki's wife (Otsuna's "aunt") becomes even more obvious as Bunkō reports that Watanabe no Tsuna hailed from Mita (in Musashi, Adachi-gun) and Amagasaki's wife comes from the section of Edo also known as Mita (in present-day Minato-ku, Tokyo). Watanabe no Tsuna's aunt in *Tale of the Taira* is from Settsu no kuni (in present-day Osaka and Hyōgo prefectures), the former name of which is "Tsu no Kuni," the same name as the teahouse to which Amagasaki's wife goes to retrieve her husband. These obvious allusions to *Tale of the Taira* add another important satirical element to Bunkō's "Otsuna at the Tsu no Kuniya Inn." Now the reader sees that Amagasaki's wife transforms herself, posing as Otsuna's aunt, in order to retrieve not her arm but her husband. Amagasaki's wife thus represents a demon.

In this very intricate satire the three characters, Amagasaki Ikkō, his wife who poses as Otsuna's aunt, and Otsuna herself, are three parts of a love triangle that was sustained by the pathetic weakness of Ikkō and the jealousy of two women. Bunkō took the theme of the love triangle that was popular in later Edo-period gesaku and made it into a narrative that incorporates historical and fictional elements from both China and Japan.

The love triangle theme, which Bunkō uses, is found in *Spring Love: A Plum Blossom Almanac* (*Shunshoku umegoyomi*, 1832–33) by Tamenaga Shunsui (1790–1843). Tanjirō, a handsome but weak-willed ne'er-do-well, is pursued by two motherly but passionately jealous women, Yonehachi, who is Tanjirō's principal lover, and Ochō, who tries to manipulate the indecisive protagonist. Amagasaki Ikkō, like Tanjirō in *Spring Love*, is incapable of defending himself against two powerful and manipulative women. Tanjirō is also a lazy lout who neglects the family business. He makes no effort to earn a responsible living to support his wife, even though she has remained faithful to him. He is little more than a vagabond, who exhausts his financial resources to frequent the bordello in order to pursue an affair with the courtesan Ochō.

However, it is the confrontation between the two women that reveals more clearly the spinelessness and cowardliness of Amagasaki. His indecisiveness is a trait that appears in the male character Tanjirō, who wants to please both Yonehachi and Ochō and who is unable to make a choice between them, just as Amagasaki is unable to choose between Otsuna and his own wife. In spite of the strength of the women, Bunkō writes that their jealousy and deception show them both to be "monsters." Deceit, cheating, fraud, and trickery—these are the vices that turn people into "monsters" in many of Bunkō's satires.

Bunkō's social satire incorporates fictional elements from Chinese and Japanese classical literature, as well as from the contemporary popular gesaku. He uses this literary heritage to penetrate the secrets of actual people and the significance of heretofore unknown events. Bunkō's use of various literary genres to satirize the political and cultural milieu of the time exposed the scandals of the samurai class.

A Satire of Self-Sacrifice

Bunkō's satirical view of the purported samurai ideal of self-sacrifice is humorously presented in an allegory titled "The Valor of the Self-Sacrifice of Tanaka Kyūguemon" (*Tanaka Kyūguemon hitomi o osonae ni sonawarishi buyū no koto*, 1756).[10] Kyūguemon (1662–1729) had been born of peasant stock but managed to become a wealthy merchant who secures a government post and becomes an even wealthier bakufu official. The manner in which he was able to be so successful is closely scrutinized in this tale. Even though some of the circumstances of the story are fictional, the contemporary reader would know Tanaka Kyūguemon as a person who had been able to advance from his status as a lowly peasant to the position of a retainer in the service of Shogun Tokugawa Yoshimune. The story of his advancement illustrates the weakening of the formerly strict social boundaries in the Tokugawa class system. It is also a disparaging satire on reputed samurai ethics and ideals.

As the story goes, Kyūguemon is walking along a mountain path one day on his way to the home of his nephew. He is bringing a fish with him as a gift, when suddenly he sees a pheasant caught in a hunter's snare, wildly flapping its wings, trying to escape. Thinking that a pheasant would make a much nicer gift than the fish he has brought and finding the hunter nowhere in sight, Kyūguemon decides to break open the trap, take the valuable bird, and leave the fish in its place.

The hunter meanwhile has been going around checking a number of traps he had set. When he comes to the trap in which Kyūguemon has left his fish, the foolish hunter exclaims in surprise: "I can't believe it! How could a fish that lives in the sea climb up the mountain and get trapped in my snare?" Bunkō explains that he is a superstitious man and has concluded that this strange event might be some kind of curse by an evil spirit. Frightened, he shouts out, and a crowd gathers to see the unusual phenomenon. Though no one is able to explain how this has happened, the peasants, like the hunter, accept what their eyes tell them and believe that the fish has somehow either gotten into the trap of its own accord or was put there by an evil spirit.

10. Baba, *Tōji chinsetsu yōhiroku*, 217–19.

A fortune-teller from the neighboring shrine of the great guardian Shintō god Daimyōjin steps forward and proclaims that the fish is a sign that the mountain gods are angry.[11] He demands that everyone now must worship the fish in order to avert divine wrath. The seer's words throw everyone into a panic. They immediately put the fish in a wooden bucket filled with water lest it die and begin building a miniature Shintō shrine over the bucket. A tiny *torii* (shrine gate) is put in front of the bucket, and the villagers begin to pray to the fish. Every day they continued to pray and to offer flowers to Daimyōjin to honor the fish-turned-god. Some days after that a shocking oracle comes from Daimyōjin through the mouth of the seer: "I command you to take one man and one woman from the village and bring them as human sacrifices. If you do not comply with this command, the entire village will be destroyed." Following much discussion and debate, the villagers conclude that they have no choice but to follow the god's directions and proceed to look for two people who would make suitable human sacrifices.

Meanwhile, Kyūguemon has been visiting his nephew for a few days. Both of them enjoy a delicious meal with the pheasant he has stolen from the trap. As Kyūguemon is returning home, he goes into the village and is quite amused to see what has transpired. He hears that the peasants are looking for a volunteer to be a human sacrifice, so he devises a plan to trick the villagers again. He tells the people, "If you agree, I will sell you my life and be the human sacrifice. I'm the kind of person who doesn't get along well with other people anyway. Besides, I am still living with my old mother, and she is getting on my nerves." On hearing Kyūguemon's offer, everyone feels relieved that they have found their human sacrifice. "Certainly after you die," they say, "we will take the money owed to you for your sacrifice and give it to your mother as payment for your life." The villagers then proceed to prepare Kyūguemon for the sacrifice.

The reader would notice that the preliminaries for the sacrifice are done in the manner of a samurai preparing for ritual suicide. The villagers bathe him, dress him in a new white linen kimono, and cut his hair. They then build a large wooden platform, decorate it, and lead

11. Daimyōjin is a generic name that includes a myriad different Shinto deities. Inari Daimyōjin was the most widely worshipped in early modern Japan.

Kyūguemon up to the top. As this is being done, *yamabushi* (mountain monks) begin praying and chanting sutras in honor of Daimyōjin, then continue their chants throughout the night.

By dawn, everyone has returned home, the monks have stopped chanting and are fast asleep. Kyūguemon, having waited for everyone to leave, gets down from the platform, opens the tiny shrine, and takes out the bucket that contains his fish. He is so hungry that he slices it up, eats it, and washes it down with the saké that the monks have brought as an offering to Daimyōjin. Kyūguemon, having just eaten, feeling clean with a fresh haircut, and all spruced up in his new white kimono, peacefully walks away.

The protagonist of the tale, Tanaka Kyūguemon, was known to be a commoner who had come to Edo from an impoverished area in Kawasaki to try his hand at merchandising.[12] He became quite successful in business and in government, and Bunkō acknowledges his resourcefulness and ingenuity. Bunkō satirized what he sees as the foolish and superstitious beliefs of Shinto and shows that Kyūguemon was wise enough not to be taken in by the delusions of Shinto believers. The allegory also shows Bunkō's belief that the god the villagers worshiped, Daimyōjin, was no benevolent guardian at all, as was commonly thought, but a demon who demanded human sacrifice. The old Shintō beliefs are discredited, shown to be no more credible than the advice of the fortune-teller in the story. The real Tanaka Kyūguemon was rewarded with a position as an official of the bakufu for pointing out abuses in the government of Shogun Tokugawa Yoshimune. As explained above, Yoshimune, instead of having him punished, rewarded him for his honesty and courage (see chapter 5).

As Bunkō saw it, Tanaka's promotion to the office of intendant was the good fortune of one who was sensible, unlike the vast majority of samurai, as well as commoners, who simply went along with what they were told, worshiping the Shintō gods and giving credence to the words of fortune-tellers.

It is important to note here that Bunkō is showing contempt for Shinto

12. Tsuji Tatsuya, *Kyōhō tsugan*, 348.

"superstitions" and is highly critical of its rituals and religious practices, using both fictional elements and actual history to declare his opposition to native beliefs in an amusing but also derisive manner. Undoubtedly, Bunkō holds opinions that are unique among the educated writers of his time. The kokugaku (national learning) scholars, for example, were sometimes critical of the bakufu but supportive of Shinto. The Neo-Confucians were supportive of the bakufu and critical of Buddhism. As the reader will see, Bunkō was critical of the bakufu and denounced not only Shinto beliefs but the Buddhist faith as well.

The allegory also provides evidence that by this time status and rank were no longer unalterable. Bunkō views the system of Tokugawa class divisions between commoners and samurai as simply another superstition that has been advanced by the regime in its continued desperate attempt to preserve the status quo. Putting one's faith in rank and privilege is no different from believing that a fish could climb a mountain and get itself caught in a trap.

The samurai's traditional power of life and death over commoners is shown to be no different from a "fictitious" Shinto god demanding human sacrifice. In the story a samurai's privilege of being able to demand anything of a commoner, including the sacrifice of his own life, suffers a startling reversal. It is now the peasants who are demanding the life of a samurai. Traditional subservience to the samurai class, Bunkō suggests, is the result of an illusion held by both the ruling class (the Shinto god of the allegory) and the ruled (the foolish villagers). The widely held assumption that samurai have the right to special privileges and are supposedly more intelligent and inherently more worthy of respect than commoners, simply by virtue of their birth, is the result of ignorance and superstition.

Other Edo Satirists

What is known of other satirists of the early modern period will further illustrate by comparison the unique characteristics of Bunkō's writings. Asai Ryōi (1612–91), author of a number of chapbooks (kanazōshi), took up some of the same themes as Bunkō: the wastefulness of the samurai, the greed of merchants, the mistreatment of peasants. However,

Asai presented these themes in general terms, without implicating specific individuals in corruption. Ihara Saikaku (1642–93), the best-known of the early satirists of the Tokugawa period, wrote fictional caricatures of a very guarded type that were so carefully crafted that no one would be seriously offended. The samurai officials in Saikaku's stories are practically immune from attack. The merchant class, whom Saikaku perceived to be a safe target, does not fare as well, but Saikaku is not overly critical even toward them. In *The Japanese Family Storehouse* (*Nippon eitaigura*, 1688), merchants are portrayed as moral weaklings who are led astray by their own greed and by the carnal temptations of the pleasure quarters, but they are harmlessly foolish. Considering the trend in his day to enforce stricter censorship, it is not surprising that Saikaku regards as inappropriate the writing of direct satire about members of the samurai class. He does not explore in any depth the results or the moral implications for their lack of discretion, dishonesty, or cruelty, as Bunkō does.

What is more, in contrast to Bunkō's characters, Saikaku's protagonists are not real people. Saikaku kept his stories solely on the level of fiction and did not attempt direct political commentary about actual events or actual members of the elite ruling class. His satirical barbs were primarily reserved for making light of the famous classics or for mocking society in general rather than directing attention to specific government officials or their policies. The division of his novel *Tales of an Amorous Man* (*Kōshoku ichidai otoko*, 1682) into fifty-four chapters, as is often cited, parodies *The Tale of Genji* (*Genji monogatari*, eleventh century), which has the same number of chapters; but he pokes fun at concepts rather than people. He never ventures to parody any work or any author closer to his own time. Saikaku's modern-day prince, Yonosuke, unlike the hero of Murasaki Shikibu's classic, is unencumbered by sentiment or the obligations of aristocratic pedigree. His "nobility" originates not from his breeding but from his wealth and amorousness. This could be interpreted as a slap at the samurai elite of Saikaku's time, and their propensity to be greedy, but the contemporary lack of filial piety and virtue among actual persons, their vendettas, and the frequent violations of their codes of conduct were only hinted at indirectly in Saikaku's works. He writes from the perspective of the detached observer when composing tales about the samurai. This is what most clearly contrasts him with Baba Bunkō, whose satirical barbs about actual samurai, rather than fictional characters, were direct and unmistakable.

After Saikaku's death, Ejima Kiseki (1666–1735), relying heavily on his predecessor's style as well as content, wrote a type of commentary that provoked laughter but could not be considered social or political satire. Kiseki has been described as "a satiric realist whose humor is without bitterness."[13] His tales, as described by Conrad Totman, of "misers, flatterers, drunkards, boors, braggarts, gluttons, and lechers" have some similarities to the content of Bunkō's essays, but Kiseki rarely takes offense at the inappropriate conduct of officials or corruption in the government. Kiseki's purely fictional characters contrast sharply with Bunkō's descriptions of real people and actual situations. Unlike Bunkō, "Kiseki had too much of an unreflective Genroku spirit," which kept his writing on the level of entertainment and prevented him from engaging in deeper social scrutiny.[14]

The famous playwright Chikamatsu Monzaemon (1653–1724) came close to social satire in his accounts of disturbances in the houses of the daimyō (*oiemono*), but the dramatic plots were fictionalized versions of history. Bunkō, however, reported such disturbances as actual events. Chikamatsu's play *Love Suicide at Sonezaki* (*Sonezaki shinjū*, 1703), for example, was based on the recent suicide of a shop attendant and a prostitute in Osaka. Chikamatsu could have used this and other plays to teach a moral lesson or to criticize the Tokugawa status quo, but he chose instead to dwell simply on the pathos of the situation.[15] Bunkō saw a deeper political and social significance in such incidents.

Chikamatsu did satirize shogun Tokugawa Tsunayoshi (1646–1709) in his play titled *The Sagami Lay Monk and the Thousand Dogs* (*Sagami nyūdō sembiki inu*, 1714), but it was a rather indirect censure of the shogun and more of a criticism of the "Laws of Compassion for Living Things" (*jōrui awaremi no rei*), which stipulated that the killing of a dog or cat, even if accidental, was punishable by death. In his article "Chikamatsu's

13. Totman, *Early Modern Japan*, 216, 217.

14. Howard Hibbett, *The Floating World in Japanese Fiction* (London: Oxford University Press, 1959), 50, 62–63.

15. Totman, *Early Modern Japan*, 219–20.

Satire on the Dog Shogun," Donald Shively finds it surprising that such a satire would have been written in this period when the shogunate "ruthlessly suppressed political criticism, ... safeguarded itself with a network of censors, secret police, and informers, ... [and] even forbade private authors to discuss events involving the ruling class more recently than the sixteenth century."[16] For this reason, Chikamatsu took none of the risks that Baba Bunkō did. Shively admits that Chikamatsu made oblique references to recent scandals involving high personages, but he cloaked his satire by transferring the events to an earlier century and changing the names of the characters accordingly.[17]

Bunkō, however, almost never made oblique references to corrupt officials. He never changed names in order to disguise them, nor did he set his satire in an earlier period. As has already been seen, Bunkō satirized Tokugawa Ieshige and City Magistrate Tsuchiya Masasuke while they were still in power. By contrast, Chikamatsu's satire targeting Tsunayoshi was written after the shogun had been dead for five years. The policies of Tsunayoshi that Chikamatsu criticized had already been repudiated by the succeeding shogun, Tokugawa Ienobu (1662–1712), who "made a statement to the corpse [of Tsunayoshi] before the burial, explaining the necessity of repealing the laws [of compassion for living things] immediately."[18] Chikamatsu wrote his play after Ienobu had released over eight thousand men imprisoned for violating the animal laws, so the playwright would not have been in any danger of being punished for mocking Tsunayoshi or his policies. It is surprising that Donald Shively was surprised at Chikamatsu's "satirical" criticism of the shogun.

Among artists, Hanabusa Itchō (1652–1724) produced a work of political satire in 1690 in the form of a painting that supposedly presented Tokugawa Tsunayoshi riding a boat in the company of his favorite mistress. The painting does indeed poke fun at the shogun but does not draw any conclusions or make any judgments about his conduct. Itchō was exiled in 1698 for his alleged *lèse majesté*.[19]

16. Donald H. Shively, "Chikamatsu's Satire on the Dog Shogun," *Harvard Journal of Asiatic Studies* 18, no. 1/2 (June 1955), 159.

17. Ibid., 160.

18. Ibid., 162.

19. Ibid., 161.

Bunkō's Literary Heritage in Kōshaku

The roots of Bunkō's satirical style can be found in the long tradition of kōshaku (oral presentation) that arose in the Muromachi period (1336–1568). At that time, knowledge was considered to be private or secret learning that was passed down through oral instruction by artisans, poets, teachers, and aristocrats from father to son or from master to senior disciple. Knowledge was kept within families or private literary circles. The lessons or morals of kōshaku that could be applied to contemporary life were also for private consumption.[20] Teachings on literary composition or artistic techniques were given only to high-ranking or privileged persons who had been born into educated families or who could purchase the expertise. Commoners were usually excluded from this transmission of knowledge and skills, and hence were prevented from taking full advantage of the fruits of the traditional arts and scholarship.

By the early Edo era important changes were taking place in this view of knowledge as the property of the elite, and learning began to be dispersed to a wider audience who had no traditional claim on the "secret" knowledge of the wealthy families. Matsunaga Teitoku (1571–1653) was one of the first to take the unprecedented step of lecturing publicly on teachings that he had received privately.[21] His lectures on literary masterpieces, such as "Poems by One Hundred Poets" (*Hyakunin isshu*, thirteenth century) and the collection of essays titled *Essays in Idleness* (*Tsurezuregusa*, c. 1330), marked a new beginning in pedagogical theory; and education was becoming less a transmission of secrets to a select few and more instruction and information that could be shared by all classes.

In 1692 Akamatsu Seizaemon (dates unknown) came to Edo from Kyoto and began public readings of selections from the *Tale of the Taira* with commentary for a commoner audience. Before Akamatsu, storytellers and itinerant preachers (kōdanshi) would recite the tales, but any explanation or application of the lessons of the tale to contemporary life was

20. Nobuhiro Shinji, "*Kōdan, jitsuroku, kōshaku*," in *Nihon bungaku zenshi, kinsei*, ed. Ichiko Teiji et al. (Tokyo: Gakuteisha, 1978), 4: 589.

21. Donald Keene, "Characteristic Responses to Confucianism in Tokugawa Literature," in *Confucianism and Tokugawa Culture*, ed. Peter Nosco (Princeton: Princeton University Press, 1984), 121.

still not part of kōshaku recitation. The traditional teaching method of kōshaku instruction would develop into the technique of early modern kōdan, which was well-suited to Bunkō's personality and his unconventional ways of expression. Like Akamatsu and Fukai Shidōken before him, Bunkō would use a fan as a prop to develop the intensity of his story through gesture or to hit the fan on a stand to create sound effects in order to create an atmosphere of suspense or excitement for his listeners. Even in Bunkō's own time knowledge was still guarded, but commoners had become aware of their ability to access learning and information that had previously been forbidden to them. The tradition of the early modern kōdanshi grew out of the seeds that Matsunaga Teitoku, Akamatsu Seizaemon, and others had planted. Bunkō took from them the concept that information that had once been kept private should now be disseminated as widely as possible, but he was much more fearless in reporting the facts he discovered than previous kōdanshi had ever been.

The oral tradition, as it evolved by the late Edo period, is particularly evident at the end of *Contemporary Edo: An Album of One Hundred Monsters*. Bunkō has a list of five short, unedited pieces that appear to be the introductions to longer oral presentations.[22] The notes are characterized by short sentences divided into three or four phrases, each of which would be read aloud in approximately the space of one breath. These four short paragraphs mention four different people, all of whom Bunkō designates as "monsters" because they have somehow managed to deceive by their dishonesty an unsuspecting public.

In the first piece, one Kimura Sehei has managed to become an instructor of sumo wrestling, even though his eyesight is very poor. A cadence of an oral format, rather than a style of written literature, is apparent in the short text. As it has been translated in the appendix in full, one can easily imagine the kōdanshi announcing the phrases in short, poignant bursts, and by hitting his fan on the podium at the end of each phrase, could easily catch the attention of his audience and of those who might be walking by.[23] Bunkō refers to anyone who has cheated or deceived people, such as the sumo referee with "bad eyesight," as "one of

22. Baba, *Tōdai Edo hyaku bakemono*, 40–42.
23. Ibid., 41.

those monsters." Kimura had the reputation of throwing sumo matches to the contestant who offered the best bribe. This is how he was supporting himself and his extended "family." It is also why he had no need of a government stipend.[24] This short text is only an introduction or starting point from which a longer satirical presentation could develop.

Bunkō's reference here to Kimura Seihei's "bad eyesight" would immediately bring to mind an actual person, Kimura Kyobei, who did not only have bad eyesight, he was totally blind. His ability to deceive and defraud others is shown in one of Bunkō's other anecdotes, "The Illicit Affair of the Daughter of Honjō Yamato no kami."[25] Before looking more closely at this work, which will be discussed in chapter 9, there are three other very short introductions from which Bunkō could have begun oral presentations. They appear immediately after "Kimura Sehei, the sumo referee."

The second deceitful character or "monster" in the list of four that Bunkō speaks about is Kamiya Gorōbei, a commoner who does a successful business selling inferior paper products.[26] The third is Toshimaya Jūemon, a saké shop owner whose attempts at robbing his customers are apparently well known. The fourth note concerns one Tanbaya Gorōbei, who makes money hand over fist without doing much work. This last, which is more developed than the other three, introduces Murata Gobei, a merchant who does a good business at his saké shop in spite of his propensity to borrow exorbitant sums of money. This piece satirizes an attitude that came to be common among the samurai class in the eighteenth century: that it was better to borrow money and pay exorbitant interest charges than to be, or even appear to be, poor.

These four pieces are so short as to appear cryptic, remaining in the form of a kōdanshi's notes but ripe with possibilities for satirical development. The different degrees of development in these notes are important because they illustrate the process by which oral kōdan stories gradually evolved into the written literary forms of Edo-period sermonizing known as *dangibon*, which began to develop in the Shōtoku (1711–16) and Kyōhō periods and flourished in the Hōreki and Meiwa periods (1764–72).

24. Ibid., 41.
25. Baba, *Tōji chinsetsu yōhiroku*, 241–42.
26. Baba, *Tōdai Edo hyaku bakemono*, 41n17.

Bunkō's Literary Heritage in Dangibon

Bunkō's unique satirical style can be traced to a wide variety of Japanese literary traditions. The dangibon (satirical sermon) genre was a further development of kōshaku, and its influence is evident in many of Bunkō's anecdotes and tales. The most notable work of dangibon in Bunkō's time was Jōkanbō Kōa's *A Clumsy Sermon on the Present Age (Imayo heta dangi*, 1752), discussed above. This satirical sermon was written at the time the genre was beginning to reach the height of its popularity. Bunkō followed the dangibon style in its basic format and content, presenting colloquial, often humorous, examples of societal decadence in order to give moral instruction and to elicit a response of condemnation for the moral failures of the elite classes.

In Bunkō's "The Short Bow of Oguri Mataichi" in *Contemporary Edo: An Album of One Hundred Monsters*, the ghost of Oguri Mataichi, a hatamoto, rails against the moral dangers of gambling, warning that anyone who indulges in such a diversion will quickly fall victim to its addictive powers.[27] The story begins in the typical dangibon style by introducing the status, the origin, and the primary characteristic or talent of the protagonist. The conclusion, also written in the manner consistent with dangibon, offers a simple moral lesson.

The protagonist of the story, Oguri Mataichi, is a samurai who has a residence in the Honjo area of Edo. Skilled in the martial arts, particularly in the use of the short bow, he would frequently attend archery competitions around Edo, showing off his ability and teaching his art. However, he became acquainted with a beautiful prostitute called Oshun and met her every morning at the Utamato archery site in Ryōgoku, Yonezawa-chō. Consequently, he began to neglect his art. In fact, Mataichi became so infatuated with Oshun that he eventually abandoned the short bow altogether, and, as Bunkō reports, became a great "monster." The lesson Bunkō draws from Mataichi's moral fall is that becoming acquainted with a prostitute will bring about the destruction and the loss of the purpose of one's life. The anecdote is meant to be a warning for his readers.

27. Baba, *Tōdai Edo hyaku bakemono*, 33–34.

Bunkō goes on to develop the details of the circumstances that caused Mataichi's moral collapse. After Oshun died unexpectedly, Mataichi was so upset that he broke his short bow, which Oshun had given him, and threw his arrows away. The bow was the type called the "Yang bow" because in T'ang China the lover of Emperor Hsüan Tsung, Yang Kuei-fei, had such a bow. In addition to Mataichi, who abandoned the way of the samurai, Oshun, who led him astray, is also given the designation "monster."

Before his downfall, Mataichi had long been dedicated to his practice of swordsmanship (*kendō*), as well as archery. He had made his living teaching these skills to young samurai and wealthy commoners until the beautiful Oshun seduced him. After Oguri met her at the Utamato archery grounds, he became lazy and "did nothing from dawn to dusk." Samurai were, of course, officially forbidden by the bakufu to associate with the courtesans of the Yoshiwara, but that did not deter Mataichi. He frequented the quarter, seeing Oshun as often as possible until she died. After her death, Mataichi despaired of life and never returned to his former samurai devotion to the martial arts.

The purpose of this tale, a dangibon-like anecdote about the undoing of a samurai who falls in love, is to show the reader the kind of events that will lead up to a samurai becoming a "monster." He abandons everything that makes him a samurai, his weapons along with his virtue and honor, all marks of his status. The prostitute Oshun, a "monster" as well, was the reason the samurai lost his honor and gave up his pursuit of the martial arts. What Bunkō saw as the contemporary samurai surrender to immorality and vice is symbolized by Mataichi's falling in love with the prostitute and renouncing the symbols of samurai status.

Bunkō uses the character of Oguri Mataichi to represent an actual hatamoto, Oguri Nobuaki,[28] a famous archer and a contemporary of Bunkō. In addition to mocking the samurai, Bunkō is also satirizing the so-called Oguri School (*Oguri ryū*) of martial arts, one of the more popular martial arts academies of the period. The school's technique of combat, founded early in the seventeenth century by Nobuaki's ancestor, Oguri

28. Tajihi Ikuo, *Tōdai Edo hyaku bakemono*, 33n14.

Jin'emon Masanobu (1582–1661), was a style of training that first focused on Japanese swordsmanship and later expanded to instruction in other martial arts, eventually specializing in archery. The number of samurai who practiced the Oguri method during the Tokugawa period is reputed to have been over three thousand. Bunkō shows that the decline in samurai virtue was reflected in the increasingly fragile commitment of the school's samurai to the martial arts.

The influence of Chinese folktales and Chinese history, characteristic of the dangibon genre, is evident in this story. "Oshun had the heart of Yang Kuei-fei," the Chinese empress and legendary seductress. Oguri, of course, represents Emperor Hsüan Tsung, who was a failure as a statesman and disgraced himself because of his infatuation with Yang. In deep mourning at the time of her death, Emperor Hsüan was blamed for having demoralized the T'ang court and for having opened the way for the rebellion of An Lu-shan (703–57). The emperor was forced to abdicate in 755. Bunkō concludes that samurai are fickle and vacillating, lacking in moral fiber, and willing to abandon their virtue as quickly as their martial arts.

Bunkō's Literary Heritage in Setsuwa Bungaku

The fourteenth-century anecdotal narrative literature known as *setsuwa bungaku* (folktales) originated as oral stories that were subsequently put into written form. This genre included tales based on myths and legends as well as short anecdotes about ordinary life. A mixture of mythical stories from the past with contemporary gossip about actual people and rumor about current events, setsuwa bungaku is easily distinguishable from the more refined literary prose genres of the classical period. With its simplicity and popular appeal, what the *setsuwa* lacked in lyricism and elegance, it made up for in strength and directness. Commoners of the Edo period largely abandoned the elegant literary genres of earlier periods, such as the poem-tales (*utamonogatari*), which were characterized by their reliance on poetry to sustain the prose narrative. The *waka* poetry and diaries (*nikki bungaku*) of the Heian period were likewise of little interest to the urbanites of Edo in the eighteenth century. Bunkō's works, like setsuwa, relied on a wide variety of both fictional elements combined with real-life content. Informal chats and contemporary anecdotes, which were foundations of setsuwa literature, also characterized the simple, straightforward style of Bunkō's stories about famous people of his own day.

Contemporary Edo: An Album of One Hundred Monsters was Bunkō's most popular and most important collection of satirical anecdotes in the tradition of setsuwa bungaku. This collection is reminiscent of the style, content, and formation of the well-known setsuwa collection *Tales of Times Past* (*Konjaku monogatari shū*, twelfth century) of the late Heian period. Minamoto no Takakuni (1004–77), considered to be the principal editor of that collection, had gathered anecdotes and stories from various sources, including from people to whom he spoke, as well as from literary works. Though much of *Tales of Times Now Past* is comprised of Buddhist legends or based on stories from China or India, there are also secular pieces that deal with a variety of types of characters, ranging from high-ranking personages of aristocratic lineage to common criminals and even ghosts and monsters. This was precisely the subject matter of Bunkō's anecdotes in *Contemporary Edo: An Album of One Hundred Monsters*, and like some of the selections of *Tales of Times Now Past*, Bunkō's satires are humorous and gossipy. Fact and fiction are melded together in both collections and give the reader a glimpse into how popular culture was influenced by the politics of the respective periods.

Even after setsuwa bungaku came to be written down, it still contained the vestiges of its past oral tradition. The closing sentence of a number of the anecdotes in *Tales of Times Now Past*, "Thus it has been handed down" (*to nan katari tsutaeru to ya*), is evidence of the oral source of the tales. The word "*toka*" (and so forth) and the verb suffix of past recollection and admiration "*keri*" are further indications that the roots of the anecdotes are to be found in oral discourse. Elements of oral literature are clearly evident in Bunkō's written style as well. His sentences are composed of the type of short phrases and ellipses that were more common to the spoken language of eighteenth-century Edo than to any formal literary language. Also characteristic of the setsuwa are the additions that appear to have been inserted by a later editor. In particular, the one- or two-sentence didactic summaries that give a word of warning or a moral lesson and are often composed in an informal style are indications of such additions. The moral lessons that conclude the short stories in *Tales of Times Now Past* warn the reader of impending disaster, sometimes give instruction on how to avoid hell and attain salvation, or offer instruction on the importance of obeying the Buddhist law.[29] Bunkō's concluding remarks at the end of some of his essays, such as "Beware! This person is a monster," or "This man in particular must be a great fiend," or "This moral must be passed on to everyone," all have a didactic function similar to the short conclusions at the end of the anecdotes in *Tales of Times Now Past*.

Bunkō's Literary Heritage in Gesaku

The popular literature of the Tokugawa period (gesaku) is sometimes considered to be a superficial, even decadent form of literary expression that has little artistic value, at least compared to the great literary works of the Heian period. Literary critic Hashimoto Osamu (1948–), for example, has naively stated that "the townspeople [in early modern Japan] lived disconnected from any *ism*" to refer to a supposed ignorance or lack of interest in the politics of the period. His shortsighted comment that "the most important characteristic of commoner culture was the 'joke' (*jōdan*)" is indicative of his negative evaluation of the literature of the period.[30] If one overlooks the satirical element in gesaku, one might indeed come to a negative conclusion about its value, but one would also be denying the Edo reader the sophistication that he or she must have had in order to appreciate such works as *Contemporary Edo: An Album of One Hundred Monsters*. Likewise, if an historian were to describe the early modern culture only in ideological or intellectual terms and ignore the importance of gesaku as social and political commentary, he or she would, as a result, fail to grasp the subtleties of the popular culture and misunderstand the conventional view of the politics of the period.

A dismissive appraisal of the popular culture of early modern Japan developed as the country was "modernizing" during the Meiji period

29. Yamada Yoshio et al., eds., *Konjaku monogatari shū* (Tokyo: Iwanami shoten, 1977), 2: 85, 86, 158, 306.

30. Hashimoto Osamu, *Edo ni Furansu kakumei o*, 3 vols. (Tokyo: Chūō kōronsha), 1: 40.

(1868–1912) and Western literature was being imported and translated into Japanese. Japanese authors of the late nineteenth and early twentieth centuries were studying the literary masterpieces of the West and writing in styles and genres that were modeled on Western fiction. The view of Western literature as modern and praiseworthy and Edo-period gesaku as old and decadent has persisted until today. This dismissive assessment of Edo-period literature has been in large measure due to a misunderstanding of the function and purpose of literature in the Edo era. Contrary to common assumption, gesaku was not only for entertainment. As the popular writings of Baba Bunkō clearly demonstrate, gesaku came to be an expression of dissent and a method of venting frustration with the Tokugawa government and the ruling elite. Bunkō retained the characteristics of entertainment contained in gesaku, but he made notable contributions to popular literature's political and social significance by incorporating contemporary history and biography into his satire.

From the mid-1700s to the fall of the shogunate in 1867, there was never a sustained revival of the government's political influence, in spite of the bakufu's attempts to impose various reforms. The gradual political decline continued for over a hundred years until the bakufu's eventual fall. It was not gesaku that was a dormant or exhausted literary genre; it was rather the Tokugawa regime and its ideology that were slowly decaying. Baba Bunkō stood squarely within the literary tradition of gesaku and used its conventions to create a literature of dissent that not only showed contempt for the Tokugawa authorities, but also openly attacked Tokugawa ideological orthodoxy.

Wolfgang Schamoni at the University of Heidelberg has argued that Hiraga Gennai (1728–80) is the founding father of the gesaku tradition and that writings before him should not be classified as gesaku.[31] It is certainly true that it was Gennai who first coined the term "gesaku" in 1770 (long after Bunkō) and used it to refer to his puppet play *The Miracle at Yaguchi Ferry* (*Shinrei yaguchi no watashi*). However, Schamoni's argument that Gennai was the first writer of gesaku cannot stand in light of the fact that Masaho Nokoguchi's *A Comprehensive Mirror on the Way of*

31. Itasaka, *Kodansha Encyclopedia of Japan*, 3: 28–29.

Love (*Endō tsūgan*) was written in 1715, long before Gennai coined the term "gesaku," but it has nonetheless long been considered a work of the gesaku genre, since it is a collection of lectures interspersed with amusing anecdotes about the "pleasure" districts. It is quite legitimate then to consider Baba Bunkō a writer of gesaku as well on the basis of the characteristics of his style and the content of his writings, even though he also wrote before Gennai. What is more, if gesaku is viewed as a form of satirical writing, Baba Bunkō must certainly be considered a writer in that tradition, and perhaps an even more important writer of gesaku than the much more widely known Hiraga Gennai.

The renowned Japanese critic of Edo literature Nakamura Yukihiko (1911–98), while affirming Gennai's place as a writer of gesaku, actually questions his importance as a satirist and even argues that his work is not really satire at all. He makes this surprising evaluation for two reasons: First of all, Gennai hid his satire, an important element of Tokugawa-period gesaku, behind a laborious grammatical style and a thick screen of oblique metaphors; and secondly, it is doubtful that Gennai actually experienced any kind of passionate conflict within himself which, Nakamura insists, is a prerequisite for the kind of satirical expression that is characteristic of gesaku.[32]

In his satirical work *The Dashing Life of Shidōken* (*Fūryū Shidōken den*, 1763), for example, Gennai writes that three retainers of Minamoto no Yoritomo (1147–99)—Wada Yoshimori (1147–1213), Sasaki Takatsuna (d. 1214) and Chiba Tsunetane (1118–1201)—did nothing to advance themselves or cultivate their literary or military skills after their victory over the Heike. Instead, they went to the theater and engaged in other frivolous pursuits. Gennai's intention was to use these three Kamakura-period warriors as representations for two shogunal officials of his own day, Matsudaira Munenobu (1729–82), the daimyō of Matsue, and Mizoguchi Naoatsu (1714–80), the daimyō of Shibata, both of whom claimed descent from these three illustrious Genji warriors.[33] By setting the context of his satire in the Kamakura period (1185–1333), Gennai gave himself an important safety valve. In the opinion of critic Masuda Osamu (1927–2004), a

32. Nakamura Yukihiko, *Kinsei sakka kenkyū* (Tokyo: Shobō, 1961), 187.
33. Ibid., 168.

work should be evaluated as a gesaku composition only if it is being used effectively as a political force or social "weapon" against a particular person or group, but Gennai's satire had little such effect on the contemporary society.[34] Gennai's prose was successful for questioning the popular belief that the samurai were inherently intelligent and moral, but it failed to raise effective criticism against the specific individuals that he wished to target.

Literature in the first half of the eighteenth century reveals the significant place that popular gesaku played long before Gennai in providing a platform for dissent. Gesaku was already transformed from being "playful literature" (a common but inaccurate translation for the word "gesaku") into a political and social force long before Gennai. The townspeople's discontent with political officials was articulated with minimal success by Hiraga Gennai, perhaps in part because he was a samurai himself. One conclusion that might come from this comparison of Baba Bunkō and Hiraga Gennai as gesaku authors might be that Bunkō's gesaku was political satire for the masses while Gennai's satirical writings were entertaining tracts for the elite.

Gennai's satire *The Legend of the Tengu's Skull* (*Tengu sharekōbe mekiki engi*, 1778), for example, was intended to be a criticism of the commoner class and of the superstitions and false beliefs that commoners held.[35] Gennai's work was written in a ponderous, highly literary style with parallelisms more typical of classical Chinese than the colloquial language of the common people. His allegory ridicules the gullibility and foolishness of samurai but does not specify anyone in particular. As *The Legend of the Tengu's Skull* opens, several young samurai are trying to identify a strange round object that one of them has found. One says the object is probably the head of a large bird, another that it is perhaps the skull of a monster fish. The person who found it suggests that it must be the skull of a *tengu* (mountain goblin). No one is able to identify the object with certainty, but everyone agrees that it is the work of the "evil spirits of the mountains and the sea" (*chimi mōryō*).

Gennai ridicules the superstitious foolishness of the young samurai, claiming that it is more typical of commoners than samurai. However,

34. Matsuda Osamu, *Edo itan bungaku nōto*, 190.
35. Irita Seizō, ed., *Hiraga Gennai zenshū* (Tokyo: Ogihara seibunkan, 1935), 1: 378–89.

in this case it is the blindness of the samurai that prevents them from discerning the simple, obvious explanation that the object is man-made, something constructed as a practical joke by someone who wanted to fool them. Unlike the satires of Bunkō, however, there are no actual names, dates, or places mentioned. Thus, Gennai does not give his reader the opportunity to identify the characters of satire with actual people.

Bunkō, on the other hand, was a master at the use of the gesaku technique of creating satirical meaning by comparing and contrasting two or more totally different persons or situations. This is the early modern literary device known as mitate, discussed below, which presents a surprising or shocking visual contrast. His contrast between City Magistrate Tsuchiya Masasuke and his predecessor in office Ōoka Tadasuke, for example, had clear political and social implications.

Some modern printed versions of Bunkō's *Contemporary Edo: An Album of One Hundred Monsters* can easily give the reader the false impression that Bunkō's works are completely different from traditional gesaku. The use of *katakana* and Chinese characters in modern printed editions gives the appearance of a formal document that is to be read with the Sino-Japanese pronunciation (*kanbun yomikudashi*) of words rather than in the colloquial language of the period. In contrast to the printed editions, however, extant manuscripts of this work that were printed from woodblocks are written with very fine, flowing *hiragana* characters in a hand similar to the characters in the gesaku subgenre known as "tales of the floating world" (*ukiyozōshi*). These booklets, which were portrayals of the exploits of young men in the "pleasure" districts, were in vogue during the one-hundred-year period between the publication of Ihara Saikaku's *The Life of an Amorous Man* (*Kōshoku ichidai otoko*) in 1683 and Fukugūken Asei's novel *Self-satisfaction in the Various Arts* (*Shogei hitori jiman*) in 1783. Bunkō took advantage of the ukiyozōshi literary style by mixing popular informal colloquial expressions with formal three-character and four-character Chinese compounds. This created a comical literary duality: a mixture of the formal and the informal, the high and the low, the classical and the contemporary in language, form, and content.[36]

36. Sumie Jones, "Language in Crisis: Ogyū Sorai's Philological Thought and Hiraga Gennai's Creative Practice," in *Principles of Classical Japanese Literature*, ed. Earl Miner (Princeton: Princeton University Press, 1985), 244–45.

Bunkō's Literary Legacy in Kabuki and Kyōgen Drama

Emura Shōsuke (dates unknown) was a stagehand at Ichimura Hanzaemon's theater in Osaka in the 1750s. He had become a successful moneylender and acquired a considerable fortune. Shōsuke was not only popular among the Osaka theatergoers for his skill in the construction of stage sets and scenery, he was also a devout Buddhist. Bunkō takes him to task, revealing Shōsuke's dark side, which few people knew anything about. In an anecdote in *Contemporary Discussions of Worldly Affairs in Musashi*, Bunkō describes Shōsuke's cruelty to his poor mother:

> Shōsuke is such a great believer in the Nichiren [Buddhist] sect . . . that people call him the "Honorable Saint." But for all that, his own mother, who works as a cleaning woman, lives in a tiny rear tenement in Matsushima-chō with her younger sister and younger brother. It's a place unfit for human habitation. They do not even know whether there will be enough food for them to eat or anything for them to wear. What could be more cruel than a son allowing this to happen to his mother![37]

Bunkō reports that Shōsuke was actually quite wealthy and perfectly able to take care of his mother, but he was a hypocrite whose external behavior gave people the impression that he was a "saint." Few saw him as he really was: a "monster," whose sense of morality was perverted and not at all saintly. Bunkō could write about Emura Shōsuke from his own personal observations because Bunkō also was a resident of Matsushima-chō. They lived in the same neighborhood.

Bunkō's interest in drama was not limited to the stagehands and actors of the kabuki theater. He uses the characterization and plots of well-known kabuki and kyōgen (comic drama) plays to intensify the impact of his satire. The kyōgen play *The Female Narukami* (*Onna Narukami*, 1743), for example, which contains elements of paradox and dramatic character reversals, provided Bunkō with the foundation for his own version of the same story, which he titled "The Case of the Narukami Nun" (*Narukami bikuni no ben*, 1758) in *Contemporary Edo: An Album of One Hundred Monsters*.[38] Many of Bunkō's readers would have been familiar with *The*

37. Baba, *Tōsei Buya zokudan*, 373–74.
38. Baba, *Tōdai Edo hyaku bakemono*, 15–16. This kyōgen was first performed in 1696.12 at

Female Narukami and also with the original production on which it was based, known simply as *Narukami*, first performed in 1696.[39]

The original 1696 kabuki drama is the story of the pious monk Narukami, who is actually a demon in disguise. Out of pure maliciousness, Narukami has plunged all of Japan into a terrible drought by holding the Dragon-god captive in his cave in the mountains, preventing it from flying to the sky to form rain clouds with its breath and bringing the needed rain. In order to save the farmers from the drought, the emperor dispatches Princess Taema to Narukami's mountain retreat. The emperor instructs her to pretend to fall in love with Narukami, seduce him, and then release the Dragon-god from his captivity. She makes the journey to the monk's cave as commanded. Narukami is successfully drawn into the princess' embrace and finds himself unable to resist her seduction. After he has given himself over to sexual pleasure, Narukami falls fast asleep, providing the opportunity for the princess to go to the chamber where the Dragon-god is kept captive. She cuts the cords that bind the creature and frees him from confinement. The Dragon-god returns to his place in the sky, forms clouds with his breath, and rain soon begins to fall again. The farmers' crops are saved, and Princess Taema returns to the emperor.

On awakening from his sleep, Narukami sees what has happened. His plan to keep the country forever in drought has been thwarted. He screams out in rage and curses the princess for her trickery. His anger is so intense that his real form is exposed. He stands before the audience, no longer as a monk but in his true manifestation as a horrible demon.

The later kyōgen play of 1743, titled *Onna Narukami*, maintains the same plot, but the gender roles are reversed. Instead of a monk being seduced by a princess, it is a nun, a female Narukami, who is seduced by an imperial prince, Kumo no Taemanosuke. (The suffix "suke," which indicates the name of a male, is added to "Taema," the name of the princess in the earlier version of the play.) After falling in love with Taemanosuke and being seduced by him, the nun Narukami falls asleep. The Dragon

---

the Nakamuraza theater. The 1743 play was titled "*Onna Narukami omoi no takitsuse*," written by Tsuuchi Kuheiji (dates unknown) and first performed at Ichimuraza theater.

39. "Narukami" is one of the "Eighteen Favorites," written by Ichikawa Danjirō I (1660–1704).

escapes. The enraged nun reveals her true identity, which had previously been hidden behind the appearance of a saintly Buddhist nun, and appears on the stage in the form of a terrible she-demon.

In Bunkō's version, the Narukami nun, as the reader might now suspect, is not simply a fictional character.[40] Bunkō explains that she is a real woman, the widow of Kanemaki Genjun, a samurai-pediatrician who had a practice in Tachibana-chō (in present-day Sumida-ku, Tokyo). Bunkō uncovers her real identity and exposes her to be a "monster" and a "demon," just like the male and female Narukami characters in the kyōgen and kabuki plays. Bunkō describes in detail the character and the behavior of Lady Kanemaki. She is a highly placed person, a member of the elite, who has long been admired and respected in her community. However, the truth is she is actually a hypocritical woman whose virtue is little more than a sham. Like the monk Narukami and the nun Narukami in the plays, Lady Kanemaki is admired for her ostensible holiness, but Bunkō exposes her for what she really is: a horrifying demon.

Even while her husband was still alive, Lady Kanemaki had affairs with other men on numerous occasions. After her husband's death, she professed her desire to become a Buddhist nun; and to show everyone her sincerity, she did not simply shave her head as was customary: she pulled her hair out by the roots. Hearing that she had done this in order to defend her chastity, everyone praised her for her outstanding virtue. However, as Bunkō points out, she was a "monstrous fraud." In reality, she was a woman of easy virtue and spent much of her time going alone to the theater in the pursuit of illicit affairs. Her exploits at the theater involved a liaison with the famous actor Segawa Kikunojō II, also known as Rokō (1741–73).[41] Whenever she went to the theater, Bunkō reports, she was attractively dressed as a nun, wearing a black kimono and black obi sash. Inside, however, she was filled with lustful desire for Segawa.

The kabuki actor was not her only love interest. She had an ongoing illicit love affair "with an unknown man of low class." Wanting only to

40. Baba, *Tōdai Edo hyaku bakemono*, 15.

41. Kikunojō II took the stage name Rokō in 1756. Kikunojō I (1693–1749) had also been famous for performing "Onna Narukami" roles.

give a good impression and to show herself off as an admirable woman, she did the best she could to present herself as a holy nun. As part of her ruse, she made pilgrimages to various shrines and temples. She often visited the three prominent Buddhist holy places: Asakusa Emma Hall, Kayadera, and the stone image of the Bodhisattva Manjusri, where she was seen listening to sermons and hearing edifying stories preached by the monks. Bunkō concludes that in appearance, she shows herself to be on the Buddhist path and apparently lives according to the Buddhist law. However, he says, when it comes to licentiousness, this "monster" has no equal.

When Lady Kanemaki promised on the death of her husband to shave her head as a sign of her intention to become a Buddhist nun, she gave her word that she would never again marry, as a pledge of eternal marital fidelity to her deceased spouse. There was no reason for anyone to doubt that her sole motivation for entering religion was to protect her virtue. Lady Kanemaki followed through with her promise, and pulling out her hair made her action even more convincing.

Bunkō noted that nearly everyone considered her to be a saint, though some thought that pulling out her hair at the roots was probably due to her impulsiveness. In the eyes of most people, however, she had always shown herself to be a devoted wife while her husband was alive, and now she was proving herself to be a model of Buddhist devotion. This was the general impression, but Bunkō exposes the shocking truth that Lady Kanemaki had been having the affair with the seventeen-year-old Segawa Kikunojō II, even while her husband was still alive. Ironically, Segawa was the onnagata who had played the role of the nun in the kyōgen play *Onna Narukami*. Using Segawa's stage name, Bunkō calls Lady Kanemaki "Rokō's nun." The plot of the drama was being played out in real life, Kikunojō in the role of Prince Taemanosuke and Lady Kanemaki as the demon-nun.

The Tokugawa law code obligated members of the samurai class to avoid the kabuki theater, as well as the Yoshiwara and other "pleasure" districts.[42] They were expected to keep themselves pure and free

42. Wm. Theodore de Bary, *Sources of Japanese Tradition*, 336.

from the corruption of the commoner class, but it was all a hypocritical charade. Many samurai would disguise themselves as commoners, hide their identity under large wide-brimmed hats, and enter the Yoshiwara. Members of the elite class who frequented the quarter incognito were much like Lady Kanemaki, who identified herself with the actors and the characters of the kabuki stage, trying to imitate the lovers and heroes of the theater. In Bunkō's view, these samurai were "monsters," just like Lady Kanemaki.

In his tale of the demon-widow, Bunkō again availed himself of the favorite gesaku literary convention known as mitate. The use of an incongruous comparison or contrast between what is true and what only appears to be true suited Bunkō perfectly in his description of the contrast between what Lady Kanemaki appeared to be and what she really was. Her hypocrisy is displaced by reality to reveal a shocking truth. In "The Case of the Narukami Nun" religious devotion evaporates and is displaced by the revelation of Lady Kanemaki's past and present love affairs. Faithfulness is displaced by infidelity; nice impressions shift and are proven to be false.

While she was married, Bunkō informs the reader, Lady Kanemaki had everyone fooled by going to a number of shrines and temples every single day to hear sermons and edifying stories. Actually, her motivation for going to these holy places was not to pray or be instructed. As Bunkō explains, she made her visit to the temples "with the intention of shamelessly committing adultery with licentious men." Bunkō is quite aware that the three popular pilgrimage sites, Asakusa Emma Hall, Kayadera, and the shrine of Manjusri, were considered to be among the most sacred places for Buddhist devotion in Edo. This makes the widow's story even more scandalous. By her infidelity she transforms these holy sites into three more Edo brothels. It is again through the use of the literary technique of mitate, displacing lovely appearance with stark and shocking reality, that Bunkō is able to establish a correlation between Buddhist temple and brothel and suggest that in Edo the sacred and the profane have become indistinguishable.

The literary convention of mitate might also be defined as an association of persons or places that, under normal circumstances, would have nothing in common—in this case, a "faithful" wife, a kabuki actor, a nun, a demon, a Buddhist temple, and a Yoshiwara brothel. Thus, Bunkō has used mitate to displace or dislodge common perceptions and favorable opinions. The "virtuous" are displaced from their high status, and a scandalous reality has been exposed. Mitate allows the author to direct the reader's attention to such a seemingly unbelievable revelation. It is an asymmetric association that would not be so readily obvious unless the reader were familiar with the plots of the plays on which Bunkō has based this satire. The comparison created between "Buddhist nun" and "demon," a masterful use of mitate, is only one expression of Bunkō's fundamental assertion that, along with politicians, government officials, scholars, artists, and even shoguns, Buddhist monks and nuns may appear to be respectable but are actually "monsters."

There are many other examples in Bunkō's works of the use of such paradoxical associations that reveal the hidden hypocrisy rampant in society. In "The Case of the Villainous Haikai Master" in *Contemporary Edo: An Album of One Hundred Monsters*, Bunkō reveals that the well-known and highly reputed teacher of haikai, Yūrin (flourished from 1752 to 1756), plagiarized the verses of other poets and sold them as his own compositions to wealthy connoisseurs of poetry.[43] Among his customers was the famous master of kabuki stage effects, Ōtani Hiroji (1717–57). Bunkō observes that Yūrin "looked like a Bodhisattva on the outside," but "deep down he was a demon" who made his living deceiving people. He was a respected member of the elite whose plagiarism went undetected for years until finally his deceptions were exposed and shame was brought on the art and profession of haikai poetry.

Yūrin used his ill-gotten gains to frequent the kabuki theater and the Yoshiwara "pleasure" district. For a time he had been intimate with the courtesan Tōryō of the Omiya Inn so that he could take advantage of her kindness. One day he asked to borrow several of her heirloom kimonos and then used them to dress his favorite low-class prostitute in style and accompany her to the festival at the Hikawa Shrine. Instead of returning the borrowed garments to Tōryō, however, Yūrin sold them after the fes-

43. Baba, *Tōdai Edo hyaku bakemono*, 18.

tival and pocketed a sizable profit. He told Tōryō that prostitutes had stolen the kimonos, and he could not be responsible for her loss. It was not uncommon, Bunkō suggested, for Yūrin to ingratiate himself with high-class courtesans, pledge his fidelity, and then betray them to satisfy his own particular preferences for common street walkers. Yūrin was known to spend his time with prostitutes rather than with the courtesans of the elegant Yoshiwara establishments, not because he found the cheap prostitutes more of a bargain for his money, but because he was no match for the courtesans' intellectual conversation, nor was he capable of appreciating their artistic achievements.

The incongruous association between Yūrin's supposed love of beautiful poetry, for which he was admired, and his deviant side, of which few people were aware, is another example of mitate. Bunkō concludes his anecdote, putting Yūrin in his list of the "monsters" of Edo: "Just imagine! Behavior like this in a man thought to be a refined poetry master.... Isn't it true that on the outside he looks like a Bodhisattva, but inside he is a demon?"

The satirical pieces analyzed above, "Otsuna at the Tsu no Kuniya Inn," "The Valor of Tanaka Kyūguemon and His Self-Sacrifice," "The Short Bow of Oguri Mataichi," "The Case of the Narukami Nun," and "The Case of the Villainous Haikai Master," were all composed within the literary traditions and with the popular conventions that were characteristic of various genres of early modern literature. At the same time these works were biographical accounts of prominent individuals. Fiction is used to serve historical fact. The profane and the sacred, which at first might appear to be quite different, are shown to be analogous in the world of Tokugawa society.

The Bordello and the Shogunate

A final example that best illustrates Bunkō's use of mitate or incongruous associations is his satire in *Contemporary Edo: An Album of One Hundred Monsters* titled "The Case of Hanabusa Itchō" (*Hanabusa Itchō no ben*, 1758).[44] His subject is the famous and well-respected artist Hana-

44. Baba, *Tōdai Edo hyaku bakemono*, 36–37.

busa, who was commissioned by the proprietor of the Tomoeya bordello in Yoshiwara to paint two portraits in the ornate Momoyama style. The subjects of his paintings are the two most beautiful female characters in the classical military epic *Tale of the Soga Brothers* (*Soga monogatari*, fourteenth century): the glamorous courtesan Tora Gozen, the mistress of Jūro (Sukenari, 1172–93), one of two brothers who are on a journey to avenge the murder of their father, and Keiwazaka Shōshō, a lovely shamaness and prostitute who accompanies Jūrō and his brother Gorō (Tokimune, 1174–93). The proprietor of the bordello hopes to hang the portraits at the entrance of his establishment for the pleasure of the clients.

Unfortunately, Hanabusa misunderstands the instructions of the bordello owner because of a confusion of homonyms in Japanese and mistakenly thinks that the owner has directed him to paint a tiger (*tora*) in a bamboo grove rather than the courtesan, whose name is Tora; and instead of a portrait of the shamaness, Keiwazaka Shōshō, Hanabusa understands that he is to paint a lovely scene of the Xiao River and the Xiang River (in Hunan province China). ("Xiao-Xiang" is read "Shōshō" in Japanese.) Consequently, instead of doing the portraits of the beautiful courtesans for which he had been commissioned, Hanabusa presents two completely different paintings to the proprietor: one of a tiger and the other of the two rivers.

A comic situation created by such confusion and misunderstanding was a standard convention in early modern popular literature. Bunkō uses it here not only for humorous effect but as a powerful condemnation of Buddhism, the bakufu, and the shogun, along with compliments for the women of the Yoshiwara district. Unlike the characters of gesaku, Bunkō's protagonist is not a fictional character but a real person. When Hanabusa arrives to display his paintings of a tiger and the Xiao and Xiang rivers, the courtesans of the Tomoeya brothel mock and jeer at him. Bunkō writes, "All the courtesans of Yoshiwara died of laughter over Hanabusa's foolishness and ignorance."

After exposing Hanabusa's idiocy, Bunkō abruptly shifts his focus in the anecdote to the current shogun, Tokugawa Ieshige, who has also commissioned Hanabusa to do a painting, intending to present it as a gift to the Nishi Honganji Temple. This was a very important temple for the bakufu, having been established by Tokugawa Ieyasu in 1602, and through the patronage of the shoguns it had become the principal Buddhist temple of the True Pure Land Sect in Kyoto. It was already beautifully decorated by artists of the Kanō school with the gold inlay and bright colors of the Momoyama period (c. 1568–1603), and Ieshige wanted to donate a painting in the same style in honor of his illustrious predecessor, Tokugawa Ieyasu. Bunkō informs the reader that Ieshige, however, does not understand what a Momoyama period painting is. He has simply heard that Hanabusa was trained in this style and that he was a master of the technique. Because of his lack of knowledge of the term "Momoyama," the shogun requests instead a portrait of Momotarō (the Peach Boy), the young hero of the children's folktale that was having a revival in popularity in the 1750s. The comical identification of Momoyama and Momotarō is meant to be more than humorous. It is biting sarcasm and an insult directed at Tokugawa Ieshige that exposes his appalling ignorance.

The reader familiar with the literary device of mitate will immediately see the contrasting parallel between the two persons who commissioned Hanabusa to do paintings. The first was the owner of the Tomoeya bordello, followed by the Tokugawa shogun, Ieshige. Another incongruous parallel is made between the Tomoeya bordello and the Nishi Honganji Temple. A third use of mitate is the comparison made between the epic classical tale *Soga monogatari* and the boy hero of the simple children's folktale *Momotarō*.

These outrageous and even scandalous comparisons between a bordello operator and the shogun makes the brothel keeper, who requests paintings from classical literature, appear to be more cultured and educated than the shogun, who requests, out of ignorance, a painting of a character from a children's storybook. What is more shocking is that Bunkō associates the Tomoeya, a thriving house of prostitution, with a religious institution—the Nishi Honganji Buddhist temple. The appallingly incongruous connections that are drawn between temple and bordello, pimp and shogun, classical literature and a simple children's story are masterful examples of satirical style and the use of mitate. The result of these various juxtapositions is a combined satirical attack on the Buddhist establishment, represented by the Nishi Honganji, and the bakufu, represented by Shogun Tokugawa Ieshige. The Tomoeya bordello, along with its courtesans and proprietor, emerge unscathed.

Conclusion

As observed above, Western literature is often categorized in terms of fiction and nonfiction. Fiction is imaginative, and nonfiction is presumed to contain literal, objective, or scientific truth.[45] Even in the genres of "historical fiction" or "alternate history," it is presumed that the author and informed reader know what data are historical and what are the imaginary creation of the author. This Western distinction between fiction and history, though useful for categorizing, was shown in the introductory chapter of this book to be a false distinction. In Edo-period popular literature there are a variety of genres, but the difference between fiction and nonfiction was never clearly distinguished. In the 1870s Nishi Amane (1829–97) used the word *bungaku* to translate the European word "literature," but it was not until 1885 when Tsubouchi Shōyō (1859–1935) made an effort to define the meaning of fictional literature in *The Essence of the Novel* (*Shōsetsu shinzui*) that the Japanese became explicitly aware of a strict division between fiction and nonfiction.[46]

The modern Western reader who is familiar with the cultural peculiarities of early modern Japan and its literature is comfortable with reading the satirical essays of Baba Bunkō as both history and fiction, without having to make a clear distinction between the two. This way of reading and understanding the fictional and historical elements in Bunkō's writings is really no different from the manner in which we should understand satire as well as any so-called historical text. Attention to historical and biographical detail and fictional literary elements can be, and often are, combined in a single, coherent text. This is what Baba Bunkō has successfully done. His designation of contemporary political figures as "monsters," for example, is typical of the hyperbole that would not be found in modern historical narrative, but that is not to say that his satire

45. Haruo Shirane and Tomi Suzuki, eds., *Inverting the Classics: Modernity, National Identity, and Japanese Literature* (Stanford: Stanford University Press, 2000), 251n8.

46. Ibid., 252n9.

should not be considered authentic history. Bunkō's anecdotes and essays are documented, factual reports but, as the reader has seen, also bear the characteristics of the various genres of contemporary popular literature.

The combination of simplicity and straightforwardness makes Bunkō's writing style appear less refined than the works of the many philosophical writers and historians of the period and not quite as polished as some of the more renowned writers, such as novelist Ihara Saikaku or playwright Chikamatsu Monzaemon. The simplicity and frankness of Bunkō's writing are not only due to its origin in oral performance but are also the result of his determination not to sacrifice historical fact for literary polish. Bunkō's writings, such as *Contemporary Edo: An Album of One Hundred Monsters* (in the appendix), are best analyzed and understood only if read as both history and literature, without trying to make the modern Western distinction between "fact" and "fiction."

8 | KABUKI ACTORS, MONKS, AND COURTESANS

I find there [in Yoshiwara] so many kind hearts, and I have discovered that even the women people call "trashy whores" are in a true sense the really authentic high-class courtesans.

BABA BUNKŌ, 1756

Liaisons at the Kabuki Theater

The propensity of not a few samurai to become romantically involved with a male onnagata actor or with a courtesan of one of the "pleasure" districts did not go unnoticed. Bunkō speculates that their illicit liaisons was one reason that so many samurai were no longer proficient in the traditional martial arts or took any interest in scholarly pursuits. What was worse, many were completely unconcerned about leading a life of virtue. The visits of samurai, and even daimyō, to the kabuki theater and the scandalous manner in which they conducted themselves while there are highlighted in Bunkō's story in *Contemporary Edo: An Album of One Hundred Monsters* titled "The Monster Who Switched from Being a Lover of Young Boys to Loving Women" (*Shūdō henjite jodō no bakemono*, 1758).[1] This anecdote is a satire on the Tokugawa government's hypocritical condemnation of prostitution and of the theater.

Epigraph is from Baba, *Tōsei Buya zokudan*, 403.
1. Baba, *Tōdai Edo hyaku bakemono*, 7–8.

The "monster" here is Mizoguchi Naoatsu (1714–80), a government official and the holder of an aristocratic court title.[2] He is the daimyō of Shibata in Echigo, so Bunkō refers to him as Shibata Baikō, since he was the head of a well-established family that had resided in Shibata since 1598. The Shibata domain had never completely recovered from the results of a devastating earthquake that had occurred in 1687. The rebuilding of the domainal castle alone, which started the year following the earthquake, lasted until 1704, a period of sixteen years. By 1715 the domain was still in serious financial difficulty. In 1719 a fire destroyed part of the newly rebuilt castle, and 837 dwellings were razed. The second rebuilding of the domainal castle prolonged the financial crisis. Continual crop failures, the result of year after year of overly wet weather, prevented Shibata from ever enjoying full recovery from the 1687 earthquake. Insolvency was not unusual among the daimyō, most of whose domains suffered periodically from earthquakes and fires, but Mizoguchi not only had to spend large sums of money on the obligatory alternate-year attendance (*sankin kōtai*) in Edo, he was also indebted to a number of wealthy merchants. Surprisingly, however, these financial burdens did not seem to be a major concern for Mizoguchi Naoatsu.

In spite of the poor prospects for the economic viability of his domain, Mizoguchi freely spent his money on the sexual favors of the kabuki actor Segawa Kikunojō I (1693–1749). Kikunojō was a beautiful female impersonator of the kabuki theater and was trained in the acting traditions and according to the directives of Yoshizawa Ayame (1672–1725), the famous Genroku-period onnagata. Ayame believed that since it was very difficult for a man to simulate a courtesan's innocent loveliness and guileless grace, he must practice the courtesan's role constantly, even when he was not on stage.[3] This was precisely what Kikunojō did. His constant imitation of the manners and gestures of a courtesan attracted Mizoguchi and allowed the kabuki actor to ensnare him in a virtually inescapable relationship.

Shibata Baikō had always been fond of young boys, and ever since Segawa was a youth he was completely infatuated with him. He would also go from time to time to the house of Segawa Sengyo, Kikunojō's

2. Mizoguchi held the aristocratic title of Junior Fifth Rank, Lower Grade (*jugoige*), from 1723.

3. Cecilia Segawa Seigle, *Yoshiwara: The Glittering World of the Japanese Courtesan* (Honolulu: University of Hawaii Press, 1993), 106.

younger brother (1715–56), where Baikō gave sumptuous banquets and funded other kinds of pleasurable diversions. Baikō showered his favors on both brothers and spent a great deal of money sponsoring various ceremonies, including coming-of-age ceremonies and the name-changing ceremonies at the kabuki theater, which were very expensive affairs.

Baikō's fiscal irresponsibility and his support of Kikunojō are the primary focus of this satire. Secondary points of interest are the many samurai who, penniless as they were, availed themselves of expensive diversions offered at the kabuki theater and the Yoshiwara. When Bunkō calls attention to Shibata Baikō's sexual involvement with kabuki actors, he is taking a dangerous political position, given the interest of many powerful officials in the theater. But Bunkō's satire is not limited to the theater. He criticizes Baikō for the disastrous economic situation in his domain, which never improved, not only because of the daimyō's engagement in diversions at the theater and his financial support for Kikunojō and his brother, but also because of his fiscal policies. His extravagance led to the imposition of an exorbitant tax burden on the peasant population. Bunkō concludes his satire asserting that Baikō, who spends most of his time with the most popular kabuki actor of the day, is really no better than an entertainer himself, regardless of his high samurai status and his court title. Bunkō's intention is to draw attention to the hypocrisy of the Tokugawa government in its tolerance of Baikō's behavior, particularly of his intimacy with Kikunojō, while at the same time expressing its public disapproval of samurai patronage of the kabuki theater.

Bunkō was of the opinion that Segawa Kikunojō was as much of a hypocrite as Baikō himself. In the year before his death (1748), Kikunojō had become completely fixated on doing all he could to remain forever beautiful in the eyes of his adoring public. As he aged, he had never wanted anyone to see him without his make-up, but in the last year of his life this obsession became an irrational fear. One of the haikai verses that the actor wrote is indicative of his terror that he would be seen either in the morning before he had put his make-up on or at night after he had taken it off: "Neither my rising nor my retiring: I will not let anyone know."[4]

4. "*Waga okifushi o hito ni shirarena*," in *Nihon engeki zenshi*, ed. Kawatake Shigetoshi (Tokyo: Iwanami shoten, 1959), 548.

Shibata Baikō would also make up his face, not simply to look younger but to disguise himself in preparation for his excursions to the theater district to meet Kikunojō. Bunkō writes that these two were of the same ilk and makes reference to a satirical haikai to describe Baikō's behavior. "Among all the fools in Edo there is this one called Shibata Baikō. This little ditty," Bunkō continues, "fits him perfectly: 'White face powder thrown on the fire; look at that fool's face.'[5] I would say it refers to those, like Baikō, who often powder their faces and go out in search of erotic exploits."

The word "fire" in Edo popular verse meant "passionate love," and so "powder thrown on the fire" refers to the purpose for putting on face powder in the first place—to anticipate passionate love. In other words, Baikō powdered his face in order to be ready for lovemaking. The powder also served as the disguise that allowed him to get backstage after performances, so that he could meet Kikunojō for whom he was "on fire" with passion. Bunkō adds another verse to describe the tragicomedy of their liaison: "His face powder, which should be white, is burnt black in the fire." By referring to the Baikō's face powder, which did not remain white, Bunkō is alluding to the failure and shame this daimyō would eventually have to endure. Shibata Baikō's affair with the kabuki onnagata ends unhappily. When he is finally jilted and sees that his plans to win Kikunojō's love backfire, his face powder only makes him look foolish. The metaphor of white face powder burnt black also conveys Baikō's "loss of face" because of the economic disasters that his lifestyle has caused, in addition to his rejection at the hands of his beloved Kikunojō.

After Segawa Kikunojō passed away, Baikō focused his total attention on the much younger Kikunojō II. He attended Kikunojō II's onnagata performance, playing the role of Koshizuka in the drama *Warrior Woman's Return to Yashima Camp* (*Onna musha kaijin Yashima*), in the eleventh month of 1757, and afterwards sent him an end-of-year gift of one hundred ryō. The next day the sixteen-year-old actor went to Baikō's domainal mansion in Misaki-chō (in present-day Chiyoda-ku, Tokyo) to express his thanks. The daimyō greeted him personally saying, "You must

5. *Hi ni kubaru hakufun mita ka baka no kao.* Bunkō applies this haikai to Mizoguchi. Its original source is unknown.

have been thrilled with the one hundred ryō that I sent you." Kikunojō II is reported to have smiled and replied, "Yes, but not as thrilled as you were to give it to me." The daimyō's attendants, overhearing this exchange and seeing the arrogant expression on the face of the lovely onnagata, shook with rage. Their hands immediately went to their swords, ready to cut him down.[6] Baikō's retainers considered Kikunojō's audaciousness before their powerful lord an affront not only to the daimyō himself but also to the proud clan of Shibata. Though humiliated, Baikō prevented his men from harming the lovely boy. Since Kikunojō II was the most highly acclaimed female impersonator of Edo kabuki at the time, he was quite confident of his ability to stand before even the highest classes of samurai.[7]

It was generally believed that the economic failures in Baikō's domain of Shibata and the shock of his humiliations in Edo at the hands of the arrogant young Kikunojō II led him from being a lover of kabuki actors to becoming a devoted follower of the Buddha. Bunkō, however, gives a different story of Baikō's "conversion," informing the reader in *A Confidential Record of Current, Little-Known Facts* that Baikō's remarkable turnaround took place under the instruction of a monk who reputedly had miraculous powers and was able to cure the sick.[8] Baikō had a son who had been born mute, so he begged the monk to offer prayers for him. When the boy was miraculously healed and was able to speak, Baikō became a devout Buddhist believer. His life changed, and he stopped pursuing beautiful young kabuki actors. Instead, he resolved to support the monks at Banzuin temple (in present-day Taitō-ku, Asakusa, Tokyo) where his son had been cured. He even pledged to donate his mansion for the exclusive use of religious ceremonies to be performed by the monks of the temple.

The monk at Banzuin who had cured Baikō's son was not as holy as he was purported to be, however. Bunkō reports that he arranged for prostitutes to come from Komyōji Temple (southeast of Kamakura station in

6. Itsuwa Kenkyūkai, eds., *Edo itsuwa jiten* (Tokyo: Shinjinbutsu Ōraisha, 1989), 243.

7. In May 2001 Yamamura Kunijirō (1957–) took the prestigious name of Segawa Kikunojō VII at the National Theater, playing the role of Chiyo in the "Terakoya" scene of the drama *Sugawara Denju Tenarai Kagami.*

8. Baba, *Tōji chinsetsu yōhiroku*, 230–31.

present-day Kamakura city) and stay at Baikō's mansion to provide diversion and female entertainment for the monks who were charged with conducting religious rites there. Baikō had "switched from loving young boys to loving women." That was his real "conversion."

> There is a rumor going around about something unusually evil (*gaiaku*) happening at the Banzuin temple. For whatever reason, there appears to be more going on there than meets the eye. The talk among those who know the situation well are saying that the Buddha was from the beginning just an average man. And when the respected Buddhist holy men diligently apply themselves to their religious duties, there is a prostitute with them from the Flaming Jewel Inn (*Kaen gyokuya*) whose name is Sanwaro. She was first brought to Komyōji Temple in Kamakura and then went to Edo. Imagine a Buddhist monk scheming to have a prostitute in a monastery![9]

Bunkō describes how the monks would call out to the prostitutes, "Dance, dance!" and the girls would pull up their kimonos around their necks and dance. Baikō, who began after his conversion to frequent this temple as a devoted follower and offer his prayers, soon lost any faith and devotion he might have actually acquired after the cure of his son. He was quickly drawn into the scandalous conduct of the monks, throwing himself wholeheartedly into the entertainment offered by the prostitutes at Banzuin temple. Bunkō shows that Shibata Baikō's initial conversion to Buddhism had led him down a path that was fraught with moral peril, leading him from devotion to promiscuity.

The Monster of Matsue

Shibata Baikō was not the only daimyō who was infatuated with kabuki actors. Matsudaira Munenobu (1729–82), the daimyō of Matsue, was also seen from time to time bringing groups of kabuki performers into his Edo mansion. There were stagehands and even playwrights, such as Horikoshi Nisōji (1721–81), the popular composer of comic drama (*kyōgen*), who frequented Munenobu's mansion. Bunkō reports in "The Monster of Matsue" in *Contemporary Edo: An Album of One Hundred Monsters* that no one had noticed at first anything peculiar about Matsudaira's behavior.[10]

9. Baba, *Tōji chinsetsu yōhiroku*, 231.
10. Baba, *Tōdai Edo hyaku bakemono*, 32–33.

He had seemed, on the surface at least, to conduct his affairs in a dignified and diligent manner. Things changed sometime in 1757, however. It was that year that Matsudaira had a side entrance installed in his official residence so that people could enter and leave without being seen.[11] Soon after, Matsudaira invited Mizoguchi Naoatsu, the Buddhist "convert," to his mansion and asked him to call on his young friend Segawa Kikunojō II and request a special favor. "I would like so much to have Kikunojō come to my Edo residence," Matsudaira said, "and perform the role of Oshichi from the play *Yaoya Oshichi.*" Mizoguchi was just as anxious to see Kikunojō again himself, in spite of the humiliation he had suffered, and quickly consented to making the request. He was confident that the young kabuki actor would consent to a private performance because Mizoguchi had long supported Kikunojō financially and saw himself as something of a foster father to the boy. Because of the close relationship that Mizoguchi imagined he had with the young kabuki actor, Arima Yoriyuki (1714–83), the daimyō of Kurume, made fun of him, calling Mizoguchi by his nickname, "Hey, old foster father, old foster father."[12] In the end, Kikunojō refused to perform as requested, again giving his "foster father" a stinging rebuff and disappointing Matsudaira.

The Tail of the Demon

Just as there were samurai, government officials, and even daimyō who flocked to the kabuki performances to see their favorite actors, there were also those who enjoyed the entertainment quarters. Since the bakufu ostensibly considered the kabuki theater and the "pleasure" quarters sources of social pollution, they usually went in disguise, but for all practical purposes the Tokugawa government looked the other way and resigned itself to the presence of the "notorious places" (*akusho*) as necessary evils.[13]

The 1693 ban against daimyō and hatamoto visits to the Yoshiwara

11. "*Nezumikido*" was a narrow entrance made of lattice work that was common in the Edo period.

12. Baba, *Tōdai Edo hyaku bakemono*, 32–33.

13. Jurgis Elisonas, "Notorious Places: A Brief Excursion into the Narrative Topography of Early Edo," in *Edo and Paris: Urban Life and the State in the Early Modern Era*, ed. J. L. McClain, J. M. Merriman, and K. Ugawa, 253–91 (Ithaca: Cornell University Press, 1997).

district was virtually ignored, so the law was implemented again in 1735, but again to little effect.[14] Though the possible harmful influence of these institutions on society and on samurai morality continued to be a source of consternation to the bakufu, the desirability of keeping the samurai content and of maintaining civil order in Edo made it essential that their access to these entertainments be tolerated. Based on practicality, rather than on principle, the government's control over prostitution was part of its overall policy to keep power centralized, but in fact the government exercised no firm authority over the morality or the conduct of samurai in spite of the law, and this state of affairs continued until the end of Tokugawa hegemony in the nineteenth century. In actuality, the Yoshiwara and the Kabuki theater were not simply tolerated by the bakufu. Both institutions were, in fact, supported by the patronage of highly placed officials of the government and favored as gratifying diversions that became more and more a part of the life of the ruling class.

Eighteenth-century popular literature commonly dealt with life in the "pleasure" quarters, often making it the principal subject matter. Contemporary guidebooks to Yoshiwara, for example, described the rules of etiquette, the language, and the customs of the quarter, as well as providing the names of the famous courtesans with short introductions. The guidebooks were extremely popular and even considered indispensable for the discriminating aficionado. Bunkō's descriptions of the courtesans and of the inner workings of the Yoshiwara district were much more than just another guidebook among the many already available. His personal anecdotes present the popular diversions of the day in a completely different light, offering a depth of feeling and compassion that allowed the reader to see that, even though the government officially deplored the Yoshiwara and scorned the prostitutes who were leading "virtuous" men into immorality, it was more the hypocrisy of the government that was the real cause of social pollution. The Yoshiwara that Bunkō describes may have been unsavory, but the immoral activity was not primarily the activities of the courtesans. It was the wealthy elite, the samurai, and particularly public officials, rather than the courtesans, who made the

14. Seigle, *Yoshiwara: The Glittering World of the Japanese Courtesan*, 272.

Yoshiwara a place of immorality. The quarter was one of the "notorious places" not because of the presence of the women who had been forced into prostitution, but because of the officials of the bakufu who were perpetuating a system that kept those women enslaved.

Bunkō expresses this opinion in *Contemporary Edo: An Album of One Hundred Monsters* with his short piece about Aoyama Yoshinaga (1707–60) titled "The Case of Aoyama San'emon" (*Aoyama San'emon ga ben*, 1758).[15] Aoyama is identified as the comptroller of finance (*kanjō kinmyaku*). He is presented in Bunkō's satire as very similar to a stock character of popular fiction commonly known as the *yabo*, a lazy oaf, who somehow manages to get what he wants by lying or, if possible, through bribery. Before attaining his position, he was employed as a night watchman at the shogunal castle under Tokugawa Yoshimune. Not only was he totally incompetent in his job as a night watchman, but he was also a corrupt scoundrel. Even though he was always short of money, he frequented the Yoshiwara district and spent nearly everything he earned on the courtesans and prostitutes. On one occasion he claimed to have lost his guard's uniform and his two swords. That was a lie, of course. He had actually pawned the uniform and the swords so that he would have enough money to continue his jaunts to the Yoshiwara "pleasure" quarters.

Aoyama may have been lazy and a liar, but he was also clever enough to fool and successfully bribe two of the highest officials of the bakufu in order to advance his career. The shogun's close advisers, Senior Counselor Hotta Masasuke (1712–61) and Junior Counselor Itakura Katsukiyo (1706–80), were among those tricked into thinking that Aoyama was diligent and capable. Aoyama, however, had only two things on his mind—political advancement and the courtesans of Yoshiwara.

Bunkō attributed Aoyama's political success not to his diligence, as others did, but to his familiarity with low-class prostitutes whom he would introduce to government officials for a small fee, but the prostitutes were not the only women he used for his own purposes. He sent one of his two younger sisters to Senior Counselor Hotta to serve as one of his concubines, and the other sister he sent to be a concubine for

15. Baba, *Tōdai Edo hyaku bakemono*, 21–22.

Junior Counselor Itakura. As a result, Aoyama was promoted, first from the post of night watchman to that of assistant inspector, then to the office of superintendent of construction and repair. Not long after, he was promoted again to the position of manager of provisions. Finally he was promoted to the high office of comptroller of finance and given a stipend of three thousand koku. Bunkō predicted that this "monster" would very likely advance to one of the three major magisterial positions, either as commissioner of shrines and temples, city magistrate, or magistrate of finance. Bunkō scorns the gullibility of government officials like Hotta and Itakura who could be fooled even by a *yabo* like Aoyama. These two advisers of the shogun were greatly appreciative, Bunkō writes, and in debt to Aoyama for allowing his two sisters to entertain them. But this was just another lie. The two women Aoyama had claimed were his sisters were actually cheap prostitutes, the daughters of a flower peddler who lived in a slum in the area of Tachibana-chō. If Hotta and Itakura had known the two girls were simply low-class prostitutes, they would have been humiliated.

By revealing how Aoyama had used these two women to procure his own promotions and how two high bakufu officials had been susceptible to offers of sexual favors, Bunkō exposes hypocrisy and gullibility at the highest levels of the Tokugawa government. He provides concrete evidence that promotion and rank are acquired not by ability but through manipulation and deception. He makes it clear that Aoyama's "sisters" are not the ones responsible for deceiving the officials, however. It was Aoyama himself who had forced the women to carry out his wicked plan for his own ends. Bunkō brings his story to a conclusion, informing his reader that Aoyama has recently acquired a good-looking wife, along with a number of other female companions. "The tail of the demon has become visible," Bunkō writes. "The monster's skin has been peeled off and his real appearance has been revealed." Aoyama is just one of the great monsters; there are many others still around today, Bunkō warns, and "without a doubt, the world is becoming even more filled with these great deceivers."[16]

16. Baba, *Tōdai Edo hyaku bakemono*, 22.

Although Aoyama is the central protagonist of the satire, the author's treatment of bakufu officials Hotta Masasuke and Itakura Katsukiyo is also noteworthy. These were two of Tokugawa Ieshige's closest advisers, but they are presented as typical gesaku playboys who act out the role of the musuko character (spoiled son). They are both taken in by the boorish Aoyama and used in his strategy for advancement. Though senior officials, they are presented as spoiled children from wealthy backgrounds who are deceived at the hands of the manipulative expert (*tsū*), Aoyama San'emon.

The Courtesan Segawa V of the Matsubaya Inn

The characters of courtesans and their clients, who were portrayed in gesaku prose and in the kabuki drama of the period, dominated Edo popular culture. Bunkō, however, presents a picture of the courtesans that is quite different from that of other writers of popular fiction. He depicts many of the women of the quarter as educated, more worthy of respect, and more virtuous than the politicians and officials who patronized their establishments while at the same time condemning them for their immorality. Daimyō and samurai, as well as wealthy merchants and even Buddhist monks, frittered away their resources in the brothels of Yoshiwara and the unlicensed entertainment sites, but the women they frequented often dedicated much of their time to developing the traditional arts and perfecting their talents. A number of the women whom Bunkō introduces to his reader were models of kindness and religious devotion, quite unlike their clients.

Bunkō expresses his particular admiration for the renowned courtesan (*keisei*) Segawa V, who was at the Matsubaya Inn from 1751 or 1752 until 1755.[17] Bunkō considered her unsurpassed in elegance, refinement, and talent:

> Segawa is now at her zenith, and there has been no one in the fifth block of Shin Yoshiwara in the last ten years who could compare with her.[18] The

17. Segawa V was a courtesan of the Matsubaya when Eichiya Sōsuke ransomed her. She was then called Eichiya Segawa (see *Mitamura Engyo zenshū*, vol. 19, 102). Segawa is listed in *Yoshiwara shusse kagami zen*, ed. Yagi Keiichi, folio 13, in *Hōreki ki Yoshiwara yūjo hyōbanki saiken yonshu* (Tokyo: Kinsei fūsoku kenkyūkai, 1975).

18. The old Yoshiwara district burned down, along with much of the city, in the Meireki fire of

> daughter of an impoverished family from Shimōsa Omigawa, she was recruited by Matsubaya Hanzaemon, who taught her well. She became proficient at samisen and jōruri, of course, also at the tea ceremony, haikai, *go*, *sugoroku*, and *kemari*. In addition, she could play the hand drum and flute, as well as sing and dance.[19]

Bunkō explains that Segawa also acquired proficiency in the art of divination as a disciple of Hirasawa Sanai (a.k.a. Zuitei, 1690–1780), the most famous fortune-teller of the day, but that her greatest accomplishments were in poetry and music. These talents were the result of her own hard work, determination, and intelligence. She had received no formal education in these arts in childhood.

In spite of all her achievements and the recognition she was given, however, she never found real happiness. This is particularly evident in a letter that she wrote in beautiful Kōtaku-style calligraphy in the spring of 1755.[20] The letter was addressed to her friend and fellow courtesan, Hinazuru of the Chōjiya Inn in Edomachi, Yoshiwara. When Hinazura's contract was bought out by a wealthy merchant by the name of Yanasaki Tosen and she left Yoshiwara, Segawa was no longer able to meet her daily, as she had for a number of years. Segawa herself would later be ransomed by the merchant Eichiya Sōsuke. Bunkō cites Segawa's letter to her friend Hinazuru:

> I have heard that you have been ransomed by your lover and are leaving this place of worldly sorrows to go into the lovely city. I am jealous of you, going to live with someone who truly loves you. Your lover is like a strong tree, and you are the soft soil. He is the yang, who will nurture you, and you are the yin. You will have many servants to wait on you. It will be a wonderful life for you. Congratulations.[21]

Bunkō was privy to this letter at least by the summer of 1755, just a few months after Hinazuru had received it. Quite moved by the letter's con-

---

1657. It was rebuilt in the new location and renamed "Shin Yoshiwara" (New Yoshiwara). Eventually the designation "Shin" was dropped, and the new district was known simply as Yoshiwara.

19. Baba, *Tōsei Buya zokudan*, 382. Sugoroku is a Japanese board game similar to backgammon. Kemari, which was popular in the Heian period, is similar to kickball.

20. Hosoi Kōtaku's (1658–1735) style of calligraphy was characterized by the almost exclusive use of *kanji* and the very sparse use of Japanese *kana*.

21. Baba, *Tōsei Buya zokudan*, 383.

tent, Bunkō writes, "I have cited this letter for the reader's pleasure. Segawa was a good and kind person who never mistreated her customers and did not have the slightest bit of iniquity in her heart."[22]

Segawa's Buddhist Client

Bunkō's respect for Segawa as a person, as well his admiration for her as an accomplished artist and calligrapher, stands in sharp contrast to the disparaging picture he presents of one of her clients, the Buddhist monk and poet Teramachi Sanchi (a.k.a. Hyakuan, 1695–1781). Bunkō calls the monk "a great playboy" and a "monster-monk."[23] Like the courtesan Segawa, Hyakuan was reputed to be a master of the Kōtaku school of calligraphy. "He used the calligraphy paper and the brushes of this school," Bunkō writes, "but his characters are poorly written and much inferior to the beautiful characters of Segawa."[24]

In "The Case of Teramachi Sanchi (Hyakuan)" (*Teramachi Sanchi Hyakuan no ben*, 1758) in *Contemporary Edo: An Album of One Hundred Monsters*, Bunkō gives a summary of some of the major events that took place in Hyakuan's artistic and political career that led up to a government position as an official monk of the bakufu (*bakufu hyōbōzu*).[25] As a young monk, Hyakuan spent quite a lot of money on his excursions to the "pleasure" quarters, and Segawa was one of his favorite courtesans. His position as an official bakufu monk was compromised by his associations with her, but his career survived because his love of the "pleasure" quarters, as great as that was, did not equal his ambition for political power. Hyakuan tried to use his office of official monk as a steppingstone to further advancement in the Tokugawa hierarchy. He particularly coveted the title of "poetry master of the bakufu" (*bakufu renkashi*), but he was thwarted in his designs and never received the appointment.[26] He submitted a request to the representative of the retired shogun, Tokugawa Yoshimune, to be invited to the New Year's poetry party at the shogunal palace as Yoshimune's representative. However, not only was he never extended an invitation, the shogunal representative admonished

22. Ibid., 384.

23. Baba, *Tōdai Edo hyaku bakemono*, 12.

24. Ibid., 12–13.

25. Ibid., 12.

26. Ichiko Teiji et al., eds., *Nihon koten bungaku daijiten* (Tokyo: Iwanami Shoten, 1984), 5: 183.

Hyakuan for even making the request. From that time, Hyakuan fell into disfavor with the bakufu authorities.[27] Bunkō was of the opinion that Yoshimune had been able to see through Hyakuan's ruse, had him sternly admonished, and forbade him to come to the poetry party, knowing that he was nothing but an ambitious fraud. As a result of his ambitious nature, Hyakuan was eventually demoted from his post of official monk to the lowly position of "drum monk" (*taikobōzu*), whose task it was to simply signal the time of day at the monastery with a drum and to keep the rhythm in the chanting of prayers.

Hyakuan remained a proud man even after his demotion, which made him a particularly inviting target for Bunkō's satirical barbs. Bunkō shortened his official title, *taikobōzu*, referring to him simply as the "*taiko*," or "the drum," a term which also meant a jester or a fool. The drum bearer (*taikomochi*) took a secondary position to the chime player (*kanemochi*) in the Buddhist prayer ceremonies and rites. The inferior position taiko was apparent in a popular saying of the day: "The monk who carries *kane* (money) will have a *kane* (bell) around his neck, but the monk who has no kane (money) will carry a taiko (a drum)."[28]

In spite of his aspirations to hold a high office, Hyakuan had become a man of no real importance and was now being ridiculed for having little money. He had spent much of his financial resources at the bordellos. Bunkō subjected Hyakuan to the same criticisms that townspeople would commonly direct toward the samurai of the day: they were proud and arrogant even after having exhausted their fortunes in frivolous pursuits.

Bunkō highlights other incidents in the life of Hyakuan to explore various dimensions of the monk's character. It seems that on a certain New Year's Day, Hyakuan put out a guest book at his temple so that worshippers could sign it. The paper in the guest book was the Chinese rice paper used by the masters of the Kōtaku school of calligraphy. Hyakuan thought of himself as a master of that school in spite of his lack of any real talent. It was impossible for Bunkō to imagine that Hyakuan could have had any standing as a member of such an exclusive group. The training for the Kōtaku school demanded long years of dedicated study in calli-

27. Baba, *Tōdai Edo hyaku bakemono*, 13.
28. Mori Senzō et al., eds., *Zoku enseki jisshu* (Tokyo: Chūō Kōronsha, 1980), 3: 27.

graphic techniques. Unlike Segawa, who was an excellent calligrapher, Hyakuan could not have marshaled the dedication and hard work that would have been demanded. He was a Buddhist monk who squandered his stipend to carouse with courtesans and prostitutes and a bureaucrat who used much of his energy to try to gain titles and positions. By associating Hyakuan with "the rice paper of the Kōtaku school," Bunkō shows the monk to be an ambitious hypocrite who is all pretense and no substance—an accurate representation of Edo-period Buddhism as Bunkō saw it. The satire directed against Hyakuan is unrelenting. The monk is set up as a representative of the shogunate and a symbol for the Buddhist establishment that the shogunate supported. Hyakuan is a *yamanba*, Bunkō writes, "like one of those female demons who go prowling around the mountains." The anecdote ends with a warning: "Hyakuan is still at large fooling the world."[29]

A Monk Enamored with Women

Bunkō extolled the virtues and the integrity of the women of the entertainment districts whom many maligned and vilified, and among those he denounced for immorality and lack of virtue were samurai who considered themselves honorable and righteous. Bunkō presents his views on the Buddhist establishment by focusing on the vices of monks with whom he was familiar. He points out the monks' character weaknesses and moral flaws, takes a close look at their conduct at the various Buddhist institutions in the capital, and satirizes the contrasts between "the sacred" and "the profane" aspects of their lives.

A monk of the Tendai Buddhist sect by the name of Donkai Shūten was one such monk, who "attracts people with beautiful sermons but is extremely immoral."[30] In his essay satirically titled "Donkai Shūten: Renowned Teaching and Skilled Preaching at the Indomitable Yōdenji Temple" (*Donkai Shūten dangi ni kōmei no koto Yōdenji tetsujō seppō jōzu no koto*, 1756), Bunkō scrutinizes Shūten's scholarship and methods of textual criticism.[31]

29. Ibid., 13.
30. Baba, *Tōsei Buya zokudan*, 351.
31. Yōdenji Temple is a Nichiren sect temple established in 1680.

The "beautiful sermons" that Shūten composed to draw crowds of people to the temple were constructed, Bunkō claims, on a type of literary criticism that the monks frequently used to analyze and explain the ancient Buddhist sutras. Their method emphasized the minute study of every single character in a text in order to find the hidden meaning or the mysterious religious significance of the words and phrases. Bunkō ridicules this time-consuming and "fruitless" method of scholarship: "There are many monks like Shūten who go around preaching, but have no learning at all. If this scandalizes you, you should ask me, Ba Bunkō [sic], about it. I will give you some good instruction. The truth is, when this evil monk is at his dais preaching, all he can come up with is mundane sayings, puns, and jokes." Bunkō cites one occasion when Shūten analyzed the meaning of the term "*Myōhō renge kyō*" (*Lotus Sutra*).

> Let us look at the first character "*myō*" (妙) [mystery, fascination]. One will see that it is actually a combination of two other characters. On the left side we have the character for "woman" (女), and on the right side we have the character for "a little" (少). The meaning of the title of the sutra, *Myōhō renge kyō*, then is quite clear: The monk Shūten is a little enamored with women.[32]

Bunkō clearly insinuates that Shūten, who purported to be a man of virtue and a scholar, is actually a covert client of the "pleasure" districts. More importantly, however, Bunkō offers the reader a satirical illustration of the method of literary criticism actually practiced by Shūten and other Buddhist monks. This parody of Buddhist literary analysis mocks the scholarly methodology of the Tendai sect as a whole. The secret doctrines and oral transmissions that had supposedly been passed down from Nichiren (1222–82) are mocked as well. The petty literary squabbles with other sects, as well as the debates within the Tendai sect itself, over methods of interpreting the sutras were, what Bunkō called, insignificant matters: "Shūten, just like his colleague Ryokai, does not bother to explain the sutras at all. He is nothing but a no-account monk who goes to the theater to enjoy the jokes. Everyone has been taken in by him. He is a source of evil."[33]

32. Baba, *Tōsei Buya zokudan*, 354.
33. Ibid., 351–52.

Bunkō points out that Nichiren, who taught devotion to the *Lotus Sutra*, had devoted his energies largely to faux scholarship and subsequently based his preaching exclusively on error. Bunkō writes that Nichiren had vehemently criticized monks of the Pure Land (Jōdo) sect of Buddhism for their interpretation of the *Lotus Sutra* and, as a result, was banished into the wilderness of Izu (from 1261 to 1263). While in exile, Nichiren was forced to make clothing from the skins of deer that he had killed himself, a clear violation of Buddhist law.[34] Bunkō is quite harsh in his criticism of Nichiren for having done this:

> Nichiren came from a family of boatmen. He killed deer and made robes from the hides. In a passage in the *Minobushō*, written in Nichiren's own hand, he admits precisely that.[35] Working with animal skins is the task of eta [outcasts], so Nichiren must be the descendant of eta and a shameless brute. His only point of pride is his beard and the mandalas that he draws. But what is a mandala worth anyway?[36]

Bunkō's intent is not only to show that Nichiren was a hypocrite who did not live by Buddhist principles, but also to point out that the conflicts between Nichiren Buddhists and the other sects, which were violent at times, were of little importance to him. Nichiren died in obscurity. His followers divided themselves up into many different sects, each claiming the exclusive possession of true Buddhist doctrine. Tendai, Pure Land, and Nichiren Buddhists had often in the past taken sides against each other and even engaged in armed conflict, but during the Tokugawa period the various Buddhist sects had become docile. This was thanks in part to the nationwide Buddhist parish system that the government created to ensure religious peace and to eradicate Christianity. The weakening of Buddhism that resulted played a part in the acceleration of the moral decline of the ruling class and of society in general.

34. Ibid., 352.

35. Mt. Minobu is the location where Nichiren spent his last years. Minobu Kuonji Temple is the most sacred place of worship for Nichiren sect followers. Nichiren wrote two documents at Minobu, "On the selection of time" (*Senji Shō*, 1275) and "Recompense of Indebtedness" (*Hōon Shō*, 1276).

36. Baba, *Tōsei Buya zokudan*, 352.

Komechō's Sorrow

The longing to be ransomed and to be free of their servitude was constantly on the minds of the courtesans, who had spent most of their lives as virtual prisoners in the confines of the various "pleasure" districts. Bunkō captures their feelings beautifully in an analogy about a caged bird that is finally set loose. His moving description of an incident in the life of the courtesan Komechō shows his affectionate respect for the Yoshiwara courtesans and his compassionate concern for their well-being:

> The beautiful courtesan Komechō, elegantly walking along the streets of Hachiman-chō one sunny afternoon, noticed a shopkeeper who was selling songbirds. The shopkeeper, seeing that she was obviously a woman of means, called to her and proudly exhibited his finest bird, a brown-crested bulbul (*hiyodori*) from Korea valued at thirty ryō. It was kept in a birdcage that was made out of pure silver and had once belonged to a samurai.
>
> Komechō stood in front of the shop for a while, captivated by the beauty of the bird's feathers and the sorrowful look in its eyes. Her only desire was to release the bird from its cruel captivity and let it fly away over the fields. "If only this bird had not been born so beautiful," she thought, "it would not be confined in this cruel prison." Komechō felt that the freedom of the bird was worth far more than gold or the price of thirty ryō. Though the price was exorbitant for a songbird, at that moment the huge amount of money seemed like a mere pittance. She said to the shopkeeper, "Release the bird into the sky. I will pay for its ransom."
>
> Though very surprised at the strange demand, the shopkeeper immediately opened the cage, and the bird flew up to the sky. Komechō paid the thirty ryō, and she and the shopkeeper together watched the beautiful bird disappear into the clouds. The people standing around who saw what had happened were astonished. Word spread around the neighborhood that Komechō was a very virtuous person.[37]

Bunkō saw Komechō herself as that beautiful songbird that had been held captive in the silver cage. Her beauty, her talent, her greatest longing, and her sorrow are all captured in this anecdote. The womanly compassion, depth of feeling, and sensitivity that was evident in Komechō's

37. Ibid., 391.

good deed was, in Bunkō's view, characteristic of many of the high-class courtesans of the quarter.

Otsuya of the Ōtomoeya Inn

To draw a comparison between a courtesan of the "pleasure" district and a Buddhist monk might seem to be highly inappropriate or even shocking. Bunkō, however, does precisely this in "The Woman of the Ōtomoeya Inn who is Called a Bed-hopping Slut" (*Ōtomoeya dora musume to adana o torishi koto*, 1756).[38] The monk with whom this courtesan is compared is a Buddhist bonze by the name of Enoki. He has the same name, Bunkō points out, as the monk in the classical collection *Essays in Idleness* (*Tsurezuregusa*, 1330–32). Bunkō sees both monks as proud men who have a reputation for holiness but whose character flaws stand in sharp contrast to the virtues of Otsuya, a courtesan of the Yoshiwara. Bunkō first points out a few of the monk's unpleasant personality traits: "In the *Tsurezuregusa* [Section 45] mention is made of a high-ranking and proud monk (*sōjō*) by the name of Enoki. He is extremely selfish and narrow-minded. Since there is a tall nettle tree (*enoki*) in front of the house of the monk I am talking about, people call him by his nickname 'Nettle tree monk.'"[39]

The courtesan of the piece is Otsuya, who was employed at the Ōtomoeya Inn, a bordello in operation for a short time between 1751 and 1764:

> In Shin Yoshiwara there is a courtesan, Otsuya at Ōtomoeya. She is self-effacing and has a very good disposition. . . . A certain monk called Enoki, who knew the various establishments in Yoshiwara very well, would often come to the front of the Ōtomoeya Inn and revile Otsuya, yelling at her in a loud voice: "You bed-hopping slut!" He went everywhere calling her by that name. As the saying goes, "One dog barks and a thousand others take up the cry," and so rumors about Otsuya and a bad reputation began to spread. This is how the courtesan got her nickname, "bed hopping slut," and it has stuck. Otsuya was deeply hurt and mortified. She thought about various ways she might put an end to her life, but she knew that killing herself would cause her parents unbearable sadness. So out of fidelity to them she endured the scorn.[40]

38. Ibid., 387.
39. Ibid., 387–88.
40. Ibid.

It was not only the monk Enoki who denigrated and ridiculed Otsuya. Many other people made fun of her because she was physically unattractive. Bunko writes, "People were saying that Otsuya was ugly and looked like a squash." In fact, a bawdy song called "The Great Squash" was composed about her, but ironically, she did not let that bother her. Bunkō confesses he used to think that "the jokes and songs about Otsuya were funny," but he also sympathized with her, aware that the teasing which came her way hurt her deeply in spite of the strong front she put up. "She was never unpleasant and always mannerly," Bunko wrote. "There was nothing lacking in her personality, and she could even calm the hearts of street ruffians." Otsuya eventually became one of the most successful and sought-after courtesans of the Ōtomoeya.[41] Young men who lacked the confidence to meet the more beautiful courtesans went to the Ōtomoeya to see Otsuya, and as a result, Bunkō reports, her business flourished. "It was all thanks," he said, "to the fame she acquired for being physically unattractive."

The story of Otsuya ends happily. "Heaven has had mercy on Otsuya, and people now see her gentleness and chastity (*teisei*). Recently, a man named Yamamoto, who lives at Kyōmachi 2-chōme in Yoshiwara, ransomed and married her, and she is now prospering and living a happy life."[42] Otsuya's life radically changed after she married Yamamoto. Bunkō praises her, however, not only because of her "chaste" life after she left Yoshiwara but also because of the virtues she exhibited even while working at the Ōtomoeya Inn, in particular her fidelity to her parents, her longsuffering, and her patience.

An Insider's Information

Reflecting on the comings and goings at the various establishments in the "pleasure" district, such as the Matsubaya Inn, the Ōtomoeya Inn, the Tsu no Kuniya Inn, the Ōmiya Inn, and so on, Bunkō provides information throughout his writings about the Yoshiwara and the courtesans that is not available from any other historical or literary source. He recounts, for example, some of the secret words and phrases that the cour-

41. Ibid.
42. Ibid., 388.

tesans used to refer to their clients. Many of the patrons who were not experts would have been ignorant of the private language that was used at the Matsubaya Inn and other houses of the quarter.

The courtesans' "secret" words and expressions were often taken from the names of characters in the eleventh-century romance, the *Tale of Genji*.[43] "Asagao," for example, meant "the morning after." "Aoi" designated the fee that the client would be charged. Other code words were used for different types of customers. "Yūgao" was the name the courtesans used to refer to a reticent samurai who entered the establishment by the back door with his face hidden. "Yomogifu," the title of the fifteenth chapter of the *Tale of Genji* and a term that designated the overgrown area where Prince Genji visited the aged virgin Suetsumuhana, referred to an older gentleman who arrived with his face made up with white powder in order to disguise himself or appear to be younger. The courtesans laughed when they heard that "Kumogakure" was entering the building. This term, which was also a chapter title in the *Tale of Genji*, was used by the courtesans to refer to someone who seemed to be particularly dull-witted. "Kagaribi" had long been a designation in Yoshiwara for a courtesan with few skills, but the women at the Matsubaya Inn also used it when speaking of a client whose personality was hyper and passionate at some times, and cold and withdrawn at other times.[44] These commonly used "secret" words were euphemisms for the more vulgar or derogatory terms that could be heard in the lower-class establishments.[45]

The bakufu despised all the courtesans, from the low-class women of the unlicensed districts to the sophisticated and educated courtesans of the expensive establishments of Yoshiwara. However, this contempt did not stop government officials from taking full advantage of these women for their own amusement. The attack on this hypocrisy continued to be an important feature of Bunkō's satirical exposés about the "pleasure" districts.

Bunkō's reflections on the quarters and the women imprisoned there show him to have been sympathetic and understanding of their predicament. Their lives were far from the glamorous role that was portrayed in

43. Ibid., 385.

44. Ibid.

45. Ibid.

much of the gesaku literature of the period. Young girls of twelve or thirteen, and some younger, entered the way of the courtesan often against their will, becoming the objects of men's fantasies and playthings for the pleasure of those who could afford it. Bunkō was concerned about the unjust treatment of these women and spoke out in their support: "The life of the courtesan in Fukagawa is extremely frightening. Other women, after being arrested by the high court (*kōtei*) are reduced to slavery and sold in the Shin Yoshiwara. They all enter the way of the geisha (*geidō*) against their will."[46] A few of the women did manage to escape the enforced confinement of the so-called pleasure quarters but most had no safe place to which they could flee. Bunkō informs his reader:

> Many of the women escaped to the hut of an old farmer by the name of Nuiemon, whose wife had been a prostitute herself in the unlicensed quarter of Fukagawa. One time seventy-eight geisha were rescued, brought to Nuiemon, and stayed with him more than forty days. Every day they sang and played the samisen. They were no longer afraid, even though they were in the countryside (*inaka*), and were able to live freely. In all humility, I can say that I know about this incident in some detail.[47]

Bunkō's compassionate feelings for the women who worked in the entertainment districts, his familiarity with their secret language and codes, his inside information on what happened to some of those who had escaped, and even his knowledge of the content of some of their private letters all point to a familiarity with the comings and goings of the women of the Yoshiwara that went much deeper than that of many other writers of popular literature. As an itinerant lecturer and writer, Bunkō could never have afforded to pay for the services of the Yoshiwara even if he had wanted to, but he was known to all classes of courtesans from the great ones, such as Segawa V of the Matsubaya, the famous ones, such as Komechō and Otsuya of the Ōtomoeya, and even the lowliest streetwalker, such as Omatsu:

> In Shiba, Mita-chō in the alley behind Nagazaemon's house there is a cheap prostitute everyone calls Omatsu of the Rubbish Heap.... As Kenkō wrote in *Tsurezuregusa* [section 72], "The oxcart may be ugly, but books in the oxcart

46. Ibid., 391–92.
47. Ibid., 392.

> are not." If one's purity of heart protects these five: chastity, piety, beauty, the wife, and the womb, then one can certainly be called a courtesan in the true sense.[48]

Bunkō seemed not to care in the slightest what other people thought about his close associations with the courtesans and prostitutes and defended himself against accusations that were made because of his seemingly scandalous inside information. People may have found it strange that, in spite of his moralizing about the behavior of samurai who frequented the quarter, "he himself was accused of going to every little establishment in Yoshiwara."[49] Bunkō explains the reason why he went to the quarter: "I find there so many kind hearts, and I have discovered that even the women people call 'trashy whores' are in a true sense the really authentic high-class courtesans (*tayū*). A common streetwalker with a kind heart is superior to an unfeeling *tayū*.... Money does not have anything to do with truth or falsehood, nor does it determine the real worth of a woman."[50]

48. Ibid., 403
49. Ibid.
50. Ibid.

9 | THE BREAKDOWN OF SOCIAL ORDER

Learning and military skill, loyalty and filial piety must be promoted, and the rules of decorum must be properly enforced.

SHOGUN TOKUGAWA TSUNAYOSHI (1646–1709)

Moral Decline

The shogunate in the mid-eighteenth century looked for ways to safeguard the traditional status relationships in Japanese society, hoping that this would help protect samurai virtue. Tokugawa Tsunayoshi (r. 1680–1709) and Tokugawa Ienobu (r. 1709–12) had been dedicated to the study of the Confucian classics in their interest to preserve the hierarchical distinctions among the different classes. Tokugawa Yoshimune (r. 1716–45), who is considered to be among the more successful of the Tokugawa shoguns, studied the ancient Chinese classics as well, in order to deepen his understanding of the proper relationship between lord and retainer. These three shoguns sought to discover the correct moral norms that would guide the political order, but in spite of their efforts, the positive influence that Confucianism previously had on society continued to weaken. The collapse of the Confucian intellectual and philosophical tradition and the resulting moral decline of the samurai class

Epigraph is from Tsunayoshi's revision of *Rules Governing the Military Households*; Maruyama, *Studies in the Intellectual History of Tokugawa Japan*, 114.

continued apace through the eighteenth century. The downward spiral gained momentum in the years after Yoshimune, during the shogunate of Tokugawa Ieshige.

The lord-retainer relationship, which was clearly on the point of breaking down in the 1750s, was the central doctrine of Japanese Neo-Confucian orthodoxy in the Tokugawa period. If this pillar of society were to collapse, as Baba Bunkō claimed had already happened, then the other Confucian relationships of father and son, husband and wife, elder and younger brother, and friend and friend, as well as the stability of society in general, would be in jeopardy. A peasant would no longer be submissive to the landowner; an apprentice would not be subject to his master. The Confucian social order by which even commoners lived had its primary foundation in the interdependent relationships between a daimyō and his samurai. The morals at every level of society were only as strong as the lord-retainer relationship, but Bunkō correctly perceived that there were fundamental and obvious flaws in the relationships at the upper strata of society. He points out that it was becoming more and more common for low-ranking samurai to be disrespectful of the daimyō and for daimyō to have little compassion or understanding of what it meant to act with justice and good judgment toward his retainers.

A Bannerman Forces a Concession from a Daimyō

Bunkō describes a confrontation between a low-ranking samurai and a powerful daimyō that illustrates the breakdown in the Tokugawa hierarchy. In "The Case of Hatamoto Tosai Kosuke" (*Goto Tosai Kosuke kijō no koto*, 1756), the bannerman Kosuke and his father, Shigebei, challenge the status and authority of the powerful daimyō Tachibana Sadayoshi (1698–1744), lord of Hida domain.[1]

Old man Shigebei was returning home from his bath one day and passed in front of the residence of Lord Tachibana. Some of the daimyō's men were outside sprinkling water in front of the mansion to keep the dust down. As Shigebei was walking by, they accidentally splashed him. The old man went home quite angry and told his son Kosuke what had

1. Baba, *Tōji chinsetsu yōhiroku*, 236–39. Sadayoshi was daimyō of Yanagigawa in Chikugo (present-day Fukuoka prefecture) from 1721 (Kyōhō 6) 7. 9 to 1744 (Enkyō 1) 5. 25.

happened. Kosuke was incensed at this affront to his family's honor and concluded that his father must have been deliberately sprayed with water. Kosuke was determined to get revenge for this perceived insult and immediately headed to the Tachibana mansion to protest. Arriving at the guardhouse, he explained to the gatekeeper, "I am Tosai Kosuke. Some men from your lord's mansion splashed water on my father as he was walking by. I find that very hard to excuse. If Lord Tachibana is here, I would like to express my thoughts about the matter, if you don't mind. I intend to ask, humbly of course, that he behead the men responsible."[2] The samurai guard at the gate thought all of this rather amusing. Kosuke continued to press his case and insist that he be given an audience with Lord Tachibana, so Kosuke could demand that the men responsible for the insult to his father be condemned to death and beheaded.

Bunkō records this incident well aware of the unreasonableness of Kosuke's demand. The guard's amusement at Kosuke may reveal the author's amusement as well. Even if the accidental splash of water could be considered an insult, it was hardly an offense punishable by death. Kosuke's demand is an example of the samurai's distorted sense of self-importance. The fact that Kosuke would insist on seeing the daimyō personally also reveals his lack of knowledge of proper protocol and decorum. Low-ranking samurai did not see daimyō at will, just as the daimyō who came to Edo for their alternate-year attendance would not have the automatic right to see the shogun in person.

Communication was done through the use of messengers and attendants, or in the case of the shogun, through his counselors. Another gaffe that Kosuke was making was to put himself in the place of judge over Lord Tachibana's retainers and even over the daimyō himself, thinking he could decide what action Tachibana should take. The contrast between Kosuke's polite and formal language, as recorded in Bunkō's text, and his outlandish demands adds to the irony of the situation and further illustrates the breakdown in relationships among the elite, in which there is politeness on the level of verbal exchange but, in actuality, disrespect. The anecdote continues with the gatekeeper's well-mannered re-

2. Baba, *Tōji chinsetsu yōhiroku*, 236.

sponse to Kosuke's inopportune request: "Lord Tachibana is occupied at present, but I will inform him of your business, and a messenger will be sent to you with an answer." The polite language of the gatekeeper's accommodating response matches the language of Kosuke's request.

As promised, Lord Tachibana's messenger arrives the next day with a reply from the daimyō: "The men responsible for the insult to your father will offer their apologies." Kosuke, of course, does not feel that this perfunctory response is adequate, and he goes again to the Tachibana mansion to try to speak to the daimyō in person. As before, the retainer at the gate meets Kosuke and cordially listens to the same request but insists again that an audience with Lord Tachibana is impossible. Trying to be discreet, he offers a polite excuse: "Lord Tachibana has a slight cold today and is laid up in bed." Kosuke immediately counters, "That is unfortunate. I was refused an audience with Lord Tachibana once before. You obviously think that I am of little importance, and so you have not respected my request, but I will have a chance to meet Lord Tachibana when he comes to the shogunal castle. For, you see, I am stationed there by appointment of the shogun himself."[3]

Kosuke plays his trump card. He has a position at the shogun's castle. His rank would still not entitle him to an audience with the daimyō, and this vague threat is further evidence that he has no sense of propriety. On hearing that Tosai Kosuke is a retainer at the shogunal castle, the gatekeeper shows surprise and fears that Kosuke could perhaps cause some trouble for the daimyō after all. The retainers of Lord Tachibana consult with one another and decide that it would be prudent to again send one of their number, Toda Gozaemon, to Kosuke's residence to try to explain the protocol and convince him that a samurai such as himself cannot just speak directly to a daimyō anytime he wishes. When Toda arrives at the bannerman's residence and asks to speak with Tosai Kosuke, he is met at the door by a companion of the hatamoto who says to him, "Tosai Kosuke is occupied at present. I will inform him of your business." The messenger has no choice but to leave, but later the same day he goes back to Kosuke's house to try to speak with him and is again met by Kosuke's companion,

3. Ibid., 237.

who says, "An audience with Kosuke is impossible at this time. He has a slight cold and is laid up in bed. You won't be able to see him today."[4] This, of course, is the same excuse that had been given to Kosuke for not being able to see the daimyō. It is now repeated to the messenger in exactly the same words. Kosuke has essentially put himself on the same social level as the daimyō. The humor and irony of the parallel excuses emphasize Bunkō's point that this samurai, and even samurai in general, are not only ignorant of proper protocol but are droll figures that people can laugh at almost with impunity. While the story of Kosuke's callow ignorance is entertaining, there is a more serious implication behind the situation. The purpose of the anecdote is to underscore the decline in the Tokugawa status system and the lord-retainer relationship.

Lord Tachibana's presence in Edo and his appearance in attendance at the shogunal court in 1756 actually turned out to be an auspicious time for Tosai Kosuke. The daimyō brought the customary tribute gifts for the shogun, Tokugawa Ieshige, and also had presents for Kosuke and his family. "The house of Tachibana sent messengers with financial recompense for Kosuke consisting of thirty pieces of silver, scrolls, twilled fabrics, and other gifts, all in rare and expensive boxes." In fact after that, whenever Kosuke or his family had any kind of need, there would be a visit from Lord Tachibana. Bunkō adds, "This stroke of luck was quite strange."[5]

In spite of having been offered generous gifts, Kosuke refused to relent in his demand for the executions of the men who had "insulted" his father. Even though Tachibana never conceded to Kosuke's petition, Bunkō's conclusion is that a mere low-ranking bannerman, who had little understanding of his obligations and rights under the lord-retainer relationship, had gained a kind of victory over the powerful daimyō, Tachibana Sadayoshi. The story is an excellent illustration of Bunkō's argument that the most important Confucian relationship and the bedrock of Tokugawa Neo-Confucianism was in shambles. This historical record of an actual interaction between a daimyō and a hatamoto also challenges the image of a solidified, static society in the Tokugawa period.

4. Ibid.
5. Ibid., 236–37.

Gift Giving Replaces the Samurai Ethic

In 1756 the daimyō of Morioka domain (in present-day Iwate prefecture), Nanbu Toshikatsu (1725–79), was returning to his castle after having spent a year in residence in Edo, as required under the provisions of the alternate-year attendance system. Soon after arriving home, he dispatched his messenger, Ōzaki Tomoemon, to return to Edo to inform the shogunal authorities that he had arrived back safely in Morioka. (Tokugawa law mandated giving notice of the arrival of a daimyō in his home domain to prevent the daimyō from diverting his travel to another area for the purpose of plotting with other provincial lords against the bakufu.) Morioka was a domain of one-hundred thousand koku but was given the political ranking of a domain twice its size. This was because the Nanbu clan, under Nanbu Toshinao (r. 1599–1632), had sided with Tokugawa Ieyasu at the Battle of Sekigahara. According to Toshikatsu's status and the size of his fief, Ozaki should have been met personally by the senior counselor on duty, Nishio Tadanao (1689–1760).[6] However, according to Bunkō's account titled "The Tribute from Morioka" (*Morioka mitsugi monogatari*, 1757), the senior counselor was extremely busy that year, and a chamberlain met Ōzaki instead.[7] Ōzaki considered it an insult not to be allowed to see the senior counselor personally. As a protest against this indignity, the messenger immediately returned to Morioka without having left the customary tribute gifts for the shogun. The bakufu then accused the daimyō, Nanbu Toshikatsu, of having insulted Shogun Tokugawa Ieshige by not having offered any gifts, and the daimyō was ordered confined to house arrest in his castle in Morioka as punishment.

Almost a year later, Lord Nanbu, still confined to his castle, dispatched Ōzaki to Edo a second time with orders to present the tribute gifts that he had refused to leave the year before. On arriving at the shogunal castle in Edo, the messenger was properly received by the senior counselor, who accepted the gifts in the name of the shogun and recip-

6. Nishio was the daimyō of Yokosuka (in present-day Shizuoka prefecture) from 1713 to 1760.

7. Baba, *Morioka mitsugi monogatari* in *Kaitei shiseki shūran*, ed. Kondō Heijō (Tokyo: Rinsen shoten, 1984), 440–49. This story is written primarily in *kanbun* (sinified Japanese). The details of the story also appear in the official chronicle, *Tokugawa jikki*, 45: 288.

rocated with gifts for Lord Nanbu. Satisfied that the senior counselor had made proper amends for the insult of the previous year, Ōzaki returned to Morioka with the gifts from the shogun. The order was then given that Lord Nanbu was to be freed from house arrest.

Bunkō claims that the alternate-year attendance system was a cause of such petty quibbling among daimyō and shogunal officials. The exchange of gifts had become a mere pretense of loyalty to Tokugawa Ieshige and had replaced the traditional samurai virtues of true loyalty and fidelity.[8] For Bunkō, this incident was another clear indication that the samurai ethic of duty and self-sacrifice was continuing to break down.

The Marriage of a Daimyō's Daughter to an Illiterate Commoner

The beautiful daughter of Honjō Michikata (1733–60), the daimyō of Shinano-Takatomi (in present-day Nagano and Gifu prefectures), enjoyed the pleasures and pastimes available to the young women of her status. She took sightseeing excursions, was given instruction in dancing, samisen, and traditional flower arranging, and also studied the Chinese and Japanese classics. Unfortunately, her impressive education in arts and literature did not seem to have the desired effect on her character. As she grew older, she continued to act in an untrustworthy and irresponsible manner. Her studies, contrary to expectation, apparently did nothing to enhance her virtue. Even though she was brought up in a daimyō household, she was far from the noble and refined woman of status that everyone had expected she would become.[9]

In a humorous account titled "The Illicit Affair of the Daughter of Honjō [Michikata], Lord of Yamato" (*Honjō Yamato no kami sokujo fugi no koto*, 1756), Bunkō tells the story of this young woman, who appeared to the casual observer to be serious in her cultural pursuits and a devout Buddhist, but was really an uncivil, ill-mannered, and immature girl.[10] She often spoke about the donations she offered to build Buddhist pago-

8. Kondō Heijō, ed., *Kaitei shiseki shūran*, 447.
9. Baba, *Tōji chinsetsu yōhiroku*, 241.
10. Ibid., 241–42.

das, the pilgrimages she made to temples, and her faithful recitation of the Buddhist *nenbutsu* prayer.[11] However, Bunkō informs his reader that her piety and benevolence were only for show. She was really a boor and a hypocrite who often spoke in a vulgar manner and had a loud, affected laugh that erupted at inappropriate times, a trait quite unbecoming for a daimyō's daughter. Bunkō reminds his reader how ironic it is that a typical criticism samurai would have of commoners, that they laughed out loud, could be seen in a daimyō's household. A young woman of elite status had the same fault of laughing boisterously, with mouth wide open.

One day when this young woman was on a pilgrimage to a Buddhist temple, she passed quietly in front of a young man who was praying and discreetly dropped a pornographic book into his lap. The young man, whom she did not know, had been devoutly chanting the nenbutsu prayer, but he stopped, picked up the book, and put it inside his kimono. He looked around, intrigued by this not too subtle proposition. Since there were other people praying in the temple, she had not wanted to speak to the young man directly. After all, he was a commoner; she was the daughter of a daimyō. The reader learns that the young man's name is Bunshichi, and he hails from Sakai-chō, not far from the "pleasure" quarter near the center of town at Nihonbashi. Bunshichi did menial jobs at the kabuki theater in Sakai, which was one of the three famous Kabuki theaters of Edo.

Even though he did not know who the woman was who had dropped the book into his lap, Bunshichi decided that he must immediately ask someone to pen a love note to her. The boy was unable to write himself. His illiteracy indicates that he was a poor commoner with few prospects, not even a member of the rising merchant class. Bunkō does not disclose the contents of his letter, but Lord Honjō's daughter was quick to reply to it and even gave Bunshichi precise instructions on how he was to visit her without being noticed.

On the day planned for the secret tryst, one of the maids acted as a lookout (*monomi*). Bunshichi came dressed up as a woman, and the maid led him into the daimyō's mansion. There were repeated rendezvous that took place in precisely the same way, and the two continued their illicit

11. A prayer of the jōdo sect of Buddhism: "I take refuge in the Amida Buddha."

affair in secret for quite some time. Bunkō comments sarcastically: "Such incidents among samurai women are really few and far between!"[12] After a time, the two lovers, suspecting that they could not continue the affair for long under such circumstances without being noticed, decided to run away together.

His daughter's decision to run off with a commoner was a great shock to Lord Honjō and to his household, including the maids who had aided her. The daimyō realized that his reputation could be ruined if news of it got out, so he summoned his retainers and ordered them to use any means necessary to bring his daughter back. There was only one caveat, however. The search must be carried out covertly so that the honor of the domain and its lord's integrity would in no way be tarnished.

As the story continues, the confused retainers have no idea how to go about trying to find their lord's daughter. A variety of suggestions are made. Some propose that they should bring the matter before the bakufu, thinking that neglecting to inform the officials of the situation could bring serious repercussions. Others, realizing that taking such action would not only be a risk but would also be a violation of their lord's order to keep the matter confidential, decide to go out into the streets themselves and ask random commoners if anyone had seen the daughter of Lord Honjō and her companion, Bunshichi. Telling insignificant and ignorant commoners that their lord's daughter was missing, they reasoned, would not actually violate their promise to keep the matter a secret. Bunkō masterfully brings out the irony of samurai, members of the elite class of Tokugawa society, having to appeal for aid from any mere commoner whom they happen to come across to carry out their lord's command.

The first person they approach is the retired sumo referee Kimura Kyobei. (The reader will remember from chapter 7 that Kimura is blind.) After telling Kimura what had happened, Lord Honjō's retainers listen in astonishment to Kimura's reply. "It will be no trouble at all for me to bring her back safe and sound in a palanquin. Have no worry. I'll be sure to keep the whole thing secret so that your reputations will not be harmed." The samurai gratefully accepted the old man's offer. To their amazement,

12. Baba, *Tōji chinsetsu yōhiroku*, 241–42.

it was not long before the daimyō's daughter was found and brought back. Everyone in Lord Honjō's residence was quite relieved that there had been no dishonor to the domain or disgrace to their lord and that his daughter had been brought back without anyone knowing where she had been or what she had done. Lord Honjō's retainers seemed to have preserved their own reputations as well, and all seemed to have ended happily—that is, until Bunkō reveals that Honjō Michikata promised Kimura an annual stipend of rice, enough to support two people for the rest of his life. Even if not a large stipend, receiving an annual subsidy from a daimyō makes Kimura Kyobei, a commoner, in effect the equal of a samurai retainer. "Kimura Kyobei was the poor blind beggar everyone used to see sitting on the corner at Bakuro-chō 4-chōme. Now, thanks to the stipend he receives from the Honjō house, he has all the food and money he needs."[13]

Bakuro-chō, where Kimura used to sit and beg, was the neighborhood where Bunkō himself had lived for a time. He and the people of the locale were apparently familiar with the sight of this old retired sumo referee begging by the side of the road. The irony of the story, of course, is that it was a blind man who was able to do what healthy "sharp-eyed" samurai could not do. The Honjō clan assumed that its reputation had been left intact, but actually the opposite occurred. Because of the inability of the retainers to recover the daimyō's daughter themselves, the reputation of the domain and of its lord and retainers was exposed to public ridicule. Honjō Michikata was not even aware of the derision and scorn that was being spread about him around town. Bunkō uses the example of Honjō's foolish retainers and his household as a microcosm of the samurai class as a whole, an example of the inability of samurai to carry out their duties and fulfill their obligations to their lord in a manner expected of their class. The incident of a daimyō's daughter courting and then eloping with an uneducated commoner again shows the collapse of the social boundaries and discredits the purported order of the Confucian hierarchical society.

13. Ibid., 242.

Undisciplined Tokugawa Retainers

In late 1754 a retainer from Yamashiro domain (now part of Kyoto prefecture) was walking alone in the Edo neighborhood of Shiba Rōgetsuchō.[14] Suddenly and without warning, eight samurai who were retainers of Tokugawa Munekatsu (1705–61), the powerful lord of Owari, stopped him and complained that he was blocking their way.[15] Though retainers of an illustrious Tokugawa branch family, these eight samurai behaved no better than street ruffians. On a number of occasions they had attacked and even beaten people to death with impunity. Bunkō writes about this incident in *A Confidential Record of Current, Little-Known Facts:*[16]

> There is no one in Edo who does not tremble in fear when they see the Owari seal. The retainers of that domain are rogues who will beat half-dead anyone who happens to bump into them by accident. On one occasion a samurai was walking along, minding his own business. He was unaccompanied by servants, and he was not wearing hakama and haori [the formal samurai attire]. A procession of samurai from Owari came up behind him and started cursing him for blocking the way. The lone samurai tried to let them pass peaceably, but they kept taunting him and then beat him up.[17]

As Bunkō reports the incident, the Owari men repeatedly tried to provoke the samurai with crude language and insults and finally knocked him to the ground. Such incidents, he says, were not uncommon in Edo. There were samurai from all over Japan residing in the capital under the provisions of the alternate-year attendance system. It is not surprising that the retainers of the larger, more powerful domains would sometime harass and intimidate samurai who had come to Edo from the smaller, less significant provincial fiefs.

When Mizuno Tadahide (1697–1756), the daimyō of Yamashiro, heard about this insult to one of his retainers, he was understandably angry

14. Ibid., 188.

15. Located in present-day Aichi Prefecture, Owari was the largest domain belonging to a member of the Tokugawa clan, apart from the areas directly under shogunal control. The daimyō of Owari was the highest in rank among the three branches of the Tokugawa who descended from the three youngest sons of Ieyasu: Yoshinao, Yorinobu, and Yorifusa.

16. Baba, *Tōji chinsetsu yōhiroku*, 188–90.

17. Ibid., 188.

and went immediately to the Owari mansion of Tokugawa Munekatsu in Edo and requested that the eight men from Owari who had beaten his retainer be punished by decapitation. Munekatsu tried to appease Lord Mizuno, promising that the one who was responsible for the incident would indeed be executed. Mizuno, however, was not placated by the Tokugawa promise and insisted that not just one but all eight of the samurai who had accosted and injured his retainer should be beheaded. As things turned out, none of the eight Owari samurai were ever punished or even reprimanded. This injustice, which Tokugawa Munekatsu permitted, was indicative not only of Tokugawa Munekatsu's unwillingness or inability to control and discipline his own retainers but also a symptom of the decline in samurai discipline that was prevalent at the time.

Self-Indulgent Daimyō

In another short essay titled "The Disgrace of Toda, Lord of Echizen" (*Echizen no kami bujoku no koto*, 1756), Bunkō reports that the signs of systemic collapse in the social order can be found even as far to the south as Hizen (in present-day Nagasaki and Saga prefectures). The situation there was a clear example of a daimyō's inability to govern.

> Toda Tadami [1689–1746] was the father of Toda Tadamitsu [1730–81], the present daimyō of Hizen and lord of Shimabara castle. Tadami himself was from birth a bit of an ass (*umare tsuki gudon nashi hito nari*), and his retainers at Shimabara castle were no different: lazy louts who, along with the old daimyō himself, had long since succumbed to a life of debauchery. The retainers of his son Tadamitsu, the present daimyō, are no different from his father's retainers. Although they are supposed to protect and defend their lord, they spend all of their time doing menial tasks, such as preparing his meals and cleaning dishes. All the while, Tadamitsu is spending his time in various diversions and entertainments.[18]

Tadamitsu looked down on his retainers to such an extent that he had them do the work of common servants rather than encourage them to train in the martial arts or take up the educational pursuits that would have benefited them and been more appropriate to their status. Bunkō describes the samurai spending their days being lackeys for Tadamitsu

18. Ibid., 237–38.

and his guests. All the while the daimyō himself was doing nothing in his Edo mansion. Bunkō believed that this was not unlike the general lifestyle of many of the daimyō from the provinces and was yet another example that proved that the samurai class, which was no longer focused on living according to their professed martial spirit, was in swift decline.

Bunkō explains that on one occasion when the elder Toda was absent from the castle, nine of his retainers, including his son Tadamitsu, decided to have some entertainment. When he returned, Lord Toda learned how much money they had wasted eating, drinking, and carousing with prostitutes. Rather than disciplining the samurai himself, however, Toda reported the matter to Senior Counselor Matsudaira Nobutoki (1683–1744). Matsudaira decided that the nine retainers should be punished by being confined to house arrest.

Toda Tadami's son, Tadamitsu, and the other retainers had engaged in precisely the same kind of wasteful spending and debauchery of which the daimyō himself had long been guilty. Bunkō provides clear evidence that the old daimyō is not only a hypocrite, he is also a moral weakling unable to exercise the discipline needed to rein in his own samurai. Bunkō reports, "The behavior of Toda Tadami, lord of Echizen, made him the butt of jokes among the people of Edo."[19] The laxity in samurai discipline and the ineptitude that daimyō such as Toda Tadami and Toda Tadamitsu exhibited were weaknesses that, in Bunkō's opinion, were not only shameful, but "monstrous." This again was a case of the social breakdown that Bunkō claimed was widespread.

In his collection of anecdotes titled "Sketches of Worldly Bannermen" (*Seken o-hatamoto katagi*, 1754), Bunkō asserts that the conditions of peacetime had actually rendered the samurai class superfluous and caused them to become not only corrupt and soft, but immoral as well.

> We have the example of [Toyotomi] Hideyoshi [1536–98] who, having been a lowly servant of Matsushita [Yukitsuna, 1538–98], rose up from obscurity and even attempted to seize control of the whole world.[20] In those days samurai were brave and proficient in the martial arts. Nowadays, however,

19. Ibid., 238–39.

20. Matsushita Yukitsuna (1538–98) was daimyo of Kuno (in present-day Shizuoka prefecture) from 1590 to 1598.

> samurai are brandishing only ceremonial swords in processions. In these times of peace it is only samurai who get rich who are admired. Take for example Yanagisawa [Yoshiyasu, 1658–1714].[21] He managed to move up from being a minor samurai who lived in a small house in Yotsuya with a two- or three-hundred koku income to becoming a daimyō of a 150,000 koku domain. After becoming wealthy he moved into a great mansion. But what is admirable about that? His formerly great mansion today is occupied by Ōtaka Sukeshirō, a shogunal guard, who is a drunkard and who wastes his three hundred koku stipend on loose women.[22]

In the mid-eighteenth century, townspeople saw the samurai strut around arrogantly but aimlessly, often with no skills and no inclination to engage in productive work, making it more and more obvious that many samurai lacked any meaningful purpose. Bunkō criticized the samurai of his own day by expressing his admiration for samurai of former times, such as Toyotomi Hideyoshi, and emphasizing how different they were from the dissolute samurai and daimyō with whom he was familiar.

Bunkō describes other daimyō and samurai he had seen in Edo who, unlike their noble predecessors, had abandoned discipline and led lives of debauchery. He laments that samurai who are promoted to high office are only interested in wealth. The newly-appointed shogunal guard, Ōtaka Sukeshirō, for example, was typical of many in the warrior class. According to Bunkō, he was shallow, soft, and immoral. Each individual Bunkō exposes is a symbol of the corruption of the regime. Some advisers to the shogunate, such as Arai Hakuseki (1657–1725), also judged that the samurai were failing in moral integrity and virtue, and this was a cause of the economic and social problems that plagued Tokugawa society. Bunkō was of the same opinion, but expressed it publically and much more forcefully. His stories and anecdotes illustrate the continued waning of virtue and the degradation of the putative samurai ethic.

21. Yanagisawa Yoshiyasu was son of a low-ranked samurai who had been the daimyō of Kawagoe, a 112,000 koku domain (in present-day Saitama prefecture). He was subsequently transferred to Kofu, a 150,000 koku domain (in present-day Yamanashi prefecture) and was eventually promoted to the office of senior counselor under Shogun Tokugawa Tsunayoshi (r. 1680–1709), serving from 1706 to 1709.

22. Baba, *Seken o-hatamoto katagi*, in Okada Satoshi, *Baba Bunkō shū* (Tokyo: Kokusho kankōkai, 1987), 84.

Fire and Fireworks

Date Yoshimura (1680–1752) was known as the "Great Lord (*taishu*) of Sendai."[23] This accolade was due to his long rule and also because Sendai, with an income of almost two million koku, was one of the largest in the country, comparable even to the great domains of Satsuma and Kaga in the south. As disdain for the samurai class intensified in Edo, Bunkō found an opportunity to satirize this "Great Lord" when one summer evening it was announced that he was to sponsor a fireworks display at the Ryōgoku Bridge.[24] Bunkō sets the scene in an anecdote in *Contemporary Edo: An Album of One Hundred Monsters* titled "The Monster Enjoying the Cool of the Evening" (*Yūsuzumi no bakemono no ben*, 1758).[25] Everyone went out to the bridge, enjoying the cool of the summer evening, and waited to watch what was expected to be a marvelous display provided courtesy of the "Great Lord" himself. There were commoners and samurai all flocking to the bridge to get a good position to see the fireworks. Others were boarding large pleasure barges and some little flat boats, and the whole surface of the river was covered with boats. In fact, Bunkō reports, there was not an empty boat in all of Edo.[26]

Since the Manji period (1658–61) wealthy merchants had vied with one another to see who could fill the night sky with the most color and produce the largest, most beautiful fireworks displays. Unfortunately, because of a series of fire disasters in the subsequent Kanbun era (1661–73), fireworks began to be more strictly regulated and were forbidden in urban areas except over water. People were allowed to shoot off only simple hand-held fireworks from the bridges or from boats. But this restriction was temporary, and by Bunkō's time large fireworks displays were again common. It was customary in the summer months for groups of people to gather along the Ryōgoku River to watch the fireworks, and on this particular occasion the display was expected to be especially spectacular

23. Date Yoshimura was the daimyō of Sendai from 1703 to 1743.

24. The Ryōgoku River, one of the first *sakariba* that became popular in the Kyōhō period (1716–36), was a place where people would gather for ceremonies, moon viewing, fireworks, or other pastimes throughout the year. It is the present-day Sumida River, which was the boundary between Musashi and Shimosa, and hence referred to as the Ryōgoku (two countries) River.

25. Baba, *Tōdai Edo hyakubakemono*, 10.

26. Ibid.

because the Great Lord of Sendai was the promoter, at least according to the announcement.

As things turned out, there was nothing to be seen of the Great Lord's fireworks. Evening came, and people waited and waited, but nothing happened. Then finally there was an announcement from the bridge: "Business in Lord Date's official residence has forced a postponement of the display. This evening's fireworks will be held two evenings from tonight." The people who had rented boats and waited all along the banks went home disheartened and upset, but two nights later they came out again, hoping to see a magnificent fireworks display. The vendors, selling food and drink, were doing a thriving business. People were laughing and shouting in excitement. However, the same thing happened, and again there was nothing to be seen. Excitement turned to anger, and people saw that they had been duped a second time by the Great Lord of Sendai. No one thought to ask the person who had made the two announcements why the fireworks had been canceled a second time. This man was a boat owner who rented pleasure boats at Edo Bridge.[27] His name was Kazusaya San'emon, and it was he who had made the announcement about the fireworks display so that he could make a lot of money on those two nights renting out his boats.

This is one of Bunkō's more subtle satires, because he says nothing directly in criticism of the "Great Lord" of Sendai. The boat owner who deceived the people and announced a fireworks display is the one Bunkō calls a "monster." On another level, however, it becomes clear that the satire is indeed directed against Date Yoshimura. Fireworks displays were sponsored by merchants, like Kazusaya San'emon, not by daimyō. It would have been highly inappropriate, especially for a powerful daimyō like Date Yoshimura, to stoop to the position of a "lowly" merchant and sponsor such a display for commoners. The reader is not aware until the end of the anecdote that Yoshimura is not sponsoring the fireworks, but it would have been quite believable if he had, since daimyō conducted their affairs more and more often like merchants. People had become ac-

27. Edo Bridge (Edobashi) is to the east of Nihonbashi on the Sumida River in present-day Chūō-ku, Nihonbashi Honmachi 1-chōme.

customed to the blurring of social boundaries and to seeing samurai and even daimyō giving themselves over to merchant values, trying to raise needed cash.

Bunkō referred to the boat owner, Kazusaya San'emon, as "the monster enjoying the cool of the evening." This reference is quite ironic, because it becomes obvious that the real monster is Date Yoshimura himself. He had the reputation of being the lord of a domain where there were a frequent number of fires in residential areas of Sendai. People had repeatedly suffered the loss of their homes and property as a result. Yoshimura had done nothing to relieve their suffering, nor had he taken any measures to prevent such periodic conflagrations from occurring at an increasing rate.

A short history of the daimyō who succeeded him in office will illustrate this point. Date Munemura (r. 1743–56) was Yoshimura's immediate successor. During the thirteen years that he was daimyō there were only three major fires in the domain. Date Shigemura (r. 1756–90) followed and was daimyō for only two years when Bunkō wrote his story about the anticipated great fireworks display at Ryōgoku Bridge in 1758. Up to that time Sendai had seen no major incidents of arson or of destruction by fire. By contrast, the time that Yoshimura was in office was a period of unprecedented disasters. The domain experienced the incredible number of twenty major conflagrations in which thousands of residences and businesses were destroyed and thousands of lives were lost. Even considering his longer tenure in office, the number of fires was a scandal, and so he is the real "monster" of Bunkō's anecdote.

Of course, Date Yoshimura was lord of the domain for forty years, a much longer tenure than that of either Munemura or Shigemura, but in the forty-year period there were an unprecedented number of large, destructive fires. There is dark humor as well as irony in Bunkō's account of the "Great Lord of Sendai" having allegedly ordered a fireworks display in Edo, and the irony is actually enhanced by the fact that it was only a rumor started by a merchant.

A history of Yoshimura's predecessors in office will perhaps illustrate the point even further. In the forty-three-year rule of Date Tsunamura (r. 1660–1703), a tenure even longer than that of Yoshimura, there were no major fires recorded in the domain, except for the burning of Zuihōji Temple in 1671 and the fire that destroyed the domain's Kyoto mansion (*yashiki*) in 1689. Yoshimura may not have actually planned to sponsor a fireworks display at Ryōgoku Bridge in Edo, but he was held responsible for many horrendous "fireworks displays" in his home domain of Sendai.[28] Bunkō brings out the irony in the contrast between the great number of fires in Sendai during the rule of Date Yoshimura and the relatively small number during the rule of his immediate successors and his predecessors in office.

"Kazusaya San'emon," the merchant who rented boats at the Sumida River, is a fictional but significant name. "Kazusaya" is an allusion to one of the most prestigious bordellos of the Yoshiwara district of the same name and was commonly associated with the name of another first-class Yoshiwara establishment, the Tamaya Inn. Both were at the top of the list of the most elegant establishments in Yoshiwara.[29] Coincidentally, "Tamaya" was also the name of one of the best-known mass producers of fireworks in Edo. The allusions to the Yoshiwara district suggest that the rumors about Great Lord of Sendai's diversions in the "pleasure" district are certainly true—as true as the fact of the terrible fires in Sendai, even if the rumor that he was going to provide fireworks entertainment in Edo proved to be false.

Bunkō associates Date Yoshimura and the catastrophic fires during his tenure as daimyō with the avarice of the merchant class, as well as with the diversions of the "pleasure" quarters, illustrating how a satire can operate on a number of different levels at the same time. None of these associations are explicit in Bunkō's anecdote, but the implication that there is a breakdown in the understanding of proper status relationships (daimyō being confused with merchants) and a failure of morality (the lack of measures to prevent fires and frequent appearances in the "pleasure" quarters) shows that this great daimyō was a "monster" in both his private life and in his public rule.

Even though in the 1750s there was no clamor for a popular revolt that

28. Kimura Motoi et al., eds., *Hanshi daijiten* (Tokyo: Yuzankaku, 1989), 1: 113–15.
29. Seigle, *Yoshiwara: The Glittering World of the Japanese Courtesan*, 121.

would overthrow Tokugawa rule or radically change the political status quo, a rebellion of sorts was indeed taking place. There was deep and growing skepticism about the government's capacity to operate under the norms of the social hierarchy and by its own professed ethical standards. Confidence in the shogunate's legitimacy was slowly but surely fading away.

10 | THE CHRISTIAN QUESTION

Not only is there no religion without secrecy, but there is no human existence without it.

KEES W. BOLLE

Was Baba Bunkō a Christian?

After Bunkō renounced his samurai status, resigned his government post, and began giving lectures criticizing various aspects of the prevailing culture of Tokugawa Japan, he turned to writing satirical essays and anecdotes directed against those in high office in the government and in the Buddhist and Confucian establishment. He denounced as "monsters" anyone in a position of authority who did not live up to specific standards of conduct and morality. Whether a person was a samurai or commoner, a Confucian scholar or Buddhist monk, a prostitute or an outcast, he looked upon them all as subject to the same objective moral criteria. His denunciations of religious, civil, and educational leaders were unique in the literature of the Tokugawa era, and his analysis of Tokugawa society can only be described as unprecedented for Japan at the time. His particular concern for oppressed peasants and Yoshiwara courtesans was also unparalleled in the history of the period. Even the civil authorities were able to see the challenge to their authority that Bunkō repre-

Epigraph is from Kees W. Bolle, ed., *Secrecy in Religions* (Leiden: E. J. Brill, 1987), 1; cited in Peter Nosco, "Secrecy and the Transmission of Tradition: Issues in the Study of the 'Underground' Christians," *Japanese Journal of Religious Studies* 20, no. 1 (1993): 24.

sented, as is clearly evidenced by the fact that he was the only person during the Tokugawa period to have been executed for what he had said and what he had written.

Ralph Waldo Emerson's words cited in the first chapter, "All history becomes subjective; in other words, there is properly no history, only biography," are as true for Bunkō as for any other historian. Bunkō's historical accounts and personal anecdotes make up his own unique history of Tokugawa Japan. As a writer who actually lived in Edo during the period about which he is writing, even his personal reflections and subjective opinions are as much a part of the history of Tokugawa Japan as are the writings of any modern Western historian who claims to be completely objective. Modern historians are writing from a detached outsider's perspective, while Bunkō is an eyewitness to the events he is recording. The influence from his culture and from the literary styles and traditions of many contemporary writers are apparent in Bunkō's works, but his ability to make value judgments about the culture and to point out the differences between his views and those of other writers of the period is striking.

The perspective that he offers is a challenge to modern historians of the period to look again at the place of Christianity in Japan in the eighteenth century, when a Christian would carefully guard his beliefs behind a veil of secrecy. It is obvious from Bunkō's direct references to Christianity in "A Collection of Useless Grumblings" that he was not only familiar with the religion but held it in high regard. As the reader will recall, Bunkō referred to the flag of the Shimabara rebellion as "the principal image of the Christian Lord of Heaven," which "should replace the imperial and shogunal crests." The banner, which Bunkō describes as "the body of a person," was actually a representation of the host and chalice of the Catholic Eucharist. His description of the banner is evidence of a clear Catholic understanding of the meaning of the doctrine of the Eucharist.

The opinions expressed in "A Collection of Useless Grumblings" put all of his writings in a context that allow them to be interpreted as Christian writing. Even if this key text were missing from the corpus of his work, the reader would still be drawn to reflect carefully on his motivation for attacking the political, religious, and social institutions of the period and his rationale for defending those segments of the population that were commonly despised. His positions on important issues are not found in the writings of any other salient author of the period. His anecdotes, which put Buddhism, Confucianism, and Shintoism in a disparaging light, challenge the historian and the literary critic to ask further questions about Bunkō's religious convictions. The thesis that he was a hidden Christian puts many of his satirical essays into an understandable context.

Bunkō would not have been unlike the tens of thousands of other hidden Christians who were scattered throughout Japan in the eighteenth century, whose faith remained completely hidden or only partially and very guardedly expressed. Baba Bunkō is evidence that a Christian view of society did exist and did find expression even in the middle of the Tokugawa period, a century after Christianity was banned and a century before Christians came out of hiding and began again to freely practice their religion.

There is no question that Bunkō ever openly professed to being a Christian. No baptismal certificate will ever be found to prove beyond a doubt that he was a Christian. No hidden Christians were ever issued any document that resembled a baptismal certificate. The existence or nonexistence of such a document has no bearing on the issue of whether he was a Christian or not. He lived in a time of persecution when his convictions and beliefs as a Christian were necessarily kept secret. This secrecy was an important aspect of the daily life of Christians and a significant characteristic of Christianity in Japan in the Tokugawa period. However, it is apparent that in addition to his writings in "A Collection of Useless Grumblings," Bunkō's open praise for the virtue of the lowly and despised and his condemnation of the powerful and influential as "monsters" bring his hidden convictions into the light. These beliefs were not based on any common principles that people held in Tokugawa Japan; rather, they reflect fundamental Christian values.

Japanese Contact with Christianity in the Eighteenth Century

The Italian Jesuit missionary Giovanni Battista Sidotti (1668–1714) had long heard accounts of the Christians in Japan who had been martyred for their faith. With a desire to follow in their footsteps, he asked permission to go to Japan and was sent by his superiors, but almost immediately on landing at Yakushima (in present-day Kagoshima prefecture) in 1708, he was arrested and detained in Nagasaki. The following year, he was taken to Edo and questioned by bakufu adviser and Confucian scholar Arai Hakuseki. This was the first time in almost a century that there had been a civil meeting and conversation between a Christian and a Japanese official. Sidotti impressed Hakuseki with his cultured demeanor and his intelligence, and over time the two men developed a mutual respect. Sidotti attempted to explain to Hakuseki that, contrary to what the Japanese believed to be true, missionaries would not be the first wave of an invasion force of Western armies.

After their conversations, Hakuseki recommended that the priest be deported rather than executed, even though he was guilty of the capital crime of entering Japan. The bakufu found Hakuseki's suggestion of leniency to be without legal precedent, but instead of handing down a sentence of death, it was decided that Sidotti should be imprisoned for life. He was sent to the *Kirishitan yashiki* (Christian mansion) in Myōgadani (present-day Kohinata, Bunkyō-ku, Tokyo). Hakuseki recommended that Sidotti not be treated in the manner of other prisoners but be given proper care and respect. Six years later, however, in the autumn of 1714, Sidotti was found dead in his cell from exposure and starvation.

News of Sidotti's death affected Hakuseki deeply. He wrote his reflections on the experience of his encounter with the missionary in *Information about the West* (*Seiyo kibun*, 1715), a three-volume study of the "five continents" with an overview of some of the main tenets of Roman Catholicism. Since this work contained explicit references to Christianity, the bakufu did not allow it to be published, even though the references were not particularly favorable to Christianity.[1] Hakuseki wrote: "When

1. Fujita, *Japan's Christian Encounter with Christianity*, 237, 238.

he [Sidotti] came to speak about his religion, it appeared to me to be not in the slightest respect like the true way.... At first I thought him very intelligent, but when he began to explain his doctrine he became like a fool."[2] Hakuseki, of course, would have had no choice but to condemn Sidotti's religious beliefs, and consequently his statements were perfectly in line with the government's anti-Christian policy. Hakuseki was also disturbed by Sidotti's motivation for coming to Japan in the first place. There was some optimism in the West that Japan might be a fruitful area for conversions to Christianity because loyalty to the bakufu had weakened due to the poor economic situation. Hakuseki reported, "When he [Sidotti] lived in his own land, he heard that gold and iron coins had become altered in Japan, and thought, perhaps people may have become poor there; if so, there will certainly be distress. When the people are suffering, the command of the government prohibiting the religion of Yaso [i.e. Jesus] will not be kept."[3] Though not apparently fearful of Christianity himself, Hakuseki's explanation caused alarm in the government.

Hakuseki's writings about the first priest in sixty-five years to enter Japan resulted in a renewed crackdown on Christianity and the reproclamation of the anti-Christian edicts. An increased monetary reward was offered to informants of the whereabouts of Christians, and public notice boards (*kōsatsu*) that called on the public to report the presence of Christians began to reappear. A year before Bunkō was executed, the publication of *The Real Record of the Arrival of the Christian Sect in Japan* (*Kirishitan shūmon raichō jikki*), cited in chapter 2, reflected this resurgence of the fear of Christianity. This terror of the Western religion was doubtless a factor in the decision to put Bunkō to death for no legally justified reason.

The fear of Christianity continued to persist in the decades following Bunkō's death. By the 1820s, there was still alarm that a military invasion by European powers was imminent. It was believed that Christianity was, in the final analysis, the main cause of this threat. Aizawa Seishisai argues in *New Thesis* that the secret of Western military strength lies in Christianity. He labeled the foreign religion a state cult and said that

2. Arai Hakuseki, *Seiyō kibun*, cited in Murdoch, *A History of Japan*, 306.
3. Ibid., 308.

Western leaders propagate it in order to cultivate voluntary allegiance both of the people in their own lands and in the territories that they colonize overseas. Aizawa's words, which expressed the lingering fear of Christianity that existed throughout the Tokugawa period, were a warning to Japan's leaders:

> For close to three hundred years now the Western Barbarians have rampaged on the high seas. Why are they able to enlarge their territories and fulfill their every desire? Does their wisdom and courage exceed that of ordinary men? Is their government so benevolent that they win popular support? . . . Do they possess some superhuman, divine powers? Christianity is the sole key to their success. It is a truly evil and base religion, barely worth discussing. But . . . they can easily deceive stupid commoners with it. . . . Once bewitched by Christianity, they cannot be brought back to their senses. Herein lies the secret of the barbarians' success.[4]

For Aizawa as well as for the bakufu, Christianity was a belief system that had the power to subvert the social order of nations and topple governments by force. He warned the government in 1825 that the Christian threat had never ended and that the Westerners would someday in the future again bring Christianity to Japan. "They [the Western nations] propagate Christianity to subvert it [Japan] from within. Once our people's hearts and minds are bewitched by Christianity, they will greet the barbarian host with open arms, and we will be powerless to stop them."[5]

What Aizawa had warned would take place seemed to actually happen only two years later, when in 1827 Toyota Mitsugi (as discussed in chapter 2) was arrested for the possession of Christian books that had been smuggled into Japan from China. The government simply charged her with sorcery and illegally making money by performing exorcisms of fox-spirits, and made no mention of her apparent Christian affiliation or of the fact that the group she had organized had been in existence forty years before it was discovered. Among the members of her group who were also arrested was Iwai Onseki (d. 1829), who under torture confessed that that he had seen Christian books in the possession of other members. One of those was Fujita Kenzō (1771–1829), a physician and

4. Wakabayashi, ed., *Anti-Foreign and Western Learning in Early Modern Japan*, 200.
5. Ibid.

scholar who studied astronomy, science, geography, and religion, who was also arrested along with Toyota Mitsugi and Iwai Onseki. All of them were executed, even though there was no official mention of their Christian affiliation.

It cannot be determined precisely when, but at some point the shogunal high court ceased making any direct references to Christianity at the time of arrest or during the trials of suspected Christians. Such was the case in the trial of Toyota Mitsugi and her companions. As mentioned above, people in Osaka and Kyoto, the area from which Toyota came, who knew of the details of the incident, referred to the arrest of Toyota and other members of her group as "the Christian affair," but there is no record of any such accusation having been brought up at her trial.

As time passed, Christianity was not simply a forbidden sect. By the 1700s a fear of Christianity was widespread among both officials and commoners, and that fear continued to be a characteristic of the Japanese mentality throughout the Tokugawa period and even as the country moved toward the Meiji Restoration. An 1868 pamphlet titled *Gossip about the Rise and Progress of the False Religion in Nagasaki* informed readers that even though the Christian sect had been strictly prohibited for many years, "the tainted ones" do not disappear.[6] Christians, the pamphlet reported, have power over the fox-spirits and the ability to cast spells and to bring down curses. The French missionaries at Oura Church in Nagasaki "make converts either by giving money to the poor, by performing magic for those who love wonders, or by appealing to the emotions of people to disregard all the social mores of mankind [i.e., of Japan]. This is a fearful state of things indeed."[7] The Japanese took these accusations seriously. Hidden Japanese Catholics had emerged from hiding only three years before *Gossip about the Rise and Progress of the False Religion in Nagasaki* appeared, and soon thousands of them would be held in concentration camps.

6. Paske-Smith, *Japanese Traditions of Christianity*, 103–12, 126.
7. Ibid., 126.

A Definition of Christian Literature

Bunkō's essay "A Collection of Useless Grumblings," which was discussed at length in chapter 2, has never been listed among works of Japanese Christian literature, even though it deals with specific Catholic themes. This is probably because it is outside the time frame in which Japanese Christian literature was supposed to have been written. Scholars in the West have restricted the genre of Japanese Christian literature to the so-called Christian century of the late sixteenth and early seventeenth centuries and have assumed that an eighteenth-century Christian literature could not have been produced. It has incorrectly been taken for granted that there were no Japanese Catholics alive in the eighteenth century to write anything. Historians acknowledge that some sixteenth- and seventeenth-century Christian texts were still extant in the 1700s, but to suggest that Christian writings were actually being composed at that late date, when being a Christian was a capital offense, would not be compatible with the history of Christianity in Japan that modern historians have constructed.

References to Christianity, formulated as anti-Christian polemics, do appear all through the seventeenth, eighteenth, and nineteenth centuries, surfacing in the writings of well-known scholars, such as Hayashi Razan, Suzuki Shōsan, Kumazawa Banzan, Arai Hakuseki, Miura Baien, and Aizawa Seishisai. But historians have not seriously considered the fact that if Christian texts had indeed not been composed in Japan after 1640, then there would have been no reason for these anti-Christian attacks or a fear of Christianity. A Christian text was written as late as 1800, when Fujita Kenzō, the physician arrested with Toyota Mitsugi in the "Christian affair" recounted above, wrote: "Truth seems to lie in the teaching of Jesus (*Yaso*). Thus, the grace of God is given to everyone equally."[8] Such indisputably Christian proclamations of faith challenge historians to reexamine the question of whether or not texts actually composed in the eighteenth and early nineteenth centuries, such as those of Baba Bunkō, should be considered "Christian texts." If

8. Cited in *Osaka Nichinichi Shinbun*, September 30, 2005, http://www.nnn.co.jp/dainichi/rensai/naniwa/naniwa050730.html

it can be acknowledged that "A Collection of Useless Grumblings" is an eighteenth-century Christian work, then Bunkō's other writings can also be read as the reflections and observations of a Christian author. It is obvious, simply judging from the content and tone of this work, that it is a Christian text.

What about the other writings of Bunkō, many of which have been analyzed above, that offer no specifically Christian content or terminology? Can they be said to be Christian writings as well? For those historians who continue to assume that there could not possibly have been any Christian writings in the middle of the Tokugawa period, a different approach, rather than simply analyzing the content of the works, might be more convincing. A methodology in which one begins with the question, "What would Christian discourse look like in the 1700s, if it did exist?" would allow the historian to first create a definition of Christian literature and then see if Bunkō's writings would fit that definition. Of course, one would first need to construct a definition of Christian literature that would apply to the particular historical circumstances of the period under study. One would then ask: "What would be the characteristics of a Christian literature composed in Japan in the 1700s during a period of persecution when Christianity had to be kept secret?" One might answer that such a literature would, among its characteristics, reflect opposition to the religious persecution that was being perpetrated by the Tokugawa shogunate and would be a literature of political dissent. Such a literature might also advocate an alternative set of values that would go against the prevailing culture and be directed against much of the religious and philosophical underpinnings of the political regime that sustained a policy of persecution against Christianity. But perhaps the most important characteristic of such a literature, particularly in Japan, would be its secretiveness and enigmatic quality. In other words, the Christian characteristics of such a literature would purposely be indirect and would usually avoid specifically or directly advocating Christian doctrine. It would not use Christian vocabulary or make references to Christianity, except possibly in an oblique way or in a way that could be understood only by Christians.

Japanese Christian texts written during the "Christian century" consisted of explicit teachings that were uniquely Christian, and so one might insist that any Christian writings everywhere and for all time must do the same. However, a Christian literature in a time of persecution would not necessarily be obviously Christian to the outside observer. One should also remember that it was not always the case that the main thrust of Christian writings even in the "Christian century" was to explain Christian theology or doctrine. Often the purpose was more to nourish the moral life of the individuals in the Christian community.

Scholars have been unanimous in their judgment that *Dialogue between Myōshū and Yūtei* (*Myōtei mondo*, 1605), for example, is a Christian text that was written in the "Christian century." However, if the author, Fabian Fucan (1565–1621), were not known to have been a Christian and a Jesuit scholastic (seminarian) at the time of the writing, modern readers may not necessarily reach a consensus that the text was without doubt written by a Christian. Ebisawa Arimichi (1910–92), historian of Japanese Christianity, has drawn attention to the fact that the author of *Dialogue between Myōshū and Yūtei* was a person who, in fact, did not actually possess a firm Christian faith, nor did he, though intellectually gifted, give evidence of an ability to grasp the basic tenets of Christian doctrine.[9] Fabian's eventual renunciation of Christianity and his authorship of the anti-Christian tract *Deus Destroyed* (*Ha Daiusu*, 1620) certainly supports Arimichi's argument that he had never been a fully committed Christian. If that is true, his writings might be termed "Christian-influenced" but not genuinely Christian literature. If such literature is defined as that which has been written only by a devout and totally faithful Christian, *Dialogue between Myōshū and Yūtei* would not meet the criteria of Christian literature because it was not composed by a knowledgeable, fully committed Christian. It could just as well have been written by an intellectual whose heterodox interpretation of Confucian philosophy drew him into the religious debates with Buddhists, Shintoists, and Neo-Confucians that are recorded in the book.

In order to understand why *Dialogue between Myōshū and Yūtei* has been assumed to be a Christian work, Kiri Paramore, professor at Leiden

9. Ebisawa Arimichi, *Kirishitan kyōrisho* (Tokyo: Kyōbunkan, 1993), 512.

University, has made a close reexamination of the work and has pointed out that the general opinion concerning why it is held up as an example of Japanese Christian literature is clearly based not on the work itself or on an objective assessment, but on an imagined universal standard of Catholic doctrinal works.[10] According to that standard, it is assumed that Christian literature must use specifically Christian terminology and teach Christian doctrine to be classified as a work of Christian literature.

The author of *Dialogue between Myōshū and Yūtei* uses the structure of a conversation between two upper-class Buddhist nuns to explore Buddhist, Confucian, and Shinto beliefs and then to present the Christian perspective in comparison. He points out that all the Buddhas, including Gautama Siddhartha, were no more than ordinary human beings whose understanding and intelligence did not qualitatively differ from the mental abilities of other people. Consequently, the Buddhas would never have been able to give trustworthy religious testimony any better than anyone else. They could not have guaranteed the existence of an afterlife, for example, or make any other religious pronouncement with complete certitude. Since all the Buddhas are only human beings, according to Fabian, and Buddhism lacks a supreme guide who is able to definitively determine what is morally right and morally wrong, people can only do whatever they judge for themselves to be good. He considers this a serious flaw in Buddhism because the religion is unable to present any absolute moral principles. Everyone is left to his or her own devices to try to live a moral life. Fabian's arguments in this so-called Christian text are based on logical assumptions rather than on any Christian doctrines or beliefs. According to Fabian, all the Shinto deities, like the Buddhas, are simply human beings or representations of natural phenomenon. They have been excessively honored and made "divine." Faith in the buddhas and Shinto gods, as well as the belief that Japan is a divine country and "the land of the gods," are political rather than religious ideologies. The text then should not necessarily be termed "Christian."

Turning to Confucianism, Fabian counters the belief that the Great Ul-

10. Paramore, "Hayashi Razan's Redeployment of Anti-Christian Discourse," 188.

timate (*taikyoku*) is the source of all things and that human beings originate from the same source as animals and plants. The author concludes from this teaching that the Confucians must hold that human beings are no different from plants, animals, or inanimate objects and that they are in no way unique. The implication of this Confucian belief, Fabian asserts, is that there is no such thing as a human essence. This argument, rather than being specifically Christian or even religious, is based only on philosophical assumptions.

All this is meant to show that Fabian's writings need not be viewed as genuinely Christian but simply criticisms based on reason to counter the cultural beliefs and practices of Buddhism, Shintoism, and Confucianism in an age when such criticism was allowed. Scholars who hold that *Dialogue between Myōshū and Yūtei* is a Christian work would do well to consider that Bunkō also criticized the three religions, but with arguments based in morality and not in the academic and scholarly terms that Fabian used. Bunkō can be said to have gone beyond Fabian in the area of Christian ethics in his moral criticisms of the government and in his condemnation of hypocrisy in religion. Fabian's writings, which are consistently classified by modern historians as Christian writings, actually fall short of a profound Christian awareness of such doctrines as sin or of an existential appreciation of the Eucharist, important doctrines that do appear in Bunkō's work and which were emphasized in authentically Christian tracts, such as *Christian Doctrine* (*Doctrina Kirishitan*, 1591, 1592, 1600). Fabian's discourse on Christianity remains on a purely rational, intellectual level.[11] The emphasis in *Dialogue between Myōshū and Yūtei* on abstract values contrasts with the emphasis on faith and morals in *Christian Doctrine* and other Japanese Christian texts written in the "Christian century," including *Japanese Catechism* (*Nihon no katekizumo*, 1586), *Understanding Christianity* (*Kirishitan kokoroesho*, 1586), and *Summary of the Sacraments* (*Sakuramenta teiyōfuroku*, 1605).[12]

Whether one considers *Dialogue between Myōshū and Yūtei* a Christian text or not, Christian writings of the early seventeenth century,

11. Fujita, *Japan's Encounter with Christianity*, 215. I am indebted to Neil S. Fujita for his reading and explanation of *Myōtei mondo*.

12. Paramore, "Hayashi Razan's Redeployment of Anti-Christian Discourse," 192.

when Christians could practice their religion openly, would necessarily be different from writings of a Christian author a century later when the religion was persecuted. The earlier materials could deal explicitly with Christian beliefs and use Christian terminology. The latter Christian writings would have to hide the beliefs and avoid using any expressions that could be construed as Christian. The point is that the definition of what we mean by "Christian literature" must change depending on the social and political conditions at different times. During an age of persecution, Japanese Christian literature would have the characteristics cited above that would be entirely different from those of an earlier, more open period. This is why Christian writing in an age of repression may not even be considered Christian literature compared to the literature written in a time of religious freedom. Thus, *Christian Doctrine* and other Christian works of the late sixteenth century are entirely different types of works from those of Baba Bunkō. The former is academic, concerned with philosophical or theological questions that are explicitly Christian; the latter is focused on contemporary ethical and moral issues.

Dana Gioia, a former chairperson of the National Endowment for the Arts, offers a definition of some modern Catholic literature that might serve to define Christian literature in Japan that was written in the eighteenth century and even to define Bunkō's works as Catholic. Catholic literature, he says, need not be explicitly religious—even less would it need to be devotional. Most of it would touch on profane rather than sacred topics. In general, Catholic writers see humanity struggling in a fallen world and have a deep sense of human imperfection.[13] Their writings reflect that vision. A reading of the complete translation of *Contemporary Edo: An Album of One Hundred Monsters*, which is included as an appendix at the end of this volume, will allow the reader to see that Gioia's definition of Catholic literature would certainly apply to the essays and anecdotes of Baba Bunkō in this regard.

13. Gioia, "The Catholic Writer Today," 34.

Characteristics of Christian Writings in the Eighteenth Century

It is clear that the definition of Christian literature that is written during a time of repression cannot be restricted only to literature that is directly related to the propagation of a Christian religious message. Christian literature must also encompass those works that bear the marks of Christian influence and exhibit a Christian perspective but are not necessarily explicitly Christian either in word or in content. This would be the type of literature that Baba Bunkō wrote. There are also eighteenth-century essays and books that were written openly about Christianity and contain more explicit references to the religion than the works of Bunkō. These works, however, should not be considered Christian writings.

The national learning scholar and Shinto theologian Hirata Atsutane (1776–1843) borrowed extensively from texts written by Jesuit missionaries who had worked in China in the early part of the seventeenth century, in particular Matteo Ricci (1552–1610), Diego de Pantoja (1571–1618), and Giulio Aleni (1582–1649). Since the bakufu attempted to ban books by Christian authors, it is not known with certainty exactly how Atsutane might have obtained copies of these religious tracts written by three Jesuits. Donald Keene speculates that Atsutane may have borrowed copies from scholars of the Mito domain, where there was a collection of Christian books and objects.[14] In whatever manner he may have acquired Christian books, Japanese scholars, such as Tahara Tsuguo, have acknowledged that the Christian orientation in Atsutane's writings is unmistakable.[15] Christian influence is particularly clear in Atsutane's work titled *Outer Chapters of Our Doctrine* (*Honkyō Gaihen*, 1806), in which his explanation of an afterlife appears to have developed from Christian teachings. It could not have come from Shintoism because the "indigenous religion" lacked the tradition of belief in a paradise and a hell after death.[16] Tahara wrote: "The definite influence of Christian writings in the

14. Donald Keene, *The Japanese Discovery of Europe, 1720–1830* (1952; Oxon: Routledge, rev. ed., 2010), 108.
15. Tahara Tsuguo, *Hirata Atsutane, Ban Nobutomo, Ōkuni Takamasa*, 593.
16. Keene, *The Japanese Discovery of Europe, 1720–1830*, 109.

cosmological formulations of Hirata's thought cannot be ignored. The influence of Christian writings from *Honkyō Gaihen* to *Koshiden* [Commentary on early Japanese history, 1825] is a matter of fact."[17]

As a consequence of his activities, Atsutane was exiled to Akita. Although he was not a Christian, Christianity certainly influenced his scholarship. The government's dealings with him exposed the fear and dismay concerning the Christian influence. Atsutane had made a note on his manuscript that it should not be shown to anyone. Consequently, the title "Honkyō Gaihen" does not appear in any list of his works during his lifetime. Undoubtedly, he did not want to be suspected of holding Christian views. Another of his works, *The Perpetual Calendar of the Imperial Court* (*Tenchō Mukyūreki*, 1841), was based in large part on the astronomical research of the Jesuits in China. Both Hakuseki and Atsutane give clear evidence that Christian influence had never been eliminated in Japan, even during the persecution of the Tokugawa period; however, their works cannot be called Christian texts.

The works of Hakuseki and Atsutane did touch upon certain Christian beliefs, but they were not writings of political dissent. Hakuseki's *Information on the West*, which reports his encounters with Giovanni Battista Sidotti, dealt adroitly with a sensitive subject matter but it did not criticize the regime. Atsutane's *Outer Chapters of Our Doctrine* would not have been written but for his access to banned Christian missionary texts from China, but this work did not contain political dissent either. The bakufu did consider the writings of these authors to be potentially subversive and threatening to the social order because of the punishments these authors were given. Hakuseki's *Information on the West* was banned; Atsutane was banished from Edo and sent to Kubota, his birthplace, where he died two years later in 1843.[18] There was no evidence that either had been sympathetic toward Christianity, and both men had done their best to avoid sanction. In spite of that, both were punished simply because the references to Christianity in their works, though written in a detached and dispassionate tone, aroused the bakufu's appre-

17. Information about the Christian influence on Hirata Atsutane is taken from Richard Divine, "Hirata Atsutane and Christian Sources," *Monumenta Nipponica* 36, no. 1 (1981): 37–54.

18. Ibid., 37, 39.

hension. Certainly, the case can be made that these works are evidence that there was a Christian influence in important Japanese literature of the eighteenth century, but the authors were not Christian, and the writings would not be described as Christian writings because there was no expression of agreement with Christian beliefs or indication of a familiarity with Christian morality.

The writings of Baba Bunkō, however, show more than just Christian influence. There are clearer references to Christianity that give evidence of a precise understanding of its doctrines; and furthermore, there are direct denunciations of oppressive government policies and of its officials. It is more of a literature of dissent. Throughout his career, Bunkō continued to broaden his repertoire until those he accused of immorality, hypocrisy, and corruption included even the shogun himself. Almost no well-known official in the 1750s escaped his satirical barbs. Bunkō's writings are unquestionably subversive of the political and social order in a way not seen in the writings of any other author of the period. His critical attitudes toward the elite, based on moral and ethical criteria, are apparent in his essays and anecdotes. His interpretation and recognition of virtue, quite unlike the opinions of his contemporaries, could be easily identified as Christian. Though any explicitly Christian beliefs remain hidden behind a veil of secrecy in much of his writing, his last work, "A Collection of Useless Grumblings," gives clear evidence not only of Christian influence but also of his own Christian beliefs and convictions.

Absolute Principles in Japanese Morality

Were Baba Bunkō's moral principles and ethical judgments actually evidence of the influence of Christianity, or were his convictions simply the result of training in Neo-Confucianism? The Neo-Confucianism that developed in Song dynasty China (960–1279) under the inspiration of Chu Hsi (1130–1200) was the official philosophy of the Tokugawa shogunate from the time of the first shogun, Tokugawa Ieyasu. Though its influence waxed and waned, it continued to be the intellectual and moral underpinning that supported the shogunate. The classic texts of Neo-Confucianism emphasized the importance of moral rectitude in all human relationships and affirmed the virtues of obedience, loyalty to authority, and living within the social class into which one was born. Many of the virtues of Neo-Confucianism could be said to be common to Christianity; however, the "virtue" of conformity to one's social status and a strict adherence to one's place within the class hierarchy would not be considered Christian. This was the aspect of Neo-Confucianism that Baba Bunkō vehemently attacked. He could not therefore be called a Neo-Confucian. He revolted against one of the main tenets of that philosophy.

Already in the late 1600s Japanese scholars argued that Neo-Confucian moral principles were only the product of a particular historical moment. That historical moment was the era of Song China. The moral tenets of that period were not principles that were valid for all times and in all situations. By the 1700s Neo-Confucianism was still official orthodoxy in Japan, but for all practical matters, it was not taken seriously in the increasingly commercialized environment of the later Tokugawa period. Government officials and even Japanese Confucian philosophers were questioning the practicality of the traditional Neo-Confucian emphasis on virtues as absolute principles inherent in the universe. The idea of absolute moral doctrines or eternal metaphysical truth, though important in Song Neo-Confucianism, never caught on in Japan.

Neo-Confucian concepts that were popular in Japan were not elements that could be used to construct transcendent ethical theory that would permanently guide Japanese society, much less be the principles that governed the universe.[19] Making the same point, Maruyama Masao writes that Japanese morality, far from being absolute or based on eternal, unchanging principles, has always been and is still today what one might call an "empty bag" in which one can put into it what one wishes. Morality in Japan has always been like a container, the contents of which were at one time largely of foreign (i.e., Chinese) origin. As a consequence, there is no history of indigenous Japanese ethical thought as such. There is only a history of the reception of various foreign ethical and moral systems.[20]

19. Susan L. Burns, *Before the Nation: Kokugaku and the Imagining of Community in Early Modern Japan* (Durham, N.C.: Duke University Press, 2003), 38.

20. Kenneth B. Pyle, *Japan Rising: The Resurgence of Japanese Power and Purpose*, 58.

Historical examples are sometimes raised to refute this contention that there are no absolutes in Japanese morality. Japanese militarism during the early and middle decades of the twentieth century, for example, has been understood as a system of beliefs that many of Japan's elite and common people are said to have held as absolute. However, there was actually no such thing as an absolute principle of militarism or even of loyalty to the emperor. The role of ideology, if it can be called such, prior to and during World War II has been grossly overemphasized. As Kenneth Pyle has observed in his book *Japanese Rising: The Resurgence of Japanese Power and Purpose*, the only ideology that drove Japan's military leaders was the opportunistic pursuit of power, but such a limited ideology is not actually a moral principle that can govern the entire range of human actions.[21]

Even before Maruyama's view of Japanese morality and ethics as an "empty bag," the early twentieth-century philosopher Nishida Kitarō (1870–1945) used the expression a "formless form" (*katachi ga nai katachi*) to illustrate how the relative, rather than absolute, morality of the Neo-Confucianism of the Tokugawa period has remained the dominant ethic in Japan even until the present.[22] This means that for at least four hundred years Japan has had no legacy of universal values or moral norms. There may have been an ethos of the samurai in an earlier age, but by the Tokugawa period, the only "absolute" in the eyes of the ruling elite was status, privilege, power, and prestige. Kenneth Pyle argues that today the very idea that the nation could be governed by abstract principles is scarcely credible to the Japanese.[23] Pyle cites Yoshino Sakuzō (1878–1933), a professor of political science at Tokyo Imperial University and a Christian, who argued that during the Taisho period (1912–26) the Japanese government's domestic and foreign policies were never based on abstract principles but rather on the concrete practices of the dominant countries in the world. Women's rights in the Taisho period, for example, were not promoted because such rights were of moral or ethical value but because equality for women had become by that time a "natural world trend" pursued by other countries, and it was expedient to

21. Ibid., 188.

22. Ibid., 58.

23. Ibid., 147.

move with the tide.[24] Katō Shizue (1897–2001), the first woman elected to Japan's parliament, confirms Pyle's analysis:

> Japanese men have not changed their behavior in my lifetime. They remain samurai—only now camouflaged in business suits.... Japanese men are tangled up in *shigarami*, i.e., vines of obligation from which they cannot escape. I was once asked [during the 1990s] to speak at a prominent men's university about human rights. They asked me, "What is this thing called human rights?" They did not understand the principles of democracy, or human rights, or privacy.[25]

Kōsaka Masataka, the biographer of Yoshida Shigeru (1878–1967), the immediate post–World War II prime minister, observed the absence of absolute moral principles in Japan, explaining that even after adopting its "peace constitution," the promotion of peace was never and has never been an absolute principle that Japan supported as a moral imperative.[26] Japan has simply taken advantage of the international order and the relationship among nations created by stronger states. According to Kōsaka, Japan has never stood for fixed principles but has merely adapted to whatever the situation might require. Prime minister from 1991 to 1993, Miyazawa Kiichi (1919–2007) told an interviewer in 1980, "Japan's foreign policy precludes all value judgments.... The only value judgment is to determine what is in Japan's interest. Since there are no real value judgments possible we cannot say anything."[27]

Karel van Wolferen, a Dutch journalist who is recognized for his expertise in Japanese history and politics and author of *The Enigma of Japanese Power*, has also observed that firm, absolute moral principles and values were absent in the Tokugawa period, and this continues to be true to the present. He writes:

> The most crucial factor determining Japan's socio-political reality... is the near absence of any idea that there can be truths, rules, principles, or mor-

24. Ibid., 150–51.

25. Michael Zielenziger, *Shutting Out the Sun: How Japan Created Its Own Lost Generation* (New York: Doubleday, Nan A. Talese, 2006), 122.

26. Yoshida served as prime minister of Japan from 1946 to 1947 and from 1948 to 1954. He was the architect of Japan's postwar foreign policy, which depended on the military power of the United States for the defense of Japan.

27. Pyle, *Japan Rising*, 267.

> als that always apply, no matter what the circumstances.... Concepts of independent, universal truths or immutable religious beliefs, transcending the world reality of social dictates and the decrees of power-holders have, of course, found their way into Japan, but they have never taken root in any surviving [Japanese] world-view.[28]

Tanaka Kōtarō (1890–1974), an important intellectual of the twentieth century and chief justice of the Japanese Supreme Court from 1950 to 1960, is an example of someone who shows that, in fact, it is possible for a Japanese person to hold absolute principles. He maintained a vigorous defense of human rights and was an advocate for the importance of universal and eternal truth. However, this conviction may well have been a result of his belief as a Catholic in the universality of Catholicism.[29] It did not come from Neo-Confucian or Buddhist influence in Japan. However, it is still true to say that a belief in universal truth, absolute moral teachings, and unconditional ethical principles has never been a factor in Japanese or Confucian moral traditions.

Baba Bunkō also stands out in sharp contrast to the subjective Japanese view of morality and ethics. Though he did not use the term "absolute," he adamantly held that justice for all classes, fair treatment of women, care for the poor and the hungry, and honest religious devotion were unchanging principles by which society should be guided and governed. He openly defied the local Edo city magistrate and confronted the senior counselors of the bakufu, other officials, Confucian scholars, Buddhist monks, and even the shogun himself and charged them with the violation of the principles of impartiality, integrity, and honesty in politics, education, and religion. His principles applied in every situation and to every person, no matter what his or her social standing might have been. He filled the "empty bag" and gave shape to "the formless form" of Japanese moral relativism.

28. Karel van Wolferen, *The Enigma of Japanese Power* (New York: Vintage Books, 1990), 9.

29. Atsushi Shibasaki, "Christianity and the Making of a Modern Worldview in Japan: International Thought of Tanaka Kotaro (1890–1974)," *Journal of Global Media Studies* 7 (2010): 31–40.

The Legacy of Baba Bunkō

In 1827, the same year as the "Christian affair," a document with the title *Mori no shizuku* (Raindrops falling in the forest) was published. This document had the same title that Bunkō had given to his lecture series on the Gujō peasant uprising that led to his arrest almost seventy years earlier. This newer work, written long after Bunkō had been executed, is attributed to the authorship of one "Baba Bunkō" and relates the circumstances surrounding the same Gujō uprising and the Itoshiro disturbance.[30] The treatise expounds in a concise form, similar to Bunkō's own written style, many of the same defiant assertions of government mishandling of the situation in Gujō that Bunkō himself had made. The 1827 *Mori no shizuku* also scrutinizes evil officials who take advantage of their position to deceive the public. Matsudaira Sadanobu, in particular, is attacked for his vulgarity and rudeness: "The vassal (*ason*) of the emperor, Matsudaira Sadanobu, is offensive in his speech and uncouth in his behavior. From his youth he was never reared to discern moral right from moral wrong."[31]

The anonymous author asserts that Matsudaira should have gone to hear lectures (kōshaku) every day when he was young, so that he could have become better educated and able to discipline himself with solid moral principles. The document also condemns scholars who extort money from people by selling their learning, teachers who traffic in false doctrines in order to deceive people, and monks who spend money lavishly on alcohol and prostitution.[32] These are all themes found in Bunkō's lectures and writings as well. Why would an anonymous author take as a pseudonym the name of an executed criminal and reproduce for a later age that criminal's opposition to government officials and their policies? It would only be because he felt a considerable loyalty and devotion to that individual, agreed with his views, and considered his teachings important for his own time. He would otherwise not have been willing, at

30. Morisue Yoshiaki, Ichiko Teiji et al., eds., *Hoteiban Kokusho sōmokuroku* (Tokyo: Iwanami shoten, 1989–90), 7: 725.

31. Cited in "Baba Bunkō," in *Edo monogatari* (Tokyo: Sanseisha, 1927), 2–3.

32. Ibid.

risk to his own safety, to try to preserve the legacy of Baba Bunkō. This 1827 document shows the long-term influence of Bunkō's insistence on the necessity of concrete ethical principles and preserves his belief in the Christian idea of moral absolutes.

Though the author is anonymous, the name "Ezoe Inosuke" appears as the publisher in the preface of this 1827 *Mori no shizuku*. There was, in fact, a contemporary of Bunkō who had this name. He had been a commoner who lent his verbal support to the peasants' revolt in Gujō in 1758 and was arrested and charged with being a leader of that revolt.[33] The real identities of the author and the publisher of this document remain a mystery; however, the document, which provides factual information about the Gujō uprising, is conclusive evidence not only that Baba Bunkō was still known much later in the Tokugawa period, but also that his work was considered important enough to preserve. The anonymity of the work is an indication the author was aware that he was disseminating forbidden information, even though the content of the document was no longer about a "current government investigation," a crime with which Baba Bunkō had been charged. The 1827 *Mori no shizuku* would no longer have been considered a subversive document. It was about an incident that had occurred seventy years earlier and was never included on any list of banned books. The author still wanted to keep his identity a secret. The only reason for secrecy at this late date would have been the fact that the anonymous author was knowingly disseminating the opinions of a Christian, which was still a crime in 1827. The lack of a clear justification for Bunkō's execution can only be satisfactorily explained by affirming that he was a Christian. No one else had ever been executed for the crimes of which Bunkō was explicitly accused. Capital punishment was, however, passed down for the "crime" of being a Christian.

Thinking that Bunkō was just another kōdanshi whose popularity would quickly pass, the government at first ignored his lectures and writings. The bakufu seemed to have at first been caught unawares by Bunkō, but it became apparent after his arrest that a powerful conviction lay behind his satire. The execution order of the High Court clearly shows that

33. Hayakawa, *Uzu no hirogari*, 104.

in the end the bakufu realized that Bunkō was not just another kōdanshi who was trying to attract an audience or provoke a reaction from local officials.

Baba Bunkō presents a problem for the historian today. How can such a person have existed in the culture of eighteenth-century Tokugawa Japan? How can there have been a dissident such as he who not only acquired a sense of the meaning of absolute moral principles but insisted on trying to communicate them in spite of the predominance of the "formless form" and the "empty bag" of Japanese morality? His writings reflect a moral perspective that modern scholars have assumed was nonexistent in the works of Tokugawa-period writers. Even the possibility of a Christian writer in Tokugawa Japan challenges the historian to reevaluate the entire period, in order to see whether or not we have created a Tokugawa history that ignores some important historical and literary artifacts because they do not contribute to a consistent and coherent tale in which events easily fit together and move toward a preconceived formulation that "makes sense." The historian must now abandon the traditional preconceptions and assumptions that have been erroneously projected onto the history of Christianity in Japan in the Tokugawa period.

CONTEMPORARY EDO

An Album of One Hundred Monsters
(*Tōdai Edo hyaku bakemono*)
Baba Bunkō

Table of Contents

16. The Case of the Short Bow of Oguri Mataichi
17. The Case of Nakamura Kichibei
18. The Case of Hanabusa Itchō
19. The Case of Katsuma Ryōsui
20. The Case of Yamamoto Kunai
21. In Search of the Real Shidōken
22. Descriptions of Various Monsters
    a) Kimura Sehei, the Sumo Referee
    b) In Bakuro-chō, Gorōbei, the Paper Merchant
    c) At the Kamakura shore, Toshimaya Jūemon
    d) In Tenma-chō, Tanbaya Gobei
    e) In Osaka-chō, Murata Gobei

Preface

In this world, a monster is someone who grotesquely transforms his appearance in order to manipulate society and other people. He is someone who, just when you think he is in one place, has already moved to another. His position is always changing. He is the sort of person that never acts in broad daylight, but at night he makes his presence known. Under the guise of being human, he ensnares people in his deceptions.

All together, my tales actually number fewer than one hundred, but I use this number in the title of my book anyway.

Signed,
Ba Bunkō,
a hermit of Katsushika[1]
Early autumn, in the year of the tiger, 1758

This translation is based on *Tōdai Edo hyaku bakemono*, in *Tōdai Edo hyaku bakemono, Zaishin kiji, Kana sesetsu, vol. 97 of Shin Nihon koten bungaku taikei*, ed. Tajihi Ikuo and Nakano Mitsutoshi (Tokyo: Iwanami shoten, 2000), 1–42. The word *ben* ("the case") is used in the title of almost every story. It refers to a genre of writing, the purpose of which is to discern the truth or falsehood, the sincerity or deception, in human words and actions. This one word could perhaps sum up Bunkō's purpose for writing *Tōdai Edo hyaku bakemono*.

1. Katsushika designates the low-lying area between Edogawa, Nakagawa, and Arakawa in present-day Tokyo.

1. The Aunt Who Went to Visit Tsuna at the Tsu no Kuniya Inn

Among the women who work at the inn in Shinagawa called the Tsu no Kuniya is one called Otsuna.[2] Around Edo she is always called by her alias, Keishi-Tsuna. She was given this nickname because, as everyone says, she resembles Nakamura Keishi.[3]

It so happened that a wealthy townsman from around Odawara-chō by the name of Amagasaki Ikkō, by some chance, fell in love with this Tsuna.[4] He paid no attention to his parents' protests nor to the scandal he was causing and went every night to her house. He was at her side all the time and became more and more negligent of the family business.

Without doubt, Tsuna felt just as attached to Amagasaki as he did to her and sincerely loved him. It had nothing to do with her business obligations. She even made a sincere vow to the gods never to be unfaithful to him.

Amagasaki Ikkō had a wife who was quite smart and not at all bad looking. She was two or three years older than Ikkō, however. On autumn nights she slept alone, listening to the repeating sound of the temple bell, grieving that her husband spent all his time with Tsuna. She was just like Lady Han who, so attached to the keepsake fan in her bedchamber, complained about the heartless man she desired, while the jealousy in her heart grew ever more insufferable. Ikkō's wife sent people over to Shinagawa to the Tsu no Kuniya Inn to have them fetch her husband. But they could never bring him home.[5]

She even sent a letter to Tsuna asking, "Why in the world do you detain my husband Ikkō and refuse to send him home? Out of regard for his parents, public opinion, my own grief, and for other reasons, if you truly love my husband Ikkō, you really ought to send him home." But no mat-

2. Tsu no Kuniya Inn is located in Mita, a district in present-day Minato-ku, Tokyo.

3. Nakamura Tomijūrō (1721–86), who was famous for his feminine-like beauty, was a female impersonator (*onnagata*) in kabuki plays.

4. Odawara-chō (Odawara town) was a district in Edo two blocks northeast of Aramebashi and the site of a large fish market.

5. The expression *Hanjo ga kei,* referring to the bedchamber of a woman forsaken by her lover, is an allusion to the Noh play by Zeami titled *Hanjo* (Lady Han). Lady Han is the poetess of the Former Han Dynasty, Han Shōyo (Pan Chieh-yu), who was a favorite of Emperor Ch'eng Ti (r. 36–32 BC), but was eventually replaced in his affections by another.

ter how many letters appealing to her sense of obligation Tsuna received, she lied and answered that Ikkō had never come there, but all the while detaining him still longer.

After a while, since the messengers she had sent could do nothing, Ikkō's wife thought, "Now what shall I do? When I write a letter, there is hardly an honest reply. When I send a messenger, he is ignored. So I will make a visit to Tsu no Kuniya Inn myself, meet face to face with Tsuna, speak reasonably, and bring my husband back."

So she left for Shinagawa, but then had second thoughts. "No, no. If I go as my usual self, she won't ever meet me." Ikkō's wife formulated a plan. She would make a costume. It would be a very fine two-layered cotton kimono with a narrow black satin obi. In this attire she set out for Tsu no Kuniya Inn.

On arrival she summoned a young male attendant and said to him, "If you do not mind, I would like to meet the woman who works in this establishment and goes by the name of Tsuna. Actually I am her aunt. I live in Shiba-Mita.[6] She calls me her auntie from Mita. Since it has been such a long time since I have seen Tsuna, I just had to come to meet her. Would you be so kind as to tell her that I am here?"

When the attendant took the message to Tsuna, she was lying with Amagasaki. Tsuna said to the young messenger, "Actually, I do have an aunt in Mita. She must have come to ask me for money again. Just send her away."

Ikkō's wife overheard this and, acting quite hurt, replied in a loud voice so that Tsuna could hear her, "I came all this way to visit. What an insult your way of speaking is! When you were young and abandoned by your mother, I brought you up. During the midsummer heat I made a breeze for you with folding fans and round fans, I fanned you all day long on the hot days. On the cold days of midwinter I warmed you with my body. To have raised you so kindly was all in vain. How regrettable! It is so sad that 'the little swallow' who took food from me, now that the summer has advanced, has forgotten the care her aunt gave her."

When Amagasaki Ikkō heard his wife's voice, he felt sorry for her and

6. Shiba and Mita are in present-day Minato-ku. See "Hakidame Omatus ga den" (The story of Omatsu of the rubbish heap), in *Tōsei Buya zokudan*, Yūhōdō bunko, 402–3.

said, "Hearing those words, we couldn't possibly forsake her now. Show her in. I will appease her and offer a little consolation."

Before he could call her in, Ikkō's wife, still disguised as the aunt, ran into Tsuna's room and grabbed Amagasaki, pulling him up by the collar. "Because you didn't come home when I sent people to get you, I, your wife, have had to come to get you myself."

She kicked up the room, making a mess of everything, and took her husband home. Tsuna was completely dumbfounded. "What are you doing?" she cried. But she could do nothing. She had to let this man go home to his wife since she herself was in service to the brothel.[7]

Actually, isn't it sad that among all of Tsuna's customers Amagasaki Ikkō was her best client? Really a man of unrivaled abilities!

His wife had come to the inn in disguise, lying that she was Tsuna's aunt. She was like the monster who disguised herself as Watanabe no Tsuna's mother and who retrieved the arm that Watanabe had cut off of the demon but was actually the demon herself.[8] Tsuna of Tsu no Kuniya Inn and the auntie from Mita were quite the strange, lying duo. They are both to be counted among the hypocrites who take the form of human beings and deceive people.

2. The Case of the Monster Who Switched from Being a Lover of Young Boys to a Lover of Women

Among all the fools in Edo there is the one called Shibata Baikō.[9] If I were to explain the meaning of the ditty, "White face powder thrown over the fire; look at that fool's face,"[10] then I would say it refers to those who often powder their faces and then go out in search of erotic exploits. Nowadays Baikō often powders his face and does precisely that: goes out in search of erotic exploits. He is fond of young boys, and ever since Sega-

7. A prostitute was the property of the brothel and would be allowed to leave only if she were purchased by someone who would either marry her or set her up as a concubine for his exclusive use. Amagasaki obviously did not have the means to do this.

8. Watanabe (953–1025) was a retainer of Minamoto Yorimitsu. At the entreaty of his mother, Watanabe showed her an arm that he had cut off of a demon. On seeing it, his mother suddenly exposed herself as the demon.

9. This is Mizoguchi Naoatsu (1714–80), the seventh lord of Shibata, Echigo domain. He was daimyō between 1732 and 1761.

10. *Hi ni kubaru hakufun mita ka baka no kao.*

wa Kikujirō Hamamuraya was a boy, Baikō has been intimate with him.[11] Baikō, in total disregard of his highly respected position as a daimyō, also goes from time to time to the house of Segawa Sengyo, to take part in banquets and engage in his usual pleasurable diversions.[12]

When Segawa Kikunojō II was young and called Kichiji, Baikō lavished his favors on him as well and invested a great deal of money as the sponsor of his name-change ceremony so that he could take the name of Kikunojō.[13] Kikunojō's introduction under his new name was at the opening of the season.[14] Baikō took care of Kikunojō financially and spent a lot of money so that the actor could take the style-name Rokō.[15]

Also, the year before last, when Sengyō Kikujirō was sick, as well as at the time he had been ill earlier, Baikō paid for the services of a physician and brought ginseng root and other medicines for Sengyō. The repertory company was, of course, grateful to him.

Sengyō eventually died, and at that time Baikō provided even more services. He had him buried in Oshiage Daiunji in Honjo.[16] On the seventeenth day Baikō, accompanying Sengyō's wife, Oryū, went to visit the grave. By that time, Sengyō had become known as Kudokuin. Generally, gentlemen of the samurai class who make visits to the graves of entertainers are, without doubt, monsters.[17]

After Sengyō, Baikō became the patron of the current Kikunojō and had been going to his residence quite often. However, the way things look now, Baikō no longer prefers young boys. It seems he has become fond of a woman—Sengyō's widow, Oryū. But no one has been paying any attention to this love nest. It was rumored that Baikō had been spending the night at Sengyō's house at the time the fire broke out in an area along the Yashiro river bank and Baikō's house burnt down.[18] He is a great monster.

11. Segawa Kikujirō Hamamuraya (1715–56).

12. Segawa Sengyo is a stage name for Segawa Kikujirō Hamamuraya, who was the younger brother of Segawa Kikunojō (1741–73). He took the name Kichiji in 1750.

13. Segawa took this name in 1756.

14. *Kaomise*, literally "showing faces." The theater season opened in the eleventh month and was the occasion for introducing the actors under contract for a year. This practice began in Kyoto in the 1650s and 1660s.

15. This name was also adopted in 1756.

16. Honjo is an area in present-day Sumida-ku, Tokyo.

17. The word "entertainers" is the translation of *Kawara no mono* (the people of Kawara).

18. The fire on the Yashiro River bank started on Hōreki 6 (1756) 11. 23. Fanned by high winds, it burned down the homes of many daimyō.

Recently the Hamamuraya repertory company has had a lot of orphans to provide for, and everyone is saying that they are the children of Baikō. On top of that, the current Kikunojō's stage costumes are all designs that Baikō thought of. All in all the "great daimyō" Baikō is no better than a lowly entertainer himself. Nothing could be more fiendish than having one occupation while engaging such a sideline.

3. The Case of the Monster Magistrate

"Yao and Shun, as well as the Buddha, were quite successful at convincing people that they were virtuous, even if deep down they were nothing of the kind."[19] So wrote Masuho a while back.[20] I think since these three people spent their whole lives trying to appear to act virtuously, then they were simply perpetuating a deception.

Today there was a proclamation on Nasu paper from a recent magistrate.[21] (N.B., This magistrate models himself on Ōoka Echizen, but is considerably inferior to him. His name is Tsuchiya something-or-other.) Maybe it's Tsuchi "Dirt" Echizen, the imitator of the great Ōoka Echizen. Tsuchi deals placidly with litigation and finance. It is said that he acts leniently in all affairs, even giving criminals a merciful punishment, as Ōoka had mercy on the innocent. As far as real ability goes, however, "Tsuchi" is as different from Ōoka as heaven is different from earth. Moreover, one might say that Tsuchiya's feelings are easily swayed. When he is doing his imitation while hearing cases, he pulls at his beard, trying to look like the real Ōoka Echizen. But if a person who had actually known Ōoka shows up, the imposter's facade evaporates, and the monster is unmasked.

When Sakai Sanuki no kami was the magistrate in Kyoto, he looked coldly upon Tsuchiya, and witnessing his strange disposition, tried to keep him in obscurity.[22] How did Tsuchiya manage to rehabilitate him-

19. Confucius selected these legendary sage kings, Yao and Shun (twenty-second century BC), as models of virtue and wisdom.

20. Masuho Nokoguchi (1655–1742) was a Shinto moralist of the Edo period. See Watanabe Kunio, ed., *Shintō taikei*, vol. 22, *Masuho Nokoguchi* (Tokyo: *Shintō taikei hensankai*, 1975).

21. Nasu paper is made in Echizen. Tsuchiya Masasuke, south city magistrate of Edo (*minami Edo machi bugyō*) from 1754. 12. 24 to 1767. 5. 19, used this type of paper in imitation of Ōoka Tadasuke (1677–1751), the city magistrate from 1717 to 1736, who was legendary for his just and wise judgments. Tsuchiya Masasuke was the official responsible for Bunkō's arrest.

22. Sakai Sanuki no kami Tadamochi (1722–75), the thirteenth lord of Wakasa, was daimyō

self so suddenly? He has again reared his ugly face and is trying to deceive all of us! He has in fact deceived the entire capital with his imitation.

4. The Case of the Monster in the Cool of the Evening

The happiest-looking people in the world are to be found around the sixth month of the year, during the early summer when the evenings are cool, along the banks of the Ryōgoku River.[23] When word spread around Edo that the great Lord of Sendai would order a fireworks display one evening, everyone, high and low, wanted to go out and watch it.[24]

Everything from the large pleasure barges, of course, to even the small flat boats were all rented out, and there was not an empty boat to be found in all of Edo.[25] The whole surface of the river was covered with boats. However, when people came that night, there was nothing to be seen of the Lord of Sendai's famous fireworks. There was an announcement: "Business in the lord's official residence has forced postponement of the display. This evening's fireworks will be held two evenings from tonight." The people who had waited at the river all went home.

They came out again two nights later, but again there was nothing to be seen. They had been duped twice, and they would never forget it. The monster who had duped them was not only the Lord of Sendai. It was also a boat owner at Edo Bridge by the name of Kazusaya San'emon.[26] He had schemed to let all of the boat owners around Edo make a lot of money by renting boats on those two nights. It really turned out to be a successful deception!

---

between 1740 and 1757 and magistrate of temples and shrines from 1747. 3 to 1747. 12. He was the bakufu representative in Kyoto (*Kyōtō shoshidai*) from 1752. 4. 7 to 1756. 4. 7.

23. Ryōgoku River is the present-day Sumida River in Tokyo.

24. The "great lord of Sendai" is Date Yoshimura (1680–1752). Fireworks were popular in summer at the Ryōgoku Bridge, which today is a highway that spans the Sumida River between Chūō-ku, Higashi Nihonbashi 2 chōme and Sumida-ku, Ryōgoku 1 chōme.

25. The "small flat boats," or *Hirata kobune,* were long boats used in the Edo period primarily for the transportation of stone or other heavy building materials.

26. Edo Bridge, or Edobashi, is to the east of Nihonbashi on the Sumida River in present-day Chūō-ku, Nihonbashi Honmachi 1 chōme.

5. The Case of Teramachi Sanchi (Hyakuan)

Among the official monks of the bakufu is Teramachi Sanchi, who is also called Hyakuan, and who is very well known.[27] He is a great playboy and has acquired quite a reputation at the houses of ill repute. For years, he has changed his residence five or six times every year. When you think he's really in one place, he has moved to another.[28]

If he admires the cherry blossoms here in the spring, in summer he enjoys looking over a riverbank somewhere else. In autumn, he goes to Yamanote where the leaves have fallen, then moves on to snow-covered Honjo in the middle of winter.[29]

Because he is a scandalous fellow, he is like one of those female demons who go prowling around the mountains.[30] So around town he has acquired the name "monster-monk." In recent years, he associates with the wealthy townsmen in the shogun's city, pretending to be a master of haiku poetry and making a living as an entertainer. He also plays the fool, accompanying the tile maker, Yanagibashi, to the Nakaōmiya Inn.[31]

When Miyakoji was ransomed, it was through the efforts of Hyakuan.[32] When Eichiya Segawa of the Matsubaya Inn was ransomed, the agent was again Hyakuan.[33] He received a commission and put the money in his own pocket. Miyakoji of the Nakaōmiya Inn was set up in the residence of the tile dealer Heihachi. She died from an illness last year,

27. Hyakuan (1695–1781) was a student of Reizei Tamehisa (1686–1741) and Reizei Tamemura (1712–74), leading figures among the court poets.

28. This sentence has been repeated from the preface.

29. Yamanote is a relatively high area in present-day Bunkyō-ku and Shinjuku-ku, Tokyo. Honjo is in present-day Sumida-ku. It is one of the original fifteen districts of Tokyo.

30. The *yamanba* appear in legends and folklore as female demons that devour human beings and at other times pretend to be humorous, stupid old hags.

31. Nakaōmiya Inn was a bordello in Shin Yoshiwara, Kyōmachi 2 chōme. The proprietor was one Taskejirō. An area in present-day Tokyo, Taitō-ku, Shin Yoshiwara was famous in the Edo period for its bordellos and *sakariba*, drinking establishments where people gathered for entertainment.

32. Miyakoji is one of the seven courtesans at the Nakaōmiya Inn who is listed in Yagi Keiichi, ed., *Hōreki ki Yoshiwara yūyo hyōbanki saiken yonshu, Yoshiwara shusse kagami zen*, 1754, folio 13 front. She is described as having a rather severe expression but being kind and quite talented. Her price for one evening is designated by the customary symbol for three bun in *Daishukubai*, 1756.

33. Segawa V was a courtesan of the Matsubaya Inn (Yoshiwara, Edo-chō 1 chōme) from the beginning of the Hōreki period until 1755 when Eichiya Sōsuke ransomed her. She was then called Eichiya Segawa (see *Mitamura Engyo zenshū*, 19:102). She is listed in *Yoshiwara shusse kagami zen*, folio 13 reverse, as expert in fortune-telling and the Kōtaku school of calligraphy.

Hōreki 7 [1757]. When Hyakuan acquired a memento of her, he thought it was magnificent.

It should be said that for a monk to receive rice as a stipend from the bakufu is strange. Hyakuan is a great monster. This New Year's, when I passed Hyakuan's home in Hama-chō, a visitor's notebook was put out, but the paper which accompanied that notebook was rice paper of the Kōtaku School.[34] Hyakuan is a scoundrel who tries in this way to delude people.

At New Year's, I hear, he prepared an elaborate tray of food and had two beautiful prostitutes decked out in silks carrying it. He is, indeed, a weird character. One year, he put a request before the representative of the retired shogun, Yoshimune: "Please include me in the linked verse party at the palace on the eleventh day of the first month." But he was admonished for this and fell into disfavor with the shogunal authorities. He was subsequently assigned to the lowly position of drum bearer.[35] He is still at large, trying to fool the world.

6. The Case of the Monster in a Duel

After the middle of the third month, the month of cherry blossoms, there was a large crowd of temple-goers made up of both the high-born and the low, all going in a group to the temple of Kannon in Asakusa. One was a samurai sporting a braided hat and carrying long and short swords that had vermilion-lacquered sheaths decorated with silver.[36] A handsome boy of sixteen or seventeen, an amiable youth dressed quite elegantly, approached the samurai and said, "Hey you, wait. You are certainly Shinoda Gunzaemon. I am Shimizu Sōzaemon's son, Sōjirō. You are the samurai who made a fool of my father, killed him, and ran away. I left my job to look for you and have been searching all over the place. It's by divine mercy that finally I have been led to you today. This has been a dream of mine to meet you. Let's have a duel right now. I see that I am destined to challenge my father's enemy in a duel."[37]

34. Hosoi Kōtaku (1658–1735) was a man of letters especially talented in calligraphy.

35. "Drum bearer" (*Otaiko bōzu*) was an official bakufu rank.

36. The "braided hat" (*fuka-amigasa*) is a straw hat that was used to hide one's face, particularly when venturing into the "pleasure" quarters.

37. In the *Li chih* (Book of rites) it is written, "With the enemy who has slain his father, one

The samurai calmly took off his hat and said, "Indeed I remember your father. But aren't you violating etiquette? I am not a samurai who runs away. Yes, we will have our match," and praising the boy said, "I wish I had a son like you. It's too bad, but I really ought to strike you down right here and now. Unfortunately, however, I also have a destiny; and today I must serve my master and be out on his business. So let's put off this vendetta for a while. I will finish my master's work, then take some time off, and meet you at Takadanobaba tomorrow.[38] Then I'll simply put you to the sword. Now, there's nothing to disagree about, is there?"

"That sounds completely reasonable; nothing out of the ordinary," the young man said; and he accepted the samurai's proposition, firmly promising to meet him at Takadanobaba the next day. Then each went his own way.

The crowds that had been gathering around had witnessed this exchange, and so everyone heard that there would be a duel the next day at Takadanobaba. The word, in fact, spread all over Edo and even around the countryside.

Early in the morning on the next day, a huge crowd of people, young and old, men and women gathered at Takadanobaba. They waited from morning to afternoon and from afternoon until evening, expecting that there would see a vendetta at any time. But nothing happened! Then, this great crowd of people started complaining that they had been fooled. Finally, they gave up and went home.

The "vendetta" was all a scheme that that petty thief, the samurai, had planned just so that he could get things like people's towels. There was no one in that large crowd who did not have something stolen: a purse or a medicine box, a towel or a small dagger. It's amazing that even very wise people were made fools of in this way.

By the way, the very next month, hearing there would be a samurai duel in a cherry tree field in Hongo, the same large crowd of people from all over Edo assembled again to watch the "vendetta." That was a false rumor, too; and they were fooled again.

---

should not lie under the same heaven." See James Legge, ed., *The Sacred Books of the East*, (Oxford: Clarendon Press, 1885), 27: 92.

38. Takadanobaba, a well-known place for vendettas, is in present-day Shinjuku-ku, Nishi-Waseda 3 chōme, Tokyo.

7. The Case of the Narukami Nun

In the environs of Hama-chō there lived a woman who is called the Narukami nun.[39] She was the wife of the physician, Kanemaki Genjun of Tachibana-chō.[40] After Genjun died from an illness, Takane Genryū took the name of this deceased physician, and then he became known as Kanemaki Genjun. The wife of the deceased Genjun was then taken in by this new Genjun, the former Takane Genryū.

After her husband died, Genjun's widow pulled out by the roots all of her raven-black hair in order to become a nun. Everyone thought it was much too soon to do this since she was still very young. To decide to do such a thing was going to extremes, and she may have done it because of an excessively impulsive temper. But everyone said right away that she had done it in defense of her womanly chastity and that it was admirable and praiseworthy.

But this woman is a monstrous fraud. She is exceedingly fond of the comic interludes (*kyōgen*) at the theater and never misses the change of the program at the kabuki. She is a woman of easy virtue and conducts her life in every way as if it were theater. Recently she had an illicit affair with an unknown man of low class.

Not long ago, she was advised to leave the present Genjun and remarry a third time with a supposedly virtuous man from Kanagawa Hongo.[41] She was distressed over the fact that if she went to Kanagawa Hongo, it would not be possible to meet the aforementioned low-class rogue with whom she was having an affair.

One day she went to the ballad drama *Kanadehon Chūshingura* (The treasury of loyal retainers) and saw how Osono, the wife of Amakawaya Gihei, was pressed by her father to remarry.[42] But in the trick devised by

39. The name "Narukami nun" would remind the reader of *Narukami*, a kabuki play first performed at the Nakamuraza in 1684. It is one of the "Eighteen Favorites," written by Ichikawa Danjirō I (1660–1704). She lived in Hama-chō, present-day Chūō-ku, Nihonbashi 1-3 chōme where there was a high concentration of daimyō mansions during the Edo period.

40. According to *Imayo ika jinmei roku* (List of contemporary physicians) in the National Diet Library, Kanemaki was a pediatrician in Ryōgoku, Muramatsu-chō. Bunkō gives his address as Tachibana-chō, in present-day Chūō-ku, Higashi Nihonbashi 3 chōme, Tokyo.

41. Kanagawa Hongo is in present-day Totsuka-ku, Yokohama.

42. This would be act 10 of *Kanadehon chūshingura*.

Ōboshi Yuranosuke, Osono, cut off her hair to become a nun and the proposal of marriage had to be canceled.

Just as she had seen in this drama, Genjun's wife cut off her hair to become a nun, but it was only for outward appearance. It was all to show herself off as a praiseworthy woman who refused to remarry. All the while she is carrying on an affair. She is a great monster. Since last year at the Festival of the Dead when she attended the drama in which Segawa Kikunojō performed the role of the Narukami nun in *Onna Narukami*, she has maintained the appearance of a nun, but she is really filled with sexual passion.[43] Called Rokō's nun, she is quite shameless.

At that performance she was wearing beautiful jewelry under her sheer black kimono, which had a matching black satin obi and a black velvet waist sash. Her head was almost completely covered in black crepe.

Accompanying her were two very beautiful servant girls, whom she dressed in plain kimonos with a flower pattern showing the foot of a mountain. On the shoulder of the kimono of one of the girls she had dyed the characters for "white cloud," and on the other girl's shoulder the characters for "black cloud." They were dressed like Narukami's disciples in the play, Hakuun (white cloud) and Kokuun (black cloud).[44]

Every single day this deceiving woman goes around attended by these maidservants to such places as Asakusa Emma Hall, Kayadera, and to the stone image of Manjusri where she listens to sermons and edifying stories from the monks. She committed adultery in those holy temples with licentious men and in broad daylight.

In appearance, she shows herself to be like one who has set out on the path of the Buddha and living according to the Buddhist law. It must be said, however, that in licentiousness this monster has no equal.

8. The Case of the Monstrous Haikai Master

Even if the man is called a master of haikai poetry, he can be numbered among the various kinds of fools. It must be fate that the fool I am

43. *Onna Narukami* is a *kyōgen* first performed in 1696.12 at the Nakamuraza. The play referred to here is *Onna Narukami omoi no takitsuse*, written by Tsuuchi Kuheiji (dates unknown) and first performed at Ichimuraza in 1743.3.

44. Hakuun and Kokuun are two comic priests who stand guard over Narukami as he prays.

speaking of now is also an incessant beggar who wants to be paid for making up verses for other people. His name is Yūrin, and he always wants to try to make verses for Ōtani Hiroshi, but the lines he supposedly fabricates are plagiarized from other so-called "expert" fools.[45]

In fact, Yūrin is a fiend. He performed well at the New Yoshiwara, on the fifth block, and attracted handsome guests for the prostitutes from all around. The guests quickly became intimate with the famous courtesans. Among the courtesans was Tōryō of the Ōmiya on Shinchō Avenue.[46] Even now it is said she is a renowned courtesan and one who is more famous than the likes of Miyakoji, Hakudayū or Handayū.[47]

One day "master" Yūrin came and announced, "The Hikawa Festival is to be held on the fifteenth day of this month."[48] Some of his friends who were going to the festival made a request of him, "Our prostitutes must wear yukata and dyed kimonos with wide sleeves for the festival. So have the courtesans you know lend us ten narrow obi and ten light morning kimonos for them. That's what the courtesans like to wear."

Yūrin asked Tōryō: "Would you lend me attire that courtesans would wear from the clothing you have on hand." Since he made this request so boldly, Toryō did not refuse and complied with his wishes.

Yūrin actually made a good living by "borrowing" clothes from the courtesans. He never returned any of them. He sold off all of the yukata and obi he borrowed. Of course, he wanted to avoid any harmful repercussions to himself, but still he never returned the articles of clothing to Tōryō.

Just imagine! Behavior like this for a man thought to be such a re-

45. Yūrin contributed to a haikai collection, *Shin rokkasen* (1756), with five other composers of haikai. Each imitated the works of a different *Shin kokinshū* poet. Yūrin based his work on Fujiwara Ietaka (1158–1237). He was also a contributor to the collection *Edo jūyokasen* (1752). Ōtani Hiroji II (1717–57) was a puppeteer and inventor of the *seriage* (trapdoor) and *hikinuki* (quick costume change).

46. The Ōmiya was a well-known bordello on Shinchō Avenue, one of the main streets of Yoshiwara. Its most famous courtesan was Handayū. (Seigle, *Yoshiwara*, 121.)

47. These three courtesans are named after schools of balladry (*jōruri*) set to be played on the samisen. Handayū is Edo Handayū (?–1743), who began the light, elegant style of samisen jōruri music called by that name. A *tayū* narrated the *bushi*, a type of dramatic and descriptive poetry.

48. In present-day Tokyo there are fifty-nine shrines that bear the name Hikawa. There is a Hikawa shrine, which can be located on a map dated Kan'ei 2 (1625) in the Asakusa district. On the map is also the date of the festival: the fifteenth day of the sixth month. It is the Hikawa shrine closest to the Yoshiwara district.

fined gentleman and master! One who admires the moon and sings of the beauty of nature! As the saying goes, "On the outside he looks like a Bodhisattva, but inside he is a demon!"[49] For appearance sake he wears the clothing of a scholar of poetry, but deep down he is a fraud.[50] This man in particular is without doubt a great monster.

9. The Case of Hayashi, Head of the Confucian Academy

The scholar Nobumitsu, a great Confucianist with a prestige title and a member of the Hayashi family, is presumed to indeed be upright in his personal conduct.[51] It goes without saying that he is also blameless in conducting the affairs of his office. So no one would ever suspect that he is a monster.

First of all, he is slow witted and, one might say, even stupid. He is usually carrying around a Buddhist rosary and reading Buddhist sutras even though the Hayashi family is nothing if not Confucianist. Recently, at the very gates of the Confucian Academy, he said that he detested the way of the Buddha and called it heretical nihilism. Why would he say something like that?

Not long ago when I was writing haikai, I saw this funny verse: "Heartfelt prayer is a Confucian scholar reading Buddhist sutras." Nobumitsu is a great monster who prays only for appearance sake. He teaches benevolence and righteousness, but this leading Confucian scholar, known to the entire country, often brings two or three prostitutes and numerous dancing girls and entertainers up to the front room on the second floor of his house from where he has a view of the bank of the Yayosu River.[52] On more than one occasion, the raucous laughter of courtesans and the commotion of *jōruri* singing and samisen playing could be heard coming from Hayashi's quarters.

Last year, there was a gathering at the house of the chamberlain Ōkubo

49. *Gemen nyō bosatsu, naishin nyō yasha.*

50. "The clothing of a scholar of poetry," or *jittoku*, is a *haori*, or coat, worn by Confucianists, physicians, and artists.

51. Hayashi Nobumitsu (1681–1758) was *daigaku no kami*, (head of the Confucian Academy) and held the title *Chōsantaifu*, a T'ang court title equivalent to the imperial rank of junior fifth rank, lower grade. This honor was bestowed for literary or military accomplishment, but was not an official position.

52. This is the east bank of the inner palace moat going from Hibiya to Wadakura gate.

Ise no kami, the house next to Nobumitsu's, where opinions opposing the Confucian scholar and Confucianism were presented.[53] The upshot was that everyone agreed that Hayashi's term in office had not been edifying. Hayashi felt most embarrassed at their accusations and suggestions that he be a little more reserved in his conduct. Afterwards Hayashi took a low profile, no longer interfering so much in people's affairs. But again and again, even after Ōkubo's resignation, Hayashi continued in a lot of scandalous behavior without any hesitation.

As a consequence, the year before last in the eleventh month on the day when Lady Chiyo was going to the palace, a fire broke out in Hayashi's residence.[54] His own home burnt completely to the ground, and all of the Marunouchi area burned with it.[55] He had nothing left and no excuses for his failed term in office. The fire was heavenly retribution for the misdeeds during his tenure as head of the Confucian Academy.

His last deed was the worst of all. He requested that a bronze offering bowl that had belonged to Miura Gorōzaemon, whose daughter was a concubine of Ieshige, be dedicated to the Asakusa Kannon Temple and engraved with a prayer in gratitude for the goddess' marvelous wisdom.[56] It was inappropriate for a Confucian scholar to do this, and honest people laughed at him in scorn. He makes himself out to be a great Confucian, but he is no Confucian at all. He is rather a big Confucian monster who makes his living deceiving the high and the low of the world. Isn't it unbelievable?

10. The Case of Aoyama San'emon

At the present time, Aoyama San'emon is the comptroller of finance.[57] Before acquiring this office, he was a samurai of insignificant family background and made a basic government stipend of thirty hyō.[58] He also had

53. Ōkubo was chamberlain (*gosobashū*) from 1751 (Horeki 1.7) until 1760 (Hōreki 10.5).

54. Lady Chiyo was the daughter of Tokugawa Iemitsu by the concubine Ofuri.

55. This fire occurred in 1756 (Hōreki 6) 11. 25 and burned the Kōjimachi and Yayosugashi areas as well as Marunouchi.

56. Miura Gorōzaemon's daughter, Oyū (1721–89), was the mother of Tokugawa Shigenori (or Shigeyoshi, 1745–95), who was Ieshige's second son. Gorōzaemon had worked in the operation of a brothel in Kyōmachi 1 chōme where the famous Takao was a courtesan.

57. Aoyama San'emon was also known as Aoyama Nobunaga. He held the office of comptroller of finance (*kanjō ginmiyaku*) from 1757 (Hōreki 7. 3. 15) until 1760 (Hōreki 10. 2. 21).

58. "Hyō" was 0.4 koku of rice. Thus, thirty hyō was equivalent to twelve koku.

an income of three hyō from his work on guard duty outside the shogun's castle. He worked for twenty years in that position.

During those years he was a night watchman he led a totally debauched life and consequently was always strapped for money. In spite of that, he was seen quite often going to the bordellos in the New Yoshiwara district. Not only was he totally incompetent as a watchman, he was a reprehensible scoundrel. He would put on an act of being reliable and did not appear to be neglecting his guard duty, particularly when someone was looking. No matter how inclement the weather might be, he stayed at his post. One day he reported that his official uniform and his two swords had been stolen. Actually he had pawned the uniform, and probably his two swords as well, so that he would have money to go to the Yoshiwara pleasure quarters.

What happened was this: when he went on guard duty at the Tokiwabashi Gate one day, he was waiting for his replacement, his colleague Sekine Yaichi.[59] Aoyama was not wearing his uniform at the time (he had already pawned it), so he told Sekine that he would be glad to take his watch if he could borrow Sekine's uniform. "I'll take your place on the next watch. Just let me borrow your uniform for today," he said. Sekine was only too happy to comply. Aoyama put his uniform on and continued that day's watch.

"What a kind, stouthearted fellow that Aoyama is!" everyone said. Because of the impression he gave, Aoyama was promoted to the post of assistant inspector and continued to make a show of performing his services quite faithfully just as he had always done.

In the position of assistant inspector, Aoyama sent one of his two younger sisters to be a secondary concubine for Senior Counselor Hotta Sagami no kami.[60] He sent his other sister to be a concubine for Junior Counselor Itakura Sado no kami.[61] Both of his sisters put in a good word for their brother and tricked Hotta and Itakura in various other ways as well. Aoyama was quickly promoted from the post of assistant inspector

59. Tokiwabashi Gate was on the northeast side of the outer palace moat.

60. Hotta Masasuke (1712–61) was senior counselor (*rōjū*) from 1745 (Enkyō 2. 11. 13) to 1761 (Hōreki 11. 2. 8).

61. Itakura Katsukiyo (1706–80) was junior counselor (*wakadoshiyori*) from 1735 (Kyōhō 20. 6. 5) to 1760 (Hōreki 10. 4.1).

to superintendent of construction and repair and soon after was again promoted to manager of provisions.[62] Until recently he was holding this position, which required no official rank, and not long after he rose to fame as the comptroller of finance, which has a stipend of three thousand koku. It is obvious now that he is going to continue to advance even to the three highest magisterial positions in the realm and, though he has no rank now, acquire the court honor of junior fifth rank, lower grade.[63] He is indeed a monster.

His high promotions were all the doing of his two sisters. But, in fact, they are not Aoyama's real sisters. These two girls were the daughters of a florist by the name of Saburōbei, a slum resident in the town of Tachibana-chō. From their youth, the two girls were pupils of Ichinotani Sangoshichi and practiced dance and samisen under his direction. Their father, Saburōbei, died leaving mother and two daughters to make a living on their own.

In their desperate straits, Aoyama bought them out, along with their mother and let them stay in his own home. He then legally adopted the two girls, so that he could prepare them to be geisha with the intent of sending them as prostitutes for Hotta and Itakura. The two lords fought over them, and the two went in and out of both houses.

Junior Counselor Itakura sings Edo ballads very well. The two sisters had acquired such a command of the samisen that they rival even the famous San'emon himself. This whole family has little by little pulled the wool over everyone's eyes.

Aoyama has recently acquired a good-looking young woman as his wife, and he also has a number of other female companions who are with him around town. He obviously doesn't realize that, as the saying goes, "his monster's tail is showing." There have been great monsters in the past, and obviously they are still around today. Without a doubt, the world is becoming even more filled with these great deceivers.

62. The position of superintendent of construction and repair (*kobushin*) was assigned to a bannerman who had a stipend of less than three thousand koku and who was incapable of taking on a more responsible position because of age, illness or incompetence. (*Kodansha Encyclopedia of Japan*, 4: 239). Manager of provisions (*makanai gashira*) was Aoyama's position immediately preceding his appointment to the office of comptroller of finance in 1757.

63. The "three highest magisterial positions" are commissioner of shrines and temples (*jisha bugyō*), city magistrate (*machi bugyō*), and magistrate of finance (*kanjō bugyō*).

11. The Case of Takahashi Genshū

Takahashi Genshū is known as "the hunchback doctor."[64] He is a great monster of long standing. Once when lieutenant of the Inner Palace Guards Matsudaira Norimura was senior counselor, Genshū's true character became evident, and he was banished to a distant island.[65] But even after he had been discredited for his dishonesty and Norimura removed him from office, he was still able to deceive officials again and again on his island of exile. Eventually a pardon was handed down, and he was allowed to come back home. This is very strange. He has to be called a monstrous fiend.

Now he is again living in the capital again, in Hattchōbori and is admired as a prominent physician.[66] I don't know how many countless numbers of times people have been fooled by his remedies and his way of preparing medicine.

It is said that he became infatuated with the "floating world" of the licensed quarters and interested in that above everything else. Visiting the courtesans got to be more important to him than giving medical care. He taught his medical students the same values that he had.

Recently as he was lecturing his students on medical texts, he completely transposed the topic of physical health with physical pleasure. The care of physical health is a subject that has been passed down from antiquity. Physical pleasures is what is practiced nowadays. It takes long study to provide the proper medical treatment according to the ancient methods, and it is here that a physician's work should begin.

However, one of Genshū's medical lectures went like this:

"If one wishes to know modern methods of medicine, one should go see the comic *kyōgen* performances on the stage. In one of the comic performances of the old days Yaoya Oshichi is captured.[67] According to the

64. Genshū was the well-known personal physician (*goban isha*) of Tokugawa Ieshige.

65. Matsudaira Norimura (1686–1746) was made lieutenant of the Inner Palace Guards (*sagon shogen*) in 1722 (Kyōhō 7. 7) and was *rōjū* from 1723 (Kyōhō 8. 4. 21) to 1745 (Enkyō 2. 10. 9) when he lost his fief.

66. Hattchōbori is in present-day Chūō-ku.

67. The third novelette in *Kōshoku gonin onna* (Five women who loved love, 1686) by Ihara Saikaku is the story of Oshichi and Ōnogawa Kichisaburō. It was based on an actual event that had taken place four years before the novel was published. Oshichi decided that if her house were to burn down a second time, she would be able to visit the temple page with whom she had fallen in love when her family had been forced to flee there after their home had been destroyed by fire

magistrate's investigation, it was because of her innocent stubbornness that she started a fire so that she could meet her lover Kichisaburō. This is the old-fashioned style of love. If young women nowadays feel like falling in love, it ought not to be like this.

"This spring Kikunojō's lines in the role of Osome went like this: 'If you have a different opinion from mine put it aside.[68] Even if Hisamatsu and I play hide and seek with each other, we have to eventually bare ourselves.' In the same way, contemporary women need to be forthright and determined. This is the natural way of behavior for living in the world today. If you women don't take that attitude but instead behave in the old style, playing hide and seek, surely whatever you do will never turn out well."

This is unquestionably a lecture he gave only to become popular with his students. The medical students who studied under Genshū went home having been completely fooled.

There was also the case of the woman from Hyōgōya in Koami-chō who was suffering from consumption. She went to the Inoue Kotai Hospital, but she never got any better. When she showed herself to Takahashi Genshū, she, of course, got worse and was confined to her bed.

"Oh, this is not the beginnings of consumption," he had said to her. "If a young girl becomes ill and does not regain her health, it is her parents' fault. Here's what you should do: Steal your father's house key and run away with his money. Make up your mind to go off by the new road to Yoshi, and then you will recover your health. After you take four or five of my pills, go see Rokō's performance of *Mugen no kane* (The eternal bell).[69] You will immediately start feeling better," he said. The patient laughed out loud. Her parents in Hyōgōya were beside themselves with joy that their daughter was finally laughing for the first time in fifteen days.

Incidents like this were talked about all over town. Genshu exam-

---

in 1681. 12. 28. On the second day of the Third Month in 1682 she tried to set fire to a building. She was captured and on the twentieth day was burned at the stake on the execution grounds of Suzugamori. The story is the basis of the plot of the *jōruri* play *Yaoya Oshichi* (Oshichi of the greengrocer) by Ki no Kaion (1663–1742).

68. The *shinjū* (double suicide) play *Osome Hisamatsu tamoto no shirashibori* (Dappled sleeves, Osome and Hisamatsu) was written by Ki no Kaion in 1711.

69. *Mugen no kane* is a *nagauta*, first performed by Kikunojō I in spring of 1731 at the Ichimurazura.

ined patients but often didn't have them take any medicine. When they started feeling better, he received the credit and got much respect from many people. This was his skillful deception. Is there anyone who has not heard of the great monster of Hattchōbori, the hunchback demon?

One time an old woman went to another famous old physician, Dōsan, who was also called Enjuin, and said sorrowfully, "I have one child, and the boy has fallen victim to a very serious and incurable disease.[70] His life is now in danger." She beseeched him in tears for some medicine. Dōsan listened as the mother spoke about the condition of her child. "Please prepare some kind of remedy," she begged. "My son goes into houses at night and steals. This is his serious illness. You might be able to prevent my son's stealing with some kind of medication." Dōsan then gave her some medicine. The mother gratefully accepted it and departed. She made up the concoction for her son as the doctor had directed and gave it to him to drink. Amazingly, his stealing stopped.

When she understood the kind of good effects this mysterious medicine had, she took a large dose of it herself. Just as her son had been cured of his propensity for sneaking into people's homes and stealing, she no longer cared anything about entering other people's houses either, and she stopped stealing, too.

12. The Case of the Aged Geisha

There is a renowned geisha by the name of Oroku, who used to reside in the unlicensed prostitute district in Fukagawa-nakachō.[71] A while back, there was a police raid in Fukagawa, and she was arrested and sent to the New Yoshiwara licensed district where she gained employment at the Kyōmachi Nagasakiya Inn.[72] She worked in Yoshiwara twenty-four months, but on the twenty-fifth month her term of employment ended. She went back again to work at Fukagawa and after a year and a half, because of another police raid, was again arrested and brought again to

70. Dōsan Gensaku (1551–1633) took the name of Manase Dōsan II after his uncle, Manase Dōsan (1507–94), adopted him. Gensaku is the author of *Igaku tenshōki* (Medical record of the Tenshō period), his medical journal of the years 1576–1606.

71. The central part of Fukagawa was the expansive unlicensed prostitute district. The Fukagawa prostitutes prided themselves on being exclusively young and beautiful.

72. The police raid in Fukagawa took place in 1753.

Yoshiwara. After going back and forth like this a number of times, her bid to stay at Yoshiwara on permanent contract was finally accepted at Tawaraya Inn on Kyōmachi Avenue.

However, she didn't stay. After she had spent twenty-four months working in Yoshiwara, she went back again to Fukagawa. Her comings and goings went on for as long as nine years. She was nineteen years old the first time she was taken to Yoshiwara. From the age of nineteen, the additional nine years made her twenty-eight years old. It's been four years since she again returned to Fukagawa to perform as a geisha, so she must be thirty-two. However, she tied her obi at the back just like a girl much younger. In her heart she was always a show-off, and her willfulness was just like that of a child. There has never been so foolish a person as this cheap prostitute Ōroku, until now. But for a year now this woman has been called one of the sophisticated and chic geisha.

Her father makes his living in the book-lending business, and she helps him. It seems her fate is to do two jobs. She is completely resigned to this and works with the attitude of a child, leaving everything up to fate.

She thinks of herself as young, but for a geisha she's practically an old woman. She doesn't hesitate to compare herself to the young male prostitutes in skill and energy. This is a great deception. It is just like the kabuki actor Nakamura Shichisaburō, whose real age nobody knows.[73] He has an exceedingly young appearance and has never really lost his fame as quite the lady-killer. That's because ordinarily no one ever sees him without his make-up on. Once when his appearance was quite disheveled as the result of an illness, a doctor went to help him, but Shichisaburō would not see him. Even if he had been on his deathbed, he wouldn't have seen any other person because of his appearance. It is said that at the time he actually looked quite frightening and was so wasted away that he didn't even accept an audience with the shogun. He was determined never to expose his true appearance. He managed to do this very skillfully; and as a result, a lot of people would praise him for his beauty, not knowing what he really looked like.

The female impersonator Nakamura Kiyosaburō was in a similar sit-

73. Nakamura Shichisaburō II (1703–74) was an actor accomplished in performing love scenes (*wagoto*).

uation.[74] He was one of the younger actors and was quite talented. His wife, Oiwa, was a beauty from Ōsaka, Tatamiya-chō. Although she was born beautiful, it was actually Kiyosaburō whom everyone admired as having a far more lovely complexion. Kiyosaburō was so attractive that even when he was asleep he was unsurpassed in beauty. His wife tried to show how beautiful her husband was by never putting on make-up herself so that she would never detract from her husband's beauty. Everyone said that she never failed to be modest. But it is all a big hypocritical act. Those who know what is really going on do not think she is modest at all.

I will end this section here with a warning not to trust what people are saying about these two, Nakamura Shichisaburō and Nakamura Kiyosaburō, since they are both vain frauds.

13. The Case of Uno Chōsai

The player of the hand drum at the Ichimuraza playhouse Fukiya-chō is Uno Chōsai.[75] He is considered to be an extraordinary master. Even the talented headmaster Kanze Shinkurō and Kōsei Jirō could not surpass him.[76] At least that's what people were saying. So everyone admires Chōsai for his supposedly incomparable skill at playing the drum at the theater. Originally he was an Owari actor and later completed his initiation into the secrets of the hand drum. It is said that he was a disciple of Uno Chōgen in Kyoto.

Well, one day Chōsai was summoned before the headmaster, Kanze Shinkurō, who had requested that he do a drum performance. Chōsai did his best, but he had to stop short. "Excuse me," he said, "but I am not able to complete this traditional Kumano ballad for you. I'd like someone to accompany me in performing a ballad I am more familiar with."

Then Kanze called the nagauta singer Matsushima Shōgorō, who could sing all the songs from the hunting scene in *Asaina Saburō*.[77] While

74. Nakamura Kiyosaburō I (1721–77).

75. Also known as Uno Choshichi (1713–66), he was a master of the hand drum used in accompaniment for kabuki. He performed mostly at the Ichimuraza.

76. Kanze Shinkurō ryū was a school of the Noh hand drum. Many of the masters of this school were called Shinkurō. Kōsei Jirō ryū, or simply Kōsei ryū, was another school of the hand drum in which there was more fluctuation in rhythm patterns and voice.

77. Shōgorō I, famous for his beautiful voice, had a performing career from 1726 to 1736.

Chōsai performed the piece on the hand drum, Shōgorō sang, and everyone praised them both for their renditions of highlights of the past and the present.

Kanze Shinkurō and Kōsei Jirō are performers of traditional theater who are heads of their own schools. So why is it that when asked to play traditional pieces, they have to play popular music? It's because Uno Chōsai couldn't do anything else. Besides Shinkurō and Jirō know that people today will give them a lot more money for playing the popular rather than the traditional music. As a matter of fact, Shinkurō was very happy to play with Chōsai since he was often given greater remuneration. It must be said that Uno Chōsai as well deceived people, making them think he had talent.

14. The Case of Nakamura Hachiemon

Nakamura Hachiemon is a master samisen player of the Handayū-bushi style today. Since the demise of Yamabiko Genshirō, Hachiemon has become the leading performer of this style.[78] According to some reports, however, Hachiemon is one of the foremost monsters in the world.

Last night I was taken in by this impudent demon. You might ask, "How did that happen?" Well, last night he was hired to play samisen on a pleasure boat. Before he began someone gave him flowers, and we were quite touched by this, but his performance on the boat was nothing but a recitation of an amusing story about sumo wrestling taken from an Edo jōruri ballad and some other stories about people on a boat. Everyone on the riverbank and in the boat had been straining their ears waiting to hear a samisen tune. They were not interested in his talk. He never played anything. This incident showed that he is a devious monster.

The same evening an unknown fellow by the name of Segawa Hisashi who now works for Koshirō at the Enshūya Inn in Izumi-chō was doing voice imitations of Segawa Kikunojō on another boat. And he did them quite well. Nakamura claimed that since everyone was captivated by

Asaina Saburō Yoshihide is a character in the folktale *Asaina shimameguri* (c. 1660). He travels in the land of one-eyed monsters, the land of midgets, etc. The folktale became a play.

78. Yamabiko Genshirō (?–1756), also called Yamabiko Masayumi, was the founder of the style of bushi (traditional folk music) known as Edo-bushi. (*Tōsei Buya zokudan*, 342.)

Segawa's imitations, he was not able to play the samisen. "What a despicable fellow Segawa is!" he said.

But who is the despicable one? Nakamura was hired that day for the large sum of one thousand hiki.[79] That voice imitator was hired for a pittance of two hundred mon. The difference in the quality of the entertainment was obvious. Segawa Hisashi recited the elegant lines from dramatic pieces, while Nakamura Hachiemon only ad libbed. After all, is not correct poetic style superior to incorrect? What happened is like dark clouds hiding for a moment the light of the sun or the moon.

Since Nakamura is such a strange monster and has an evil influence such as I have described, those in their apprenticeship should not let such a monster get too close to them. Since people who distinguish between truth and falsehood and good and evil are rare, everyone is deceived. It is said that this is the way things are in the world now. It is certainly true that amateurs can sometimes overshadow masters. This ought to be passed on to everyone.

15. The Case of the Monster of Matsue

Among all of the nobles, Matsudaira Dewa no kami, the lord of Matsue castle in Izumo, has been notorious for a long time for being a monster.[80]

Now there is a strange affair going on, but where it begins and ends no one knows for sure. Matsudaira's performance in office was apparently conducted in a dignified manner, and so absolutely no one suspected anything was amiss. However, Matsudaira is nothing if not a foxy old skinflint.

Last year, for the usual kyōgen plays, he had a brand new entrance put in his official residence.[81] An east-west reviewing stand was built, and he ordered many theatrical attractions to be presented for the commoners. He summoned a number of actors and sent for the composer of comic drama, Horikoshi Nisōji, who was commissioned to write a play by the lord himself.[82]

79. Traditionally, the price of one koku of rice was equivalent to one hiki of silk. In the Edo period one hiki remained more or less the equivalent of ten mon.

80. Matsudaira Munenobu (1729–82) was daimyō of Matsue from 1731 to 1767.

81. The *nezumikido* (side entrance) usually referred to a narrow opening in a show tent. When used in homes, it was made of latticework and was common in the Edo period.

82. Horikoshi Nisōji (1721–81) was a composer of kyōgen.

Just at that time, Segawa Kikunojō II had been, for a number of years, playing the part of Yaoya Oshichi in Fukiya and in Sakai. When Mizoguchi met Matsudaira in Izumo, Matsudaira said, "Let's have Rokō perform the performance of Oshichi for us."[83] Mizoguchi replied, "I would be grateful and indebted to you for doing me such a favor. I would so much like to see Kikunojō performing the role of Oshichi."

Indeed, asking for a private performance was a most uncommon imposition to put on an actor. What could possibly be the meaning of putting such an imposition on Kikunojō? But actually, Matsudaira took care of Kikunojō as if he were his foster father. After that incident Lord Arima made fun of Matsudaira, referring to him by the nickname, "honorable foster father."[84] He was implying that there was not an altogether proper relationship between the great lord of Matsue and the kabuki actor.

What a gathering of monsters, a collection of old washrags![85]

16. The Case of the Short Bow of Oguri Mataichi

There is a bannerman in the Honjo area called Oguri Mataichi who loves the short bow.[86] Evidently, he is quite skillful with it. Carrying his bow in a cotton bag, he goes to various archery competitions around Edo to show off his ability and to teach his art.

There was a very beautiful prostitute called Oshun at the Utamato archery site in Ryōgoku, Yonezawa-chō. She was at Mataichi's side every morning before dawn and followed him around wherever he went. Mataichi was so completely infatuated with her that he did nothing from dawn to dusk. He has become a great "monster." I am writing about him so that many people will take warning.

On the 25th of last month Oshun died from an illness, and Mataichi was so upset that he broke his bow in two and threw his arrows away.

83. Mizoguchi refers to Mizoguchi Naoatsu, who is the subject of "The case of the monster who switched from being a lover of young boys to a lover of women."

84. Arima Yoriyuki (1714–83).

85. The phrase "a collection of old washrags" (*tenugui no kumiawase*) is used in the haikai anthology of Yokoi Yayū (1702–82) titled *Uzuragoromo* (Patched clothes), which was composed of haiku he wrote from 1727 to 1779). The phrase refers to old people who cover their heads with washrags, dance, and do tricks.

86. *Yōkyū* (literally, willow bow) was a small bow, about 90 cm long, shot from a seated position.

This is quite perplexing. He held a memorial service for her and began his eulogy with these words: "How could this bow that you gave to me, Oshun, have now become my enemy? Now this bow and arrow have no meaning, and I discard them."

The bow Mataichi had received from Oshun was the kind that is called the "Yang bow" because in T'ang China, the lover of Emperor Hsüan Tsung, Yang Kuei-fei, first began to practice archery with such a bow.[87]

Mataichi had the heart of Hsüan Tsung, and Oshun had the heart of Yang Kuei-fei, and they had lived a happy life together. Now that she was dead, Mataichi was in deep mourning and decided to rid himself of both bow and arrow, feeling that these weapons could no longer have any place in the "way of the samurai."

"Now, if I were to take up the bow, I would feel sad," he said. "If I do not take it up though, I feel bitter. The bow and arrow—the samurai must be detached from them."

This was the strange state of his feelings for a samurai. Both of them, Mataichi and the prostitute Oshun, were monsters.

17. The Case of Nakamura Kichibei

As the proverb goes, "Even if a sparrow lives for one hundred years, it will not forget how to jump." This is certainly not a meaningless saying. An actor who forgets how to perform would not be well received by his public.

There is a former kabuki actor by the name of Nakamura Kichibei.[88] He is quite knowledgeable in the ways of the world. He left his theatrical troupe fourteen or fifteen years ago. This year he is almost eighty years of age but still hale and hearty, serving the daimyō as a professional jester and regularly receiving gifts of money and wearing expensive apparel. This notorious old monster, whom everyone is talking about now, poses as a blind storyteller in the temple precincts. He is a fraud who gets the parts of his stories mixed up and puts the end at the beginning. This is because he drinks too much.

87. Hsüan Tsung (685–762), the sixth T'ang emperor, was enamored with the empress Yang Kuei-fei (719–56), who was killed during the An Lu-shan Rebellion (705–57).

88. Nakamura Kichibei (1684–1766) became a professional jester after he retired from the kabuki stage in 1739.

Until he was fifty years old, he really ran wild, but it is true that he still commits lewd acts, even though recently he has become more discreet in the matter of alcohol and sex. However, he has gone through life so superficially that he pays no attention to what is deep down in the heart. Since he has not lost any of his health or vigor, he still manages to fool everybody. This is a deceiver whom even the enchanted white fox should worship.[89]

18. The Case of Hanabusa Itchō

When Itchō was a student, he was only one of a hundred foolish masters.[90] All of them are strange monsters who often change their appearance, but Itchō is the one who is really an old fox.

He was asked to do paintings of Tora and Shōshō that were to be displayed in the New Yoshiwara district.[91] In the room where he was supposed to paint Tora he painted instead a tiger in a bamboo grove. In the room where he was supposed to paint Shōshō he painted a scene of the evening rain on Xi Hu.[92]

While doing these paintings at the Tomoeya Inn, Itchō was munching on dumplings. On one occasion he ate a plate of eighty-one dumplings in about a minute—a monster of great accomplishments. Now it is said that everyone in Yoshiwara died of laughter over this.

Not long ago, when the shogun was traveling from the capital, he commissioned Itchō to do a painting on a scroll so that he could present it to the Jōdo sect temple, Nishihonganji.[93] The painting was to be a biographical scroll of Momotarō. The Honganji was extremely pleased with the painting.

As a reward for his effort, Itchō received a request for an audience be-

89. The white fox, a creature of Shinto and Buddhist legends and folklore, was known for its sexual prowess.

90. Hanabusa Itchō (1652–1724) was born in Osaka and came to Edo at the age of fifteen to receive painting lessons from Kanō Yasunobu (1613–85) and took the name Kanō Shinkō. Having published a collection of satirical designs that offended the shogunal government, he was banished to Miyakejima in 1698, where he lived for twelve years. It was after his exile that he took the name Hanabusa Itchō.

91. Tora Gozen and Kewaizaka Shōshō are two characters in *Soga monogatari* (Tale of the Soga brothers, 1361–88).

92. Xi Hu, a lake in Chekiang, China, is one of the eight views of the Xiao and Xiang (Shōshō) Rivers, which flow through eastern and southern Hunan province. It is an area famous for its beautiful scenes and many historic sites.

93. Nishihonganji was the headquarters of the Pure Land sect in Kyoto.

fore the shogun where he was given one serving of soba, which he ate in the shogun's presence. It is said that the food lay very heavy on his stomach, and he complained about it. There were a lot of people in attendance including the son-in-law of Nakamura Ribei of Sakai and Yamagataya Sōemon of Shinmuragi-chō.[94] These fellows are also a couple of the great monsters of Edo.

19. The Case of Katsuma Ryōsui

As for Katsuma Ryōsui, I exposed his life in another work—Tōsei *Buya zokudan* (Contemporary talks on worldly affairs in Musashi).[95] He is an exceedingly odd person and a monster of great accomplishments. His son is a landlord but conducts himself in an immoral manner and has been told that he should give up his responsibilities.

While he was living as a monk, Ryōsui was called by the name Riemon. He owned property and rented it out. He is a great monster.

20. The Case of Yamamoto Kunai

There is one monster of long standing who often passes by the rice storage facility at Asakusa. He is Yamamoto Kunai, an extraordinary individual known all over Edo. He walks around the shops acting like a great *tengu*.[96] He wears the mask of a little tengu and sports a big wooden sword.[97] Since he has been devoted to going on pilgrimages to Mt. Ōyama for years, his heart is naturally like that of a tengu, and he is tremendously proud of his no more than ordinary talents. He is a strange monster.

People say that last year on his way home, he hacked off one of his own arms. Word got around that after that happened, he grafted his right arm back on by using some kind of ointment; but, of course, there is no one who actually saw it. In spite of the lack of eyewitnesses, the story continues to be told. What in the world is all this about? Was it like the incident in *Tsurezuregusa* (Essays in idleness) that was supposed to

94. Nakamura Ribei and Yamagataya Sōemon were two well-know merchants in Shinmuragi-chō, which is in present-day Shibuya, Tokyo.

95. Katsuma Ryōsui, an instructor of calligraphy in Shin-Izumi-chō, was a miser who salvaged the waste paper from his calligraphy students and sold it. (See *Tōsei Buya zokudan*, 361–62.)

96. The expression "a great tengu" (*daitengu*) is used for someone who is arrogant.

97. "A little tengu" (*kotengu*) refers to a young man of small stature who excels in the martial arts.

have taken place during the Ōchō period?[98] There was a woman who was thought to be a demon. "I saw it," said one person. "I've seen the demon, too," said another. But actually, it was all a hoax. The stories about Yamamoto were the same: a case of some people just fooling others.

21. In Search of the Real Shidōken

In the precincts of the Asakusa Kannon Temple there is a pseudo-monk by the name of Shidōken who tells war stories.[99] He has been deceiving people around here for a long time. Recently, a piece called *The Biography of Shidōken* has been published on the sacred mountain of the Tendai sect.[100] It's an extremely bungling work without any merit. Could this monk who authored it have any redeeming features? The general public has been completely fooled by him. Even though it is true that Shidōken knows things by heart just as a scholar would, he is actually ignorant of good and evil. How despicable it is for people to praise him. People with learning, whatever they might do, are completely lacking in common sense. Should foolish jabber be the means by which one earns his living?[101] Everything he says is a repudiation of the sound sense of Heaven. Whether he is relating philosophical views on nothingness or on existence, what he has to say about the really important matters in Confucianism, in Buddhism, or in Shinto appears to be heresy. What makes this so terrible is that he is leading the world astray, destroying the love between fathers and sons and between older and younger brothers. He is a criminal, no different from the most heinous of villains. If we were living in the age of the Chinese sages, we would have to take that guy, crucify him, and then chop off his head. That guy would have been better off having been born in the Kannin period.[102]

98. The Ōchō period was from 1311 to 1312. The section in *Essays in Idleness* that is referred to is section 50.

99. Fukai Shidōken (1680–1765), professional storyteller of the Edo period, popularly known as Fukai Eizan, also known as Ichimudō, and *Kyōto no hito* (the man of Kyoto). He became famous in Edo for his recitation of military tales and other stories on the grounds of the Asakusa Temple.

100. Kinryū Dōjin, *Shidōken den*, in *Nihon shomin bunka shiryō shūsei*, Sekiyama Kazuo et al., eds. (Tokyo: Sanichi shobō, 1976), 8: 277–79. The sacred mountain of the Tendai sect is Mt. Hiei. Kinryū Dōjin (1712–82) was a monk of the Tendai sect and lived at Asakusa Temple.

101. The word *tawake* (foolishness) is used ten times in the author's preface of *Fūryū Shidōken den* to describe Shidōken.

102. The Kannin period (1017–21) was the age of Michinaga (966–1027), the most powerful of the Fujiwara regents. Goichijō (r. 1016–36) was emperor.

I myself began my career by sitting at the feet of street vendors at Gojiin Temple.[103] I became a young itinerant monk without being able to read a single word and was totally uneducated. My parents, who were born in the Jōkyō period, were knowledgeable in the arts, so I acquired a talent for telling stories.[104] So I know what I am talking about. People nowadays are being deceived by Shidōken. They go to his gatherings every night to hear the evening lectures and have no sense of shame at listening to all the foolishness. It is often said that Shidōken should not be allowed to speak in front of women and children. There is no virtue at all in what he says.

Some people say that when Shidōken was summoned before the shogun, he spoke to him directly. If that is the case, this guy is very manipulative. But according to other people, Yoshimune, the young son of the shogun Ietsugu, was escorted into the Asakusa Kannon Temple.[105] He was there to make an inspection of the area. He watched the performances and antics of the outcasts and the beggars who were in the temple precincts. At that time, Shidōken was also on the grounds, and when called forward said something idiotic that gave grave offense to the son of the shogun: "I would like you to make my two children administrators at the Ueno imperial tomb."

Yoshimune showed his appreciation for the skills of the beggars, some of whom did juggling acts with small shells. But when it came to Shidōken, a professional storyteller, the young prince thought him rude and wicked. As the saying goes, "The songs of Chang do not fit with the imperial music, and the manner in which purple takes away the luster of vermilion is disgusting."[106] These are incongruities that the wise person hates. But what is even more hateful is that this Shidōken, who is very foolish, somehow gets the better of even a strong warrior.[107]

103. Gojiin is a Shingon sect Buddhist temple in Shikoku, Matsuyama-shi, in present-day Ehime prefecture. It is number fifty-two on the popular pilgrimage of eighty-eight temples on the island of Shikoku.

104. The Jōkyō period was from 1684 to 1688.

105. Tokugawa Ietsugu (1709–16) was shogun from 1713 to 1716.

106. This is taken from *Analects*, Bk. 17, "Yang Ho." See James Legge, ed., *Confucian Analects, The Great Learning the Doctrine of the Mean* (New York: Dover Publications, 1971), 326.

107. Bunkō is referring to Yoshimune as "a strong warrior."

22. Descriptions of Various Monsters

a) *Kimura Sehei, the Sumo Referee*

This person, the son of Matsukaze Sehei, was a sumo wrestler in former days but is now retired. Twenty years ago both of his eyes went bad.

Fourteen or fifteen people lived in his home in Tachibana-chō. It's strange that somehow he managed to support them all even though he received no rice stipend from the government. In that area, he is one of those unheard-of monsters.

b) *In Bakuro-chō, Gorōbei, the Paper Merchant*

Speaking of the Gorōbei paper, none of it is of particularly outstanding quality. However, Gorōbei's business is flourishing. How is he able to deceive everyone?

c) *At the Kamakura Shore, Toshimaya Jūemon*

Last year, at the time of the dredging of the canal, Jūemon opened a new liquor store.[108] In addition to gradually fooling people about the quality of his bean curd baked in miso, he also became a tonsured demon-monk who now travels around all of Edo.

d) *In Tenma-chō, Tanbaya Gobei*

For a while, since his day-to-day work was very light, Gobei just walked around aimlessly.

He lived next door to Eichiya Sōsuke.[109] Both Gobei and Sōsuke had the same strong point: they worked hard for each other. One day they agreed not to meet again until they had each made one thousand ryō. Sōsuke and Gobei then parted and went to work. Only after they had made ten thousand ryō did they attempt to meet again, both wanting to outdo the other.

108. Jūemon operated a drinking establishment that was located between Edogawa and Shinnakagawa in Katsushika on the Kamakura shore (see *Mitamura Engyo shū*, 14: 151).

109. Eichiya was a merchant in Yomezawa-chō in the Genroku period (1688–1704). He invented the Eichiya lattice (*Eichiya gōshi*), a paper covering over doors and windows in which triangular slits were cut to allow a person inside the room to see out but which prevented a person outside from looking in.

Gobei held a lavish banquet for Sōsuke and treated him to bean curd soup with two dried horse mackerel in it. It was a meeting of old friends. They were big, fat monsters.

e) *In Osaka-chō, Murata Gobei*

Money is lent at daily interest to the bosses of each and every unlicensed prostitute quarter in Fukagawa, Hikawa, Takainari, Tamagawa, Otowa, Hitotsume, and Ōhashi. For a loan of one ryō an interest charge of two hundred mon is charged each day.[110] If one day ten ryō are lent out, the next day a clerk will come to demand payment on the principal. After the principal is paid back, an interest charge of two *kanmon* is charged.[111] If the customer is a nightly visitor to the quarter and the interest payment is not overdue, everything goes smoothly. This is the way it always works at the brothels.

The unlicensed brothels are open today, but it is hard to foresee what tomorrow will bring. What might happen even tonight is uncertain. There could unexpectedly be no one to lend you money when business does not go well.

This was the case with Murata Gobei, who is supposed to be very clever. There was some "emergency," and he spent ten thousand ryō without any hesitation. However, as the interest rate and principal gradually got higher and higher, he found himself all of a sudden on a lower social scale.

He has a tabi shop in his house and a sake shop on the banks of the river in Fukiya-chō. It is an imitation of a sake shop on the Jinyō River and has become more and more famous, doing an increasingly good business.[112] What a fantastic deceiver he is!

With my deepest respects[113]

110. After the Genroku period the price of one koku of rice was one ryō. One ryō was equal to 4000 mon. See Chie Nakane et al., eds., *Tokugawa Japan: The Social and Economic Antecedents of Modern Japan* (Tokyo: University of Tokyo Press, 1990), 233.

111. Kanmon (or kan) was equivalent to one thousand mon.

112. Jinyō River refers to Yōsukō (Yangtzechinag) in Chianghsi, China.

113. The phrase "with my deepest respects" (*anakashiko)* was often written at the end of a letter.

List of Names and Terms

Abe Masachika 阿部正允
Abe Masatake 阿部正武
adauchimono 仇討物
Aizawa Seishisai 会沢正志斎
Akamatsu Seizaemon 赤松清左衛門
Akimoto Suketomo 秋元凉朝
akusho 悪所
Amagasaki Ikko 尼ケ崎一潮
Amagasaki Ikkō 尼ケ崎一候
Amakusa Shirō 天草四郎
Andō Nobutada 安藤信尹
Aoi 葵
Aoki Jirōkurō 青木次朗九郎
Aoyama San'emon 青山三右衛門
Aoyama Tessan 青山鉄山
AoyamaYoshimichi 青山幸道
Aoyama Yoshinaga 青山宜長
Arai Hakuseki 新井白石
arige kenmi 有毛検見
Arima Yoriyuki 有馬頼徸
Asagao 朝顔
Asai Ryōi 浅井了意
Asakusa Emma Hall 浅草閻魔堂
Asakusa 浅草
Asano Naganori 浅野長矩
Atagosan 愛宕山
Awa 阿波

Baba Bunkō 馬場文耕
bakufu hyōbōzu 幕府表坊主
bakufu renkashi 幕府連歌師
bakuhan 幕藩
Bakuro-chō 馬喰町
bakushin 幕臣
Bansei hyaku monogatari 万世百物語
Banshū sarayashiki 播州更屋敷
Banzuin 幡随院
bateren 伴天連
Benkei 弁慶
Bishū 尾州
Bokuteki ruisō 牧笛類叢
Buke shohatto 武家諸法度
Bunchō 文長
bunraku 文楽
Bunshichi 文七
burei-uchi 無礼打ち
bushi 武士

Ch'eng 城
Chao Fei-yen 趙飛燕
chaya 茶屋
Chiba Tsunetane 千葉常胤
Chikamatsu Monzaemon 近松門左衛門
chimi mōryō 魑魅魍魎
Chōjiya 丁子屋
chōme 丁目
chōnin 町人
chōsan taifu 朝散大夫
Chōsui 長水
Chu Hsi 朱熹
Chūō-ku 中央区

daikan 代官
daimyō 大名

Daimyōjin 大明神
dangibon 談義本
Date Munemura 伊達宗村
Date Shigemura 伊達重村
Date Tsunamura 伊達綱村
Date Yoshimura 伊達吉村
degawari 出替り
Dewa 出羽
Doi Toshikatsu 土井利勝
Donkai Shūten 頓海秀天
Dōsan 道三
dōshin 同心

Ebiya 海老屋
Echigo 越後
Edo 江戸
Ehime 愛媛
Eichiya Sōsuke 江市屋宗助
Ejima Kiseki 江島其磧
Ekōin 回向院
ema 絵馬
Emura Shōsuke 江村庄介
Enjōji 円成寺
Enkyō 延享
Enoki 榎
eta 穢多

fudai 譜代
Fujita Kenzō 藤田顕蔵
Fujita Tōko 藤田東湖
Fujiwara Ietaka 藤原家隆
Fujiwara Kintō 藤原公任
Fujiwara Hidehira 藤原秀衡
Fujiwara Shunzei 藤原俊成
Fukagawa 深川
Fukai Shidōken 深井志道軒
Fukugūken Asei 福偶軒蛙井
Fukushima 福島
fumie 踏み絵

geidō 芸道
Genroku 元禄
gesaku 戯作
Gifu 岐阜
go 碁
goke sōdōmono 御騒動物
gosanke 御三家
Goshikizumi 五色墨
Gujō 郡上

Hachijōjima 八丈島
haikai 俳諧
haiku 俳句
Hakusan Chūkyo 白山中居
han 藩
Hanabusa Itchō 英一蝶
Hasegawa Hanzaemon 長谷川半左衛門
hatamoto 旗本
Hatchōbori 八丁堀
Hattori Kenzui 服部見瑞
Hayashi Nobumitsu 林信充
Hayashi Razan 林羅山
Hayashi Shihei 林子平
Heike monogatari 平家物語
Higekiri 髭切
Hinazuru ひな鶴
hinin 非人
Hirasawa Sanai 平澤左内
Hirata Atsutane 平田篤胤
Horikoshi Nisōji 堀越二三次
hiru 晝
hitsuke tōzoku aratame 火付盗賊改
hiyodori 鵯
Honda Masayoshi 本田正珍
Honda Tadanaka 本多忠考
Honda Tadateru 本田忠央
Hongo 本後
Honjō Michikata 本庄道堅
Horibe Taketsune 堀部武庸
Horikawa 堀川
Horikoshi Nisōji 壕越二三治
Hosoi Kōtaku 細井広沢
Hotta Masasuke 堀田正亮
Hyakuan 百庵
hyaku monogatari 百物語
hyōbushōyu 兵部少輔
Hyōgo 兵庫
hyōjōsho 評定所

Ihara Saikaku 井原西鶴
Inoue Hisashi 井上ひさし
inshi 隠士

Ise 伊勢
Iseya Sōshirō 伊勢屋宗四郎
Ishibe Kinkō 石部琴好
Ishida Baigan 石田梅岩
Itakura Katsukiyo 板倉勝清
Itō Jinsai 伊藤仁斎
Itoshiro 石徹白
Iwai Onseki 岩井温石
Iwakitaira 磐城平
Iyo 伊予
Izumiya Yohei 和泉屋与兵衛

jin 仁
jisha bugyō 寺社奉行
jitsurokutai shōsetsu 実録体小説
jōdan 冗談
Jōkanbō Kōa 静観房好阿
Jōkyō 貞享
jōmen 定免
jōruri 浄瑠璃
jugoige 従五位下

kabuki 歌舞伎
kabu nakama 株仲間
kachi 従士
Kagaribi 篝火
kagoso 駕籠訴
Kaibara Ekken 貝原益軒
kaikidanmono 怪奇談物
Kaikoku heidan 海国兵談
Kajō ruiten 科条類典
kakikomi-uttae 書き込みで訴え
Kamakura 鎌倉
Kaminoyama 上山
Kamio Haruhide 神尾春央
Kamiya Gorōbei 紙屋五郎兵衛
Kanamori Yoritoki 金森頼時
Kanamori Yorikane 金森頼錦
kanazōshi 仮名草子
kanbun yomikudashi 漢文読み下し
Kanda 神田
kane (bell) 鐘
kane (money) 金
Kan'eiji 寛永寺
Kanemaki Genjun 印牧玄神
Kanematsu Matashirō 兼松又四郎
kanemochi 鐘持ち
kanjin 寛仁
kanjō bugyō 勘定奉行
kanjō kinmiyaku 勘定金脈
kaomise 顔みせ
karyō 過料
katakiuchi 仇打ち
Katō Shizue 加藤 シヅエ
Katsuura 勝浦
Kawasaki 川崎
Kayadera 茅寺
Kazusaya San'emon 上総屋三右衛門
kemari 蹴鞠
kenshin daishi 見真大師
Ki no Kaion 紀海音
kibyōshi 黄表紙
Kichisaburō 吉三郎
Kikaigashima 鬼界ヶ島
Kimura Kiyobei 木村清兵衛
Kinsho mokuroku 禁書目録
Kirishitan yashiki キリシタン屋敷
Kiritsubo 桐壷
Kishimojin 鬼子母神
Kishū 紀州
Kobayakawa Hidekane 小早川秀包
Kobayakawa Takakage 小早川隆景
Kobikichō 木挽丁
Kōbō Daishi (Kūkai) 弘法大師 (空海)
kōdanshi 講談師
Kojiki 古事記
koku 石
Kokubyaku mizukagami 黒白水鏡
kokugaku 国学
Komechō 米蝶
Kōmyōji 光明寺
Konishi Yukinaga 小西行長
Konjaku monogatari 今昔物語
Kōsaka Masataka 高坂 正堯
kōsatsu 高札
kōshaku 講釈
kōtaku 広沢
kōtō 公盗
Kozukappara 小塚原
Kumazawa Banzan 熊沢蕃山
Kumeno Heinaibyōe 久米野平内兵衛
Kumogakure 雲隠

Kumo no Taemanosuke 雲の絶間介
Kuno 久野
kunshi 君子
Kuremasa-chō 榑正町
Kurōbei 九郎兵衛
Kurosaki Saichiemon 黒崎左一衛門
kyōgen 狂言
Kyōhō 享保
kyōka 狂歌
Kyōwa 享和

machi bugyō 町奉行
Manji 万治
Manjusri 文殊師利
Man'yōshū 万葉集
Maruyama Masao 丸山眞男
Masaho Nokoguchi 増穂残口
Masuda Osamu 増田治
Matsubaya 松葉屋
Matsudaira Masatada 松平政尹
Matsudaira Munenobu 松平宗将
Matsudaira Nobutoki 松平信祝
Matsudaira Norimura 松平乗邑
Matsudaira Sadanobu 松平定信
Matsudaira Takechika 松平武元
Matsudaira Yasuyoshi 松平康福
Matsunaga Teitoku 松永貞徳
Matsushima-chō 松島町
Matsushita Useki 松下烏石
Matsushita Yukitsuna 松下之綱
Meiji 明治
Meiwa 明和
meyasubako 目安箱
Mikoshi Nyūdō 見越入道
Minamoto no Takakuni 源隆国
Minamoto no Yorimitsu 源頼光
Minamoto no Yoritomo 源頼朝
Minamoto no Yoshitsune 源義経
Mino gundai 美濃郡代
Mino 美濃
Misaki-chō 三崎町
mitate 見立
Miura Baien 三浦梅園
Miwa Shissai 三輪執斎
Miyazawa Kiichi 宮澤喜一
Mizoguchi Naoatsu 溝口直温
Mizuno Tadahide 水野忠秀
Mizuno Tadamichi 水野忠道
Momotarō 桃太郎
Momoyama 桃山
mon 文
monomi 物見
Morikawa Bakoku 森川馬谷
mōshiwatashisho 申渡書
Motoori Norinaga 本居宣長
Mukōsaki Jinnai 向崎甚内
Murata Gobei 村田五兵衛
musuko 息子
Myōhō renge kyō 妙法蓮華経

Nakagawa Sozui 中川宗瑞
Nakai Bun'emon 中井文衛門
Nakai Samaji 中井左馬次
Nakamura Tomijūrō 中村富十郎
Nakayama Kageyu 中山勘解由
Nanbu Toshikatsu 南部利克
Narukami 鳴神
nenbutsu 念佛
Neo Jinzaemon 根尾甚左衛門
Nihonbashi 日本橋
Nihon Shoki 日本書紀
Niigata 新潟
Ningyō-chō 人形町
Nippon eitaigura 日本永代蔵
Nishi Amane 西周
Nishida Kitarō 西田幾多郎
Nishi Honganji 西本願寺
Nishikawa Joken 西川如見
Nishinomaru 西の丸
Nishio Tadanao 西尾忠直
nobinin 野非人
Nuiemon 縫右衛門

Oguri Mataichi 小栗又市
Ogyū Sorai 荻生徂徠
Ōhashi Chikayoshi 大橋親義
ōi no kami 大炊頭
Oi no nagabanashi 老の長話
oiemono お家物
Okiku お菊

Onna Narukami 女鳴神
onnagata 女形
Ōoka Tadamitsu 大岡忠光
Ōoka Tadasuke 大岡忠相
Osadamegaki hyakkajō 御定書百箇条
Ōta Nanpo 大田南畝
Ōtaka Sukeshirō 大高助士郎
Ōtani Hiroji 大谷広次
Ōtomoeya 大巴屋
otona 乙名
Otsuna お綱
Otsuya おつや
Owari 尾張

Pan Chieh-yu 班婕妤

rakushu 落首
rōjū 老中
Rokō 路考
Rokusuke 六助
ryō 両
Ryōgoku 両国
Ryūshi shinron 柳子新論

Sagara 相良
Sakai Tadamochi 酒井忠用
Sakai Tadayori 酒井忠頼
Sakai-chō 堺町
sakariba 盛り場
sakoku 鎖国
Sakuma Saburōzaemon 佐久間三郎左衛門
sankin kōtai 参勤交代
Santō Kyōden 山東京伝
Sasaki Takatsuna 佐々木高綱
Satake Yoshimine 佐竹義峯
Segawa Kikunojō 瀬川菊之丞
Segawa Sengyō 仙魚
senryū 川柳
Sensōji 浅草寺
seppuku 切腹
setchūgaku 折衷学
setsuwa bungaku 説話文学
Shibata Baikō 新発田梅郊
shigarami 柵
Shigebei 茂兵衛
Shimabara 島原
Shimizu Sōjirō 清水惣次朗
Shin rokkasen 新六歌仙
Shingaku 心学
Shingon 真言
shinme 神馬
Shinoda Kunizaemon 篠田郡左衛門
Shinran 親鸞
Shinrei yaguchi no watashi 神霊矢口渡
Shinron 新論
Shirakawa 白川
Shirakawa shingihaku no mon 白川神紙伯の門
Shogei hitori jiman 諸芸独自慢
shoshidai 所司代
Shōtoku 正徳
Shun 舜
shuppan jōkō 出版条項
sōdō 騒動
Soga Gorō Tokimune 曾我五郎時致
Soga Jūrō Sukenari 曽我十郎祐成
Soga monogatari 曽我物語
sōjaban 奏者番
sōjō 僧正
Somaru 素丸
Sugawara no Koreyoshi 菅原是善
Sugawara no Michizane 菅原道真
Sugimoto Sakon 杉本左近
sugoroku 双六
Sūkiyabashi 数奇屋橋
Suzugamori 鈴ヶ森
Suzuki Shōsan 鈴木正三

Tachibana Sadayoshi 立花貞俶
Taema 絶間
taikobōzu 太鼓坊主
taikomochi 太鼓持
taikyoku 太極
Taitō-ku 台東区
Takadanobaba 高田馬場
Takahashi Genshū 高橋玄秀
Takechiyo 竹千代
Takeda Shukuan 武田叔庵
Takenouchi Shikubu 竹内式部
Tamenaga Shunsui 為永春水

Tanaka Heizō 田中平蔵
Tanaka Kōtarō 田中耕太郎
Tanaka Kyūguemon 田中休愚右衛門
Tanbaya Gorōbei 丹波屋五郎兵衛
Tashiro Kazui 田代和生
tayū 大夫
teisei 貞清
Tempō 天保
Teramachi Sanchi 寺町三智
Toda Gozaemon 戸田五左衛門
Toda Tadami 戸田忠余
Toda Tadamitsu 戸田忠盈
Toki 土岐
Tokugawa bakufu 徳川幕府
Tokugawa Ieharu 徳川家治
Tokugawa Ienobu 徳川家宣
Tokugawa Ieshige 徳川家重
Tokugawa Ieyasu 徳川家康
Tokugawa jikki 徳川実紀
Tokugawa Mitsukuni 徳川光圀
Tokugawa Munekatsu 徳川宗勝
Tokugawa Tsunayoshi 徳川綱吉
Tokugawa Yoshimune 徳川吉宗
Tomoeya 巴屋
torii 鳥居
Tosai Kosuke 戸際小助
Toshimaya Jūemon としまや十衛門
Toyota Mitsugi 豊田貢
Toyotomi Hideyoshi 豊臣秀吉
tozama 外様
tsū 通
Tsubouchi Shōyō 坪内逍遥
Tsuchiya Masasuke 土屋正方
Tsu no Kuniya 津ノ国屋
Tsurugi no maki 剣の巻

Uemura Buzen 上村豊前
Uemura Tsunetomo 上村恒朝
Uesugi Kenshin 上杉謙信
Uesugi Munefusa 上杉宗房
Uesugi Shigesada 上杉重定
ukiyozōshi 浮世草紙
Unemegahara 采女が原
utamonogatari 歌物語

Wada Yoshimori 和田義盛
waka 和歌
Watanabe Genshirō no Tsuna 渡辺源四郎綱

Xiao and Xiang Rivers (shōshō)瀟湘

yabo 野暮
Yamada Asaemon Yoshitsugu 山田浅右衛門吉継
Yamaga Sokō 山鹿素行
Yamagata Daini 山県大弐
yamanba 山姥
Yamashita Kōnai 山下幸内
YanagisawaYoshiyasu 柳沢吉保
Yao 堯
Yaoya Oshichi 八百屋お七
yashiki 屋敷
Yaso 耶蘇
Yasuemon 安右衛門
Yoda Masatsugu 衣田政次
Yomogifu 蓮生
yoriki 与力
Yoshida Ippō 吉田一保
Yoshida Shigeru 吉田茂
Yoshida Tenzan 吉田天山
Yoshino Sakuzō 吉野作造
Yoshiwara 吉原
Yotsuya 四谷
Yūgao 夕顔
Yūrin 由林

Selected Bibliography

The Writings of Baba Bunkō, in Chronological Order

Seken o-hatamoto katagi 世間御旗本容気 [Sketches of worldly bannermen]. 1754. 7. Edited by Okada Satoshi 岡田哲. *Baba Bunkō shū* 馬場文耕集 [Collection of writings by Baba Bunkō]. Vol. 12 of *Sōshō Edo bunko* 叢書江戸文庫 [Collection of Edo literature]. Edited by Takada Mamoru 高田衛 and Hara Michio 原道生. Tokyo: Kokusho kankōkai 国書刊行会 [National Publishing Association], 1987. 5–86.

Kindai kōjitsu genpiroku 近代公実厳秘録 [A record of contemporary public secrets], c. 1754. In Okada Satoshi, ed. *Baba Bunkō shū*. 87–176.

Kinsei kōjitsu genpiroku 近世公実厳秘 [A record of recent public secrets], 1755. (The content of this work is the same as *Kindai kōjitsu genpiroku*.)

Tōji chinsetsu yōhiroku 当時珍説要秘録 [A confidential record of current, little-known facts], 1756. 1–3. Okada Satoshi, ed. *Baba Bunkō shū*, 177–253.

Tōsei Buya zokudan 当世武野俗談 [Contemporary discussions of worldly affairs in Musashi], 1756.4. National Diet Library MS. Vol. 3 of Enseki jisshu 燕石十種、第三券 [A collection of essays from the early modern period]. Tokyo: Chūō kōronsha 中央公論社, 1980. 105–140. Also vol. 86 of *Mado no susami zen*, *Buya zokudan zen*, *Edo chomonshū zen* 窓のすさみ全、武野俗談全、江戸著聞集全. Edited by Tsukamoto Tetsuzō 塚本哲三. Tokyo: Yūhōdō shoten 有朋堂書店, 1915. 339–420.

Hōhei mitsu ga hitotsu 宝丙密秘登津 [Collected records of detailed secrets of Hōreki 6], 1756, 1757. 3. National Diet Library MS. Vol. 6 of *Mikan zuihitsu hyakushu* 未刊随筆百種 [Collection of unpublished essays]. Edited by Mitamura Engyo 三田村鳶魚. Tokyo: Chūō kōronsha, 1977. 13–31.

Kinsei Edo chomonshū 近世江戸著聞集 [A collection of tales of contemporary Edo], 1757. 9. In Tsukamoto Tetsuzō. *Mado no susami zen*, *Buya zokudan zen*, *Edo chomonshū zen*, vol. 86. Tokyo: Yūhōdō shoten, 1932. 431–520.

Morioka mitsugi monogatari 森岡貢物語 [The tribute from Morioka], 1757. Kondō Heijō 近藤瓶城, ed. *Kaitei shiseki shūran* 改定史籍集覧 [Collection of historical writings, revised]. Tokyo: Rinsen shoten 臨川, 1984 reprint of 1902 edition. 440–449.

Sarayashiki bengiroku 皿屋舗辨疑録 [A record of doubts and questions about the legend of the haunted mansion], 1758. 1. In *Waseda daigaku shuppanbu* 早稲田大学出版部, eds. *Kinsei jitsuroku zensho* 近世実録全書 [Compendium of authentic records of early modern times]. Tokyo: Waseda University, 1929. 1–22.

Yamato kaidan keijitsu zensho 大和怪談頃日全書 [A recent complete collection of Japanese ghost stories], 1758. 1. Tokyo University MS.

Tōsei shoka hyakunin isshu 当世諸家百人一首 [A collection of one hundred poems about contemporary families], 1758. 4. National Diet Library MS.

Tōdai Edo hyaku bakemono 当代江戸百化物 [Contemporary Edo: An album of one hundred monsters, 1758. 7]. Vol. 97 of *Shin Nihon koten bungaku taikei* 新日本古典文学大系 [New collection of Japanese classical literature]. Edited by Tajihi Ikuo 多治比郁夫 and Nakano Mitsutoshi 中野三敏. *Tōdai Edo hyaku bakemono, Zaishin kiji, Kana sesetsu* 在津紀事, 仮名世説. Tokyo: Iwanami shoten 岩波書店, 2000. Also in Series 2, vol. 1 of *Nihon zuihitsu taisei* 日本随筆大成 [Compendium of Japanese essays]. Edited by Sekine Masanao 関根正直, et al. Tokyo: Yoshikawa kōbunkan 吉川弘文館, 1928. 787–806.

Hōreki tōdai Edo hyaku bakemono 宝暦 [Edo today: An album of one hundred monsters in the Hōreki period], 1758.7. National Diet Library MS.

Edo hyaku bakemono 江戸百化物 [One hundred monsters of Edo], 1758. Vol. 3 of *Zoku enseki jisshu* 続燕石十種、第三券 [A second collection of essays from the early modern period]. Edited by Mori Senzō 森線増銑三, et al. Tokyo: Chūō kōronsha, 1980.

Meikun Kyōhō roku 名君享保録 [The record of a wise lord in the *Kyōhō* period [1716–36], 1758.7. In Okada Satoshi, 255–302. This work is also known as *Kyōhō roku* [Record of the *Kyōhō* period] and *Kyōhō hiroku* 秘録 [Secret record of the *Kyōhō* period].

Genmitsu keijitsu uwasa 厳密頃日噂. [An investigation of recent rumors], 1758. 7. Also known as *Keijitsu zensho* 頃日全書 [Complete writings of recent times]. Vol. 9 of *Mikan zuihitsu hyakushu*. Chūō kōronsha, 1977. 13–31.

Akita Suginao monogatari 秋田杉直物語 [Tale of Akita Suginao], 1758. In *Rekkō shimpi roku zen* 列侯深録全 [Complete record of the secrets of the daimyo]. Edited by Hayakawa Junzaburō. Tokyo: Kokusho kankōkai, 1914.

Akita chiranki jitsuroku 秋田治乱記実録 [A true record of war and peace in Akita], 1758, in Hayakawa Junzaburō, ed. *Rekkō shimpi roku zen*. Tokyo: Kokusho kankōkai, 1914.

Guchishūi monogatari 愚痴拾遺物語 [A collection of useless grumblings], 1758. 8. Vol. 9 of *Mikan zuihitsu hyakushu*. Edited by Mitamura Engyo, Tokyo: Chūō kōronsha. 1977. 11–25.

Documents Titled Mori no shizuku

Baba Bunkō. *Mori no shizuku* 杜の雫. Edo bungaku kenkyūkai 江戸文學研究会 [Edo literature research association], eds. *Edo monogatari* 江戸物語 [Tales of Edo]. Tokyo: Sanseisha 三省社, 1927.

Ezoe Inosuke 江添猪輔. *Mori no shizuku* も理のしずく. Tokyo: National Diet Library MS. 17 folios. (Same as above: Baba Bunkō, *Mori no shizuku*, in *Edo monogatari*. Tokyo: Sanseisha, 1927.).

Mori no shizuku 森の雫 [Raindrops in the forest]. Tokyo: Kunaicho shoryōbu 宮内庁書陵部 [Imperial Household Agency, Department of Documents] MS. 106 folios. Copy in Gifu Prefectural Library, 1827. Also see Morisue Yoshiaki, Ichiko Teiji 市古貞次 et al., eds. *Hoteiban Kokusho sōmokuroku*. Tokyo: Iwanami shoten, 1989–90, vol. 7, 725.

Mori no shizuku Kanamori sōdōki 毛利の雫騒動記 [Raindrops in the forest: the Kanamori disturbance]. Kyoto: Kyōto daigaku nōgakubu nōseishi kenkyūshitsu 京都大学農学部農政史研究室 [Kyoto University, Faculty of Agriculture in the department of agricultural economic history], 1900s (exact year of publication is unknown.)

Mori no shizuku 盛野志津久. Haneda Hisao Collection MS. 183 folios. Yokohama. 1756.

Primary Sources Pertaining to the Kanamori Disturbance

Gunsō jitsuroku 郡騒実録 [Record of the district disturbance]. *Gujō Hachiman chōshi shiryōhen shokiroku* 郡上八幡町史、史料編諸記録 [Various historical records of the history of Gujō Hachiman city], 1985–90. Vol. 1 of *Gujō Hachiman chōshi shiryōhen ichi* 史料編一. Edited by Ishida Masayuki 石田正之, et al. Gifu: Seinō insatsu kabushikigaisha 西濃印刷株式会社, 1985. 485–545.

Kanamori hyōbu shoyu o-jidai sōdōki 金森兵部小輔御治代騒動記 [The record of the disturbances during the rule of Minister of War Kanamori], 1889. Edited by Ishida Masayuki.607–632.

Kanamori ikken 一件 [The story of the Kanamori affair]. Gifu Prefectural Library MS. 62 folios, undated.

Kanamori ikken zen 全 [The story of the Kanamori affair, complete]. Giju Prefectural Library MS. 33 folios, 1759.

Kanamori kafu 家譜 [Geneology of the Kanamori family], undated. Edited by Ishida Masayuki. 116–37.

Kanamori ke chūfu 家中譜 [The inner workings of the Kanamori house]. Giju Prefectural Library MS. 15 folios, undated.

Kanamori ki 記. [The record of Kanamori]. Gifu Prefectural Library MS. 17 folios, 1750.

Kanamorishi kikigakiryaku 氏聞書略 [Outline of verbatim notes of the Kanamori family], undated. Edited by Ishida Masayuki. 137–139.

Kanamori sōdōki zen [Record of the Kanamori disturbance complete]. Gifu Prefectural Library MS. 114 folios, undated. Edited by Ishida Masayuki. 545–606.

Kaneshi kaseiroku 金史苛政録 [An account of the tyranny of the Kanamori family], 1759. Vol. 6 of *Kyōto daigaku zō: Taisohon kisho shūsei* 蔵大惣本稀書集成 [Comprehensive collection of rare publications held in Kyoto University]. Edited by *Kyoto daigaku bungakubu kokubungaku kenkyūshitsu* 京都大学文学部国文学研究室 [Kyoto University College of Arts and Sciences, Department of Japanese language and literature]. Kyoto: Rinsen shoten, 1994.

Other Primary Sources

Arai Hakuseki 新井白石. *Tokushi yoron* 読史余論 [A reading of history]. Vol. 35, *Arai Hakuseki* of *Nihon shisō taikei* 日本思想体系. Edited by Matsumura Akira et al. Tokyo: Iwanami shoten, 1975.

de Bary, Wm. Theodore, et al., eds. *Sources of Japanese Tradition*. New York: Columbia University Press, 2005.

Fujita Tōko 藤田東湖. "Kōdōkanki jitsugi" 弘道館記述義 [True Record of the Kōdōkan]. In *Nihon Shisō taikei*. Vol. 53, *Mitogaku* 三戸学. Edited by Imai Usaburō 今井宇三郎, et al. Tokyo: Iwanami shoten, 1973.

Fujiwara Kintō 藤原 公任. *Wakan rōei shū* 和漢朗詠集 [Collection of Japanese and Chinese poems for chanting aloud]. Tokyo: Kodansha gakujutsu bunkō 講談社学術文庫, 1982.

Fukansai Fabian 不干斎ハビアン. *Myōtei mondo* 妙貞問答. Vol. 25, *Kirishitan sho, Hayasho* キリシタン書　排耶書 [Christian writings, Anti-Christian writings] of *Nihon koten bungaku taikei* 日本古典 文学大系. Edited by Ebisawa Arimichi 海老沢有道 et al. Tokyo: Iwanami shoten, 1970.

Goryōken Arubeshi 呉陵軒可有 et al., eds. *Haifū yanagidaru* 誹風柳多留 [Collection of haikai and senryū verses], 1765. Vol. 57, *Senryū kyōka shū* 川柳狂歌集 [Collection of senryū and kyōka verse] of *Nihon koten bungaku taikei*. Edited by Sugimoto Nagashige 杉本長重 et al. Tokyo: Iwanami shoten, 1958.

Gujō Hōreki giminden 郡上宝暦義民伝 [The story of the self-sacrificing people of Gujō in the Hōreki period]. Edited by Education Committee of Shiratori-chō 白鳥町教育委員会. Gifu: Taiyōsha 太陽社, 1985.

Hiraga Gennai 平賀源内. Fūryū Shidōken den 風流志道軒傳 [The Dashing Life of Shidōken]. Tokyo: Genshisha 言視舎, 2011.

——. *Tengu sharekōbe mekiki engi* 天狗髑髏鑒定縁起 [*The Legend of the Tengu's Skull*], 1778. Vol. 1 of *Hiraga Gennai zenshū* 平賀源内全集 [Complete works of Hiraga Gennai]. Edited by Irita Seizō 入田整三. Tokyo: Ogihara seibunkan 荻原文官, 1935.

Hōsei ronsan 法制論纂 [Collection of legal treatises]. Edited by Iida Takesato 飯田武郷 and Kokugakuin 国学院. Tokyo: Dai Nippon tosho 大日本図書, 1903–4.

Hōreikan 抱嶺館. *Bokuteki ruisō* 牧笛類叢 [The reed pipe: A collection of short biographies]. Unpublished manuscript in National Diet Library, Tokyo, preface 1767.

Ihara Saikaku 井原西鶴. *Kōshoku nidai otoko, Saikaku shokoku hanashi, Honchōnijū fukō* 好色二代男, 西鶴諸国はなし, 本朝二十不孝 [Son of an amorous man, Saikaku's accounts of various places, Twenty cases of unfilial children]. Edited by Fuji Akio 富士昭雄, Inoue Toshiyuki 井上敏幸 et al. Tokyo: Iwanami shoten, 1991.

Jōkanbō Kōa 静観房好阿. *Imayo heta dangi* 当世下手談義 [A clumsy homily on the present age]. Vol. 81, *Inaka sōji, Imayo heta dangi, Tōsei anasagashi* 田舎荘子、当世穴さがし [Rustic stories, Looking for the faults of the age], of *Shin Nihon koten bungaku taikei*. Edited by Nakano Mitsutoshi. Tokyo: Iwanami shoten, 1990.

Kinryū Dōjin 金竜道人. *Shidōken den* 志道軒伝 [The story of Shidōken, 1748]. Vol. 8 of *Nihon shomin bunka shiryō shūsei* 日本庶民文化史料集成 [Collection of historical materials on Japanese popular culture]. Edited by Sekiyama Kazuo 関山和夫 , Nakamura Yukihiko 西村幸彦 et al. Tokyo: San'ichi shobō 三一書房, 1976.

Kyōhō tsūgan 享保通鑑 [Legal proceedings of the Kyōhō period]. Vol. 9 of *Mikan zuihitsu hyakushu*. Edited by Mitamura Engyo. Tokyo: Chūō kōronsha, 1977. 78–289.

Lu Chiu-yūan 陸九淵, ed. *Lu Hsiang-shan ch'ūan chi* 陸象山全書 [The complete works of Lu Hsiang-shan]. Hong Kong: Kwong chi shuchu 廣知書集, 1959.

Nakane Shuku 中根淑. *Hyakuman tō* 百万塔 [Comprehensive collection of documents]. 12 vols. Tokyo: Kinkōdō 金港堂, 1892.

Ogyū Sorai 荻生徂徠. *Benmei* 弁明 [In defense of virtue]. Vol. 1 of . *Ogyū Sorai zenshū* 全集 [Complete works of Ogyū Sorai]. Edited by Imanaka Hiroshi 今中寛. Tokyo: Kawade shobō shinsha 川出書房新社, 1973.

Ōta Nanpo 大田南畝. *Kanasogi* 金曽木 [Kanasogi]. Vol. 10 of *Ōta Nanpo zenshū* 全集 [Complete works of Ōta Nanpo]. Edited by Hamada Giichirō 濱田儀一郎 et al. Tokyo: Iwanami shoten, 1986.

The Real Record of the Arrival of the Christian Sect in Japan [*Kirishitan shūmon raichō jikki*] 切支丹宗門来朝実記, 1755. In *Japanese Traditions of Christianity: Being Some Old Translations from the Japanese, with British Consular Reports of the Persecutions of 1868–1872*. Edited by M. Paske-Smith. Kobe: J. L. Thompson & Co., 1929.

Sawa Chikane 沢近嶺. *Shunmu dokudan* 春夢独談 上下 [Reflections on the Anecdotes of Su Shih (1036–1101). Vol. 8 of *Zoku Nihon zuihitsu taisei* 続日本随筆大成 [A Collection of Japanese essays, continued]. Edited by Mori Senzō and Kitagawa Hirokuni 北川博邦. Tokyo: Yoshikawa kōbunkan, 1980.

Sekine Shisei 関根只誠. *Shisei airoku* 只誠埃録 [Humble records by Shisei]. Tokyo: Kyōiku shuppan sentā 教育出版センター [Education publishing center], 1983.

Sekine Toshio 関根俊雄. *Sekine bunko senshū, dai ikki* 関根文庫選集, 第一期 [Sekine library collection, series one]. Tokyo: Kyōiku shuppan sentā, 1983.

Edo kaidanshū zen san satsu 江戸怪談全集三冊 [Edo ghost stories in three volumes]. Edited by Takada Mamoru 高田衛. Tokyo: Iwanami shoten, 1989.

Takayanagi Shinzō 高柳眞三, Ishii Ryōsuke 石井良助. *Ofuregaki Hōreki shūsei* 御触書宝暦集成 [Collection of official records of the Hōreki period]. Tokyo: Iwanami shoten, 1976.

Tokugawa jikki, dai kyū hen 徳川実記第九編 [True accounts of the Tokugawa period, part 9]. Vol. 46 of *Shintei zōho Kokushi taikei* 新訂増補国史大系 [Outline of national history, corrected supplement]. Tokyo: Yoshikawa kōbunkan, 1976.

Hōreki ki Yoshiwara yūjo hyōbanki saiken yonshu 宝暦期吉原遊女評判記, 細見四種 [Guide to the Yoshiwara courtesans of the Hōreki period, four books]. Edited by Yagi Keiichi 八木敬一. Tokyo: Kinsei fūsoku kenkyūkai 近世風俗研究会, 1975.

Konjaku monogatari shū ni 今昔物語集二 [Collection of tales of times now past, part 2]. Vol. 23 of *Nihon koten bungaku taikei*. Edited by Yamada Yoshio 山田孝雄. Tokyo: Iwanami shoten, 1977.

Yamaga Sokō 山鹿素行. *Seikyō yōroku* 聖教要録 [Essential military teaching]. Vol. 32, *Yamaga Sokō*, of *Nihon shisō taikei* 日本思想体系. Edited by Tahara Tsuguo 田原嗣雄 et al. Tokyo: Iwanami shoten, 1970.

Yamaga Sokō. Vol. 8 of *Sōsho Nihon shisōka* 叢書日本思想家 [Collection of writings of Japanese intellectuals]. Edited by Sasaki Moritarō 佐々木杜太郎. Tokyo: Meitoku shuppansha 明徳出版社, 1978.

Yokoi Yayū 横井 也有. *Uzuragoromo* 鶉衣. Edited by Ishida Motosue 石田元季. Tokyo: Iwanami shoten, 2011. Yōkyokushū 謡曲集 [Collection of Noh chants]. Vol. 79 of Shinchō *Nihon* koten shūsei 新潮日本古典集成. Edited by Itō Masayoshi 伊藤正義. Tokyo: Shinchōsha, 1988.

Secondary Sources

Anesaki, Masaharu. *History of Japanese Religion: With Special Reference to the Social and Moral Life of the Nation*. Rutland, Vt.: Charles E. Tuttle Company, 1963.

Kaibara Ekken Muro Kyuso 貝原益軒 室鳩巣. Vol. 34 of *Nihon shisō taikei*. Edited by Arai Kengo 荒井見悟 et al. Tokyo: Iwanami shoten, 1970.

Bellah, Robert N. *Tokugawa Religion: The Values of Pre-Industrial Japan*. Glencoe, Ill.: The Free Press, 1957.

Blum, Mark L. 2008. "Collective Suicide at the Funeral of Jitsunyo: Mimesis or Solidarity?" In *Death and the Afterlife in Japanese Buddhism*, edited by Jacqueline Ilyse Stone et al., 137–74. Honolulu: University of Hawaii Press, 2008.

Botsman, Daniel. *Punishment and Power in the Making of Modern Japan*. Princeton: Princeton University Press, 2005.

Boxer, Charles. *The Christian Century in Japan, 1549–1650*. Berkeley: University of California Press, 1951.

Breen, J. L. "Heretics in Nagasaki." In *Contemporary European Writings on Japan: Scholarly Views from Eastern and Western Europe*, edited by Ian Nish. Woodchurch, UK: Paul Norbury Publications, 1988.

Burns, Susan L. *Before the Nation: Kokugaku and the Imagining of Community in Early Modern Japan*. Durham, N.C.: Duke University Press, 2003.

Cieslik, Hubert. "The Great Martyrdom in Edo 1623: Its Causes, Course, Consequences." *Monumenta Nipponica* 10, no. 1/2 (1954): 1–44.

Cullen, L. M. *A History of Japan, 1582–1941: Internal and External Worlds*. Cambridge: Cambridge University Press, 2003.

Divine, Richard. "Hirata Atsutane and Christian Sources." *Monumenta Nipponica* 36, no. 1 (1981): 37–54.

Ebisawa Arimichi. *Kirishitan kyōrisho* キリシタン教理書 [Christian doctrine]. Tokyo: Kyōbunkan, 1993.

Elison, George. *Deus Destroyed: The Image of Christianity in Early Modern Japan*. Cambridge, Mass.: Harvard University Press, 1988. First published 1973 in the Harvard East Asian Monographs Series, No. 72. Page references are to the 1988 edition.

Emerson, Ralph Waldo. *Essays: First Series*, Houghton, Mifflin Company, 1841.

Fujita Hiroshi 藤田洋. *Omoshiro kōdanbanashi* おもしろ講談ばなし [Entertaining anecdotal speeches]. Tokyo: Nihon hōsō shuppan kyōkai 日本放送出版協会, 1992.

Fujita, Neil S. *Japan's Encounter with Christianity: The Catholic Mission in Pre-Modern Japan*. New York: Paulist Press, 1991.

Gioia, Dana. "The Catholic Writer Today." *First Things* (December 2013): 33–43.

Griffin, Dustin. *Satire: A Critical Reintroduction*. Lexington: University Press of Kentucky, 1994.

Groemer, Gerald. "The Creation of the Edo Outcast Order." *Journal of Japanese Studies* 27, no. 2 (2001): 263–93.

Hall, John Carey, trans. "The Edict in 100 Sections." Part 4 of "Japanese Feudal Laws III: The Tokugawa Legislation" *Transactions of the Asiatic Society of Japan*, 41, part 5 [1913]: 683–804.

Hall, John Whitney, and J. L. McClain. *Japan From Pre-History to Modern Times*. New York: Dell Publishing Co., 1970.

——. *Early Modern Japan*. Vol. 4 of *The Cambridge History of Japan*. Cambridge: Cambridge University Press, 1991.

Hanasaki Kazuo 花咲一男. *Ōedo monoshiri zukan* 大江戸ものしり図鑑 [Illustrated dictionary of the great city of Edo]. Tokyo: Shufu to seikatsusha 主婦と生活社, 1994.

Hanley, Susan B. *Everyday Things in Premodern Japan*. Berkeley: University of California Press, 1997.

Harootunian, H. D. *Toward Restoration: The Growth of Political Consciousness in Tokugawa Japan*. Berkeley: University of California Press, 1970.

——. *Things Seen and Unseen: Discourse and Ideology in Tokugawa Nativism*. Chicago: Chicago University Press, 1988.

Hasegawa Yukinobu 長谷川幸延. *Kyōkaku chūshingura* 侠客忠臣蔵 [Tale of a chivalrous retainer]. Tokyo: Tōgensha 桃源社, 1959.

Hashigawa Bunzō 橋川文三, *ed. Nihon no meicho* 日本の名著 [Great books of Japan]. Tokyo: Chūō kōronsha, 1974.

Hashimoto Osamu 橋本治. *Edo ni Furansu kakumei wo* 江戸にフランス革命を [The French revolution in Edo]. Tokyo: Chūō kōronsha, 1994.

Hayakawa Kōichrō 早川杠一郎. *Uzu no hirogari: Hōreki sōdō to Kanamori Yorikane o chūshin ni* うずのひろがり宝暦騒動と金森頼錦の中心に [The expanse of the storm: The Hōreki disturbance, centering on Kanamori Yorikane]. Gifu: privately printed by the author, 1974.

Hibbett, Howard. *The Floating World in Japanese Fiction*. London: Oxford University Press, 1959.

Higashibaba, Ikuo. *Christianity in Early Modern Japan: Kirishitan Belief and Practice*. Leiden: Brill Academic Publishers, 2002.

Hucker, Charles O. *A Dictionary of Official Titles in Imperial China*. Stanford: Stanford University Press, 1985.

Hur, Nam-lin. *Death and Social Order in Tokugawa Japan: Buddhism, Anti-Christianity, and the Danka System*. Cambridge, Mass.: Harvard University Asia Center [Harvard East Asian Monographs], 2007.

Iguchi Hiroshi, "Yoshida Ippō." Vol. 6 of *Nihon koten bungaku daijiten* 日本古典文学大事典 [Encyclopedia of Japanese classical literature]. Edited by Ichiko Teiji et al. Tokyo: Iwanami shoten, 1984.

Ikegami, Eiko. *The Taming of the Samurai: Honorific Individualism and the Making of Modern Japan*. Cambridge, Mass.: Harvard University Press, 1995.

Inoue Hisashi 井上ひさし. *Gesakusha meimeiden* 戯作者名々伝 [Biographies of gesaku authors]. Tokyo: Chūō kōronsha, 1979.

Ion, A. H. "Japan and Christianity: Impacts and Responses by John Breen, Mark Williams." Book Review in *The International History Review* 20, no. 1 (March 1998): 160–62.

Ishii Ryōsuke. *Edo no keibatsu* 江戸の刑罰 [Punishment in the Edo period]. Tokyo: Chūō kōronsha, 1964.

Itasaka, Gen, et al., eds. *Kodansha Encyclopedia of Japan*. 9 vols. New York: Kodansha America Inc., 1983.

Edo itsuwa jiten 江戸逸話事典 [Edo dictionary of anecdotes]. Edited by Itsuwa Kenkyūkai 逸話研究会 [Anecdotes research association]. Tokyo: Shinjinbutsu oraisha 新人物往来社, 1989.

Iwahashi Junsei 岩橋遵成. *Dai Nippon rinri shisō hatten shi* 大日本倫理思想発展史 [History of the development of Japanese ethical thought]. 2 vols. Tokyo: Meguro shoten 目黒書店, 1914.

Iwao Seiichi. *Nanyō Nihon machi no kenkyū* 南洋日本町の研究 [Studies on the Japanese settlements in Southeast Asia]. Tokyo: Iwanami shoten, 1966.

Jennes, Joseph. *A History of the Catholic Church in Japan: From Its Beginnings to the Early Meiji Era*. Tokyo: Oriens Institute for Religious Research, 1973.

Jones, Sumie. "Language in Crisis: Ogyū Sorai's Philological Thought and Hiraga Gennai's Creative Practice." In *Principles of Classical Japanese Literature*, edited by Earl Miner, 209–257. Princeton: Princeton University Press, 1985.

Jones, Sumie, Kenji Watanabe et al. *An Edo Anthology: Literature from Japan's Mega City, 1750–1850*. Honolulu: University of Hawaii Press, 2013.

Kawatake Shigetoshi 河竹繁敏. *Nihon engeki zenshi* 日本演劇全史 [Complete history of Japanese theater]. Tokyo: Iwanami shoten, 1959.

Keene, Donald. *20 Plays of the Nō Theatre*. New York: Colombia University Press, 1970.

——. *The Japanese Discovery of Europe, 1720–1830*. Oxon: Routledge, rev. ed., 2010 [1952].

Hanshi daijiten 藩史大事典 [Complete history of the domains], 8 vols. Edited by Kimura Motoi 木村礎 et al. Tokyo: Oyamakaku 雄山閣, 1989.

Kitagawa, Joseph Mitsuo. *Religion in Japanese History*. New York: Columbia University Press, 1966.

Koike Shōtarō 小池章太郎. *Kōshō Edo kabuki* 考証江戸歌舞伎 [A study of Edo kabuki drama]. Tokyo: Sanju shobō 三樹書房, 1979.

Komada Shinji 駒田信二. *Edo kobanashi* 江戸小話 [Tales of Edo]. Tokyo: Iwanami shoten, 1985.

Konita Seiji 小二田誠二. "Jitsurokutai shōsetsu no genzō: *Sarayashiki bengiroku* o megutte" 実録体小説の現像「更屋敷弁疑録」をめぐって [The development of historical fiction: Analyzing *Sarayashiki bengiroku*]. *Nihon bungaku* 12 (December 1987): 49–59.

Konta Yōzō 今田洋三. *Edo no kinsho* 江戸の禁書 [Proscribed writings of Edo]. Tokyo: Yoshikawa kōbunkan, 1981.

Konuma Daihachi 小沼大八. *Iyo no kakure kirishitan* 伊予のかくれキリシタン [Hidden Christians of Iyo]. Matsuyama 松山: Ehime ken bunka shinkō zaidan 愛媛県文化振興財団 [Foundation for the Promotion of Culture in Ehime Prefecture], 1998.

Kornicki, Peter. *The Book in Japan: A Cultural History from the Beginnings to the Nineteenth Century*. Honolulu: University of Hawaii, 2001.

Laver, Michael S. *The Sakoku Edicts and the Politics of Tokugawa Hegemony*. London: Cambria Press, 2011.

Lippit, Noriko Mizuta, Sekine Eiji et al., eds. *Monogatari no Yokubō* 物語の欲望 [The desire for monogatari]. Proceedings of the Second Midwest Research, Pedagogy Seminar on Japanese Literature, November 13–14, 1993, Purdue University.

Marsh, Ian, ed. *Democratisation, Governance and Regionalism in East and Southeast Asia: A Comparative Study*. London: Routledge, 2006.

Maruyama Masao. *Studies in the Intellectual History of Tokugawa Japan*. Princeton: Princeton University Press; Tokyo: University of Tokyo Press, 1975.

Matsuda Osamu 松田修. *Edo itan bungaku nōto* 江戸異端文学ノーと [The marginalia of Edo heretical literature]. Tokyo: Seidōsha 青道社, 1993.

McClain, James L., et al., eds. *Edo and Paris: Urban Life and the State in the Early Modern Era*. Ithaca: Cornell University Press, 1994.

Mikami Sanji 三上参次. *Edo jidai shi* 江戸時代史 [History of the Edo period]. 2 vols. Tokyo: Kōdansha 講談社, 1992. Reprint of Tokyo: Fusanbō 富三房, 1943–44 edition.

Mills, Douglas E. "*Kataki-uchi*: The Practice of Blood-Revenge in Pre-Modern Japan." *Modern Asian Studies* 10, no. 4 (1976): 525–42.

Miner, Earl et al., eds. *The Princeton Companion to Classical Japanese Literature*. Princeton: Princeton University Press, 1985.

——, ed. *Principles of Classical Japanese Literature*. Princeton: Princeton University Press, 1985.

Mitamura Engyo. *Mitamura Engyo zenshū* [Complete works of Mitamura Engyo]. Tokyo: Chūō kōronsha, 1975.

——. ed. *Mikan zuihitsu hyakushu* [Collection of unpublished essays]. Tokyo: Chūō kōronsha, 1977.

Miura Baien, *Samidare-sho* 五月雨抄 [*Musings during the early summer rain*], 1784. Translated by Leon Hurvitz, *Monumenta Nipponica* 8, no. 1 (1952): 289–326.

——. *Samidare-sho II*, *Monumenta Nipponica* 9, no. 2 (1952): 330–56.

Miyamoto Ryoen, "The Acceptance of Chinese Neo-Confucianism in Japan in the Early Tokugawa Period." In *Meeting of Minds: Intellectual and Religious Interaction in East Asian Traditions of Thought*, edited by Irene Bloom and Joshua A. Fogel. New York: Columbia University Press, 1997: 238–277.

Miyamoto Tsuneichi 宮本常一 et al., eds. *Minkan shūkyō* 民間宗教 [Popular religion]. Vol. 18 of *Nihon seikatsu shomin shiryō shūsei* 日本生活庶民史料集成 [Collected sources on the history of the daily lives of common Japanese people]. Tokyo: San'ichi shobō, 1972.

Miyao Shigeo 宮尾しげお. *Edo kobanashi shū* 江戸小咄集 [A collection of Edo tales]. 2 vols. Tokyo: Heibonsha 平凡社, 1971.

Morisue Yoshiaki 森末 義彰, Ichiko Teiji et al., eds. *Hoteiban Kokusho sōmokuroku* 補訂版 国書総目録 [Supplement to the complete catalog of national literature]. Tokyo: Iwanami shoten, 1989–90.

Murai Saiai 村井早苗. *Bakuhansei seiritsu to kirishitan kinsei* 幕藩制成立とキリシタン禁制 [The formation of the bakuhan system and the ban on Christianity]. Tokyo: Bunken shuppan 文研出版, 1987.

Murdoch, James. *A History of Japan*, vol. 3. London: Routledge & Kegan Paul, 1949.

Mutō Gorō 武藤互郎 and Mishima Eitarō 三島栄太郎, eds. *Nōhoku: Hōreki giminroku* 濃北宝暦義民録 [A Hōreki-period record of the self-sacrificing men of Hokunō village]. Gujō: Gujō Hōreki gimin kenshōkai 郡上宝暦義民顕彰会 [Committee to honor the self-sacrificing men of Gujō], 1966.

Mutō Sadao 武藤禎夫. *Rakugo sanbyaku dai jo* 落語三百題上. Tokyo: Tōkyōdō 東京堂, 1969.

Nagasawa Kikuya 長沢 規矩也 et al., eds. Vol. 4 of *Nihon shomoku taisei* 日本書目大成 [Index of Japanese publications]. Tokyo: Kyūko shoin 汲古書院, 1975.

Nagatomo Chiyoji 長友千代次. *Kinsei kashihon'ya no kenkyū* 近世貸本屋の研究 [A study of early modern book lenders]. Tokyo: Tōkyōdō, 1982.

Najita, Tetsuo. "Intellectual Change in Early Eighteenth-Century Tokugawa Confucianism." *Journal of Asian Studies* 34, no. 4 (1975): 931–44.

———. "History and Nature in Eighteenth-Century Tokugawa Thought." In *The Cambridge History of Japan*. Vol. 4, *Early Modern Japan*. Edited by John Whitney Hall et al. Cambridge: Cambridge University Press, 1991.

Najita, Tetsuo and J. Victor Koschmann, eds. *Conflict in Modern Japanese History: The Neglected Tradition*. Princeton: Princeton University Press, 1982.

Najita, Tetsuo et al., eds. *Japanese Thought in the Tokugawa Period, 1600–1868: Methods and Metaphors*. Chicago: University of Chicago Press, 1978.

Nakamura Kiyozō 中村喜代三. *Kinsei shuppanhō no kenkyū* 近世出版法の研究 [Study of publishing laws in the early modern period]. Tokyo: Nihon Gakujutsu Shinkōkai 日本学術振興会, 1972.

Nakamura Yukihiko 中村幸彦. *Kinsei sakka kenkyū* 近世作家研究 [Study of early modern authors]. Tokyo: Sanichishobō 三一書房, 1961.

Nakano Mitsutoshi. *Gesaku kenkyū* 戯作研究 [Study of popular literature]. Tokyo: Chūō kōronsha, 1981.

———. *Edo bunka hyōbanki* 江戸文化評判記 [A critique of Edo culture]. Tokyo: Chūō kōronsha, 1992.

Nakane Chie, et al., eds. *Tokugawa Japan: The Social and Economic Antecedents of Modern Japan*. Tokyo: University of Tokyo Press, 1990.

Nakai, Kate Wildman. *Shogunal Politics: Arai Hakuseki and the Premises of Tokugawa Rule*. Cambridge, Mass.: Council on East Asian Studies, Harvard University, 1988.

Nam-lin Hur. *Death and Social Order in Tokugawa Japan: Buddhism, Anti-Christianity, and the 'Danka' System*. Cambridge, Mass.: Harvard University Asia Center, 2007.

Naramoto Tatsuya 奈良本辰也, ed. *Kinsei seidōron* 近世政道論 [Contemporary theses on governing]. Vol. 3 of *Nihon shisō taikei* 日本思想大系. Tokyo: Iwanami shoten, 1976.

Nester, William. "Japan's Mainstream Press: Freedom to Conform?" *Public Affairs* 62, no. 1 (1989): 29–39.

Nish, Ian, ed. *Contemporary European Writings on Japan: Scholarly Views from Eastern and Western Europe*. Woodchurch, UK: Paul Norbury Publications, 1988.

Nishiyama Matsunosuke 西山松之助. *Edo Culture: Daily Life and Diversions in Urban Japan*, 1600–1868. Translated by Gerald Groemer. Honolulu: University of Hawaii Press, 1997.

Nishiyama Matsunosuke and Gunji Masakatsu 郡司正勝 et al., eds. *Edogaku nyūmon* 江戸学入門 [Introduction to Edo studies]. Tokyo: Chikuma shobō 筑摩書房, 1981.

——, eds. *Edogaku jiten* 江戸学辞典[Dictionary of Japanese studies]. Tokyo: Kōbunkan 弘文館, 1994.

Nobuhiro Shinji 延広真治. "Kōdan, jitsuroku, kōshaku" 講談、実録、講釈 [Storytelling, histories and lectures]. Vol. 4 of *Nihon bungaku zenshi, kinsei* [Complete history of Japanese literature, early modern]. Edited by Ichiko Teiji et al. Tokyo: Gakuteisha 學燈社, 1978.

——. "Shisei airoku, kan nihyakuni, kan nihyakuroku." Vol. 202 of *Sekine bunko senshū daiikki bessatsu ni kaisetsu hen* 別冊二解説遍 [Sekine library collection, additional volume with annotations]. Edited by Ichiko Teiji et al. Tokyo: Kyoiku shuppan sentā, 1984.

Noda Hisao 野田寿雄. *Kinsei shōsetsushi ronkō* 近世小説史論考 [A study of the history of the early modern novel]. Tokyo: Hanawa shobō 塙書房, 1961.

Noda Naoharu 野田直治 and Suzuki Yoshiaki 鈴木義秋. *Gujō han Hōreki sōdō no kisoteki kenkyū* 郡上藩騒動の基礎的研究 [Fundamental studies on the Hōreki disturbance in Gujō domain]. Gifu prefecture, Ono 岐阜県 小野: Gujō shiryō kenkyūkai 史料研究会 [Seminar for researching Gujō materials], 1967.

Noma Seiji 野間清治 et al., eds. *Kōdan zenshū* 講談全集 [Complete collection of anecdotal literature], 12 vols. Tokyo: Dai Nippon yūben kai kōdansha 大日本雄弁会講談社, 1929.

Nomura Mumyōan 野村無明庵. *Honchō wajin den* 本朝話人伝 [Biographies of our country's orators]. Tokyo: Kyōei shuppan kai 協栄出版会, 1944.

Nosco, Peter, ed. *Confucianism and Tokugawa Culture*. Princeton: Princeton University Press, 1984.

——. "Secrecy and the Transmission of Tradition: Issues in the Study of the 'Underground' Christians." *Japanese Journal of Religious Studies* 20, no. 1 (1993): 3–29.

Ohashi Yukihiro 大橋幸泰. "Kinseijin to kirishitan [4] kakushi nembutsu to Kyōzaka kirishitan ikken" 近世人とキリシタン[4]—隠し念仏と京坂「切支丹」一件 [Early Modern Man and Christianity, part 4: The secret *nenbutsu* and the Kyōzaka Christian incident] 2013, 6.18, 1–2. http://www.f.waseda.jp/yohashi/atomi/nihonsyuukyo-uron/0618.pdf.

Okada Satoshi. ——. "Kokugakuin daigaku shozōhon *Meikun Kyōhō roku* no kisoteki kenkyū to honkoku: Baba Bunkō jitsurokumono no seiritsu o megutte [jō]" 國學院大學所蔵本〔名君享保〕の基礎的研究と翻刻：馬場文耕実録物の成立をめぐって(上) [The reprinting and beginning research on Kokugakuin University's manuscript of *Meikun Kyōhō roku*: On the creation of authentic studies by Baba Bunkō, Part 1]. Kokugakuin zasshi 雑誌 82, 4 (April 1981): 34–53.

——. "Kokugakuin daigaku shozōhon *Meikun Kyōhō roku* no kisoteki kenkyū to honkoku: Baba Bunkō jitsurokumono no seiritsu o megutte [ge],» (下) [Part 2]. *Kokugakuin zasshi* 82, 5 (May 1981): 60–84.

——. "*Baba Bunkō to Ōoka seidan: Ōoka Tadasuke shussedan o jikutoshite*" 馬場文耕と「大岡政談」:大岡忠相出世譚を軸として [*Baba Bunkō and cases tried by Ōoka: The successful career of Ōoka Tadasuke*]. *Kokugakuin daigaku daigakuin kiyō* 国学院大学大学院紀要 [Memoirs of Kokugakuin University] 12 (June 1981): 108–30.

——. "*Yamato kaidan keijitsu zensho shōkō*" 「大和怪談頃日全書」小考 [Summary of *Yamato kaidan keijitsu zensho*]. *Kokugakuin daigaku Nihon bunka kenkyūjo kiyō* 53 (March 1984): 294–322.

Ooms, Herman. *Tokugawa Ideology: Early Constructs, 1570–1680*. Princeton: Princeton University Press, 1885.

Palmeri, Frank. *Satire, History, Novel: Narrative Forms, 1665–1815*. Newark: University of Delaware Press, 2003.

Paramore, Kiri. "Hayashi Razan's Redeployment of Anti-Christian Discourse: The Fabrication of *Haiyaso*." *Japan Forum* 18, no. 2 (2006): 185–206.

——. *Ideology and Christianity in Japan*. Oxon: Routledge, 2009.

Pflugfelder, Gregory M. *Cartographies of Desire: Male-Male Sexuality in Japanese Discourse, 1600–1950*. Berkeley: University of California Press, 2007.

Pyle, Kenneth B. *Japan Rising: The Resurgence of Japanese Power and Purpose*. Cambridge, Mass.: Public Affairs, 2007.

Reischauer, Edwin O., and John K. Fairbank, eds. *East Asia: The Great Tradition*. Boston: Houghton Mifflin Company, 1958.

Ribeiro, Madalena. "The Japanese Diaspora in the Seventeenth Century According to Jesuit Sources." *Bulletin of Portuguese/Japanese Studies 3* (2001): 53–83.

Riffaterre, Michael. *Fictional Truth*. Baltimore: Johns Hopkins University Press, 1990.

Rubinger, Richard. *Private Academies of Tokugawa Japan*. Princeton: Princeton University Press, 1982.

Sansom, George. *A History of Japan, 1615–1687*. Stanford: Stanford University Press, 1963.

Sasama Yoshihiko 笹間良彦. *Zusetsu: Edo machibugyō jiten* 図説:町奉行辞典 [Illustrated dictionary of the office of Edo city magistrate]. Tokyo: Kashiwa shobō 柏書房, 1991.

Screech, Timon, ed. *Secret Memoirs of the Shoguns: Isaac Titsingh and Japan, 1779–1822*. New York: Routledge, 2006.

Seigle, Cecilia Segawa. *Yoshiwara: The Glittering World of the Japanese Courtesan*. Honolulu: University of Hawaii Press, 1993.

Sekine Mokuan 関根 黙庵. *Kōdan rakugo konseki dan* 講談落語今昔譚 [Discourses on professional storytelling and comic stories, past and present]. Tokyo: Yūsankaku 雄山閣, 1923.

——. *Kōdan rakugo kō* 考 [Treatises on professional storytelling and comic stories]. Tokyo: Yūsankaku, 1967.

Sekine Shisei, ed. *Teisei kaihan: Meijin kishinroku* 訂正改版：名人忌辰録 [A record of the deaths of famous people, revised edition]. Tokyo: Rokugokan 六合館, 1925.

Shibasaki Atsushi. "Christianity and the Making of a Modern Worldview in Japan: International Thought of Tanaka Kotaro." *Journal of Global Media Studies* 7 (2010): 31–40.

Shirane, Haruo, and Tomi Suzuki, eds. *Inverting the Classics: Modernity, National Identity, and Japanese Literature*. Stanford: Stanford University Press, 2000.

Shively, Donald H. "Chikamatsu's Satire on the Dog Shogun." *Harvard Journal of Asiatic Studies* 18, no. 1 (1955): 159–80.

Smith, Patrick. *Japan: A Reinterpretation*. New York: Pantheon Books, 1997.

Suzuki, Keiko. "The Making of Tōjin: The Construction of the Other in Early Modern Japan." *Asian Folklore Studies* 66 (2007): 83–105.

Suzuki Tōzō 鈴木棠三 and Okada Satoshi, eds. *Edo jidai rakusho ruiju* 江戸時代落書類聚 [Collection of graffiti from the Edo period]. 3 vols. Tokyo: Tōkyōdō shuppan, 1984.

Suwa Haruo 諏訪春雄. *Shuppan kotohajime: Edo no hon* 出版事始：江戸の本 [The origins of publication: Books of Edo]. Edo series 江戸シリーズ, no. 11. Tokyo: Mainichi shinbunsha 毎日新聞社, 1978.

Tahara Tsuguo 田原嗣郎 et al., eds. *Hirata Atsutane, Ban Nobutomo, Ōkuni Takamasa* 平田篤胤、伴信友、大国隆正. Vol. 50 of *Nihon shisō taikei*. Tokyo: Iwanami shoten, 1973.

Takada Eitarō 高田栄太郎. "Genjikki *Mori no shizuku* (1)" 幻実記 [An imaginary history of *Mori no shizuku*]. *Genya* 幻野 [Fleeting world] 17 (November 1979): 75–98.

——. "Genjikki *Mori no shizuku* (2)." Genya 18 (December 1979): 53–77.

——. Takada Eitarō. "Baba Bunkō o ou '*Hiragana mori no shizuku* no koto'" 馬場文耕を追う(1):「平仮名森の雫」のこと [In pursuit of Baba Bunkō (1): Concerning *Hiragana mori no shizuku*]. *Gujō shidanshi* 郡上史談志 [Historical newsletter of Gujō] 38 (April 1980): 1–3.

——. "Baba Bunkō o ou (2): Bunken o asatte" 文献をあさって [Searching for a bibliography]. *Gujō shidanshi* 39 (August 1980): 393–95.

——. *Gekyoku Mori no shizuku* 戯曲森乃雫 [M°ori no shizuku: a drama]. Gifu: Kyōdō bunkashi "Gujō" henshūbu 郷土分化誌「郡上」編集部, 1980.

——. "Baba Bunkō o ou (3): Bunken kaisetsu o chūshin ni" 文献解説を中心に [An explanation of the bibliography]. *Gujō shidanshi* 43 (April 1981): 433–35.

——. "Baba Bunkō o ou (4): San keitō no hon o chūshin ni" 三系統の本を中心に [Concentrating on a study of the three versions of *Mori no shizuku*]. *Gujō shidanshi* 44 (August 1981): 442–44.

——. "Baba Bunkō o ou (5): Kiita koto nado" 聞いたことなど [What has been told and other tales]. *Gujō shidanshi* 45 (April 1982): 458–60.

Takahashi Keiichi 高橋圭一. "*Seken ohatamoto katagi no haikei*" 「世間御旗本気質」の背景 [The background of *Sketches of Worldly Bannermen*]. *Kokugo kokubun* 国語国文 54 (1985): 21–36.

——. "Jitsuroku *Akita sōdōmono kō*: Baba Bunkō saku *Akita monogatari* o chūshin ni" 実録「秋田騒動物」考：馬場文耕作 「秋田杉直物語」を中心に [A study of the historical record *The Akita disturbance*, with reference to Baba Bunkō's *Tale of Akita Suginao*]. In *Yomihon kenkyū* 読本研究 [A study of the *yomihon* storybook.]. Edited by Yokoyama Kuniji 横浜邦治. Hiroshima: Keisuisha 渓水社, 1990.

——. "Bunkō chosaku shokō" 文耕著作小考 [A short treatise on the works of Bunkō]. In *Setsuwa ronshū daiyonshū: Kinsei no setsuwa* 論集 第四集：近世. Edited by Setsuwa to setsuwa bungaku no kai 説話と説話文学の会 [Committee on narrative and legendary literature]. Osaka: Seibundō, 1995.

Takayanagi Mitsutoshi 高柳光寿 et al., eds. *Shintei Kansei chōshū shokafu* 新訂寛政重修諸家譜 [Kansei genealogy of public officials]. 22 vols. Tokyo: Zoku gunsho ruijū kanseikai 続郡書類従完成会 [Editorial committee of the second series of *The Collection of Various Books According to Their Categories*], 1964.

Tanizawa Eiichi 谷沢永一 et al., eds. *Miyatake Gaikotsu chosaku shū* 宮武外骨著作集 [Collected works of Miyatake Gaikotsu]. 8 vols. Tokyo: Kawade shobō shinsha 河出書房新社, 1986.

Toby, Ronald. *State and Diplomacy in Early Modern Japan: Asia in the Development of the Tokugawa Bakufu*. Stanford: Stanford University Press, 1991.

Totman, Conrad. *Early Modern Japan*. Berkeley: University of California Press, 1993.

Toya Toshiyuki 戸谷敏之. *Kirishitan nōmin no keizai seikatsu: Hizen no Kuni Sonogi-gun Urakami-mura yamazato no kenkyū* 切支丹農民の経済生活: 肥前国彼杵郡浦上村山里の研究 [A study of the economic life of Christian peasants in the villages of Hizen Sonogi, Urakami]. Tokyo: Itō shotenkan, 1943.

Tsuji Tatsuya 辻達也. *Ōoka Echizen no kami: mei bugyō no kyozō to jitsuzō* 大岡越前守：名奉行の虚像と実像 [Echizen no kami: the famous magistrate's false image and real image]. Tokyo: Chūō koronsha, 1964.

Tsukahara Jūshi 塚原澁柿. *Kyantabi* 侠足袋 [A chivalrous monk]. Tokyo: Sakuryō shobō 佐久良書房, 1909.

Tyler, Royall, ed. and trans. *Japanese Nō Dramas*. London: Penguin Books, 1992.

Ueda Kazutoshi 上田万年 et al., eds. *Jingibu* 神祇部 [Gods of heaven and earth]. Vol. 1 of *Shinkō Gunsho ruiju* 新校群書類従 [New collection of classified petitions]. Tokyo: Naigai shoseki 内外書籍, 1938.

Urakawa Wasaburō 浦川和三郎. *Urakami Kirishitanshi* 浦上切支丹史 [History of Urakami Christians]. Tokyo : Kokusho Kankōkai 国書刊行会, 1973.

Vaporis, Constantine Nomikos. *Voices of Early Modern Japan: Contemporary Accounts of Daily Life during the Age of the Shoguns*. Boulder: Westview Press, 2014.

Wakabayashi, Bob Tadashi, ed. *Anti-Foreign and Western Learning in Early Modern Japan: The New Theses of 1825*. Cambridge, Mass.: Council on East Asian Studies, Harvard University, 1991.

Walthall, Anne. *Social Protest and Popular Culture in Eighteenth-Century Japan*. Tucson: University of Arizona Press, 1986.

Wolferen, Karel van. *The Enigma of Japanese Power*. New York: Vintage Books, 1990.

Wolff, Kurt H. *The Sociology of Georg Simmel*. Glencoe, Ill.: The Free Press, 1950.

Yagi Keiichi et al., eds. *Yoshiwara saiken nenpyō* 吉原細見年表 [Chronology of Yoshiwara guidebooks]. Tokyo: Seishōdō 青上裳堂, 1996.

Yamada Tadao 山田忠雄. "*Hiragana mori no shizuku* no yukue" 平仮名森の雫の行方 [The whereabouts of *Hiragana mori no shizuku*]. *Nihon no rekishi geppō* 日本の歴史月報 [Monthly review of Japanese history] 20 (September 1975): 12–13.

——. "Seiji to minshū bunka: Edo no shomin bungei ni tsuite" 政治と民衆文化：江戸の庶民文芸について [Politics and popular culture: The literature of the Edo populace]. *Rekishi hyōron* 歴史評論 465 (1989): 24–44.

Yoshioka Isao 吉岡勲, et al., eds. Gifu-ken no rekishi shiriizu. Vol. 5 of *Zustetsu: Gujō no rekishi* 図説：郡上の歴史 [Illustrated history of Gujō]. Gifu: Kyōdo shuppansha, 1986.

Ward, Haruko Nawata. *Women Religious Leaders in Japan's Christian Century, 1549–1650: Women and Gender in the Early Modern World*. Surrey, UK: Ashgate Publishing Company, 2009.

Watanabe Kunio, ed. *Masuho Nokoguchi* 増穂残.口.Vol. 22 of *Shinto taikei* 神道大系 [Collection of Shinto works]. Tokyo: *Shinto taikei hensankai* 編纂会, 1975.

White, Hayden. *Tropics of Discourse: Essays in Cultural Criticism*. Baltimore: The Johns Hopkins University Press, 1978.

——. *The Content of the Form: Narrative Discourse and Historical Representation*. Baltimore: The Johns Hopkins University Press, 1987.

Zhang De-Er. "A Study of the Large Scale Flooding over Eastern China in 1755." *Advances in Climate Change Research* 3 (March 2012): 128–37.

Zielenziger, Michael. *Shutting Out the Sun: How Japan Created Its Own Lost Generation*. New York: Doubleday, Nan A. Talese, 2006.

Index

A Christian Samurai: The Trials of Baba Bunkō was designed and typeset in Arno by Kachergis Book Design of Pittsboro, North Carolina. It was printed on 60-pound Natures Recycled and bound by McNaughton & Gunn of Saline, Michigan.